CAMBODIA CONFOUNDS
THE PEACEMAKERS
1979–1998

CAMBODIA
CONFOUNDS THE
PEACEMAKERS
1979 – 1998

MacAlister Brown
AND Joseph J. Zasloff

A BOOK FROM THE OAKLEY CENTER FOR THE
HUMANITIES AND SOCIAL SCIENCES, WILLIAMS COLLEGE

CORNELL UNIVERSITY PRESS

ITHACA AND LONDON

The publisher gratefully acknowledges receipt of a subvention
from the Office of the Dean of Faculty at Williams College,
which defrayed part of the cost of publication.

First published 1998 by Cornell University Press.

Printed in the United States of America.

Cornell University Press strives to use environmentally responsible suppliers and
materials to the fullest extent possible in the publishing of its books. Such materials
include vegetable-based, low-VOC inks and acid-free papers that are recycled,
totally chlorine-free, or partly composed of nonwood fibers.

Brown, MacAlister.
Cambodia confounds the peacemakers, 1979–1998 /
MacAlister Brown, Joseph J. Zasloff.
p.   cm.
"A book from the Oakley Center for the Humanities
and Social Sciences, Williams College."
Includes index.
ISBN 0-8014-3536-6 (alk. paper)
1. Cambodia—Politics and government—1979–
I. Zasloff, Joseph Jermiah. II. Title.
DS554.8.B76   1998
959.604'2—dc21   98-7448

Cloth printing   10   9   8   7   6   5   4   3   2   1

Contents

Preface

In April 1975 the triumphant entry of the North Vietnamese into Saigon was preceded by the Khmer Rouge's ruthless evacuation of Cambodia's capital, Phnom Penh. For the next four years little was known of the agrarian totalitarian regime imposed upon Cambodia, as Khmer Rouge leaders defiantly isolated themselves from the international community. Indochina watchers subsisted on isolated shreds of news until the murderous regime was overthrown by Vietnamese military forces and Khmer Rouge defectors in January 1979. The subsequent refusal of the United Nations General Assembly to seat the "puppet" regime installed by the Vietnamese served to restrict the information available to foreign scholars.

Meanwhile the Khmer Rouge armed forces reorganized themselves indisplaced persons camps along the Thai border, and China and Thailand saw to the replenishment of their arsenals. Two other resistance parties grew up, one led by the exiled Prince Norodom Sihanouk, and the rival claimants to legitimacy became stalemated both on the diplomatic front, over the non-admission of the People's Republic of Kampuchea (PRK) to the UN General Assembly, and on the military front, where Khmer Rouge guerrilla forces harassed the Vietnamese Army troops assisting the PRK. The conflict was gradually becoming ripe for diplomatic negotiation.

Brown and Zasloff jointly published studies on Indochina in the 1970s, and we were drawn to the drama emerging in Cambodia. Stimulated by visits to refugee camps on the Thai-Cambodian border in 1980, Zasloff published his observations in University Field Staff Reports. Together we wrote a case study about diplomatic negotiations in the Cambodian crisis, which was published with the support of the Pew Foundation. Brown created simulation exercises with Williams College undergraduates, in which the issue was cast as how to make peace in the face of Khmer Rouge intransigence. Successive years of role-playing students reached an outcome in which China secretly allowed the top Khmer Rouge leader, Pol Pot, to be removed from the scene, with hopes of gradual reconciliation among the Cambodian parties.

In real life, diplomatic negotiation slowly developed between the Phnom Penh regime (led by Hun Sen) and Prince Sihanouk. Talks aimed to end the civil war and settle the legitimacy question in an election conducted by the international community under the aegis of the United Nations. This decade-long peace-seeking negotiation became our continuing research enterprise, all the more engaging as it fell within our special interests in Southeast Asia, diplomacy and negotiation, and international organization. The record became more public, and after 1978 Cambodia itself became accessible. We undertook to recount and analyze the growing international effort to help Cambodia find peace, independence, and democratic political values. Episodes in the story have been told, but scholars had not yet laid out the diplomatic and political story from the routing of the Khmer Rouge in 1979 to the approach to a second national election in 1998. As the United Nations Transitional Authority in Cambodia (UNTAC) took shape and carried out its assignment, it was clear that the UN's most extensive peacemaking and peacekeeping effort was worthy of a comprehensive study, to further public as well as institutional learning about how small a gain may be considered success.

The sources of information we have used range from personal visits to Phnom Penh and border camps during the 1980s to radio transmissions from Cambodian party transmitters, translated by the Foreign Broadcast Information Service of the U.S. government. Personal interviews were conducted at the U.S. State Department and Defense Department, with Central Intelligence Agency personnel in Washington and in the field (Bangkok and Phnom Penh), and with various embassies representing the Socialist Republic of Vietnam, the Soviet Union, Democratic Kampuchea, Canada, and Thailand. United Nations personnel at the New York City headquarters, and in the UN Border Relief Operation and the various components of UNTAC in Cambodia in 1992 and 1993, greatly assisted our understanding of the unfolding drama. Journalists of various countries and affiliations contributed special insights, as well as key suggestions about whom to see for our coverage of the UNTAC operation and the post-UNTAC scene and our efforts to read the balance sheet on key actors in the struggle. An invaluable source of information about the twelve-year negotiation effort to reach a comprehensive political settlement was *The Cambodia Conflict:*

Search for a Settlement, 1979–1991, An Analytical Chronology, by Patrick Raszelenberg and Peter Schier for the Institute of Asian Affairs in Hamburg, Germany.

Our own collaboration has benefited from more than two decades of joint writing about Laos and Cambodia, with most of our field research done in tandem. Individual research regarding the writing of the Constitution was done by Zasloff with Professor Louis Aucoin, at Boston University, for which we are grateful, and both of us attended, student-mounted conferences on Cambodia at the Woodrow Wilson School of Public Affairs, Princeton University, 1982, and at the Schell Center for International Human Rights at Yale Law School, 1991. Over many years as a Khmer Rouge–watcher, and eventually as U.S. ambassador to Cambodia, Charles Twining has patiently informed us, as well as tweaked us on our deliberate pace, and we are grateful for both gestures. Among the journalists who have assisted us over time, Nayan Chanda has probably been the most helpful. The essential journals have been the *Far Eastern Economic Review* and the *Phnom Penh Post.* Their staffs are, of course, in no way responsible for our viewpoints, and their reportage has been seconded and critiqued by dozens of other observers and participants in Cambodia's struggles, whom we have identified when so authorized.

Although we cannot pretend to honor all the individuals who have shared their time and knowledge with us, over almost twenty years of observing Cambodia, we can express our appreciation to them, and specifically thank the organizations that helped to support our travel and our drafting and production. In the latter category are the ever-willing Faculty Secretarial Office at Williams College under Donna Chenail, Peggy Bryant, Shirley Bushika, and Rebecca Brassard. The research librarians at the John E. Sawyer Library, Williams College, were a dauntless source of help. The readiness of Sawyer Library to acquire timely books and journals about Indochina should also receive grateful mention.

Brown is particularly appreciative of the Fulbright Lectureship Program and the John F. Kennedy Foundation in Thailand, which placed him at Chulalongkorn University, in Bangkok, in 1980–81 and 1984–85. Zasloff is grateful to the Smith-Mundt Scholarship Program for his early introduction to Indochina as a professor at the University of Saigon in 1959 and 1960. He has been assisted in more recent years by the Asian Studies Program, the University Center for International Studies, and the Provost's Development Fund of the University of Pittsburgh. Similarly, Brown has received financial encouragement from the Williams College Faculty Research Fund and a research stipend from the Keck Foundation's grant for Global Studies at Williams College.

Another form of assistance we received was the provision of working space. Particularly rewarding for Brown was his year at the Oakley Center for the Humanities and Social Sciences at Williams College, 1994–95. Zasloff is grateful to Williams College for his appointment as a research associate during spring 1995, and for the generous provision of office space during many summers.

As these words are written the future of Cambodia remains in a delicate balance between personal ambitions, economic greed, the vagaries of health, courage, vision, and chance. We had hoped to record the international community's success story in bringing peace and democracy and development to a tortured state. Instead we have described the complex negotiation and application of a comprehensive political settlement, which unraveled with the Hun Sen coup of July 1997. All hope has not been abandoned, however, and we should not overlook the tangible impact that United Nations peacekeeping has had. Cambodia is not the same polity that it was before UNTAC's visit. UNTAC made a generous effort to sink roots for liberal democracy, a fragile plant, in barren soil. It required special attention, and probably did not receive enough. Strongman government emerged again in 1997. International support of the Cambodian people in their faltering movement toward democratic rule would be an act of mercy, and decency, and even economic feasibility. We hope that our recounting of the mistakes as well as the accomplishments will contribute to greater levels of success in future rescue efforts by the world community, which we believe should be undertaken in spite of our disappointment with the shortfalls in Cambodia.

MacAlister Brown

Williamstown, Massachusetts

Joseph J. Zasloff

Pittsburgh, Pennsylvania

Abbreviations and Acronyms

AEPU	Advance Election Planning Unit
ANS	Armée Nationale Sihanoukiste, or Sihanouk National Army
ASEAN	Association of South East Asian Nations
BLDP	Buddhist Liberal Democratic Party
CGDK	Coalition Government of Democratic Kampuchea
CivPol	UNTAC Civil Police
CNR	Cambodian National Resistance
CPK	Communist Party of Kampuchea
CPP	Cambodian People's Party (SOC)
DK	Democratic Kampuchea (Khmer Rouge)
DNUM	Democratic National Union Movement—of ex-KR Ieng Sary
FBIS	Foreign Broadcast Information Service
FUNCINPEC	United National Front for an Independent, Neutral, Peaceful, and Cooperative Cambodia
ICP	Indochinese Communist Party
JIM	Jakarta Informal Meeting
KCP	Kampuchean (or Khmer) Communist Party (same as CPK)
KNP	Khmer Nation Party—of Sam Rainsy
KNSP	Khmer National Solidarity Party, founded by Khieu Samphan (KR)
KPNLF	Khmer People's National Liberation Front
KPRP	Khmer People's Revolutionary Party
KPRAF	Khmer People's Revolutionary Armed Forces
KR	Khmer Rouge, "Red Khmers"—Communist Party of Kampuchea (KCP); also called Democratic Kampuchea, DK, or PDK
LDP	Liberal Democratic Party
MOLINAKA	Movement for the National Liberation of Kampuchea, 1979

NADK	National Army of Democratic Kampuchea (Khmer Rouge)
NAM	Non-Aligned Movement
NGC	National Government of Cambodia
NGO	non-government organization
NUF	National United Front led by FUNCINPEC and KNP
PAVN	People's Army of Vietnam
P-5	Permanent Five Members of the UN Security Council
PDK	Party of Democratic Kampuchea (Khmer Rouge)
PNGC	Provisional National Government of Cambodia
PRK	People's Republic of Kampuchea, later SOC
RCAF	Royal Cambodian Armed Forces
SNC	Supreme National Council (of Cambodia)
SOC	State of Cambodia
SRV	Socialist Republic of Vietnam
UCD	Union of Cambodian Democrats—founded by Ranariddh, 1997
UNAMIC	United Nations Advance Mission in Cambodia
UNDP	United Nations Development Programme
UNGA	United Nations General Assembly
UNHCR	United Nations High Commissioner for Refugees
UNSC	UNited Nations Security Council
UNTAC	United Nations Transitional Authority in Cambodia

Actors in the Combodia Conflict, 1975–1993

	SOC	DK	FUNCINPEC	KPNLF
Governmental identity	People's Republic of Kampuchea (PRK) 1979–89 State of Cambodia 1989–93	Democratic Kampuchea (Khmer Rouge) 1975–82 Coalition Government of Democratic Kampuchea CGDK) 1982–90 National Government of Cambodia (NGC) 1990–93	United Front for an Independent, Neutral, Peaceful, and Cooperative Cambodia (FUNCINPEC) 1981–92 CGDK 1982–90 NGC 1990–93	Khmer People's National Liberation Front 1979–82 CGDK 1982–90 NGC 1990–93
Party identity	Cambodian People's Party 1991– Khmer People's Revolutionary Party (KPRP) 1979–91	Party of Democratic Kampuchea (PDK) 1976 Communist Party of Kampuchea (CPK) 1960–81 (secret)	FUNCINPEC 1981	Buddhist Liberal Democratic Party (BLDP) 1992–
Leaders	Hun Sen, prime minister Heng Samrin, president of PRK	Khieu Samphan (foreign affairs) Pol Pot ("brother number one") Ieng Sary (China relations)	Prince Sihanouk (former chief of state) Prince Ranariddh (son)	Son Sann (former prime minister)
Regional supporters	Socialist Republic of Vietnam(SRV)	Thailand (covert border traffic) China (arms supply)	ASEAN (Brunei, Indonesia, Malaysia, Philippines, Singapore,) Thailand	ASEAN
Aligned outside powers	°USSR	°China 1975–92	Australia, °France, Japan, °USA, °UK	Australia, °France, Japan, °USA, °UK

°USSR (Russia), China, France, UK, and USA confer monthly starting January 1990, as permanent members of UN Security Council, P-5.

Chronology of Events, 1975–1998

1975

April 17   Khmer Rouge wins civil war—imposes ruthless rural communalism, names country Democratic Kampuchea (DK).

1978

December 25   Vietnam invades Cambodia to install pro-Vietnam regime.

1979

January 10   People's Republic of Kampuchea (PRK) formed in Phnom Penh.

January 11   Exiled Prince Sihanouk successfully appeals at UN to continue seating DK.

1981

July 13   International Conference on Kampuchea, New York—93 states attend, no agreement.

1982

June 22   Coalition Government of Democratic Kampuchea (CGDK) announced by three factions; Sihanouk's (FUNCINPEC), Son Sann's (KPNLF), and DK.

1985

January 14   Hun Sen becomes prime minister of People's Republic of Kampuchea.

1987

December 4–5   First meeting, in France, of Sihanouk and Hun Sen.

1989

July 25–28   First Jakarta informal meeting (JIM) of CGDK parties and PRK.

July 30–August 30   Paris Conference on Cambodia—4 factions, 19 countries, no settlement.

September 27   Vietnam announces completion of full troop withdrawal.
October   Evans (Australia) offers proposal for UN-administered transitional period preceding elections.

1990
August 27–28   Five permanent members (P-5) of UN Security Council offer "framework" for comprehensive political settlement.
September 9–10   At Jakarta informal meeting, four factions agree to form a Supreme National Council (SNC).
November 26   P-5 agree on draft Agreements on a Comprehensive Political Settlement of the Cambodia Conflict; SNC almost agrees.

1991
May 1   Voluntary cease-fire achieved in Cambodia.
October 16   UN Advance Mission in Cambodia (UNAMIC) established by Security Council.
October 23   Paris Agreements on a Comprehensive Political Settlement are signed.
November 9   First UNAMIC personnel arrive in Cambodia.

1992
January 9   Yasushi Akashi named special representative of secretary-general in Cambodia.
February 28   Security Council establishes UNTAC (UN Transitional Authority in Cambodia).
March 15   Akashi arrives in Phnom Penh.
May 15   SNC adopts Electoral Law; party registration starts.
June 13   Phase two of cease-fire begins, without Khmer Rouge.

1993
January 28   SNC sets election of National Assembly for May 23–28.
April 4   Khmer Rouge announces nonparticipation in election; campaign starts April 7, with sporadic violence.
May 23–28   Election, 90% turnout; Akashi declares it "free and fair." FUNCINPEC (led by Prince Ranariddh) wins 45 percent of votes and 58 seats; CPP wins 38 percent of votes (51 seats).
June 14   Sihanouk restored as head of state, by Constituent Assembly.
July 1   Coalition provisional government approved by assembly.
September 24   New Constitution of Cambodia promulgated; Sihanouk elected king by assembly, names new government with two prime ministers, Ranariddh and Hun Sen.
December 31   UNTAC personnel fully withdrawn; Center for Human Rights remains.

1994
February–March   Fighting between Khmer Rouge and government forces—no decisive outcome.
June   Sihanouk proposes he lead a government of national unity—prime ministers unwilling.
July   National Assembly outlaws Khmer Rouge.

October	FUNCINPEC ministers Sam Rainsy and Prince Norodom Sirivuddh harassed out of office by political rivals. Rainsy starts new political party, Khmer Nation Party (KNP), later the Sam Rainsy Party.
1995	Growing friction between the two prime ministers.
1996	
August 8	Ieng Sary and 4,000 Khmer Rouge soldiers defect to royal goverment—arranged by Ranariddh, but Hun Sen takes credit.
August 28	Sary creates Democratic National United Movement (DNUM).
September 14	King grants amnesty to Ieng Sary, after two prime ministers request it.
1997	
March 30	Demonstration led by Sam Rainsy's KNP hit by hand grenades, 16 dead; Hun Sen appears implicated.
June 6	Ranariddh negotiates more Khmer Rouge troop defections.
July 5	Troops of Hun Sen and Ranariddh fight in and outside Phnom Penh; reports of executions by Hun Sen troops.
July 6	Hun Sen dismisses Ranariddh, who has left for Europe; Hun Sen accuses Ranariddh of illegal arms and troop movements.
July 10	ASEAN postpones Cambodia entry indefinitely.
July 16	Ung Huot nominated by FUNCINPEC remnants for First Prime Minister.
July 22	Ranariddh-loyal troops reach Thai border under General Niek Bun Chhay.
July 25	Pol Pot tried for murder of Son Sen in Anlong Veng by a "Peoples Tribunal"; sentenced to house arrest for life.
August 6	National Assembly (NA) removes parliamentary immunity of Ranariddh.
	NA names Ung Huot First Prime Minister.
August 8	DNUM says it will stay neutral.
	Ranariddh and KNP and BLDP found Union of Cambodian Democrats (UCD) in Bangkok.
August 12	King receives Chea Sim, Hun Sen, and Ung Huot in Beijing.
August 18	Hun Sen denounces UN Center for Human Rights.
September	Foreign aid cut back, and IMF suspends operations.
September 19	UN General Assembly leaves Cambodia seat vacant.
October 16	Ailing Pol Pot interviewed—no remorse.
October 25	King returns to China, after a two-months' visit in Siem Reap.
October 30	Ieng Sary visits Phnom Penh; he supports the CPP line (i.e., that July 5 was not a "coup").
November 7	Hun Sen travels to Japan; he says that Ranariddh may enter

	the election, after requesting an amnesty (Ranariddh says he is not guilty of crimes).
November 18	Sam Rainsy returns to Phnom Penh for a ceremony for the March 30 grenade victims.
December 1&2	Twenty-five members of UCD arrive in Phnom Penh; they seek safe return for all exile-politicians.
December 8	Sam Rainsy and Hun Sen meet for three hours (all smiles).
December 19	National Assembly passes electoral law—election to be July 26, 1998.

1998

January	European Union (EU) pledges $11 million for election, without insisting on Ranariddh participation.
January 25	Khmer Nation Party (Sam Rainsy) open in principle to coalition with CPP after a free election.
February 2	Ung Huot founds the Populist Party, backed by five ex-FUNCINPEC national assemblymen.
February 13	National Election Commission of questionable neutrality.
February	U.S. Department of State calls for "free, fair and credible" election.
March 4	Military court convicts Ranariddh (in absentia) of arms smuggling and conspiracy. Hun Sen requests royal pardon.
March 21	King Sihanouk pardons Ranariddh of both charges.
March 30	Ranariddh returns to Phnom Penh for four days—with bravado, and melancholy—mild clash of demonstrators.
	KR factions reported fighting one another.
April 7	UN S-G Special Representative for Human Rights reports fifty opposition politicians killed since August.
April 8	UN S-G agrees to coordinate management and observation of election.
April 11	RCAF fights for control of Anlong Veng. Ta Mok, Khieu Samphan, Nuon Chea escape.
April 15	Pol Pot found dead in his sleep. Thai army does not permit an autopsy.
May 13	DK Radio goes off the air.
June–July	Voter registration and poll organization by European Union; NGOs send observers.
July 26	Election mostly free and fair. CPP wins 64 seats; needs a coalition to form a new government.

CAMBODIA CONFOUNDS
THE PEACEMAKERS
1979–1998

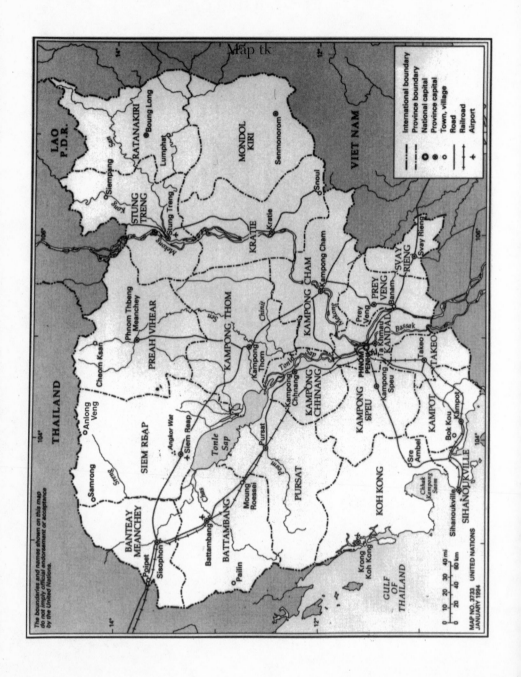

Map tk

The Genesis of a Failed State

hrough faults of its own leaders and misfortunes in abundance, Cambodia entered the 1980s as a "failed state," in need of help on an international scale.[1] A civil war between Cambodian political factions aligned with regional and superpower rivals raged in a country traumatized by three and a half years (1975–78) of atrocious rule by the so-called Khmer Rouge party. This national nightmare was imposed by the Khmer Rouge, officially identified as the Communist Party of Kampuchea (1960–81) and after 1981 as the Party of Democratic Kampuchea (PDK).[2] But as the Khmer Rouge period ended, the nation was badly divided over which set of leaders should succeed the ruthless Khmer Rouge.

The phenomenon of failed states has recently shown itself most clearly in Bosnia, Somalia, and Liberia, as well as Cambodia. The mark of a state in this condition, as Gerald B. Helman and Steven R. Ratner have said, is to be "utterly incapable of sustaining itself as a member of the international

1. This phenomenon was first addressed by Gerald B. Helman and Steven R. Ratner, "Saving Failed States," *Foreign Policy*, winter 1992–93. They designated Cambodia as clearly a "failed state," p. 14. A somewhat related concept, *state collapse* ("the literal implosion of structures of authority and legitimacy"), has been recently conceived and studied with respect to African states (in 1993), without even acknowledgment of its kinship with the concept of *state failure*. See William I. Zartman, ed., *Collapsed States: The Disintegration and Restoration of Legitimate Authority* (Boulder: Lynne Rienner, 1995). According to the latter author, state failure is not necessarily state collapse.

2. Kampuchea is the indigenous name for what Westerners called Cambodia. In this text the two names are used interchangeably. The Khmer Rouge ("Red Khmer") were officially known as the Kampuchean Communist Party (KCP), during 1960–81. In 1982 they changed their name to Party of Democratic Kampuchea (PDK).

community."[3] A pervasive incapacity of government is evident. Civil strife and a breakdown of government produce widespread economic privation, anarchy, and violence. Such was the condition of Cambodia, as summarized by Ratner in 1992: "Twenty years of civil war, invasions, outside arms supplies, gross violations of human rights, massive dislocation of its population, and destruction of its infrastructure have rendered the country incapable of governing itself."[4] How did Cambodia fall into such a condition?

Cambodia had declined over time from a proud and creative empire in the Angkor period in the ninth through fifteenth centuries to a disintegrating kingdom of peasants and fishermen by the nineteenth, century barely able to survive as a buffer state between Siam and Vietnam. Its once imperial territory had been nibbled away during four centuries of decline, until France arrived to impose a protectorate in 1863. This colonial arrangement maintained the traditional monarchy and exploited the agricultural, fish, and mineral endowment of a rump Cambodia.

During World War II, Japanese occupation of Indochina weakened the French position as protecting power. Although the French returned in 1945, they faced hostile independence movements, and by the mid-1950s France had given up trying to maintain its colonial sway in Indochina. King Sihanouk—whom the French had maneuvered to the throne in 1941—negotiated insistently for Cambodian independence, which was granted in November 1953.

The French effort to hang on longer as the colonial power in Vietnam ran out of energy in 1954 at the Geneva Conference, and the United States entered the area to maintain a barrier against the communist-led North Vietnamese. Until 1970 Cambodia, under Sihanouk's adroit leadership, avoided entanglement in the U.S.-Vietnam war next door by remaining neutral and independent. When Sihanouk could no longer orchestrate neutrality, it cost him his job. In the face of growing economic mismanagement and military impotence, Sihanouk's cousin Sisowath Sirik Matak and the prime minister, General Lon Nol, combined to secure a National Assembly vote deposing the weary Sihanouk during his absence in Europe in March 1970. This shift in leadership, however, brought the war in Vietnam openly into Cambodia, and heightened the national demoralization to the point

3. Helman and Ratner, "Saving Failed States," further define the conditions of state failure and call for expansion of the role of the UN in conservatorship for needy states. Ratner has developed this idea in his book *The New UN Peacekeeping: Building Peace in Lands of Conflict after the Cold War* (New York: St. Martin's, 1995).

4. Helman and Ratner, "Saving Failed States," p. 14. This tragic period in Cambodian history is told in brief form in Russell R. Ross, ed., *Cambodia: A Country Study* (Washington: Federal Research Div., Library of Congress, GPO, 1990), chap. 1, "Historical Setting."

that radical Cambodian communist guerrilla soldiers (the Khmer Rouge) were able to march victoriously into Phnom Penh in April 1975. They remained in power for three and a half insane years until routed by Vietnamese forces and Khmer Rouge defectors in late December 1978.

Sihanouk had manipulated his nation's politics from 1953 to 1970 by giving up the throne (in March 1955), but not his aura as prince, and leading his own national party while serving as prime minister. He tried unsuccessfully to steer clear of the war in Vietnam. North Vietnam's army and southern Viet Cong forces used Cambodia's northeastern border areas as a base for attacking South Vietnam, and the port of Sihanoukville for landing supplies destined for North Vietnamese sanctuaries. Starting in 1969, the United States systematically bombed these areas without public acknowledgment. China stepped forward as a source of economic aid.

Fortune ran out on the populist prince in March 1970, and his inept successors were unable (or unwilling) to protect the country from deadly communal violence against thousands of immigrant Vietnamese who were living peaceably within Cambodia. In addition, the Lon Nol government did not oppose the U.S. and South Vietnamese forces which thrust inconclusively (in May 1970) into the border sanctuaries of the North Vietnamese. The mercurial Prince Sihanouk, supported in exile by the Chinese premier, Chou En-lai, made common cause with the previously renounced Khmer Rouge. They named him the titular head of the National United Front for Kampuchea, whose guerrilla troops were waging a disciplined but ruthless war in the countryside. Even after the U.S.–Vietnam War ended with a nominal cease-fire on January 27, 1973, peace did not extend to Cambodia. The Khmer Rouge were determined to win their own victory without the advice or support of the North Vietnamese. By the spring of 1975, the Khmer Rouge, thought to be less than seventy thousand strong,[5] put Phnom Penh under siege, and prepared a disastrous program of social leveling and relocation for every town and city in the nation.

The Khmer Rouge had its origins in the communist Khmer People's Revolutionary Party (KPRP), established secretly in 1951 under Vietnamese mentors. Following the Geneva settlement of 1954, the party divided its forces between Cambodia and Vietnam. The stay-at-home party element established a temporary Central Committee in Phnom Penh, but the KPRP suffered grievous losses to Sihanouk's secret police through defections. Urban-oriented versus rural-oriented factions within the party struggled for

5. Elizabeth Becker puts the Khmer Rouge army at 68,000 in April 1975. *When the War Was Over* (New York: Simon and Schuster, 1986), p. 179.

power, with the urbans gaining control. Saloth Sar, the leader of this segment, became general secretary in February 1963, after the previous party leader, Tou Samouth, had mysteriously disappeared a few months earlier. In May 1966 the secret party changed its name to Kampuchean Communist Party (KCP) and sent most of its leadership underground.[6]

A small group of French-educated radicals, generally of propertied class origin, gradually acquired control of the party's destiny, even though the North Vietnamese communist leadership preferred to keep Sihanouk in power, in a neutral Cambodia. In 1953 Saloth Sar (alias Pol Pot) had returned from a study grant in Paris, after failing his exams at radio-electricity school. Already a member of the French Communist Party, he quickly joined the underground KPRP. By 1963, Pol Pot and his brother-in-law, Ieng Sary (also a Paris student and a schoolteacher), found this game so hazardous that they retreated to the forests, where their revolutionary wives (the sisters Khieu Ponnary and Khieu Thirit) joined them two years later.

More successful as students were Khieu Samphan, Hu Nim, and Hu Yuon, who worked for university doctorates in France in the early 1950s (though of these three only Khieu Samphan would survive his party's deadly factional rivalries and purges). Their challenging academic treatises on Cambodia's dependency on the international economy, and on the exploitative role of the urban elite, did not set the course of the KCP. Rather, the Pol Pot national chauvinist element of the party, doctrinaire to the point of losing touch with humanity, favored a super economic Great Leap Forward (going Mao Zedong at least one leap better) toward a millennial, industrially developed state, somehow built on the basis of forced labor in the agricultural sector.[7] Other elements of the party leadership seem to have favored more faithful use of China's Cultural Revolution model (self-reliance, agricultural emphasis, and class leveling), and keeping in touch with the international revolutionary movement. Still another group, destined for oblivion, favored the Vietnamese model of building socialism. During the party's period in power (1975–78) advocates of such links to Vietnam were ruthlessly liquidated.

6. Detailed history of the communist movement in Cambodia is found in Ben Kiernan, *The Pol Pot Regime* (New Haven: Yale University Press, 1996); Ben Kiernan and Chantou Bona, eds., *Peasants and Politics in Kampuchea, 1942–1981* (London: Zed, 1982); Becker, *When the War Was Over*; Craig Etcheson, *The Rise and Demise of Democratic Kampuchea* (Boulder, Colo: Westview, 1984).

7. Kiernan and Boua, *Peasants and Politics*, p. 228. See also the intellectual dissection of the Khmer Rouge by Michael Vickery, "Democratic Kampuchea: Themes and Variation," in *Revolution and Its Aftermath in Kampuchea*, ed. David P. Chandler and Ben Kiernan, Monograph Series No. 25, Southeast Asia Studies (New Haven: Yale University, 1981).

Thus the history of the revolutionary party which called itself (starting in 1982) the Party of Democratic Kampuchea is replete with secrecy, duplicity, and intrigue, strident chauvinism with regard to Vietnam, and compassionless purging of ideological and personal opponents. (These features persisted even in the declining years of the party.) Democratic Kampuchea, intoxicated by its military victory in 1975, brashly challenged Vietnam along its borders (some of which had been previously in dispute). As the bloodshed mounted from these punitive raids in 1977 and 1978, the party unloosed a purge of sickening brutality against its less xenophobic or utopian elements. Arrest, interrogation, torture, confessions of the most twisted sort ("I was a CIA agent"), and execution became a grisly government industry at the Tuol Sleng prison in Phnom Penh, where fallen leaders like Nim, and probably Yuon, as well as Vorn Vet were executed. The revolution was choking on its own paranoia, as well as the vicious clash of revolutionary ideas and practice among regions and among leading personalities. Up to twenty thousand innocents, high and low in importance, were brutally abused and executed at the Tuol Sleng prison alone.

Yet these tens of thousands of victims were relatively few when measured against the hundreds of thousands who died of exertion, undernourishment, social uprooting, ruthless administration, and outright execution of suspected bourgeoisie and religious minorities during the vicious years of mass mobilization of agricultural production, with drastic leveling of social class. The communes in which much of the nation was forced to live banned private property, family units, currency, news media, books, and music as well as laughter. The commune inhabitants slept in barracks and ate in canteens. From April 1975 to January 1979 it is estimated that more than a million Cambodians perished from abuse, sickness, and punitive violence, in a nation of seven million.[8]

Yet the routing of the Khmer Rouge by Vietnamese forces in early 1979 was undertaken not in the name of humanity but rather as an act of regional politics. Vietnam struck to relieve the vicious threat along its borders and to replace China as the presumptive mentor of Cambodia. After three and a half years of mounting reciprocating border incursions (up to division size), Vietnam surreptitiously spearheaded an invading force in late December 1978, which brought in its wake an organization formed largely from Khmer Rouge defectors, called the Khmer National Front for Na-

8. The most reliable estimate of the human toll seems to be Kiernan, *The Pol Pot Regime*, p. 458. A variety of estimates is summarized by the CIA in Etcheson, *Rise and Demise of Democratic Kampuchea*, table 7.1, p. 148.

tional Salvation. In this new national crisis Democratic Kampuchea reenlisted Sihanouk—who had lost all power or influence during its nightmarish rule—to plead at the United Nations in January 1979 for the condemnation of the Vietnamese invasion.

PART I

NEGOTIATION OF A
POLITICAL SETTLEMENT

CHAPTER ONE

The Diagnosis Phase, 1979–1988

I t took twelve years of shifting power relations and diplomatic maneuver to reach a settlement bringing peace and independence to Cambodia. From the earliest days of the overthrow of the Khmer Rouge in December 1978, diplomatic contact and negotiation were seen as potentially rewarding—as the Khmer Rouge/DK demonstrated by appealing to the UN Security Council to condemn and undo Vietnam's intervention. The new claimants of Cambodian national authority, however, even though installed by the People's Army of Vietnam (PAVN), preferred to treat the Cambodia question as strictly a civil war. The capture of Phnom Penh, they argued, had settled the issue in favor of Heng Samrin's newly founded Kampuchean National United Front for National Salvation—which gave way on January 10, 1979, to a self-proclaimed People's Republic of Kampuchea (PRK). With Vietnamese military backing, the PRK routed the Khmer Rouge regime. Vietnam saw no profit in subjecting that victory to diplomatic reconsideration. In its view the Khmer Rouge and other political opponents should acknowledge the new government and end the civil war. The ruthless Khmer Rouge should give way to a new, humane set of leaders, who constituted the sole government of Cambodia and were entitled to represent their nation at the UN and other international fora.

The Cambodian "resistance" to this claim wished to internationalize the issue, in order to challenge the legitimacy of the PRK and to enlist outside support for their implacable rejection of a government installed by direct Vietnamese military intervention. The Khmer Rouge, or Democratic Kampuchea (DK), like most Third World delegations to the UN, asserted that foreign aggression should not be rewarded by giving the United Nations seat of an invaded state to collaborators of the intervening state. For the PRK, however, the matter required no negotiation or compromise, but rather an acceptance of the defeat of the oppressive Khmer Rouge and the impotence of the fugitive Sihanouk and his supporters. The new rulers in Phnom Penh claimed there was nothing to negotiate except surrender and possible amnesty for political opponents of the overthrow.

Tragically, more than a decade passed before the competing players in Cambodia were able to apply negotiation conclusively to settle the Cambodian civil war cum international proxy struggle. Before diplomatic bargaining or give-and-take could be seriously applied, however, the PRK had to give up its hope that, with time, its assertion of national authority would become legitimate. Likewise, the goal of the DK and the followers of Sihanouk and Son Sann—to exclude the usurpers (the puppets of Vietnam) from international acceptability and force them physically out of power—had to reach the point of appearing more costly than a compromise solution.

The twelve-year period of moving toward negotiated agreement on a comprehensive political settlement of the Cambodia conflict swarms with detail concerning parties and players, initiatives and maneuvers, pronouncements and proposals, propaganda and dramatic journalism, conciliators and hard-liners, humanitarian assistance, and individual greed. The players and interests were so variegated that a conceptual breakdown of the years is needed to help perceive the process. We use the explanatory model of diplomacy pioneered by I. William Zartman to simplify the turbulence and maneuvering.[1]

The following treatment applies the three-phase model of negotiation conceived by Zartman, which assumes that negotiators typically undertake a phase of *diagnosis* of the issues and players, a second phase of *formula seeking* for an agreed resolution, and a third phase of settling *details* for the final agreement. The three phases seem to have occurred, in this case, as diagnosis (1979–87), formula seeking (1988–September 1990), details (September 1990–October 1991). Thus, the following account of the search for a political settlement in Cambodia is oriented to three logically related functions.

Phase One (1979–88): Diagnosis

The principal objective during the diagnostic phase is to determine whether negotiation is feasible and likely to be worthwhile. Players or par-

---

1. See I. William J. Zartman and Maureen R. Berman, *The Practical Negotiator* (New Haven: Yale University Press, 1982), especially chaps. 3–5.

ties must be available and willing to commit themselves to the process. They must be ready to talk to one another in a formal manner, even though great enmity, distrust, and disdain may exist between them. No Cambodian party, or coalition of parties, wished to "legitimize" any other, even by sitting down together, and each side claimed to be the sole legal government of Cambodia. The Cambodian parties disagreed regarding who should parley, with Sihanouk insisting on his talking directly with Vietnam and the latter asserting that the conflict was a domestic Cambodian, not an international, dispute. The People's Republic of Kampuchea (PRK) held the Khmer Rouge in contempt, yet they might be ready to talk with some of them in a neutral place if net rewards or benefits were discertible.

If the power relationships were at a stalemate, (as it seemed in the late 1980s) or slipping toward a clear disadvantage for one party, then an agreement to negotiate might become more likely. Third parties could also push the players by withholding (or promising) military or economic assistance, as occurred when both the Soviet Union and China eventually cut back their critical assistance to the PRK and the Khmer Rouge respectively. Pressure might be applied through UN General Assembly and Security Council resolutions, and regional meetings such as ASEAN conducted. A changing structure of relationships, such as the breakup of the Cold War, would surely affect the sense of what was at stake in Cambodia and probably encourage the conclusion that civil war with great power mentors was not a permanent condition. New arrangements of independence and neutrality might become feasible for Cambodia once the rapprochement of China and the USSR was achieved. The diagnosis period was prolonged in this case because the potential parties to negotiations were bitterly divided; but the world political structure was in unusual flux.

The United Nations Forum

As noted previously, the Vietnamese intervention in December 1978 left little room for diplomacy except at the United Nations, where the legitimacy of the overthrow might theoretically be established by seating the new regime (the People's Republic of Kampuchea) as the legal embodiment of Cambodia.[2] The PRK did not achieve UN representation, however. Even though the PRK claimed rulership of the nation, the Democratic Kampuchea government, however detestable its stewardship had been,

2. Acceptance of the credentials of a new government at the UN General Assembly does not bind individual states to accord diplomatic recognition, but it provides an impetus in that direction.

held onto its seat at the General Assembly. The strength of Third World nations' sentiment against outside intervention readily overrode the notion that a government as catastrophic for the nation as the DK deserved to be overthrown by its neighbor—especially if the intervention was partially masked by collaboration with dissidents and deserters. There was no regular channel of communication between the new and the defeated regime; and other aspirants to rulership such as Prince Sihanouk and one-time prime minister Son Sann wanted to be considered in any dialogue about the national future. Sihanouk, as early as August 1979, suggested a national election as a possible formula for resolving the conflict over who should rule.[3] Such a device held no attraction to the PRK leaders already in office. Thus, there was every reason to expect in 1979 that the exploratory stage of negotiation would be prolonged and acrimonious.

Many factors had to be clarified through patient exploration before negotiation of a political settlement could be considered desirable or feasible. First of all, there had to be parties willing to acknowledge one another and to address their conflicting interests and goals. Did such players exist in 1979?

A week after the Vietnamese entry into Cambodia the DK government requested, on January 3, 1979, that the UN Security Council deal with the invasion of its territory. China saw to the release of Prince Sihanouk from his doleful confinement to the palace in Phnom Penh, and flew him to UN headquarters in New York City to speak dramatically in the debate over China's draft Security Council resolution calling for the withdrawal of all foreign troops from Cambodia.[4] Singapore sounded the dominant theme in the debate when it asserted that no other country had a right to topple the government of Democratic Kampuchea however badly it may have treated its people. The Soviet Union, however, vetoed the resolution; and the prince refused any further cooperation with the Khmer Rouge, for the moment at least.

In February 1979, China launched a one-month, twelve-mile military incursion into northern Vietnam, to lay waste the infrastructure and teach Vietnam a lesson. On March 16, the Soviet Union again vetoed a UN Secu-

---

3. Sihanouk, "An Open Letter to the Summit Conference of the Non-Aligned Countries, Havana," Pyongyang, August 1979, in Patrick Raszelenberg and Peter Schier, *The Cambodian Conflict: Search for a Settlement, 1979–91* (Hamburg: Institute of Asian Affairs, 1995), p. 28.

4. Nayan Chanda, *Brother Enemy: The War after the War* (New York: Harcourt Brace Jovanovich, 1986), describes this dramatic journey by the beleaguered prince to speak for the Khmer Rouge government that had allowed the murder of a number of his children and kept himself under virtual house arrest.

rity Council draft resolution, this time sponsored by the Association of South East Asian Nations (ASEAN). This resolution expressed "regret" concerning both the "armed intervention in internal affairs of Kampuchea and the armed attack against the Socialist Republic of Vietnam"—an equating of two military actions that the Soviets did not consider commensurable, nor rightly subject to the same timetable of rectification. China nonetheless completed an announced withdrawal of its forces from Vietnam on March 15, 1979.

Having survived two Security Council debates, the DK government-in-exile faced new challenges at the UN as the Credentials Committee of the thirty-fourth (1979) General Assembly took up the DK's continuing claim to represent Cambodia. By a vote of 6-3, with the United States in the majority, the committee decided to sustain the disintegrating DK government as the representative of Cambodia. The Cuban ambassador summed up the line taken by Soviet bloc nations by calling DK accreditation an action "based on letters from a non-existent government which does not control a single inch of territory of Kampuchea." Nonetheless the PRK failed to gain much backing in the General Assembly, which voted 71-35-34 in favor of the Credentials Committee's recommendation on September 21, 1979.[5]

A permanent Cambodian mission to the UN was installed in March 1979 near the UN headquarters in New York, presumably with Chinese funding. The cosmopolitan radical Thiounn Prasith, a political associate of Pol Pot's in student days in Paris,[6] was accredited by the UN secretary-general as permanent representative of Cambodia, in which capacity he served for thirteen years. The earliest press releases issuing from this mission were awkward in a manner that suggested no native English-speaking editor. In later years this foreign taint disappeared and glossy color photographs of "liberated villages" in Cambodia were distributed on a bimonthly basis, along with foreign policy statements often attributed to the DK foreign minister, Khieu Samphan.

In November 1979 the General Assembly passed the first of what became an annual resolution appealing for a cessation of "all hostilities forthwith" and resolving "that the people of Kampuchea be enabled to choose their own government, without outside interference, subversion, or coer-

5. Ibid., p. 377. A general source of information regarding UN actions is the *Yearbook of the United Nations*, Department of Public Information, United Nations, New York.
6. Ben Kiernan, *The Pol Pot Regime* (New Haven: Yale University Press, 1996), pp. 10, 327–28, reveals little-known data on the aristocratic Thiounn Prasith's radical nationalism and loyal service to the Khmer Rouge. Prasith presided at the Permanent Mission of Democratic Kampuchea in New York as late as May 1992. Interview by M. Brown.

cion."[7] This pronouncement, supported after considerable debate by 91 members of the General Assembly (while 21 opposed and 29 abstained), prompted vehement protest by the "foreign ministry" of the People's Republic of Kampuchea, which the Soviet bloc nations and India, but scarcely any others, officially recognized. Thus a sporadic, long-range diplomatic dialogue of sorts was under way between foreign ministries of questionable legitimacy, each of which claimed to represent Cambodia on the basis of a military conquest to which the Cambodian people had not fully acquiesced. If true diplomatic negotiation was to take place the rival parties had to be willing to suspend the question of recognition under international law, and probably to involve additional participants beyond the PRK and the DK. The range of issues to be negotiated had to be acknowledged, and the parties to the discussion had to be identified and circumscribed. Eight agonizing years passed in exploring and testing issues, leadership, meeting places, conciliators, and items of exchange that might constitute sufficient bases for diplomatic bargaining.

Identification of the Parties to the Dispute

Another requirement of prenegotiation diagnosis was some sign of convergence of the parties' positions. By imaginative efforts, Cambodian leaders and outside diplomats managed to repackage some of the issues. Changing international circumstances, such as the rise of Mikhail Gorbachev and the collapse of the Soviet economy, also altered the power relationships. Some change reflected a growing weariness with warfare or a looming stalemate of military forces. Power was shifting in ways that might make a compromise more palatable for Vietnam than the rising cost of its military commitment. The years 1979–88 saw all of these factors at work, but the process of *diagnosis* of the conflict to determine whether and when it was negotiable dragged on and on. Fear and resentment, both within Cambodia and across the region, generated by Vietnam's domineering entry into Cambodia in December 1978, precluded a simple acceptance by the ASEAN neighbors of the satellite regime in Phnom Penh; and the resistance to the PRK received tangible military assistance from China, Thailand, Singapore, and the United States. Thus serious negotiation, except for the wooing of votes

7. Raszelenberg and Schier, *The Cambodian Conflict*, p. 30. This book is relied upon extensively hereafter for its recording of communications by the many parties to the Cambodia disputes, but not necessarily for its editorial commentary. It is a remarkable and invaluable compendium of radio and written output by the key media in the Cambodia conflict. Materials found in its pages 21–150 are used in this chapter.

for the annual UN General Assembly resolution on "the situation in Kampuchea," had to wait nine years before the conflict could be diagnosed as truly ripe for resolution.

The first faltering step toward a settlement through negotiationwas the plea made by Prince Sihanouk on January 11, 1979, for UN Security Council condemnation of the Vietnamese military entry into Cambodia. Sihanouk's plea prevailed over a message issued the previous day by the PRK, claiming to be "the authentic, legal and only representative of Kampuchea."[8] Yet Sihanouk rebuffed China's Deng Xiaoping's urging to join the DK government (in exile). This left unsettled the question of who would participate in any effort to negotiate a political settlement in Cambodia.

The fledgling PRK meanwhile tried to legitimize its heavy dependence on Vietnam by signing (in Phnom Penh on February 11, 1979) a treaty of friendship, peace, and cooperation with the Socialist Republic of Vietnam (SRV), which called for "fraternal cooperation" in all fields, including "national defense and construction." The PRK later invoked this treaty to validate the presence of the People's Army of Vietnam (PAVN) in Cambodia (since late December 1978) as being at the request of the PRK—which had not claimed to exist before January 10, 1979. China launched its costly punitive incursion twelve miles into Vietnam, destroying infrastructure, but fell far short of persuading Vietnam to withdraw from Cambodia or address Sino-Vietnamese disputes by means of negotiation. Nonetheless, China and Vietnam sat down in April 1979 to discuss the normalization of relations. Repeated meetings over the next eight months made no progress, however, and parleys were indefinitely postponed in December.

Equally barren were the earliest efforts by the Khmer Rouge to strengthen the depleted forces of resistance to the PRK by offering to cooperate with Prince Sihanouk and his yet unorganized followers. The prince scornfully rejected such suggestions, which Ieng Sary offered via *Le Monde* on June 1. Son Sann, a former prime minister in the 1960s, proclaimed a new Khmer People's National Liberation Front (KPNLF) four months later. The KPNLF claimed to command several thousand armed troops inside Cambodia, and its key goals for Cambodia were sovereign independence and a just and democratic social order.

Tens of thousands of Cambodians fled westward in 1979 in hopes of escaping the advancing Vietnamese and avoiding recruitment by the new regime, as well as to find food and security along the Thai border. In time they found both food and shelter in organized refugee centers hastily provided by the United Nations with private international assistance. Vietnam's

8. Ibid., pp. 21–22; Chanda, *Brother Enemy*, chap. 11.

invasion had disrupted the brutal communal economic system imposed by the DK government and threatened the nation with another catastrophe. Looming food shortages helped to drive more than half a million persons to the Thai border, where emergency food distribution was organized by the UN refugee and relief organizations and voluntary agencies from the international church and refugee relief network.[9] Months later, settled in holding camps, some just inside Cambodia, this mass of displaced Cambodians became a pool for guerrilla resistance fighters and their families. Most of them were ineligible for resettlement in France or the United States and could only hope for a comprehensive political settlement that would favor their return home to Cambodia. This return, however, was thirteen miserable years in coming.

The General Assembly Resolution, 1979–

The glimmer of a diplomatic route to a comprehensive settlement of the Cambodia conflict first appeared in the UN General Assembly's adoption (91-21-29) on November 14, 1979, of an ASEAN-sponsored resolution calling for immediate withdrawal of all foreign forces from Kampuchea. The resolution also requested the secretary-general to report on the possibility of holding an international conference on Cambodia. The secretary-general had already undertaken to organize a conference on immediate humanitarian relief for displaced persons along the Cambodian-Thai borders. The PRK government in Phnom Penh remained unrecognized at the UN General Assembly and was therefore unwilling to deal with UN relief operations. Private voluntary agencies, however, were allowed to operate in the PRK in Phnom Penh, as were the Russians. In spite of Prince Sihanouk's open letter in September to the UN member states suggesting that Cambodia's seat be declared vacant until a national government could be formed, the Credentials Committee of the General Assembly, as earlier noted, recommended (6-3) on September 19 that the DK continue to hold the seat, and the General Assembly adopted the recommendation on September 21. The United States, in order to counter Vietnam in the region, voted with the majority in both the committee and the General Assembly.

Sihanouk took other diplomatic initiatives with slightly more success. On September 23–27, 1979, he vetted a peace plan at a colloquium of followers

---

9. William Shawcross, *The Quality of Mercy: Cambodia, Holocaust, and Modern Conscience* (New York: Simon and Schuster, 1984), tells the dramatic story of relief organizations on the Thai-Cambodian border.

at his exile home in Pyongyang, North Korea.[10] He placed his main emphasis on holding a "Geneva 1954 type conference," with the resurrection of its International Control Commission (India, Poland, Canada) to verify the removal of Vietnamese troops, disarm all Khmer fighters, and provide security for the election of a truly representative government. Thus the elements of a formula for renewing the nation were in the air, if not on the UN agenda, but the serious players were yet to decide how they should confront one another.

A growing rapprochement of the United States and China, however, sustained itself during both a visit of Deng Xiaoping to the United States and also China's punitive incursion into Vietnam in February 1979. At the same time, the Soviet Union showed its unwillingness to stand up militarily for Vietnam (during the Chinese incursion). ASEAN, in mid-January 1979, expressed its deep concern about "the on-going armed intervention against the independence, sovereignty and territorial integrity of Kampuchea." The Khmer Rouge, despite the routing of their forces to the Thai border, clung to much of their following of soldiers and families in the UN-financed relief camps of bamboo thatch, with water trucks and basic food and medicine, astride the border. Gradually the Khmer Rouge impressed new young soldiers into service and replenished their Chinese-financed equipment under the permissive eye of the Thai military at the border. Refugee camp populations segregated themselves into Khmer Rouge sites and other political groupings. Prince Sihanouk, the key political asset in the pre-positioning game, continued to scorn the invitations of the DK party to join forces. A cosmetic move by the DK in December 1979, replacing Prime Minister Pol Pot with the presumably moderate Khieu Samphan, made no serious impression on the situation. Pol Pot remained fully effective as commander-in-chief of the National Army of Democratic Kampuchea notwithstanding his purported removal from the top political post.[11]

The second year of testing out the negotiability of the struggle in Cambodia concluded with a new UN General Assembly resolution, this time calling for an international conference on Cambodia in 1981, which would focus especially on withdrawal of foreign forces, free UN-supervised elections, and UN guarantees of Cambodia's independence and territorial integrity. A proto-formula for negotiation might have been visible, but the PRK foreign minister, Hun Sen, rejected UN resolutions out of hand, since there was "no international problem to be resolved." The matter, he asserted, was an internal Kampuchean problem.

10. Raszelenberg and Schier, *The Cambodian Conflict*, pp. 28–29.
11. Ibid., pp. 31, 37–39.

1980–1981:Toward a UN Conference on Cambodia

Two major events occurred in this period: the founding of a front based on Prince Sihanouk, and the International Conference on Kampuchea held in New York City in July 1981, under UN auspices.

Four months before the conference gathered in New York, Sihanouk created his own political organization. On February 9, 1981, the prince had expressed his readiness to cooperate with the Khmer Rouge against the Vietnamese occupation, but he insisted on Chinese military assistance and financial support as a precondition. A month later he conferred directly, for the first time, in his exile abode in Pyongyang, North Korea, with the DK prime minister, Khieu Samphan. China's Radio Beijing then interviewed the DK spokesman, who alluded somewhat incongruously to future UN-supervised elections and parliamentary government in Cambodia. Lack of agreement was evident, nonetheless, on the conditions under which the Khmer factions would disarm as the PAVN might withdraw from Cambodia. On March 21, 1981, a small group of Sihanouk followers, after a working meeting in Pyongyang, proclaimed the National United Front for an Independent, Neutral, Peaceful, and Cooperative Cambodia (FUNCIN-PEC, in French), with Sihanouk (living in North Korea) as president. Its military arm, the MOLINAKA movement, was already organizing, and the prince had expressed a willingness to cooperate with other resistance forces.[12] The PRK, meanwhile, had bolstered its claim to political legitimacy by unveiling a draft constitution on March 10 and electing a National Assembly on May 1, 1981.

The scene was now set for an international conference to seek a comprehensive solution—but the International Conference on Kampuchea, in New York on July 13–17, 1981, failed to bridge the gap between negotiating parties. Seventy-nine countries attended and fourteen sent observers. Vietnam, the USSR, Laos, and the PRK did not attend, since they objected to the conference's assumption of jurisdiction. ASEAN offered a draft proposal calling for immediate disarming of the Khmer factions after a full pullout by the Vietnamese forces. This idea found no favor with the DK or China, or for that matter with the absent Vietnam and PRK. China's objections to the ASEAN draft were nonetheless accommodated in the final declaration by calling for "appropriate arrangements to ensure that armed Kampuchean factions are not able to prevent or disrupt the holding of free elections, or intimidate or coerce the population during the electoral process." From the sidelines the PRK foreign minister asserted, "There is

12. Ibid., pp. 42–43.

no Kampuchea problem and hence no solution for it." Before long, the counter-chorus would sing of dark designs in Hanoi to resurrect the "Indochina Federation" (Vietnam, Laos, and Cambodia), which Ho Chi Minh had secretly referred to in 1951 as the future goal of the newly formed Vietnam Worker's Party. Events such as the 1954 Geneva Conference on Indochina had long since altered the "federation" idea expressed in 1951. The Indochina-wide approach to revolution had faded into history, as the Cambodian and the Laotian People's Revolutionary Parties took on the burden of political struggle in their own countries— with Vietnamese advice and "special relations" but not formal union.[13]

Despite its impasse, the abortive International Conference on Kampuchea registered in its declaration a basic structure for peace. This consisted of a cease-fire, withdrawal of all foreign forces, the holding of free elections under UN supervision, and international guarantees of independence and neutrality. The conference adjourned, subject to reconvening by its president advised by an ad hoc committee. The issues appeared to be not yet ripe for negotiation, but the elements of a transaction were being identified.

Formation of a Coalition Resistance "Government"

Sihanouk's anti-Vietnam policy next moved assertively toward the formation of a tripartite front embracing the parties led by himself, Son Sann, and Pol Pot. The prince first sounded out the KPNLF leader, Son Sann, in France in early August 1981 and received a very tentative reception. By September 4, however, Son Sann joined Sihanouk and the DK's Khieu Samphan in a "Singapore Joint Statement" expressing their desire to create a coalition government of Democratic Kampuchea. The three camps set up an ad hoc committee to work out the modalities of the venture. Military coordination was to be achieved via a tripartite committee, rather than a joint chief of staff, and this arrangement would permit ASEAN to distribute aid to all three of the factions without generating unnecessary mistrust. The unanimity of the three parties did not extend, however, to embracing leading Khmer Rouge personalities. Son Sann, in a speech on October 9, demanded political exile for several of them, which the DK radio promptly rejected as "completely unreasonable." The three factions asserted full agreement, however, in pledging not to interfere with the proposed UN-

13. See MacAlister Brown, "The Indochina Federation Idea: Learning from History," in *Postwar Indochina*, ed. Joseph J. Zasloff (Washington: Foreign Service Institute, U.S. Department of State, 1988), chap. 4.

supervised elections and to respect the outcome. On October 21, 1981 (Resolution 36/5), the UN General Assembly went on record again overwhelmingly in favor of withdrawal of foreign troops (100-25-19) and adopted the declaration of the International Conference on Kampuchea which spelled out the elements of a comprehensive solution of the Cambodia conflict. Once again the battle over accepting the credentials of the DK delegation to the General Assembly was won by a decisive margin, 77-37-31 in favor of maintaining the DK in its seat.[14]

The ad hoc committee for exploring the formation of a "coalition government of Democratic Kampuchea"—which the Singapore Joint Statement of September 4 had created—met ten times (starting in Bangkok) before reconvening with the foreign ministers of Singapore and Thailand (Suppiah Dhanabalan and Siddhi Savetsila) and the deputy premier of Singapore (Sinnathamby Rajaratnam) in late November 1981. The agreement had specified that the "three parties would refrain from bringing to the public their differences during the whole period of the agreement."[15] This condition did not long prevail, however, as the KPNLF let it be known that it would not join political hands with the Khmer Rouge, some of whose leaders should remain in exile. Nonetheless, the DK faction took the diplomatic offensive on November 30, 1981, by airing both a summary of the progress made by the ad hoc committee and also the proposed political program for a coalition government, which the committee members of the three parties had agreed to in principle.

The operating principle of the proposed "union" was to be "tripartitism," with a consensus required on "all major issues." The top offices of the coalition would be president, prime minister (a position that Son Sann coveted), and deputy prime minister (officially responsible for foreign affairs), a position eventually assumed by the DK's Khieu Samphan. The DK party insisted that no agreement had been signed, and the reluctant Son Sann party was given two months to consider the proposal.

At the United Nations General Assembly in October 1981 the DK had tried to fortify its position by sending Deputy Prime Minister Ieng Sary, one of its leaders whom the KPNLF had declared ineligible for joining a tripartite council, to meet in the corridors with Third World foreign ministers and to deliver the annual address of Kampuchea. Notwithstanding the abominable record of his Khmer Rouge government during the years

14. Raszelenberg and Schier, *The Cambodian Conflict*, pp. 47–49. General Assembly Resolution 36/5.

15. Permanent Mission of Democratic Kampuchea to the UN, Press Release, No. 084/81, Sept. 15, 1981.

1975–78, Sary set forth a five-point minimum political program for settling the situation in Kampuchea, which had been first announced by the DK on June 30, 1981. The proposal called for (1) total withdrawal of Vietnamese troops from Kampuchea and a UN-supervised general and free election, (2) election of a national assembly which would establish a constitution for a "parliamentary regime," (3) maintenance of Kampuchea as "independent, peaceful, neutral and non-aligned," (4) election of a national government and (5) formation of a national army. A later statement by the DK's permanent representative to the UN, Thiounn Prasith, reduced the proposal to the first three items: withdrawal, elections, and independence and neutrality.[16]

In a move designed to reduce the apparent ideological diversity within the coalition "government," the Communist Party of Kampuchea (CPK), the political core of the DK government, officially dissolved itself on December 6, 1981. Henceforth its former members were to continue "as resolute patriots" in their glorious struggle and their "noble mission to fight the Vietnamese Le-Duan clique aggressor and expansionist" (*sic*),[17] but they would not be publicly linked to communism. In Phnom Penh, as well, a change of party image was attempted on December 4, 1981, as the ruling Khmer People's Revolutionary Party (KPRP) made Heng Samrin, a 1978 defector from the Khmer Rouge, its secretary-general in place of the Vietnamese-trained Pen Sovan, a longtime Khmer communist who had lived in exile in Vietnam after 1954.[18] The ideological import of these shifts was uncertain, but they suggested a move toward a more *national*, less Vietnamese-inclined leadership.

1982: Tightening the Resistance and the Vietnamese Troops Issue

Thus, three years after the Vietnamese entry into Cambodia to expel their xenophobic Khmer Rouge neighbor, the conflict remained unsettled despite the diplomatic pressure applied by Southeast Asian nations in ASEAN and the UN General Assembly, as well as by the two rival communist great powers and the United States and its allies, particularly Australia and Japan. Among the Cambodian people, traumatized by three and a half years of

16. Ambassador Thiounn Prasith, Statement to the 36th General Assembly, Press Release, Permanent Mission of Democratic Kampuchea to the UN, New York, Oct. 19, 1981; and Raszelenberg and Schier, *The Cambodian Conflict*, pp. 41–42.

17. Commumuniqué by the Central Committee of the Communist Party of Kampuchea, No. 106/81, Dec. 11, 1981, Permanent Mission of Democratic Kampuchea to the UN, New York.

18. Chanda, *Brother Enemy*, p. 217.

brutal forced communal labor, political leaders remained ill-disposed toward both sharing power and thinking nationally (a trait that would maliciously reappear in 1997). The political factions remained dependent on outside political backers and economic donors. The fearsome dimensions of the national nightmare, the "Pol Pot time" as people called it, were being documented for the first time by scholars. Notwithstanding, the Khmer Rouge remained in a contest for power with three rival political factions, Prince Sihanouk's FUNCINPEC, Son Sann's KPNLF, and the Vietnamese-backed People's Republic of Kampuchea (PRK).

The two most prominent roadblocks to a negotiated settlement for Cambodia were the presence of the People's Army of Vietnam (PAVN) and the continuing threat of the Khmer Rouge — and each of these two armies justified its actions by the presence of the other. A pullout of the more than 100,000 Vietnamese troops in Cambodia risked a military takeover by the Khmer Rouge forces, which might spark another counter-coup by Vietnam. Key uncertainties had to be reduced by any negotiated settlement, including the presence of Vietnamese troops and the counterforce applied by China via the odious Khmer Rouge, as well as by forces supporting Son Sann and Sihanouk. Would the three resisting parties cooperate against the Vietnamese and their Cambodian allies, or would the Son Sann and Sihanouk factions attempt to exclude the most disciplined and bellicose party, the "Pol Potists"?

One consultation of statesmen after another occurred in the early months of 1982. The ASEAN states, particularly Thailand, the most exposed, and Singapore, the seemingly most endowed with diplomats, promoted a consolidation of the resistance to Vietnam's military presence in Cambodia. The Vietnamese, for their part, worked with the other two Indochina states to decry China's alleged expansionism and to promote a regional conference with ASEAN states, rather than the international conference on Kampuchea for which the UN General Assembly had repeatedly called. China demonstrated its central role in the maneuvering by hosting a meeting in Beijing in February 1982 between Prince Sihanouk and the DK's Khieu Samphan to discuss the amplification of the three-headed resistance coalition agreed to the previous September. The two parties' spokesmen agreed that each party would remain free to disseminate its own points of view; and two days later Son Sann did so, in effect, by notifying the two conferees that he could not leave Paris at the moment to join the talks. The Vietnamese party newspaper *Nhân Dân* added acid to the situation by referring to China's guests as "two public figures who had been dumped into the garbage of history"; and Radio Phnom Penh taunted Sihanouk by charging that he "knelt down, kowtowed to this genocidal clique and crawled into the same cage."[19]

Nonetheless Son Sann expressed his readiness two months later, after discussions with the Malaysian foreign minister, Tan Sri Ghazali Shafie, to work with the DK and FUNCINPEC on the formation of a coalition government. He officially accepted all four of the basic principles of the proposed government which the other coalition members had agreed to. These four principles instructed the parties to (1) abide by a "genuine union" with no monopoly of powers, (2) adopt tripartism in the structure of the coalition government, (3) decide all important problems by consensus, and (4) base the coalition on the legal status of Democratic Kampuchea, i.e., seated by the UN.[20]

The road was then open to a summit conference of the three party leaders in Kuala Lumpur, Malaysia, to ratify the agreement on a coalition, even though key issues relating to the distribution of offices remained to be negotiated. Hanoi, on June 2, offered a partial withdrawal of its troops from Cambodia, if Thailand would cease working with China to supply the Khmer resistance factions (including the Khmer Rouge) with weapons. Rather than pursue this controversy the ASEAN foreign ministers called for a total pull-back of troops and reaffirmed the declaration of the International Conference on Kampuchea. On June 22, 1982, the three coalition leaders met in Kuala Lumpur to sign an agreement establishing a Coalition Government of Democratic Kampuchea (CGDK), on the basis of the four principles. Prince Norodom Sihanouk was president, with Son Sann the premier and Khieu Samphan the vice president, in charge of foreign affairs. The three leaders repeated the ceremony on July 9 at an unidentified "historical site" inside Cambodia, near Thailand; and the new president launched an appeal to all friendly countries to bring aid and support for the "sacred cause," the restoration of peace in Kampuchea and stability and security in that part of the world. Sihanouk promised that "soon after the withdrawal of the Vietnamese occupation forces from Kampuchea the entire people shall be able to exercise fully their rights to self-determination through general and free elections and secret ballots, under the supervision of the United Nations Organization."[21] Sadly, it took eleven more years of

19. Raszelenberg and Schier, *The Cambodian Conflict*, pp. 50–51.
20. Ministry of Information of Democratic Kampuchea, "Clarification, Concerning the Talks within the Tripartite Ad Hoc Committee," Press Release, No. 092/81, Oct. 16, 1981; and Raszelenberg and Schier, *The Cambodian Conflict*, pp. 47, 51.
21. Proclamation of HRH Samdech Norodom Sihanouk, President of Democratic Kampuchea, July 9, 1982, in Raszelenberg and Schier, *The Cambodian Conflict*, p. 55.

diplomacy and military force before this seemingly reasonable promise was finally fulfilled.

In addition to announcing the "inner cabinet" of the Coalition Government, (i.e., Sihanouk, Son Sann, and Khieu Samphan), the proclamation named four coordinating committees—finance and economy, defense, culture and education, and health and social affairs — each composed on a tripartite basis. Among the Khmer Rouge personalities included in the structure was the high-ranking Ieng Sary, whom the KPNLF had earlier designated for political exile.

The Vietnamese response to these organizational moves of its Cambodian adversaries was to announce on July 15 a partial withdrawal of PAVN units. Such unverifiable token actions were to be repeated more than once in future years, but Vietnam made clear in periodic visits of its foreign minister to ASEAN nations that it retained a right to "self-defense" against hostile activities directed against Vietnam, Laos, or the PRK. At the UN General Assembly in October 1982, the resolution calling for a "comprehensive political settlement," based on the resolution and declaration of the International Conference on Kampuchea, passed by a vote of 105-23-20, a gain of five favorable votes over the previous year. Vietnam expressed vehement condemnation of the resolution, which it considered "a gross, barbarous and unacceptable interference in the PRK's internal affairs."[22]

1983: The Struggle for Recognition

The year 1983 might be called the "Year of Legitimizing." The fledgling Coalition Government of Democratic Kampuchea tried to demonstrate its international acceptability and legality by physically receiving foreign guests within Cambodia's boundaries and sending CGDK representatives (especially President Sihanouk) to foreign capitals. These official visits were concentrated in nonaligned states.

Under international law, one of the criteria for recognition as a state is "effective control over a clearly defined territory and population, an organized administration of that territory, as well as a capacity to conduct foreign relations and to fulfill international obligations."[23] In a pitiful approximation of the territorial control criterion the CGDK managed to entertain foreign ambassadors, as well as its own president, Sihanouk, in the so-called "Kampuchea Zone" or the "Phnom Malay region in Battam-

22. Ibid., pp. 56–57. UN General Assembly A/RES/37/6, Oct. 28, 1982.

23. G. Von Glahn, *Law among Nations*, 6th ed. (New York: Macmillan, 1992), p. 88, quoting the U.S. Department of State press release of Nov. 1, 1976.

bang province" (Kampuchea). This showpiece capital was the village of Phum Thmei, in the jungle close to the Thai border, which official visitors, such as foreign diplomats presenting their credentials to the president, could reach overland via adjacent Thailand. How close PAVN soldiers were to the jungle hideaway during ceremonial meetings is not recorded, but in the dry season of 1984–85 Vietnamese forces overran every civilian camp and military base along the border, forcing almost 300,000 civilian refugees to withdraw into Thai territory.[24] The second and third meetings on Khmer territory of the "Council of Ministers of the CGDK," which included the three principal leaders and the "Ministers of all Coordination Committees," occasioned photographs of a smiling prince and his wife, Neak Moneang Sihanouk, greeted by villagers and a military guard of honor (in Chinese-style uniforms). Shelter was provided by bamboo thatch roofs, but the principals were formally attired and the table setting was lavishly adorned with glass and china.[25]

After the second meeting of the Council of Ministers in Beijing, Sihanouk noted progress from one meeting to the other in "showing better harmony and friendship."[26] Thus, a token expression of authority supposed to be exercised nationwide substituted for the real thing and gave rise, in ensuing weeks, to formal visits by ambassadors from states that chose to stand up against foreign military intervention and wink at the criteria of state recognition under international law.

A subtheme in this symbolic dance about recognition of the CGDK and rejection of the PRK was attendance at the summit conferences of the Non-Aligned Movement (NAM). In 1979, the first year of the PRK, Cuba, the host state for the conference, had maneuvered to block the DK from filling Cambodia's seat. Sihanouk, then in exile in North Korea, recommended in an open letter (August 1979, that the seat be left vacant until a democratically elected government could represent the nation.[27] Three and a half years later the seventh NAM summit hostess, Indira Gandhi, prime minister of India, declined to invite either the PRK or the CGDK to attend the conference, but she did not avoid partisan rancor among the foreign ministers. Malaysia and Singapore sharply criticized India's decision, and

24. Chanda, *Brother Enemy* p. 396.
25. The earliest of the ambassadors who reached the CGDK's jungle capital, on April 30, 1983, were from Malaysia, China, Bangladesh, People's Republic of Korea, Mauritania, Pakistan, Yugoslavia, and Egypt.
26. "President Samdech Norodom Sihanouk's Visit to Democratic Kampuchea," Special Issue, Press Release, Feb. 23, 1983, Permanent Mission of Democratic Kampuchea to the UN, New York.
27. Raszelenberg and Schier, *The Cambodian Conflict*, p. 28.

this time Sihanouk's open letter to the summit and to the Indian people made a spirited case for attendance by the CGDK.

Another running controversy of this period concerned the reporting of military actions by the DK and the periodic withdrawals of "volunteer forces" announced by the PAVN. Monthly reports from the DK mission to the United Nations claimed magnificent guerrilla resistance by the National Army of Democratic Kampuchea (NADK), recording with unconvincing precision the killing of Vietnamese soldiers, the capture of weapons, cutting and mining of roads, and "liberating" of villages.[28] There were also charges, never substantiated, of the use of chemical weapons by the Vietnamese. Thailand, the ASEAN state lying closest to the running civil warfare, tried in vain to get Vietnam to pull its military forces back thirty kilometers from the border, to create a buffer zone. The military struggle seemed to have settled in, with no strategic breakthrough in sight.

Gestures or demands offered by one side to the other as enticements for reciprocating concessions registered scant progress. China released a five-point peace proposal on March 1, 1983, which included a willingness to respect the outcome of UN-supervised general elections.[29] Thus the idea of elections gained wider utility and strength. On the other hand, in a shift of position, the ever-mercurial Prince Sihanouk on May 29 restated his idea of national reconciliation through the formation of a four-party government. The negative reaction to this idea among his coalition government partners brought matters close to a resignation by the indispensable prince. In December he donned the mantle of independent, national man-of-peace again by offering to receive any Vietnamese or Heng Samrin (PRK) representative to exchange views in a nonofficial setting. The UN General Assembly, on October 5, 1983, renewed its annual ASEAN-sponsored resolution against intervention in Cambodia by a vote of 105-23-19. Vietnam, for the first time, did not bother to challenge the credentials of the CGDK delegation.

1984: Military Stalemate

The following year the four Cambodian factions, the ASEAN states, and China, the USSR, France; and United States continually tested the waters regarding possible participants in diplomatic discussions or a conference.

28. Press Releases of the Permanent Mission of Democratic Kampuchea to the UN.
29. Raszelenberg and Schier, *The Cambodian Conflict*, p. 59.

The continuation of military clashes between the Khmer Rouge forces and the PAVN showed the Khmer Rouge to be once again supplied, uniformed, and trained for guerrilla operations well within Cambodia, in the northwest provinces.[30] Meanwhile, the rival foreign ministries periodically announced the conditions under which serious talks might take place. For the CGDK the total departure of the PAVN seemed to be a precondition for talks; but the Vietnamese would offer nothing more than token withdrawals of "volunteers" serving in Cambodia, announced from time to time, so long as DK guerrillas armed by China operated out of the refugee camps and nearby "bases" along the Thai-Cambodian border. The battle claims set forth by the Khmer Rouge remained inflated and scarcely credible, yet eyewitness accounts by some journalists made clear that the guerrillas could raid the interior of Cambodia with some impunity.[31]

Nonetheless, diplomacy remained a reasonable option for any side in theconflict. In addition to the periodic meetings of ASEAN foreign ministers and Indochina foreign ministers, individual statesmen such as former Thai prime minister Kriangsak Chamanon and the Indonesian commander of armed forces, General Benny Murdani, visited Hanoi and returned with conciliatory messages that pictured Vietnam in a defensive, not expansionist, position. Australia, in March, softened its position toward Vietnam and strongly condemned the Khmer Rouge; and in February 1984, Washington sent Assistant Secretary of Defense Richard Armitage to Hanoi for the highest-ranking visit by an American to Vietnam since the U.S. departure in 1975. China did not remain passive in this contest of emissaries, however; Foreign Minister Wu Xueqian visited Malaysia in February for talks at the highest level, and emerged with a clear statement in favor of UN-supervised elections, as well as increased aid for the CGDK.[32] Sihanouk, as well, remained active by reiterating on a number of occasions his willingness to talk directly with the Vietnamese, in whatever capacity they might prefer. The Vietnamese, however, played their role of benevolent neighbor by announcing more PAVN withdrawals from Cambodia in June, made possible, as they somewhat unconvincingly claimed, by the increasing ability of the People's Kampuchean Revolutionary Armed Forces (PKRAF) to hold

30. Two Khmer Rouge raids that gained notoriety in January 1994 were the "capture" of Siem Riep city and Kompong Thom city for less than twenty-four hours, which was repeated a month later. Special Issue, Press Release, Permanent Mission of Democratic Kampuchea to the UN, Feb. 1984.

31. See *The Nation Review* (Bangkok, July 19, 1984) for Professor Stephen Orlov's account of a well-managed two-week trip inside Cambodia, with a three-person Canadian Broadcasting Corporation team and a DK combat unit, which M. Brown personally reviewed with him at the time in Bangkok.

32. Raszelenberg and Schier, *The Cambodian Conflict*, pp. 68–70.

their own.[33] A secondary propaganda contest heated up in accompaniment to the main controversy, as Khmer resistance and Thai military spokesmen asserted that hundreds of thousands of Vietnamese settlers were moving into Cambodia to "Vietnamize" the country. The numbers cited seemed quite inflated, and the threat of cultural imperialism seemed overblown.

During the annual United Nations General Assembly speech-making and caucusing season in September the CGDK's two top officials, President Norodom Sihanouk and Prime Minister Son Sann, met for a talk with U.S. President Ronald Reagan right after his address to the General Assembly. The vice president, Khieu Samphan of the Khmer Rouge, remained at a distance, lest U.S. legislators castigate their government for consorting with a Khmer Rouge mass murderer. Reagan made clear his support for ASEAN's insistence on a total withdrawal of Vietnamese forces from Kampuchea.[34] The ASEAN resolution in the General Assembly, calling for a comprehensive political settlement in Kampuchea, attracted five more votes than the year before. An effort by a French diplomat and Hun Sen, the foreign minister of the PRK, to arrange a meeting with Sihanouk in France on his way home from the UN General Assembly was vetoed by the DK element of the coalition (in accordance with the previous agreement on consensus decision making). Diplomacy would not yet supplant the clash of arms.

1985: Vietnam Promises Full Troop Withdrawal

By 1985 the lineup of parties that might seek a negotiated settlement was clearly established, even though each side hoped that its opponents could be put at odds with one another. Differences of emphasis were detectable among the ASEAN states; and Son Sann and Khieu Samphan shared precious little political ground. The Khmer People's Revolutionary Party (KPRP) itself was not immune to historical suspicions with regard to the Vietnamese, even when located in the same political camp with them. This fault line within the Phnom Penh camp was well known, but the growing revolutionary People's Armed Forces (KPRAF) found it expedient to maintain joint military operations with the PAVN, rather than strive for autonomy. All four Khmer parties depended on their military suppliers and advisors (especially China and the USSR), who had little need for more than a stalemate. Any diplomatic resolution of the struggle, however, would

33. Ibid., p. 71.
34. Press Release, Permanent Mission of Democratic Kampuchea to the UN, New York, Oct. 3, 1984.

depend in good part on the relative ability of the rival Cambodian governments to control people and territory. Thus, the PRK and the resistance armed forces probed and tested, engaging in military showmanship and presenting apparent solidarity.

For the Vietnamese the game was two-faced: on the one hand ruthless, in their shelling of refugee camps just inside Kampuchea along the Thai border, and on the other hand conciliatory, with periodic announcements of withdrawals of portions of the PAVN. Thus, a partial pullout was announced in March 1985, after PAVN shelling had scattered all the Cambodian refugees into new encampments inside Thailand. On August 22, 1985, Vietnam announced that the PAVN would withdraw entirely by 1990, whether "there is Pol Pot or not."[35] During the interim they apparently counted on no decisive change in the balance of forces. In fact, the Vietnamese eventually pulled out a year earlier, in September 1989. During the interim, the resistance forces became somewhat coordinated, via a joint military command involving the KPNLF and the ANS (Sihanouk), but this did not preclude skirmishes with the Khmer Rouge.[36] The economic and military assistance provided by the United States to the "noncommunist resistance" in Cambodia became public in 1985, as the Reagan administration began using publicly known channels rather than its previous covert ones. An aid grant of $5 million was adopted by the House of Representatives on July 10, 1985, with prohibitions against allowing Thailand to administer the funds and against any U.S. aid reaching the Khmer Rouge.

For all the escalation of military activity, the search for a diplomatic breakthrough was relentlessly explored by the foreign ministries of the regional states, the great powers, the United Nations secretary-general, and the Cambodian leaders. The PRK promoted Hun Sen (in January 1985, at age thirty-four to the post of prime minister, after his predecessor, Chan Si, died in a Moscow hospital on December 31, 1984. Hun Sen had served as foreign minister of the People's Republic of Kampuchea since its establishment in January 1979. He had reportedly started his political career, at age sixteen as a courier in the underground communist party (Khmer Rouge) following Lon Nol's overthrow of Sihanouk's regime in 1970. In military service he was wounded five times and lost one eye. After the Khmer Rouge took full power in 1975, Hun Sen rose to the level of Eastern Zone deputy regimental commander, before defecting to Vietnam in June 1977. His advancement within the anti–Khmer Rouge movement was remarkable even

---

35. Raszelenberg and Schier, *The Cambodian Conflict*, p. 86, and Chanda, *Brother Enemy*, p. 396.

36. Raszelenberg and Schier, *The Cambodian Conflict*, p. 83 (April 26, 1985).

by counterrevolutionary standards, and he has continued to display qualities of intelligence, toughness, bombast, intimidation, and boldness that
make his rapid rise to the top of his party quite credible. His career seems
to have rested upon his own shrewdness and ruthlessness, not the mentor-
ing of the Vietnamese. Opposed to the venerable Prince Sihanouk, this
youngster was seen at first as a mismatch, but he gradually impressed the
statesmen who were able to meet him, and eventually Sihanouk himself.

Package peace proposals continued to issue forth from the Indochina
states' foreign ministers, One presented on January 17, 1985, offered five
points: (1) PAVN withdrawal paired with exclusion of "the Pol Pot clique";
(2) self-determination, including elimination of "the threat of genocide"; (3)
free elections with foreign observers; (4) a zone of peace and stability; and
(5) "international guarantee and supervision" of the agreements.[37] Clearly
the proposals were reaching toward a common formula, and, in addition,
Sihanouk was winning wider backing for his effort to connect the rival parties. In February, in a message to the Cambodian people, he called on Vietnam to allow free elections *under UN supervision*, and offered to step down
as president of the CGDK if the resistance lost the vote. The Vietnamese in
return announced that Sihanouk could play a role in the PRK if he abandoned the CGDK; and the prince called for an international conference of
regional and concerned states, somewhat similar to the Geneva conferences on Vietnam and Laos in 1954 and 1961. Yet diplomatic maneuvers in
April 1985 revealed the prince to be constrained by his CGDK affiliation
and not allowed to engage in indirect talks (labeled "proximity talks") between the CGDK and the PRK, even though Sihanouk personally favored
the idea. The coalition government on May 19 formally rejected the idea as
unbalanced, so long as Vietnamese troops remained in Cambodia.[38] Hanoi
claimed in April that by 1987 about one-half of its force would have departed. By July the "proximity talks" idea had been modified to include the
admission of a PRK delegation as part of the Vietnamese delegation.

Improving the Party Images

The most hard-line of the protagonists, the Khmer Rouge, also softened
their position by claiming that they would not rule out direct negotiations
with Hanoi, whom they nonetheless accused of attempting to suppress the
Cambodian nation by sending in hundreds of thousands of Vietnamese set-

37. Ibid., pp. 76–77.
38. Ibid., pp. 81–84.

tlers and forcing the enlistment of soldiers to fight fellow Cambodian resistance troops. The Party of Democratic Kampuchea in July 1985 identified their goal to be a "liberal capitalist system" guided by a parliamentary regime. They pronounced themselves ready to maintain Cambodia in strict . neutrality and nonalignment, confirmed by a treaty of nonaggression with Vietnam, and implemented by a government elected under UN supervision. Vietnam, in March 1985, offered its own five-point plan for peace: (1) withdrawal of PAVN,(2) an international supervision and control commission (as in the Geneva Agreement, 1954), (3) internationally supervised elections with the Khmer Rouge excluded, (4) solution of the missing-in-action issue (for the USA), and (5) a freeze on military bases negotiations in Southeast Asia.

The most ingenious enticement to a change in outlook, to promote negotiation, was the DK Party's unloading of its international pariah, Pol Pot. According to DK documents issued by the office of the vice president of the CGDK, Khieu Samphan, Pol Pot announced his *retirement* from his duties in the party because of his reaching age sixty in 1985. (His few biographers have considered him just fifty seven in 1985.) Four years later, in 1989, more official correspondence was made public which purported to grant permission to Brother Number One of the movement to step down again, from his "volunteer" work as director of the High Institute for National Defense (a "research institute"), where he had been allowed to continue working as an ordinary researcher.[39] In addition, he promised that following "the complete withdrawal of the Vietnamese aggressors from Kampuchea" he would "cease all activities in all organs of the future State of Kampuchea." Indeed, if only the question of political participation by the Khmer Rouge had been truly so simple as this charade pretended, some reconciliation might have been achieved. Even if one interpreted the reduction of Pol Pot's title as a sign of flagging health, time proved his vitality to be sufficient to continue, for all the talk of retirement, not as an aging fisherman but rather as the continuing first-ranking leader of the revolutionary party struggling to transform Cambodia.

The UN General Assembly debate on ASEAN's resolution in October produced a 114-21-16 vote, a gain of four votes in favor over the previous year. The challenge to the CGDK credentials was not even attempted.

---

39. Ibid., pp. 86–87, 89; and "Letter from H.E. Mr. Pol Pot to Leaders of the Democratic Kampuchea Party," March 4, 1989, Press Release 7, June 1989, Permanent Mission of Democratic Kampuchea to the UN, New York.

1986: The Soviet Union Retrenches

By 1986 the ingredients of the Kampuchea situation were quite well known and doggedly manipulated by national, regional, and international statesmen looking for agreeable arrangements that would convert military struggle sustained by foreign assistance into political struggle supervised by international monitors. Diplomatic ingenuity was applied to getting the four Cambodian parties to agree to parley, but none of them wished to face the need to compromise before the existing situation was proven to be unrewarding. So, guerrilla warfare of the three resistance armies continued to test the will and equipment of Vietnamese "volunteers" and PRK party stalwarts and draftees, in a low-grade campaign of sabotage and retaliation.

By January 1986 the CGDK under Sihanouk had rashly attempted a joint military command embracing the Sihanouk forces (ANS) and the KPNLF (but not the Khmer Rouge). This augmented the coalition's claim to be a government, and also tried to avoid the disarray of three resisting "armies" unable to avoid skirmishes with one another. Equally disconcerting were rivalries among the KPNLF top generals, competing for leadership and indirectly for profits from commercial business conducted along the border in the refugee camps. The joint military command lasted less than a month, but in March 1986 the three coalition ministers in charge of military matters agreed to meet bimonthly to coordinate propaganda, and to study the coordination of military activity by the three factions. Within the year a symbolic meeting of the three commanders-in-chief of the resistance forces—Son Sen (DK), Sak Sutsakhan (KPNLF), and Prince Sihanouk's son Norodom Ranariddh (ANS)—took place on November 18, 1986.[40] Prince Ranariddh was entering the political realm after years in France teaching law and avoiding the deadly Khmer Rouge period. His political career was destined to be rocky.

In early 1985 the resistance forces had been estimated at 30,000 to 40,000 under the National Army of Democratic Kampuchea (NADK), 15,000 armed under the KPNLF, and 7,000 under Sihanouk's ANS.[41] The armed forces of the PRK were rated at 30,000 men integrated with Vietnamese forces—whose number was declining from 150,000 (in early 1985). By May 1986, U.S. intelligence estimated the PAVN presence at 140,000 following five partial withdrawals over the course of four years,[42] but resis-

40. Raszelenberg and Schier, *The Cambodian Conflict*, pp. 90, 95.
41. Press Release, "Meeting of the Commanders-in-Chief of the Tripartite Patriotic Forces of the CGDK," Permanent Mission of Democratic Kampuchea to the UN, New York, Nov. 26, 1986.
42. Raszelenberg and Schier, *The Cambodian Conflict*, pp. 91–97.

tance statements concerning the PAVN's announced troop withdrawals dripped with official skepticism.

In October 1986, the Vietnamese passed up their usual dry season offensive against the resistance bases and refugee camps. Negative public relations were thereby avoided, as well as unwanted casualties. Another gesture to world opinion was the Vietnamese foreign minister's expressed willingness to allow international supervision of the PAVN withdrawals, so long as this was coupled with an internationally supervised end to military assistance to Khmer factions via Thailand.

For all the effort put into the military balance of forces, much activity also developed in the political sphere. Early in the year Hun Sen, who by then had emerged as the key leader of the PRK, was again so bold as to invite the symbol of national unity, Prince Sihanouk, to join the PRK against the Khmer Rouge. At the same time, the PRK expressed its willingness to begin negotiations on internal Kampuchean issues "on the basis of the removal of the Pol Pot clique." As for the international issues—which involved Vietnam, China, Thailand, and other states caught in the Cambodian civil war — the CGDK indicated its readiness to discuss matters with Vietnam indirectly by means of "proximity talks." In a key move the CGDK put forth an eight-point proposal for the settlement of the conflict in Cambodia. Significantly, the CGDK Council of Ministers had agreed to issue this challenge at a meeting held in Beijing in March 1986.[43]

The CGDK Proposal for Settlement

In simplified terms the plan called for:
1. negotiation by Vietnam and the CGDK concerning the modalities of a strictly scheduled two-phase withdrawal of Vietnamese forces
2. a cease-fire during implementation of the withdrawal argeements
3. UN supervision of the troop withdrawal
4. formation of a quadripartite coalition government
5. organization of free elections by the quadripartite government under UN supervision
6. guaranteed neutrality, with UN troops present for two to three years, leading to a liberal and democratic regime
7. reconstruction assistance received from all quarters and countries
8. a treaty of peace, nonaggression, and cooperation with Vietnam.

43. Press Release, Council of Ministers of the CGDK, Permanent Mission of Democratic Kampuchea to the UN, New York, March 19, 1986.

The new elements in this set of proposals were the two-phased withdrawal of PAVN, rather than full withdrawal, before talks could begin, and the call for the formation of a four-party coalition interim government without indicating how to accomplish it. The talking points enunciated by CGDK leaders in press releases emphasized the recent favorable trend in military operations, in which the PAVN had reduced its dry season offensives and the resistance forces had extended their range well into the interior of the country. A very serious effort to rally nonaligned states to back the eight-point plan produced official visits to African states by CGDK vice president and foreign affairs spokesman Khieu Samphan. This Khmer Rouge stalwart showed up in Senegal, Egypt, Kenya, Rwanda, Sierra Leone, Mauritania, Côte d'Ivoire, Mali, Burkina Faso, Liberia, and Guinea, Conakry, and press interviews pumped up the case for the eight-point proposal. The ASEAN states, plus Australia, and North Korea welcomed the proposals, even though Vietnam rejected the initiative.[44]

The most obvious flaw of the plan was its failure to provide for disarming the contending Khmer parties, which omission Khieu Samphan tried to explain away as a necessary safeguard against possible Vietnamese violation of the agreements, "as in the past." In response, the Vietnamese foreign minister proposed international supervision of the PAVN withdrawal.[45] The eight points also left out any reference to the recessed International Conference on Kampuchea.

In retrospect the most significant voice in the summer of 1986 was the Soviet Union president Mikhail Gorbachev's on July 28 in Vladivostock. Gorbachev announced a great retrenchment in Soviet foreign policy on a number of fronts, pulling back troops from Afghanistan and Mongolia, preparing to confer with the People's Republic of China at any level about improving neighborly relations, and asserting that no insurmountable barriers existed regarding friendly relations between ASEAN and the Indochinese states.[46] Even though the CGDK press releases acknowledged no change of policy in the Soviet pronouncement, Chinese leader Deng Xiaoping avowed in September that "something new" was in the speech.[47] Behind the scenes decisive shifts were afoot in Soviet support for Vietnam's

44. Press Release, "Coalition Government of Democratic Kampuchea's 8-Point Peace Proposal Praised by World Community," Permanent Mission of Democratic Kampuchea to the UN, New York, April 6, June 20, 1986.

45. Raszelenberg and Schier, *The Cambodian Conflict*, pp. 94, 96.

46. Ibid., p. 99.

47. Press Release, No. 059/86, "Statement by the Ministry of Foreign Affairs of the CGDK on Mikhail Gorbachev's Speech in on Vladivostock," Permanent Mission of Democratic Kampuchea to the UN, New York, Aug. 25, 1986, and Raszelenberg and Schier, *The Cambodian Conflict*, p. 102.

military presence in Cambodia. The annual cost of Soviet aid to Vietnam in return for use of military bases was nearly $2 billion and eight thousand personnel, plus bad blood with the ASEAN states.[48] Vietnam was on the verge of facing new Soviet economic limitations on its position which could push it into negotiation sooner rather than later.

The Non-Aligned Movement prepared in the summer of 1986 for its sixth summit meeting in Harare, but the planners again were not ready to choose between the two claimants to the Cambodia seat, which remained vacant, much to the CGDK's chagrin. At the UN General Assembly, however, the annual resolution on Kampuchea prevailed again, by 115-21-13, and left a bitter taste in the mouth of the Indochina states.

1987: Bilateral Talks at Last

After nine years of inconclusive maneuver the Khmer factions and their foreign mentors, suppliers, and observers reached a turning point in 1987. In *Foreign Affairs*, Gareth Porter observed, "Last December [1987] a peace settlement has for the first time become a real possibility."[49] A prime reason for this optimism at the end of 1987 was that Prince Sihanouk, who had announced a one-year leave of absence from the presidency of the CGDK, had met privately and unofficially with Hun Sen, the premier of the PRK. The two political leaders had exchanged views frankly and laid the groundwork for future discussions, which might become four-party talks and might also engage Vietnam. Finally the stage had been set for serious presentation by the players of their needs, aspirations, flexibility, and determination. To express the situation in the language of diplomacy, the "turning point of seriousness" had been reached, and the parties had diagnosed the situation's disagreements and its actors to the point where determining a formula for settlement was the proper order of business. The issues in dispute had been laid out and the players had assumed their genuine positions. By the beginning of 1988, the diagnosis was encouraging, and the situation called for a formula about which to negotiate.

Arranging a Sihanouk–Hun Sen encounter was not a simple task. Neither party wanted to extend legal recognition to the other, explicitly or implicitly. In addition, the venerable god-king figure, Prince Sihanouk, could not disregard the social inequality in his dealings with the young prime minister. Twice before Sihanouk had cancelled meetings that had been

---

48. William Bach, "A Chance in Cambodia," *Foreign Policy*, Spring 1986, p. 76.
49. Gareth Porter, "Cambodia: Sihanouk's Initiative," *Foreign Affairs*, Spring 1988.

scheduled for late 1984 and for June 1987.[50] But on December 2–4 in Sihanouk's residence at Fère-en-Tardenois in France, the two key political figures met for the first time and aired their concerns, their ideas, and their flexibility in search of a peaceful settlement. Both made clear their unwillingness to recognize the other as legitimate chief of government, but they were ready to explore new structures that might transform the current political (and military) impasse into a viable reconciliation and consolidation of the Khmer nation.

The two protagonists carefully set the procedures, to avoid any suggestion of legitimizing the other side (the PRK or the CGDK). Sihanouk had long insisted that Vietnam was the party responsible for the military occupation of Cambodia and therefore the party with whom he should negotiate. This was implied in the first point of the CGDK's eight-point proposal for a political settlement. Yet on January 21, 1987, the Voice of Khmer radio announced that Sihanouk was willing to talk with Vietnam, with the Heng Samrin regime represented in the Vietnam delegation. Rumania had attempted unsuccessfully to set up a direct meeting of Sihanouk and Heng Samrin in Bucharest in January 1987. Rumania had advised the prince to allow Hanoi "the possibility to withdraw from Cambodia with honor, without losing face."[51] A meeting in Bucharest of Sihanouk and Heng Samrin was not to be, however. China again made known that Vietnam must pull out before talks could begin.

Following the demise of Rumanian president Ceausescu's maneuver the CGDK returned to pumping its appeals on behalf of its eight-point program, and added a fillip by withdrawing all previous demands for reparations from Vietnam. These constructive moves were somewhat diminished, however, by reversion to threadbare propaganda themes such as the "Indochina Federation" goal attributed, via tendentious reading of Indochina Communist Party history, to the Vietnamese leadership.

The time for head-to-head negotiation seemed, nonetheless, to have arrived and Hun Sen appeared to seize the initiative again in April 1987 to get Prince Sihanouk's consent. Again the prince stuck to his usual line — the Vietnamese must meet with him first.[52] The Indonesian minister of foreign affairs, Mochtar Kusumaatmadja, in May reaffirmed his invitation to the four Khmer factions to negotiate their conflict without the presence of any other parties. The efficacy of quadripartite discussions, however, was

50. Russell R. Ross, ed., *Cambodia: A Country Study* (Washington: Federal Research Div., Library of Congress, Dec. 1987), p. 235.

51. Raszelenberg and Schier, *The Cambodian Conflict*, pp. 108–10.

52. Ibid., p. 118.

threatened by the serious rifts and disarray among the leading generals of the rapidly dwindling KPNLF armed forces,[53] as well as an outright military clash between FUNCINPEC and PDK soldiers. The latter incident angered Sihanouk to the point that on May 7 he started a one-year "leave of absence" from the presidency of the CGDK. The incident was not the first of its kind, apparently, but the prince's resignation, he frankly admitted (in June), freed him to act without the veto of the Khmer Rouge holding him back.[54] Sihanouk's counterpart, Hun Sen, continued his upbeat refrain in his June 18 review of PRK policies, which he characterized as shifting priorities from the battlefield toward the negotiating table. He acknowledged that this move away from fighting-while-negotiating was a slight step back, but it would make possible a conservation of strength for the period ahead when PAVN troops would no longer be present to counter the Khmer Rouge. A week later, according to newspaper reports, Vietnam tried to arrange a Sihanouk–Hun Sen meeting, but once again Sihanouk declined. Ten days later in a conversation with Mochtar the prince set forth two conditions for a meeting: first, the request must come from the PRK directly and not Vietnam, and second, the meeting must occur at his residence (in Pyongyang); and only non-official forms of address should be used.

Sihanouk also commented favorably on the Indonesian idea of a cocktail party format and assured his participation notwithstanding his anticipation of strong PDK objections. He would like to invite Vietnam to join in, and his top preference would be a three-sided get-together of the prime ministers of Vietnam and the PRK and himself — which seemed to short-circuit the issue of mutual nonrecognition on the part of the rival governments of Cambodia.

With another UN General Assembly looming in October, Sihanouk held off on any arrangement of talks with Hun Sen, lest it weaken the support of the CGDK in the annual resolution on "the situation in Kampuchea." He declared himself ready, however, to meet Hun Sen in France in November or December. Meanwhile the PRK agreed on August 12 to join an informal "cocktail party" without any preconditions; and Laos and Vietnam expressed their readiness to join the gathering at a later stage.

53. Porter, "Cambodia: Sihanouk's Initiative." The KPNLF was believed in early 1986 to have only a thousand men inside Kampuchea and to be on the verge of becoming a "nonentity."

54. Raszelenberg and Schier, *The Cambodian Conflict*, p. 119.

The Efforts of Facilitators

The ASEAN side became a bit unsteady in the face of such progress, however, since Mochtar seemed to be operating somewhat on his own by insisting neither on the eight-point proposal as the basis for discussion nor on a format in which Vietnam would join immediately after the quadripartite meeting, to deal with international issues.[55] Hanoi objected to the eight points, since they did not call for the elimination of the Khmer Rouge. Sihanouk achieved more clarity on August 23 when he laid out two conditions for his meeting with Hun Sen: first, a written request by Hun Sen to Sihanouk; and second, agreement to let Sihanouk announce the contents of the talks.[56] The PRK leadership, for its part, announced its readiness to meet with other Khmer leaders with the exception of "the criminal Pol Pot and his close associates," to discuss "national reconciliation based on the non-recurrence ever of the danger of genocide," and an orderly repatriation of refugees. China chimed in at this point, as host to an annual Beijing meeting of the CGDK on August 27, by insisting on full withdrawal by Vietnam before national reconciliation could be undertaken. Deng Xiaoping, chairman of China's Central Advisory Committee, declared that installing Sihanouk as leader of Cambodia was the primary goal, and following the path to socialism was of secondary importance.

The atmosphere for diplomatic efforts remained favorable notwithstanding occasional angry blasts by one side or the other; and a meeting of Soviet and Chinese foreign ministers at the UN in September added new grounds for hope. A week later, on September 28, the PRK foreign minister announced the official consent of the PRK to talks without preconditions. Prince Sihanouk's address to the UN General Assembly (delivered by Son Sann) invited "the people installed in Phnom Penh" to "participate in our Coalition Government which will become a quadripartite coalition government of Kampuchea." The new four-party coalition could be formed even before Vietnamese troops were fully departed, he added. Shortly thereafter an uncorroborated French news dispatch reported that the PRK would be willing to negotiate with the Khmer Rouge's Khieu Samphan, but not with Pol Pot or Ieng Sary.

An official statement of Hun Sen's desire to talk to Prince Sihanouk was conveyed by India's foreign minister, Natwar Singh, on October 5, 1987. Three days later the PRK announced both a new five-point proposal for

---

55. Ibid., p. 130. Vietnam was officially opposed to meeting with the DK element of the CGDK.
56. Ibid., pp. 132–45.

resolution of the Khmer conflict and also its readiness to converse with Sihanouk and "leaders of other opposition groups" (with the exception of Pol Pot "and some of his close associates").

The new package of five proposals by the PRK contained no new ideas but did represent some concessions: (1) a willingness to talk with all Khmer leaders except Pol Pot and a few top associates, (2) Vietnamese withdrawal (to be paired with an end to all types of aid to the resistance), (3) general elections "with foreign supervision" after withdrawal of the PAVN, (4) a pacified border with Thailand and repatriation of Khmer refugees, and (5) an international conference to guarantee the agreements and the independence of Cambodia. This was the most comprehensive set of proposals yet offered. In spite of their desire to create a constructive image at the UN, however, the Indochina states remained blocked by the annual ASEAN resolution calling for the immediate withdrawal of Vietnamese forces. The General Assembly resolution prevailed again 117-21-16, a gain of two favorable votes.

Finally, it was time to move into direct discussions. Hun Sen telegraphed Sihanouk on November 18 expressing his readiness to meet the prince in France with no preconditions; and Sihanouk, two days later, officially invited Hun Sen to his residence in Fère-en-Tardenois, Aisne province, with a proposed schedule of two days of talks and possible continuations in France or Pyongyang, North Korea. Hun Sen agreed to Sihanouk's proposal on November 26 and inquired as to Sihanouk's preferred format. The prince chose to meet three on three, joined by his wife Monique and son Ranariddh, opposite Hun Sen, Deputy Foreign Secretary Dith Munti, and Vice Cabinet Minister Cham Prasith. The prince officially invited Hun Sen to Fère-en-Tardenois for December 2, 1987, with a working breakfast at 10:00 a.m., followed by a talk, and a working luncheon. Sihanouk always used the private form of address toward Hun Sen, so as to avoid using his political title or acknowledging a People's Republic of Kampuchea.

The long-awaited breakthrough meeting of the two main Khmer rivals took place on December 2–4, 1987. It produced a joint communiqué and an agreement to meet again in January 1988 in the same venue. (This engagement was subsequently cancelled by Sihanouk but reinstated for Saint-Germain-en-Laye on January 27, 1988.)

A handwritten summary of the December talks, signed by Sihanouk, has provided the most detailed (even though terse) account of what the principals tried to communicate to one another.

The First Sihanouk–Hun Sen Talks

Hun Sen opened with a historical account of the resistance that grew up after 1973 (*sic*) against Pol Pot, which led ultimately to a call for help from Vietnam (the SRV), since no other states were disposed to act to relieve Cambodia of the Khmer Rouge. The PAVN, however, would definitely withdraw by 1990. He then spoke up for including the KPNLF and the PDK in the talks, but if this should fail to happen, he and Sihanouk would have to continue to seek a rapprochement and a comprehensive solution to the conflict. Sihanouk declined an offer to serve in a high government position in the PRK. He made clear that he would return to Phnom Penh only as president of a new Khmer state, which would be neither "Democratic" (i.e., Democratic Kampuchea); nor a "People's Republic" (i.e., the PRK), but rather a parliamentary democracy "à la française." Sihanouk insisted again on his desire to address in person the leadership in Hanoi and Moscow, the source of the dispute in his opinion. In addition, he saw some sort of rapprochement between China and Vietnam as indispensable to any termination of the Cambodia conflict.

The following day Hun Sen made oral promises of nondiscrimination against returning Khmer residents and denied recent allegations by Amnesty International of torture and arbitrary imprisonment by PRK officials. The day's talks ended on an adamant note, however, when Hun Sen rejected any possible recognition of the CGDK or Democratic Kampuchea by his government; and Sihanouk made clear that the CGDK would never recognize the PRK or a "communist 'Cambodian' state."Nonetheless, Sihanouk invited his opponent to visit him in Pyongyang in April, with an eye to enlisting the good offices of his friend North Korean president Kim Il-Sung. The prince avowed that a rapprochement between China and Vietnam was fundamental to a resolution of the Cambodian conflict.

An interesting feature of this three-day gathering was the reported nightly conference between Hun Sen and Soviet and Vietnamese diplomats upon his return to the nearby village of Soissons, where he was lodged.[57]

On the second day of talks, Norodom Ranariddh explicated his father's message of the day to Indonesian foreign minister Mochtar, namely that he was willing to join in the proposed political "cocktail party" in Jakarta so long as his coalition cohorts, the KPNLF and the PDK, were willing to attend. The next day, Sihanouk and Hun Sen issued a joint communiqué which stipulated that their conflict "must necessarily be settled politically,"

---

57. Ibid., p. 147. These contacts were denied but published in *Asiaweek* and *Neue Zürcher Zeitung*.

by the Khmer factions themselves. No mention was included of withdrawing Vietnamese troops nor of the nature of a future political system for Cambodia.[58] In a separate interview Hun Sen saw a movement toward a "real settlement" and emphasized his PRK's willingness to engage in four-party negotiations.

China, while abstaining from comment on Prince Sihanouk's activity, did not hesitate to assert publicly that the crux of the dispute remained the withdrawal of Vietnamese troops. A spokesman for Son Sann echoed this line of thought, while welcoming the meetings, by averring that the KPNLF leader would not join any quadripartite negotiations unless Vietnam joined in. The foreign ministry in Hanoi on December 10 avowed a policy of nonintervention with respect to Kampuchean problems but envisaged an international conference, which the SRV would attend, to deal with implementing a future settlement achieved by the Khmer parties themselves.

Despite the uplift achieved by the three-day Fère-en-Tardenois conference and the announcement of a reunion there in January 1988 (and a third meeting in Pyongyang), Sihanouk momentarily slowed the pace on December 9 by canceling meetings number two and three. It would be fruitless, he said, to meet without the KPNLF and the PDK, and they were holding out until Vietnam was engaged in the negotiation. As a postscript the prince called for the simultaneous dismantling of the PRK and the CGDK and their replacement by a "State of Cambodia, a non-communist, non-socialist, neutral and non-aligned state, a free democracy à la française." His awkward coalition proposal would use four co-ministers for each ministry, and he demanded a public pronouncement by the Vietnamese that they would withdraw their troops following the formation of the quadripartite government. An international control mechanism would supervise the withdrawal. Ironically, the designation "State of Cambodia" was subsequently appropriated by Hun Sen's faction on April 20, 1989, when it abandoned the communist-associated name of People's Republic of Kampuchea (PRK) and proclaimed itself the State of Cambodia (SOC).

Sihanouk's hesitations to meet again lasted hardly more than a week, during which he experienced ASEAN's discontent with the breakdown. On December 15 the prince announced his readiness to resume two-party talks at Saint-Germain-en-Laye, and two days later Hun Sen agreed to join him, on January 17, 1988. Son Sann welcomed the meetings, but he would not himself participate in four-party talks unless Vietnam's participation was assured. Hanoi continued to treat the talks as suited for the Khmer parties alone. In mid-December Hun Sen agreed to a January 27 meeting in Saint-

58. Ibid., pp. 145–48.

Germain-en-Laye, but Sihanouk decided to propose Pyongyang for January 27. Hun Sen wanted to meet sooner, so the encounter was finally scheduled for January 20–21, at Saint-Germain-en-Laye, France.[59]

1988: The Eve of a Breakthrough

As the year 1988 began, a second meeting of the two foremost Khmer leaders was planned, and a move toward four-party conversations with Vietnam was gaining credibility. The process of diplomatic bargaining was close to the stage in which a formula for resolution of the conflict was conceivable, and the lineup of contending parties for negotiation was fixed, even though subject to change.

The preconditions to negotiation (PAVN withdrawal) had been voiced. The issues to be resolved had been designated and their relative importance had been tested. The areas of potential compromise and of intractability had been identified. The political environment (a dwindling Soviet Union) had been verified. The modalities of negotiation (an international conference in Paris) had been championed. In addition, important staff assistance was beginning to stir in the United Nations Secretariat and key foreign ministries.

59. Ibid., pp. 147–50; also Ross, *Cambodia: A Country Study*, pp. 233–37.

CHAPTER TWO

Formula Seeking and Details, 1988–1991

The second meeting between Sihanouk and Hun Sen in January 1988 opened the Cambodia conflict to a new stage — *formula seeking*. More than two and a half years later, the contending parties would finally reach a formula for agreement in the "framework" prepared by the Permanent Five members of the Security Council and accepted by the four factions on September 10, 1990. During this period of testing out formulas for ending the military conflict and restoring the divided nation, diplomatic players floated and rejected ideas, explored and organized meetings and conferences, and gradually put into place, like a mason building a wall, one stone of consensus after another.

The formula for agreement in Cambodia prescribed actions for many interested players, even though the two self-proclaimed Cambodian governments, the People's Republic of Kampuchea (PRK) and the Coalition Government of Democratic Kampuchea (CGDK), were the principal parties. The CGDK was three-headed and formally committed to deciding its actions by consensus. Prince Sihanouk, the leading figure in the coalition, was more than equal with his partners because of his royal identity. The prince, and the CGDK, insisted that the proper dispute was between the national leader President Sihanouk and Vietnam, which had invaded Cambodia in 1978. Sihanouk never managed to win this point and gradually gave way to direct discussions with the PRK regime and indirect talks with the Vietnamese.

The Basic Issues: 1988

A successful formula of agreement had to deal with numerous bones of contention.

1. Who should rule the nation, on what basis of legitimacy? In theory, the bases of legitimacy might include conquest, existing practice, international arbitration, elections. Sihanouk had proposed elections as a legitimizing device very early in the diagnostic phase, and the idea had not been seriously challenged. Yet, should the Khmer Rouge or parts thereof be treated as politically or legally ineligible to participate? What would constitute "free and fair elections"

2. How could Cambodia regain full independence, particularly from the Vietnamese "liberation" forces? The announcement by Vietnam in 1985 that it would withdraw all its troops from Cambodia by September 1990 made this issue much less contentious than an open-ended Vietnamese military occupation would have been; and eventually the issue dwindled except for questions about how to verify the PAVN departure. The CGDK insisted on total departure as the formula. The related issue of alleged imperialism conducted by Vietnamese "settlers" lacked an agreeable formula. On the other hand, Cambodians and the UN relief organizations alike believed that repatriating Khmer displaced persons from the border camps was important for the national renaissance.

3. How and when should a cease-fire take place and be monitored by an international control mechanism? What key political issues had to be settled first? How might the rival military forces be reduced by disarming requirements and procedures?

4. Should military assistance to the contending parties be terminated, and, if so, when?

In both issues 3 and 4, the fear of future betrayal inhibited agreement. The "resistance" parties feared deception by Vietnam, which in turn distrusted the Khmer Rouge. The Vietnamese/PRK side wanted a specific reference to the inadmissibility of the Khmer Rouge ever sharing in power again. The semi-secret DK party, with China's backing, strenuously objected that language characterizing the Khmer Rouge administration as "genocidal" was inappropriate and unnecessary. Since former Khmer Rouge personalities were prominent in the Phnom Penh government, the question of whether they should be excluded from future service was a fundamental and sensitive one.

5. Who should organize the elections: the current government (later called the State of Cambodia or SOC), the United Nations, or a multiparty government? The SOC option was anathema to the resistance parties, but the UN was inexperienced at organizing an election, and the PRK regarded

it as biased in favor of the CGDK. A multiparty government would be new to the job and buffeted by internecine disagreements.

6. Who should govern the nation during the interim between a cease-fire and elections? Governance could not (without bias) be left in the hands of the Vietnamese-installed party (Khmer People's Revolutionary Party), but this group would probably never agree to its own dismemberment. Could administration be shared by the resistance parties, or delegated to an international body? If shared, should it be on a two-party or four-party coalition basis?

7. Could the sovereign independence and territorial integrity of Cambodia be guaranteed by neighbors and great powers? Neutrality appeared to be the most promising foreign policy for Cambodia, but who would guarantee this condition?

8. How should a new constitution for Cambodia be composed? What model would be appropriate?

By 1989 channels of communication had been slowly created between the competing Khmer political factions, and these groups spoke to one another even while sending military forces against each other. Gradually, with the help of Southeast Asian states and the great powers, the contending factions had organized themselves into parties locked in a military stalemate and a diplomatic maze that tantalized would-be peacemakers.

In 1985 the Soviet Union had begun to change the dynamic by informing the Vietnamese that it could no longer economically sustain the PAVN presence in Cambodia; and, in addition, Chairman Gorbachev intended to improve Soviet relations with China, with an exit from Afghanistan as a major step. Vietnam's drop in power and China's consequent cut in its support of the Khmer Rouge against Vietnam was likely to make a negotiated settlement more feasible than a military contest. The Cambodian parties were at least accustomed to the idea of negotiation and had tried out a number of formats, including Sihanouk as a player.

Finding a Formula for Settlement

A formula for resolving diplomatic disputes may take a variety of forms. In some instances the critical combination of agreements is "discovered" by a process of "try and see." In other cases a solution is "invented" by a process of creative imagination and construction. Sometimes the formula can be logically deduced from a set of agreed principles, such as equal rights of states on the high seas, while in others it may be inductively put together, piece by separate piece—as in the Arab-Israeli negotiations concerning the very distinguishable issues of the West Bank, Golan, and Jerusalem. In the case of Cambodia, the parties in dispute would most likely seek a resolution through two basic principles: free and fair election of a government and noninterference by outside governments. Many side issues lay entangled in this proto-formula, which two and a half years of diplomatic maneuver finally wrapped together in a formula package.

The formula search was greatly favored by the worldwide practice of holding national elections—however unfair and unfree the actual practice might be in some nations. Also, the ideas of national sovereignty and nonintervention, that is, freedom from dictatorial interference, are universally favored—as the repeated UN General Assembly resolutions calling for the exit of foreign troops from Cambodia were to demonstrate. Third World nations, including Cambodia, having emerged from the age of colonialism, honored the international legal principle of sovereign independence with a devotion often exceeding that displayed by the Western authors of the doctrine.

Understandably, the shift of negotiations from "diagnosis" to the "search for a formula" does not proclaim itself with ringing bells or press conferences, but keen observers of diplomacy sometimes sense what is called "a turning point of seriousness." The formula-seeking phase may continue some months or years before a formula is clearly identified. Several studies of Cambodia have spoken of "a turning point," such as the first meetings of Sihanouk and the PRK leader Hun Sen, after which the parties seemed ready for give-and-take negotiation. What were the terms of trade? In the case of Cambodia, certain key ideas were ultimately accepted by all parties: that warfare should cease, that elections should determine who governs, that international guarantees should sustain independence. How to combine these instrumental notions into a package that the contestants perceived as preferable to the status quo was the essence of formula seeking. An unusual array of statesmen and civil servants from neighboring states, great powers, and the UN Secretariat devoted energy and imagination to this end between 1988 and September 1990. Their efforts would find expression in a "Framework Document" issued by the Permanent Five (P-5) members of the UN Security Council on August 28, 1990.

Not every issue can find a resolution even in the best of formula seeking. A frequent device for bridging intractable disagreements is to separate out the areas of deadlock for continuing negotiation and separate instruments. For Cambodia, "annex agreements" were added to the framework offered by the P-5. Certain key issues were left to be resolved after acceptance of the P-5 proposal, such as basic principles of a future constitution. Such a falling short of full agreement does not invalidate the general rule that a diplomatic formula should be comprehensive, as the Paris Agreements on a Comprehensive Political Settlement for Cambodia tried to be. These accords addressed the major points of disagreement, even though the provisions for governance during the preelection "transition" period remained a most serious bone of contention. Sometimes an issue can be settled by future events. For example, an agreed verification of the total withdrawal of Vietnamese forces from Cambodia was never achieved, but its salience as an issue subsided as the military conflict dwindled.

The analysis that follows does not record the full pattern of diplomatic give-and-take. The two and a half years of maneuver left intricate trails of testing out demands, of concessions, of postures and convictions, of hardness and flexibility. At best a summary of these explorations is offered here, with a reminder that the diplomatic contest by itself cannot explain the political outcome.

1988: Specific Frameworks for Settlement

Hun Sen opened the new formula-seeking phase by announcing that the final departure date of the Vietnamese armed forces from Cambodia had been moved up to September 1989. He said he was looking forward to a second meeting with Prince Sihanouk, his wife, and his son Ranariddh, which they set for January 20–21 in Saint-Germain-en-Laye, near Paris. At the meeting, Sihanouk insisted that the PAVN withdraw much sooner, while Hun Sen stressed the impossibility of dismantling his government before general elections were held.[1] Hun Sen was probably aware of the efforts by the ragged CGDK military elements to organize a coordinated "national resistance." Sihanouk asserted that a quadripartite coalition government should handle the organizing of elections, under supervision of an international peacekeeping force. The PRK called for elections first, under their own management, and only afterwards would the PRK be dismantled. The PRK was insisting upon the dismantling of the Khmer Rouge armed forces before it would enter a coalition government. Three days after the conference, the PRK's deputy premier announced a readiness to deal with the DK's Khieu Samphan as a negotiation counterpart, while ruling out any contact with Pol Pot or Ieng Sary.

After this flurry of position staking, Sihanouk trumped his "leave of absence" from the presidency of the CGDK by resigning the post altogether, partly in response to backbiting within the coalition, and partly to invite

1. Patrick Raszelenberg and Peter Schier, *The Cambodian Conflict: Search for a Settlement, 1979–91* (Hamburg: Institute of Asian Affairs, 1995), pp. 152–91.

unofficial contact with Vietnam. After a month's failure to reach this goal, Sihanouk resumed his presidency "temporarily." The mercurial prince was also the pragmatic try-and-see negotiator, and on February 4, 1988, he called off further talks with Hun Sen, which he considered to be unpromising.

The PDK tried to keep the proposal for a coalition alive, via conversations in Beijing between Sihanouk and Khieu Samphan (February 7–9). However, disagreements emerged over the prince's proposal to establish a four-party national army, amid evidence of serious rifts and a weakening leadership within the KPNLF. The resistance coalition planted a symbolic boundary by including the DK's notorious Ieng Sary at a meeting of its so-called cabinet of ministers on February 10, without Sihanouk. Their adversaries in Phnom Penh made clear that they would not deal with Sary or Pol Pot, whom they regarded as perpetrators of genocide.

In April the deputy foreign minister of the USSR endorsed the French-Indonesian idea of an informal meeting of all concerned parties in an unofficial format, which they dubbed a "cocktail party." The PRK continued to push for renewed Hun Sen–Sihanouk talks, but the prince held back, insisting on a direct engagement of Vietnam as a party to the dispute. A rumor in June suggested that China was ready to grant political asylum to Pol Pot.

Another new element in the diplomatic equation was a "working paper" by UN undersecretary-general Rafeeuddin Ahmed, who presented "specific proposals" to "provide a framework for a comprehensive settlement of the Kampuchean problem." The goals laid out by the UN Secretariat were:

1. withdraw all foreign forces
2. bar the return of "the universally condemned policies and practices which have marked a recent past"
3. hold free elections
4. establish a neutral, independent, democratic, and nonaligned Cambodia
5. guarantee respect for regional security concerns
6. create a zone of peace, freedom, and neutrality.

Many procedural questions had to be faced as well. The "framework" covered many of them, including the relative timing of the PAVN's withdrawal, the ending of foreign military assistance, a cease-fire, the sending of an international peacekeeping force, a political education program, and an elections commissioner; but detailed planning for disarming of troops and ensuring sovereignty and neutrality was not yet worked out.

The proposed cocktail party, redesignated as the Jakarta informal meeting (JIM) to assuage Moslem objections to Western drinking, was to include the four Cambodia factions and Vietnam. The CGDK stole a march on the meetings with an official statement calling for a provisional quadri-partite government, following the simultaneous dismantling of the PRK and the CGDK regimes. This new government would be responsible for organizing general elections. Phnom Penh called it "ridiculous" to require the PRK to dissolve itself. The disagreement surrounding this question was to remain unresolved for several years to come.

The First Jakarta Informal Meeting

The first JIM took place in Bogor, Indonesia, on July 25–28, 1988, with a first stage involving the four Cambodian factions reacting to a seven-point proposal by the PRK, and a second stage including the Indochina govern-ments and the ASEAN states, which started immediately thereafter. The PRK's seven points included the critical idea of a "national reconciliation council" charged with organizing general elections, while the PRK re-mained in office. They also spoke ambiguously of the "rejection" (i.e., dis-bandment) of the Khmer Rouge armed forces and the termination of external assistance. Sihanouk was present as an official guest of the Indone-sian president Suharto but not a party to the meetings. Nonetheless he dis-seminated a speech calling for a four-party provisional government, which would somehow operate with four-party ministries and a National Army of Kampuchea under a quadripartite general staff. Again, in Sihanouk's pro-posal the elections were to be organized by a hard-to-imagine provisional government and he made no reference to an international peacekeeping force.

The proposals and commentaries at Bogor did not achieve an agreement that could be expressed in a final declaration, but Chairman Ali Alatas, the Indonesian foreign minister, framed a "consensus statement" which, de-spite its name, did not reflect unanimity. In a diplomatic uplift effort he praised all sides for their work, and he singled out the key issues as (1) with-drawal of Vietnamese forces, (2) "prevention of the recurrence of genocidal policies and practices of the Pol Pot regime," and (3) cessation of external arms supplies to the factions. The Khmer Rouge blocked any agreement on the nonreturn of Pol Pot, and the PRK castigated this negative action.

Nonetheless the Jakarta press labeled the conference a "psychological breakthrough." The Khmer Rouge rejected the formation of a national rec-onciliation council under Sihanouk's chairmanship, but Hun Sen and the prince met informally during the conference and publicly announced a fur-ther rendezvous for October 1988. Indeed, Sihanouk's thinking had loosened up to the point of discussing with the Japanese prime minister, ten days after Jakarta, the possibility of a bilateral government and a military formation of his ANS and the PRK armed forces, to pit roughly seventy thousand troops against the Khmer Rouge and preclude their return to power. He would require, however, that this incongruous government be created after the PRK had been disbanded. The PDK, a week later, altered their peace plan to include the *simultaneous* dismantling of the PRK and the DK, giving way to a provisional four-party government under Prince Sihanouk, with military forces confined to barracks and an international control mechanism to ensure that "any one Kampuchea party cannot dominate the others." Hun Sen looked forward to a new meeting with Sihanouk to pursue further his unexpected anti–Khmer Rouge realignment ideas.

A very positive move was taken in late August when the deputy foreign ministers of China and the Soviet Union met in Beijing to negotiate a rapprochement, with the Cambodia conflict as the first agenda topic. They found the issue not readily subject to resolution. Sihanouk contributed four points to solve the conflict and spotlighted four major topics of disagreement: the date of the PAVN's full withdrawal, the dispatch of an international peacekeeping force, the dismantling of the PRK before elections, and the dismantling of the National Army of Democratic Kampuchea. The Soviet Union assumed a more positive role in Asia with Gorbachev's announcement on September 16, 1988, of seven proposals to strengthen security in Southeast Asia, including a Soviet departure from the Cam Ranh Bay naval base in Vietnam, if the United States would leave its Philippine bases.

ASEAN saw fit to sharpen its annual UN General Assembly resolution on Cambodia, referring to the goal of "national reconciliation among all Kampucheans under the leadership of Samdech Norodom Sihanouk" and to "the non-return to the universally condemned policies and practices of a recent past." ASEAN did not agree, however, to the Soviet proposal to leave the Kampuchean seat at the UN General Assembly vacant. The ASEAN resolution passed 122-19-13, continuing the CGDK' s occupancy of Kampuchea's seat at the UN.

Hun Sen and Sihanouk met again on November 7–8, in Fère-en-Tardenois, joined by Son Sann for the KPNLF, but without a PDK spokesperson. The PRK rejected the proposed PDK representative, a DK ambassador to UNESCO, whom they considered not an appropriate person for a summit-level conference. Hun Sen's proposals to the resistance parties included a cease-fire in place, a political status quo until elections, closing out the Khmer refugee camps, and a national reconciliation council under Prince Sihanouk[2] A joint communiqué was achieved, and Hun Sen was quoted in the press as affirming his party's acceptance of the Khmer Rouge playing a role in the political solution and joining in future four-party working groups and summit meetings.[3]

Notwithstanding this slight convergence of the parties, Sihanouk (three weeks later) announced his doubt that further talks with Phnom Penh would be possible so long as they continued to reject some seven proposals that he stood by. These provisions lay at the heart of the fundamental process of setting up elections outside the PRK framework, in a secure demilitarized environment. On the other hand, Under secretary-General Rafeeuddin Ahmed, after talking with Hun Sen in Phnom Penh, reportedly agreed with him that a full-scale dissolution of the PRK would be premature.

1989: Another Jakarta Informal Meeting and the Exit of PAVN

The new year opened with uncertainty over whether a second JIM could be organized and over Phnom Penh and Hanoi's demand that the withdrawal of Vietnam's troops (recently promised for September 1989) be linked to ending external assistance and sanctuary for resistance factions. Nonetheless, China and Vietnam were showing signs of serious dialogue, and China reportedly pledged to stop military aid to the resistance factions, in parallel with Vietnam's troop withdrawal.

ASEAN's foreign ministers encountered many obstacles in setting up a JIM II, which Sihanouk explained with the assertion that the time was not ripe for a solution, and "the Jakarta meeting is bound to fail." ASEAN, nonetheless, decided that the United States, China, and Japan should be included in the JIM. The Thai government went further, under Prime Minister Chatichai Choonhavan's new rubric of turning Cambodia "from a battlefield into a marketplace," by conducting direct talks with Hun Sen in Bangkok on January 25. Hun Sen registered his objections to an international peacekeeping force and to a dismantling of the PRK prior to elections—two issues that were never to reach a full-scale resolution. He expressed a willingness, however, to allow the voluntary repatriation of the 300,000-plus refugees living at the Thai-Cambodian border. The international legitimacy of Hun Sen, which this Bangkok meeting implied, was regretted but not precluded by Prince Sihanouk.

2. Ibid., p. 193. The proposed national reconciliation council seems to have been a forerunner of the later Supreme National Council idea.
3. Ibid., p. 195.

JIM II gathered in Bogor, Indonesia, on February 19–21, after several weeks of Chinese-Soviet discussions, which included a communiqué confirming both the end-of-September date for the PAVN withdrawal and also the principle of reducing outside military assistance in tandem with Vietnamese troop reduction. Disagreement persisted, however, concerning China's preference for dismantling the PRK during the period preceding elections, and the Soviets' objection to sending a UN peacekeeping force, despite their endorsement of an "international control mechanisn."

No joint communiqué emerged from JIM II, but again a "consensus statement" was released which made no claim to unanimous agreement on all points. Foreign Minister Ali Alatas of Indonesia summed up the exercise as ending "satisfactorily" after negotiation in a "frank and constructive atmosphere" (called "very heated debates" by Hun Sen). The DK faction, on behalf of the CGDK, issued a "draft statement" which differed here and there from the consensus statement. These persisting points of disagreement on the DK's part principally included an interim authority (quadripartite), election procedures, an international control mechanism to verify the end of foreign arms aid, and an international peacekeeping force to "prevent any Cambodian party from monopolizing power by itself." Once again the strain between the PRK and the PDK was intense and uncompromised, with the PDK refusing to agree to language (later appearing in the consensus statement) concerning "the prevention of the recurrence of genocidal policies and practices of the Pol Pot regime." Overall, the conference registered growing understanding of the irreconcilable issues, but further negotiation was postponed until China and the USSR held a summit meeting in May.

The CGDK offered to take part in a reduction of the four factions' armies to ten thousand men each, with excess weapons turned over to UN peacekeepers. Vietnam and the PRK on April 5 again announced the withdrawal date for Vietnam's forces (September 30), this time "unconditionally," while also belatedly asserting the legitimacy of Vietnam's entry in 1978 to help the people of Kampuchea against the genocidal Pol Pot regime. The three Indochina states proposed an International Control Commission to monitor the PAVN departure, but the idea was never effectively picked up, and the departure of Vietnamese forces in September was not systematically verified. Under the circumstances, Son Sen, the DK army commander, continued to claim that disguised Vietnamese soldiers constituted up to 20 percent of the PRK's army. Sihanouk publicly doubted the number was that large, but he expressed fear that an unverified one million Vietnamese settlers had infiltrated Cambodia.

More Sihanouk–Hun Sen Talks

The PRK next undertook (on April 30) to revise its constitution in the direction of private economic rights, and changed its name from the communist ("people's republic") designation to the State of Cambodia (SOC). Prince Norodom Ranariddh categorically rejected this "so-called Constitution, drafted unilaterally, by a puppet regime of Hanoi." On May 2–3, at the invitation of the Indonesian foreign minister Ali Alatas, Sihanouk and Hun Sen met for the fourth time in Jakarta. Son Sann also attended, representing the resistance coalition. Sihanouk announced on arrival that he no longer insisted upon dissolution or dismantling of the PRK. Son Sann, however, was far less flexible, accepting none of the PRK's new constitution and insisting on the creation of a four-party coalition government. Sihanouk was open to using the PRK's idea (tabled at JIM II) of a supreme council to organize national elections, but such a council's relationship to the existing SOC administration in Phnom Penh was not yet clear. Sihanouk and Hun Sen were able to agree on the cessation of outside military aid and the convening of an international conference to work out an international control mechanism for monitoring Vietnamese troop departures and for other peace agreement duties. Hun Sen nonetheless refused to agree to including the PDK in a four-party government.

Considerable give-and-take ensued, without agreement, over when a cease-fire might be achieved. China and Vietnam proved to be just as inconclusive in negotiating their own normalization of relations. China and the Soviet Union also conferred at the summit level (in Beijing), with the unscheduled accompaniment of pro-democracy demonstrations in Tiananmen Square. Notwithstanding the distraction, they discussed the resumption of friendly relations; and the two sides notably pledged "to respect the results of the general election" in Cambodia, to phase out military assistance to the factions in step with Vietnam's withdrawal of troops, and to support the convening, as soon as possible, of an international conference on Cambodia. Two weeks later France announced a Paris international conference on Cambodia for early August 1989, under the co-chairmanship of the French and Indonesian foreign ministers, Roland Dumas and Ali Alatas.

The Paris Conference on Cambodia

In a bit of window dressing, on June 3, Pol Pot was reported by the DK to have resigned from his official position directing the DK High Institute for

National Defense, to work thenceforth as an "ordinary researcher." Notwithstanding his previous resignation as secretary-general of the Communist Party of Kampuchea in 1981, and as commander-in-chief of the National Army of Democratic Kampuchea in 1985, Pol Pot was still regarded internationally as the preeminent leader of his party, "brother number one."[4] A few weeks earlier the PRK had tried to broaden and soften its own image by renaming itself the State of Cambodia (SOC).

The impending Paris conference prompted Sihanouk to outline his CGDK's position on verifying Vietnamese troop (and settler) withdrawals, verifying a cease-fire and the phased reduction of military aid, and disarming and demobilizing troops of the Cambodian parties down to forces of ten thousand men confined to barracks. These proposed actions were never fully executed, but the concept was endorsed in the final Paris Agreements. ASEAN foreign ministers also chimed in (July 4) with support for "a comprehensive political settlement," with an international peacekeeping force, under the UN, to help conduct free and fair elections. Vietnam and the SOC both rejected any role for the UN, which they saw as politically biased, but Hanoi showed willingness to compromise on the issue, if the UN ceased its seating of the CGDK.

A fifth meeting of Hun Sen and Prince Sihanouk took place on the outskirts of Paris (LaCelle-Saint-Cloud) on July 24 and 25. They discussed the idea of the four party leaders holding roundtable talks, presided over by Sihanouk and the French foreign minister, Roland Dumas. Four major points of impasse soon emerged: (1) the composition of the Cambodian delegation to the Paris Conference on Cambodia (SOC plus CGDK, or quadripartite?), (2) the participation (or not) of the Khmer Rouge in a preelection government, (3) the international control mechanism and peacekeeping force under UN auspices (or not?), and (4) the cease-fire (before or after the signing of a comprehensive settlement?)[5] Under the circumstances the second day of the talks ended quickly, but the French prime minister, Michel Rocard, persuaded Hun Sen in person to join a four-party delegation to the Paris conference, thereby enabling the roundtable talks to continue, albeit fruitlessly, on July 28.

The Paris Conference on Cambodia lasted a month (July 30 to August 30, 1989), with the participation of the four Cambodian factions sitting behind a sign labeled "Cambodge," with four separate delegations identified

4. Ibid., pp. 238–39. Press Release, "Letter from H.E. Mr. Pol Pot to the Leaders of the Democratic Kampuchea Party," Permanent Mission of Democratic Kampuchea to the UN, No. 062/89, June 7, 1989.

5. Raszelenberg and Schier, *The Cambodian Conflict*, p. 245.

by their respective leaders, Son Sann, Sihanouk, Khieu Samphan, and Hun Sen (seated in order of age). Also attending were the permanent five members of the UN Security Council (P-5), the six ASEAN states, the other two Indochina states (Vietnam and Laos), Australia, Japan, two former control commission states during the Vietnam War (India and Canada), Zimbabwe (acting chair of the Non-Aligned Movement), and the UN secretary-general, Javier Pérez de Cuéllar. The French and Indonesian foreign ministers were elected co-chairs. The foreign ministers of each of the attending states (except fractured Cambodia) quickly agreed to an "organization of work" prepared by France, which set up key research committees on specific topics under co-chairs. They also agreed to the UN secretary-general's proposal to send a fact-finding mission to Cambodia as soon as possible. The principle of unanimity for nonprocedural issues was adopted at the urging of both China and Vietnam.[6]

The First Working Committee concerned itself with a cease-fire and an international control mechanism. The Second Committee dealt with guarantees of "independence, sovereignty, territorial integrity and neutrality of Cambodia, and the cessation of arms assistance, and prevention of any recurrence of genocidal policies and practices and the return and introduction of foreign forces." The Third Committee dealt with the return home of refugees and displaced persons and the reconstruction of Cambodia. A fourth group, called the Ad Hoc Committee, examined questions of national reconciliation and the establishment of a four-party interim authority under the leadership of Prince Sihanouk, and also the organization of "internationally supervised free elections."[7] A fifth, coordinating committee was charged with drafting within a month a final document setting forth all the elements, internal and external, of a "comprehensive settlement."

The avid organization of the conference by France and Indonesia also included the distribution of "non-papers" to provide an agenda for the committees' work. The UN secretary-general and various delegations also circulated "communications" as the work proceeded. In the case of the Ad Hoc Committee on national reconciliation and interim authority in Cambodia, however, the sides were deadlocked from the very beginning and made scant progress.[8] This issue remained the most difficult to resolve as negotia-

6. Amitav Acharya et al., eds., *Cambodia—The 1989 Paris Peace Conference: Background Analysis and Documents* (Toronto: Centre for International and Strategic Studies, York University, 1991), pp. 125, 129.

7. "Organization of Work," Aug. 1, 1989, in Acharya et al., *Cambodia—The 1989 Paris Peace Conference*, pp. 129–30. A detailed insider account of the Paris Conference on Cambodia is found in Michael Haas, *Genocide by Proxy* (New York: Praeger, 1991), chap. 19.

8. Haas, *Genocide by Proxy*, p. 200.

tion continued. The other committees made real advances in refining their topics, but the conference achieved no final document, merely a "statement" issued August 20, 1989, which announced the suspension of the conference, subject to reconvening "in due time."[9]

The foreign ministers who had addressed the opening session in upbeat tones avoided the final meeting of the month-long effort to reach a comprehensive settlement. The issue of national reconciliation and sharing of power by the still intransigent political factions was not yet ripe for settlement. Within a month military struggle replaced the efforts of the thwarted diplomats. The level of mutual trust among the four factions was far from sufficient to allow compromise agreements on how to organize a national election to settle the question of who would rule Cambodia. No consensus was achievable on any substantive issue, even though the great power supporters of the factions were moving toward disengagement from their clients. The distinguished Singapore diplomat Tommy Koh attributed the failure of the conference (amid successes) to the rejection by the SOC of proposals to share power in the interim period prior to elections. Hardliners within the Hanoi leadership pulled the SOC back from compromise. The issue, contrary to appearances, was not ready for settlement.[10] More than a year was to pass before a complete formula for settlement was conceived, and a year beyond that before the Paris Agreements were achieved.

Constructive Ideas

Yet, despite the stinging failure of the Dumas/Alatas effort to wrap up the conflict, a few constructive elements were added to the problem-solving exercise. The agreement on dispatching "a preliminary short-term fact-finding mission to gather technical information on the spot" paid off within a month, with the dispatch of Lt.-General Martin Vadset of Norway, the head of the UN Truce Supervision Organization in the Arab-Israeli war, and fourteen assistants, who recommended a minimum force of at least six thousand men for the international control mechanism and a serious upgrading of the estimates of logistical needs.[11] The dispatch of this useful mission had encountered reluctance among the resistance parties, which

9. Acharya et al., *Cambodia—The 1989 Paris Peace Conference*, p. 484.

10. Tommy T. B. Koh, "The Paris Conference on Cambodia: A Multilateral Negotiation That Failed," *Negotiation Journal*, January 1990. Raszelenberg and Schier, *The Cambodian Conflict*, p. 249.

11. Haas, *Genocide by Proxy*, p. 196.

realized that a control mechanism in place before the departure of the Vietnamese forces might verify their eventual exit and seriously challenge a long-standing arguing point against Hanoi.

Another device that survived the Paris conference was Hun Sen's proposal at JIM II of a "Supreme Supervisory Council" to help manage the period between a comprehensive agreement of the parties and the holding of elections (without dismantling the SOC). This proposal, later altered in regard to the composition and duties of the council, as well as its name, survived into the final agreements of 1991. Yet the different parties perceived the council in somewhat different ways.

The attempt to resolve this issue of interim national authority during the preelection period also inspired a device that lasted through the postconference negotiations—the special supervision of those ministries that exercised power seriously affecting the political environment in favor of the government. As proposed by Sihanouk, four key ministries—defense, foreign affairs, interior, and information—would be given four-party administration;[12] but his general plan was not picked up, partly due to its practical awkwardness. The idea nonetheless survived into the final agreement (art. 6), where the UN authority was authorized to exercise such "control as is necessary to ensure the strict neutrality" of the agreed-upon agencies (with finance added to the list).

Differing proposals for the duration of the election campaign emerged at Paris, with the SOC favoring an early timetable (three months from the departure of foreign troops) and the FUNCINPEC preferring a year to get ready. The Paris Agreements ultimately called for elections within nine months of the start of voter registration.[13]

Other activities and statements of lasting impact on the negotiation process included the reception of Hun Sen by the French prime minister, even though France did not recognize the SOC[14]—a meeting that Sihanouk had worked long to preclude. The prince's behavior revealed how much the working principle of unanimity among the CGDK parties exercised a restraint on his tendency to swing from bold reconciliation gestures to narrow caution and resentment toward the Phnom Penh regime. Some of his communications seemed to be virtually composed by the DK/Khieu Samphan element of the Cambodia delegation.[15]

12. Ibid., p. 201.
13. United Nations, *Agreements on a Comprehensive Political Settlement of the Cambodia Conflict*, Paris, Oct. 23, 1991, Annex 1, Section D. See also Haas, *Genocide by Proxy*, p. 191.
14. Raszelenberg and Schier, *The Cambodian Conflict*, p. 246.
15. Haas, *Genocide by Proxy*, pp. 195–96.

U.S. Secretary of State James Baker, who attended only the opening session of the Paris Conference on Cambodia, also revealed a two-sided posture — on the one hand believing strongly that the Khmer Rouge "should play no role in Cambodia's future," and on the other hand willing to support Sihanouk's call for inclusion of the Khmer Rouge in an interim government preceding elections. The "strength of U.S. support" for such a government, Baker said, "would depend directly and inversely on the extent of KR participation, if any, in that government." In other words, the more Khmer Rouge presence in the government, the less support from the United States.[16] This oddly stated compromise position by the U.S., which had previously insisted on a four-party interim government, did not satisfy the enemies of the Khmer Rouge—some of whom spoke out in the U.S. Congress. The United States, in line with ASEAN's strategy, accepted the PDK as "a fact of life," but did not wish to have its aid to the CGDK reach the Khmer Rouge element.

This approach was riddled with tensions. Michael Haas faulted the United States for pressing the SOC for a "capitulation, a treaty of surrender, when in fact there was a military stalemate."[17] He found it surreal to envisage so-called moderate PDK members campaigning for office, while an international force suppressed the "extremist" PDK guerrillas. Yet this was the picture that ASEAN, Sihanouk, and Son Sann rested their policy upon — in what they considered a compromise, not a forced capitulation. The Paris conference also provided a forum for the SOC leader Hun Sen to insist on the "principle" of not dismantling his government before the holding of elections.[18] In any event, the Paris conference advanced the peace process only slightly, and a true formula for a "comprehensive political settlement" was yet to be fashioned.

The next significant event in the search for peace was the final departure of Vietnamese military forces on September 26, 1989. The withdrawal was dramatized with local fanfare and photographed by the international press, but not independently recorded by an international group. Prince Sihanouk, in Beijing, continued the wild charges (seconded by China) that more than 100,000 Vietnamese soldiers would remain in Cambodia disguised as elements of the Phnom Penh regime's army or militia. Consequently a cease-fire was not feasible unless it were part of a comprehensive

16. Raszelenberg and Schier, *The Cambodian Conflict*, p. 248. See also "Opening Statement of the Honorable James A. Baker, III, to the Paris International Conference on Cambodia," July 30, 1980, in Acharya, et al., *Cambodia—The 1989 Paris Peace Conference*, pp. 82–85.

17. Haas, *Genocide by Proxy*, p. 207.

18. Raszelenberg and Schier, *The Cambodian Conflict*, p. 252.

settlement, accompanied by UN control and peacekeeping forces.[19] Several tens of thousands of Vietnamese advisors were also asserted (by Son Sann) to remain in place within the SOC. Verification of these charges was never provided.

The withdrawal of Vietnamese forces in September was congruent with the fall of European communism and the Soviet empire. The collapse of the Soviet bloc was being felt in a squeeze on economic aid to Vietnam,[20] and by extension on the SOC, as well as in the readiness of the Russians to improve relations with China, which also reduced the economic burden of military overextension. The erosion of Soviet power was dictating a genuine readiness to wrap up the remote proxy war in Cambodia.

The Khmer Rouge spokesman Khieu Samphan renewed his preferred remedy for the uncertainties regarding relative military strength, proposing that an international control mechanism, assisted by UN peacekeepers, should supervise a reduction of the Khmer factions to ten thousand men each, restricted to barracks.[21] Sihanouk reiterated the proposal on November 27, in Beijing, after a Khmer Rouge military offensive had won control of the gem-mining town of Pailin in late October and provoked the SOC to ask Vietnam for reinforcements. Vietnam had made known before its troops departed that they would return if needed. At the same time Sihanouk seriously welcomed the proposal made by the Australian foreign affairs minister, Gareth Evans, just three days earlier, for a sort of UN trusteeship for Cambodia. Two weeks later Hun Sen said he was ready to consider the "Evans plan," but he insisted that Cambodia's UN seat be vacant. The UN General Assembly meanwhile adopted an ASEAN resolution calling for a comprehensive settlement, after waves of skeptical speech making about the unverified Vietnamese military withdrawal. Despite the bitter rejoinders issued by the Phnom Penh foreign ministry, the resolution passed, 124 members in favor, 17 against, and 12 abstaining. The resolution called for "the creation of an interim administering authority," and a week later Australia launched its proposal for a UN administrative role and national reconciliation.[22] China welcomed the Evans initiative in principle, while still preferring a four-party provisional government headed by Sihanouk.

---

19. Ibid., pp. 259–62. Also Press Release No. 082/89, Sept. 15, 1989, "Statement of the CGDK Denouncing the Vietnamese Claim of Unilateral Withdrawal," Permanent Mission of Democratic Kampuchea to the UN, New York.

20. Soviet and East European aid to Vietnam in 1989 was estimated at $1.6 billion but declining drastically. Raszelenberg and Schier, *The Cambodian Conflict*, p. 280.

21. Ibid., p. 263.

22. Ibid., pp. 266–67, 276–77. "The Situation in Kampuchea," UN General Assembly Resolution 44/22, Nov. 7, 1989.

The Evans (Australian) Proposal

The Australian plan for solving the preelection power-sharing issue grew out of Foreign Minister Gareth Evans's speech to his national Senate on November 24, 1989. His idea, as acknowledged in the foreword of the Australian Government "Red Book" issued in February 1990,[23] owed much to the thinking of Prince Sihanouk and the U.S. congressman Stephen Solarz, who chaired the House of Representatives subcommittee on Southeast Asia, with whom Evans conversed in early October. Soon after his speech Evans dispatched his deputy Michael Costello to promote the idea, as a diplomatic breakthrough, to the foreign ministries of the concerned countries that had attended the Paris conference. The Jakarta meeting on Cambodia held on February 26–28, 1990, under the co-chairmen of the Paris conference, faced Evans with a serious request for information and analysis, and a deadline for the preparation of "working papers" on the logistics and practicabilities of the UN trusteeship idea, even though a break in the impasse was not seriously expected at the meeting. The Australian foreign ministry quickly analyzed the costs and requirements of an international (UN) interim administration of Cambodia as a substitute for multiparty government which the four factions were unwilling to attempt. Although the "Evans plan" did not emerge from the subsequent international debates without serious modifications, the winter of 1990 saw the idea of an "enhanced role" of the United Nations, if not a "trusteeship," emerge as the most promising model for a truly "comprehensive political settlement."

The United States helped push matters in this direction by mobilizing the Permanent Five (P-5) members of the UN Security Council into a truly fruitful collaboration which provided analysis and diplomatic encouragement and language for bringing the contending parties and nations together. The vice foreign ministers of the P-5, following U.S. Secretary of State James Baker's suggestion, met in Paris on January 15–16, 1990, to discuss the possibilities for "resolving the Cambodia problem." They agreed to an enhanced role for the UN in Cambodia and issued a sixteen-point "Summary of Conclusions" which listed their working principles.[24] The Perma-

23. *Cambodia: An Australian Peace Proposal*, Working Papers for the Informal Meeting on Cambodia, Jakarta, Feb. 26–28, 1990, Department of Foreign Affairs and Trade, Commonwealth of Australia, Canberra, 1990.

24. "Summary of Conclusions of the Permanent Five Members of the Security Council on the Cambodia Problem," Paris, Jan. 15–16, 1990, in Acharya et al., *Cambodia—The 1989 Paris Peace Conference*, pp. 487–88. The principal U.S. representatives were Richard Solomon, assistant secretary of state for East Asia, and Thomas R. Pickering, permanent representative of the U.S.A. to the UN.

nent Five began meeting on a monthly basis, alternating between Paris and New York, with press statements issued at the conclusion of each meeting. The sixteen principles presented after the first get-together were well chosen and contributed phrasing that strengthened the converging thinking of the concerned parties.

Thus, the agreed goal became "a comprehensive political settlement" with a "cessation of outside military assistance," an "enhanced UN role" involving an "effective UN presence" to assure internal security in a "neutral political environment," and a special representative of the UN secretary-general. "A Supreme National Council might be the repository of Cambodian sovereignty during the transition process." These points did not address, however, the question of whether existing government structures would be retained.

The diplomatic virtue of the Evans proposal was that it avoided both the dismantling of the SOC and also the retention of *full* authority by the SOC prior to the election. It called for leaving the Cambodia seat vacant at the UN General Assembly, but this was potentially negotiable for Sihanouk. If a national council could be established, it might fill the UN seat. The UN was still regarded by the SOC and Hanoi as an unfriendly organization, but if the UN based its actions in Cambodia on the authority of the secretary-general, not the General Assembly, this difficulty might be surmounted. As for the UN as an election-supervising organ, it had gained precious experience in Namibia and Nicaragua, but not to the point of organizing the event in lieu of a government. Also, a legal obstacle came to be appreciated, namely that the UN Charter did not allow for trusteeship to be exercised by the United Nations over one of its members. Thus the UN could not undertake the full authority in Cambodia, a divided member state, pending the election of a national government.

The Australian proposal and "Red Book" of working papers nonetheless concentrated thinking on a promising and generally accepted means of distributing power to conduct a free and fair vote on the political future of Cambodia. With but a few negotiable sticking points evident and all the concerned foreign ministries taking favorable positions, the JIM III gathering in Jakarta on February 26–28, 1990, put the idea foremost on its agenda. To be sure, Hun Sen adamantly objected to dealing with the PDK leadership, and Khieu Samphan refused to agree to Cambodia's UN seat being vacant, as did Sihanouk. The prince also continued to make statements that credited the Khmer Rouge with having played a valued nationalist, anti-Vietnam role.[25] Yet the consensus of the Permanent Five

25. Raszelenberg and Schier, *The Cambodian Conflict*, p. 284.

members of the Security Council in favor of Evans's initiative made the moment quite propitious for a genuine agreement by the Cambodian factions, whose existence depended heavily on Soviet, Chinese, U.S., and UK material support, and France's diplomacy.

The 155-page collection of working papers prepared by the Australian ministry of foreign affairs and trade, after a ten-day visit by its research team to Cambodia, addressed itself to overall structure of government during the transition period and to the exercise of three key governmental functions: civil administration, electoral organization, and security. The papers also analyzed measures to guarantee a sovereign, independent, and neutral Cambodia, and its reconstruction. The most significant idea regarding structure was the Supreme National Council (SNC), to be the repository of Cambodian sovereignty during the transition and the occupant of the Cambodia seat at the UN. This idea survived, in somewhat different form, into the final agreements. The proposal called for the SNC to devolve all government authority to the UN secretary-general to use as necessary to ensure free and fair elections, and to "delegate to such existing officials or external agencies as he deemed appropriate."

The working papers outlined three variations involving the UN in the exercise of government authority: (1) substituting for existing administrations (i.e., the SOC and CGDK), or (2) adding UN authority above or alongside existing administrations, or (3) a mixture of substituting and monitoring depending on the political sensitivity of the governmental function. The working papers ("Red Book") went so far as to draft a framework negotiating text for a final comprehensive settlement and a "Summary of Resource Requirements" (based on its best-bet current assumptions), which estimated the cost for high, low, and middle-range numbers of personnel and duration of the operation. The possible personnel requirements ranged from a low-cost model of 2,500 military and 550 polling officials to a high-cost plan for 9,000 military and 22,400 polling personnel. The time period assumptions ran from twelve to eighteen to twenty-four months. The total costs of twelve-month operation at maximum strength (9,000 military and 22,400 polling personnel) would be $2.1 billion. If extended twenty-four months, the cost would be $3.6 billion. The lowest-price scenario would cost $687 million for twelve months and $1 billion for twenty-four months. These estimates were thought to compare plausibly with the costs of the UN's ongoing election monitoring operation in Namibia, which was much easier to undertake than the program suggested for Cambodia. On the other hand, the Australian research task force had been able to spend but ten days in Cambodia preparing its nine working papers.[26]

26. *Cambodia: An Australian Peace Proposal*, pp. 3, 152–53.

Notwithstanding the hasty preparation, the working papers, focused the negotiating parties on the financial costs and personnel requirements in a serious fashion. The operation under consideration was ambitious beyond any previous UN undertakings, and it depended on the agreement of bitterly contesting Cambodian parties. Such agreement was more conceivable as their great power sponsors cut back on assistance and insisted on an honest departure of Vietnamese forces. The USSR proposed a New Year's moratorium on military aid to the Cambodian parties and planned a drastic cutback on its previous year's economic aid level of $1.6 billion to Vietnam.[27] Even more emphatic pressure could be generated by a solid front on the part of the Permanent Five, and U.S. Secretary of State Baker took the initiative to regularize their consultation on the Cambodia problem.

1990: The Permanent Five Mechanism and Jakarta Informal Meeting III

The first P-5 meeting on Cambodia in Paris, on January 16, 1990, led to a second meeting and press statement in New York on February 11–12. The five permanent members of the Security Council explored two key issues: the modalities of peacekeeping and the administrative structure during the interim period. The latter was to be the most controversial. The Five posed questions to the secretary-general and welcomed his initiatives in setting up a Secretariat task force to begin contingency planning for a UN role in the settlement process. Further consultations were planned for a meeting in Paris in the first half of March. The P-5 sounded a new note in the peace process by appealing for the protection of the renowned historic buildings at Angkor.[28]

By February 1990 the groundwork for agreement was clearly being laid by the collaboration of P-5, Australian, and UN research teams. In mid-February, Hun Sen opined in an interview that the time was ripe to resolve the conflict since all the parties agreed in principle on a UN role. Five days before the Jakarta meeting Sihanouk and Hun Sen met again, for five hours in Bangkok, at the invitation of Thai Prime Minister Chatichai Choonhavan. The two Cambodian rivals signed a joint communiqué, for the first time, in which they endorsed as "essential" principles both a UN presence in Cambodia and a "supreme national body" to symbolize Cambodia's national sovereignty and unity. Notwithstanding this bare-bones consensus,

---

27. Raszelenberg and Schier, *The Cambodian Conflict*, pp. 278, 280.
28. Acharya, *Cambodia—The 1989 Paris Peace Conference*, pp. 489–90.

the two leaders remained adamantly opposed regarding the replacement of the SOC government, about which Hun Sen refused to compromise. The third Jakarta informal meeting, on February 26–28,[29] came too early in the process to settle the fateful question of power sharing by the Cambodian factions during the transition period.

The maintenance in place of the SOC, even though its administrative reach might be partially restricted or replaced by a UN authority, was not agreeable to the resistance coalition. Starting February 3, 1990, this group called themselves the National Government of Cambodia (NGC), though CGDK designation remained in frequent use.[30] The military elements of the former CGDK called themselves the Cambodian National Resistance (CNR). Hun Sen predicted "chaos" if the present administrative structures were to be dissolved. This would set the stage for a return to power of the "Pol Pot clique." Vietnam's foreign minister, Nguyen Co Thach, argued that the UN's recent election supervision in Nicaragua and Namibia had not called for sovereign UN administration, which was not permissible under the UN Charter since Cambodia was a member state, not a trusteeship. Son Sann indicated his preference for an interim government based on a Supreme National Council recruited from the four factions.

The ultimate failure of the Jakarta meeting[31] was its inability to agree on a seventeen-point draft communiqué dealing with such conflicted matters as the prevention of the return of the "genocidal Pol Pot regime," the asserted total withdrawal of Vietnamese troops, the Australian proposal versus Sihanouk's recent five point proposal as the basis for discussion, and the establishment of a Supreme National Council in conjunction with an enhanced United Nations administrative role. In mid-January Sihanouk had balked at the idea of a Supreme National Council, considering it a trap conceived by Hun Sen and Vietnam.[32] This obduracy softened quickly (in Beijing) however, as the Australian proposal gained widespread encouragement. The first meeting of the P-5 had endorsed the idea of a council; and the Jakarta meeting was ready to make the Evans proposal the basis for discussion. Even though the Jakarta talks did not produce an

29. Attending the meeting were Vietnam, Laos, ASEAN, the four Cambodian parties (with Sihanouk represented by Prince Ranarriddh), and the UN secretary-general (represented by Rafeeuddin Ahmed).

30. Raszelenberg and Schier, *The Cambodian Conflict*, p. 291. Sihanouk, as president of the CGDK, announced the new names on Feb. 3, 1990. The country was now Cambodia rather than Democratic Kampuchea.

31. The Vietnamese press called the meeting "a practical success" since only the Khmer Rouge raised objection to some parts of the draft document. Raszelenberg and Schier, *The Cambodian Conflict*, p. 306.

32. Ibid., p. 288.

agreement (as Dumas had anticipated), the concerned states retained reasons for optimism.

The monthly meeting of the P-5 in March took as its starting point the Jakarta parley, which had produced no common text but did reach a "common understanding" that the UN was needed to play an "enhanced role" in the settlement process. The UN, the Permanent Five said, should organize elections and also establish a Supreme National Council as the "unique legitimate body and source of authority in which, throughout the period of transition to elections, national sovereignty and unity should be enshrined."[33] The SNC's membership should be decided by the Cambodian parties themselves, and the SNC was expected to delegate to a United Nations Transitional Authority in Cambodia (UNTAC) all necessary powers, including those to conduct free and fair elections. The SNC would occupy the seat of Cambodia at the United Nations and other international bodies and conferences. The UNTAC was to be established by the Security Council under the direct responsibility of the secretary-general. Rafeeuddin Ahmed, the under secretary-general, consulted with the P-5, who sought technical information and advice from the UN Secretariat. Thus, the P-5 and the Australian foreign affairs ministry were pushing forward with detailed studies of the problems of creating a UN transitional authority which would derive its powers from a Supreme National Council, established by the Cambodian parties to be the "unique legitimate body and source of authority," in which national sovereignty would be enshrined.

By the end of May, the P-5 met for the fourth time and sent a letter to the secretary-general including a summary of conclusions. Rafeeuddin Ahmed had briefed them on the visits made by UN fact-finding teams in Cambodia. They welcomed the anticipated meeting of the Cambodian parties in Tokyo, in early June 1990, and hoped that their discussions would lead to the formation of a Supreme National Council and an early reconvening of the Paris Conference on Cambodia. The P-5 stipulated five specific provisions that must be included in a comprehensive political settlement:

1. verified withdrawal of foreign troops, and cease-fire and cantonment of Cambodian armed forces;
2. a supreme national council;
3. free and fair elections of a constituent assembly;
4. enshrinement of human rights;

33. "Statement on Cambodia: The Five Permanent Members of the Security Council," Paris, March 13, 1990, in Acharya et al., *Cambodia—The 1989 Paris Peace Conference*, pp. 492–95.

5. guarantees for independence, sovereignty, territorial integrity and inviolability, neutrality, and national unity.

Working papers, this time by the P-5, were under way, and the P-5 planned
to invite representatives of the Cambodian parties to their next meeting, in
Paris before mid-July.[34] Thus the process of information gathering and
working papers started by Australia's foreign affairs minister, Evans, was
now expanding in the hands of P-5 personnel and the UN Secretariat.

The Jakarta meeting had fallen short of an agreed formula for settlement, but it left the parties close enough to move discussions into the realm
of financial costs as well as procedures. A meeting of the parties scheduled
for Tokyo on June 4–5, 1990, was expected to permit Japan to play a major
role in the peace process. Unfortunately this significant reentry into Southeast Asian affairs stumbled over the issue of whether to deal with two Cambodian governments (the SOC and the CGDK) or the four Cambodian
parties. Sihanouk allowed himself to be drawn into the bilateral format, and
consequently the PDK boycotted the Tokyo conference before it could
even get started.

An Abortive Role for Japan

In the diplomatic buildup to the abortive Tokyo meeting, however, Prince
Sihanouk generated significant movement by announcing compromises of
his earlier stance. The SOC, as well, pronounced a willingness in March to
be flexible and to accept the United Nations for peacekeeping verification
operations, but it insisted on a statement forbidding a recurrence of "the
genocidal Pol Pot regime." This item had proven to be wholly unacceptable
to the Khmer Rouge. The SOC also moved into support of *both* governments (SOC and CGDK) remaining intact, not simply their own. Sihanouk,
for his part, expressed a willingness to allow some technical functions of the
SOC (such as postal and health services) to remain in operation.[35] In early
April, after a visit to Beijing, Sihanouk floated a nine-point proposal containing two major concessions. He did not insist on a dismantling of the
current governments, and he accepted a Supreme National Council with
six seats for each of the two governments (as the SOC preferred), rather
than equal seats for each of the four parties. The prince also expressed a

34. "Letter Dated 29 May, 1990, from the Representatives of China, France, the USSR,
the UK and the USA to the UN, Addressed to the Secretary General," Annex, "Summary of
Conclusions," in ibid., pp. 495–97.
35. Raszelenberg and Schier, *The Cambodian Conflict*, pp. 307–20.

willingness to meet Hun Sen in July, but quickly reversed himself in favor of four-party talks, since only such a format would be considered binding by the PDK. The SOC unconditionally rejected Sihanouk's Nine Points (flexible as they were), calling them "a maneuver to blaze a trail for the Pol Pot clique to return to power in Cambodia."

Notwithstanding this rhetorical flourish, the SOC leader suggested to visiting European Community Commissioner Claude Cheysson, on April 28, that he would accept the Khmer Rouge as part of a Supreme National Council, and as a party contesting in free elections. Four days earlier, Sihanouk had wavered, under pressure from Thailand's Prime Minister Chatichai Choonhavan, and agreed grudgingly to talk to Hun Sen in Tokyo. Thailand, Japan, and China, as concerned regional powers, were taking the initiative in the search for a settlement. Sihanouk pointed out that China and the Khmer Rouge could block any agreement they did not want. On May 1 Hun Sen accepted an invitation to talk with the Thai government, and was reported as conceding that a settlement for Cambodia "requires the participation of the Khmer Rouge."[36] Japan's Premier Toshiki Kaifu took an active role, in consultation with Indonesia's President Suharto, to invite the Cambodian leaders to Tokyo for significant peace discussions. Sihanouk characteristically declined, in favor of devoting himself entirely to the "rehabilitation" of his people and the "reconstruction" of his country. Khieu Samphan and Son Sann, as well as the Japanese, entreated the prince not to abandon politics, but Hun Sen shrewdly observed that with 70 percent certainty he expected Sihanouk to end his leave of absence and show up at Tokyo—which, of course, he did,[37] to provide a diplomatic bridge, a sort of "shuttle policy" between all the factions.

On May 17, in preparation for the Tokyo meetings, the Thai deputy prime minister, Chavalit Yongchaiyudh, obtained the initials of Sihanouk and Khieu Samphan on a document earlier approved by Hun Sen which outlined, somewhat vaguely, a preliminary cease-fire procedure. The KPNLF indicated its general consent to the idea, without having signed it.

The Japanese foreign minister, Taro Nakayama, announced on May 22 that Hun Sen and Sihanouk had agreed to meet in Tokyo on June 4–5, without a fixed agenda, and he hoped that a cease-fire could be achieved as a first step toward a comprehensive settlement. According to Nakayama, Sihanouk in attending would represent all three resistance factions.

The P-5 vice–foreign ministers held their fourth meeting in New York on

---

36. Ibid., p. 322. See also Janet E. Heininger, *Peacekeeping in Transition: The United Nations in Cambodia* (New York: 20th Century Fund, 1994), chap. 2.

37. Raszelenberg and Schier, *The Cambodian Conflict*, pp. 324–31.

May 25 with a briefing by UN fact-finders, including personnel from the office of the UN High Commissioner for Refugees (UNHCR). They issued a "Summary of Conclusions" on the need for an international force to verify, monitor, and supervise the factions' armed forces, and on the importance of establishing a Supreme National Council to be the symbol of Cambodian sovereignty and unity. The five foreign ministries' staffs were carefully preparing working papers examining the requirements for a final settlement, and informing the discussions among the factions. The P-5 were close to setting forth a formula for full agreement, and they invited the four factions to their next monthly talks, in Paris. The NGC leaders (Son Sann, Norodom Ranarriddh, and Khieu Samphan) informed the UN secretary-general of their support of the P-5's efforts, but they reiterated their demand for an effective UN international peacekeeping force. The SOC was reported to have discovered the "plotting of a coup against the regime" by twenty-one senior officials in Phnom Penh. They allegedly intended to create a "liberal democratic party"—which the SOC warned might have brought back the genocidal Khmer Rouge.

Four days before the opening of the Tokyo meeting, Prince Sihanouk, who had resumed his office as president of the Cambodian National Resistance on May 29, met with Khieu Samphan, who insisted that the anticipated agreement at Tokyo be quadrilateral, not bilateral. Sihanouk found himself facing "a possible [PDK] sabotage of the ceremony in Tokyo." The meeting without a PDK participant lasted twenty-five minutes, before devolving into informal discussions among the parties. A six-point communiqué signed by Hun Sen and Sihanouk on June 5, with four annexes, called for a cease-fire based on "voluntary self-restrained use of force by all factions," and the establishment of a Supreme National Council with equal representation of the SOC and the CGDK. Here was the key sticking point, both in the conference format and in the agreement to be signed. The Japanese foreign ministry asserted that the two-party conference format had been made clear at the start, but neither Thai nor Chinese officials could persuade Samphan to participate in the talks.

The Khmer Rouge argued that the "Document in five Points," sponsored by the Thai deputy prime minister, General Chavalit Yongchaiyudh, and signed by Hun Sen on May 1 and by Sihanouk and Khieu Samphan on May 17, was not supposed to be modified at Tokyo but rather was to be formally signed by the four factions. The Khmer Rouge claimed that the May 17 text was later altered to refer to "two parties," or "two sides," and the phrase "seeking a comprehensive political solution based on the Paris Conference on Cambodia" was deleted. After the event Sihanouk did not deny this PDK assertion. Such a text the PDK would not sign, nor would they sit at the conference in a two-governments seating format. So, the cease-fire called for by the Hun Sen–Sihanouk six-point communiqué issued at Tokyo (June 5) did not bind the Khmer Rouge. On the other hand Hun Sen quickly analyzed the Khmer Rouge's boycott as opening the door to a SOC-Sihanouk military alliance against the now isolated PDK.[38] Such a realignment was publicly disavowed by Sihanouk, however.

Almost at a Formula

The Tokyo communiqué, signed by two sides only, marked a "turning point" in the dogged Khmer Rouge effort to hang on to equal representation in the future governance of Cambodia. Even though Sihanouk announced that he would not join a Supreme National Council nor run in a presidential election, he promptly named three FUNCINPEC representatives to the gestating SNC. Hun Sen named six SOC representatives to the council on June 13, but Son Sann named only two and implied that the PDK should do likewise. Sihanouk accommodated this proposition by reducing the FUNCINPEC panel to two, leaving two seats for the PDK in the council, which would consist of six from the SOC, six from the former CGDK. The PDK, however, was not yet reconciled to the two-sided composition of the SNC, so their two seats remained without nominations, and the SNC without ignition.

China announced (June 9) that it would continue to support all three resistance factions, whereas the U.S. House of Representatives approved $7 million in aid to the two noncommunist resistance factions only. The PDK floated a seriously constructed proposal for settlement on June 29, calling for an international peacekeeping force to remain for several years, and a quadripartite Supreme National Council which would "run the affairs of the country," exercising full legislative and executive powers, and representing Cambodia at the UN.[39] In other words, the PDK was ready to delegate maximum authority to the council (at the expense of the incumbent SOC).

The next attempt to bridge the narrowing gap was the July gathering of the Permanent Five. Two regional powers, Thailand and Indonesia, had tried their best before the Tokyo breakdown, but increasingly the great powers were ready to take a leadership role, and Indonesia feared that

38. Ibid., pp. 333, 336, 339. See also Sina Than, "Cambodia 1990: Toward a Peaceful Solution?" *Southeast Asian Affairs*, 1991 (Singapore: Institute of Southeast Asian Affairs, 1991), pp. 86–88.

39. Raszelenberg and Schier, pp. 347–67.

Thailand was drifting too close to an acceptance of the SOC. At the July meeting the P-5 deputy ministers, who were expected to invite the factions to meet again, had to decide between a two-governments format and a four-factions format, which the now self-styled National Government of Cambodia (NGC) tried to arrange. Instead of choosing, the P-5 withdrew their invitation to the Cambodian parties for July 16–17, and appealed instead for an organizational meeting of the Supreme National Council, recommending Prince Sihanouk to chair it. The scope of the SNC's authority was still discussable, and China expressed a readiness to place certain "sensitive departments" dealing with political and military affairs under direct UN control. This issue remained a crucial matter in the final agreement.

At this point the United States made a major change of course. The "Baker shift," announced on July 18 after tightly guarded deliberation by President George Bush, called for no further U.S. support for seating the NGC coalition at the UN (nor recognition of its current mission to the UN), the initiation of direct talks with Vietnam (which the U.S. did not intend to recognize), and the provision of humanitarian aid to the SOC. The overriding goal was to prevent the return to power of the Khmer Rouge.

This U-turn in U.S. policy in Southeast Asia was not endearing to the NGC, nor to the ASEAN states, whose lead the United States had hitherto deferred to. The USSR and Vietnam hailed the move for opening up a gradual rapprochement between the U.S. and its former enemy in Hanoi; and a SOC Foreign ministry spokesman foresaw the achievement of an early political settlement of the Cambodian conflict, with the UN playing an appropriate role. Australia and Japan also reacted positively to the U.S. move. On the other hand, Sihanouk, Son Sann, and Khieu Samphan, bolstered by China, Singapore, and the Royal Thai Army supreme command, raised serious objections to the U.S. abandonment of the ASEAN strategy at the UN. Their leitmotif was that the Khmer Rouge, to compensate for the loss of their acceptance at the United Nations, would be obliged to undertake more military effort. Singapore in particular deplored the giving away of diplomatic denial of the SOC in return for nothing. Sihanouk called it "a fantastic reward for the SOC, a government that has betrayed its country." The PDK pounded their claims to have upheld their nation against "the Vietnamese enemy aggressors." Nonetheless, ASEAN foreign ministers, meeting on July 24–29 with invited counterparts from Australia, Canada, the European Community, New Zealand, and the United States, were able to agree upon proposing a Supreme National Council "representing all shades of political opinion" at the next UN General Assembly, where the credentials question would be raised again.

The actual formation of the SNC remained stalled despite Son Sann's invitation to Hun Sen to join in four-party talks to resolve the matter. The SOC prime minister asserted that there was nothing to discuss, since the question was settled (he believed) by the Tokyo joint communiqué — which the Khmer Rouge had not signed. The deadline (set in Tokyo on June 5) for convening the Supreme National Council was August 1, but ASEAN and the UN Security Council had provided guidelines for the formation of an SNC, "in which no Cambodian party should be dominant and no Cambodian party should be excluded." The Soviet and U.S. foreign ministers agreed in August that the Khmer Rouge should play a part in future elections provided they refrained from violence and accepted the outcome. Chinese and U.S. officials conferred in China on August 6 and agreed that the SNC should be convened before the next UN General Assembly in September, in order to avoid an ugly credentials contest. The SOC announced its intention to attend the yet-to-be-arranged inaugural meeting of the SNC but stipulated that a cease-fire must be in place. The Thai prime minister, Chatichai, reported assurances by the Chinese that they would stop supplying the Khmer Rouge militarily once the SNC was established.

Finally, a meeting of the three resistance party leaders was scheduled for Beijing on August 22–23. At about the same time Hun Sen expressed his willingness to have the UN supervise the administration of key military, foreign, and domestic affairs, after the Supreme National Council set up committees in charge of these areas of government. The Beijing meeting achieved a seven-point joint statement agreeing that Prince Sihanouk should be the president of the SNC, as "the only Cambodian statesman who is accepted by the whole Cambodian people and by the world community", and the SNC was to be "the unique legitimate body and source of authority throughout the transitional period." The resistance parties asked the co-chairmen of the Paris Conference on Cambodia to convene a four-party meeting in Jakarta as soon as possible. The Tokyo agreement in June between Hun Sen and the NGC leader Sihanouk was not regarded by all three resistance parties as binding, despite Hun Sen's insistence upon it. Yet the SNC had to be officially constituted before it could meet in Jakarta. Vietnam cleared the air a bit by expressing acceptance of the PDK as a party in the resistance coalition "with the exception of ringleaders who have committed bloody crimes."

The final breakthrough to a formula for settlement of the Cambodia conflict occurred on August 28, when the P-5 vice ministers of foreign affairs set forth a "Framework Document for a Comprehensive Political Settlement of the Cambodia Conflict," in six pages. This public draft of an agreement was duly accepted by all the parties and the *details* phase of negotiation began.[40]

The Details Phase (1990–1991) Begins

The framework document created a genuine formula for negotiation once the four Cambodian parties formally accepted it "in its entirety as the basis for settling the Cambodia conflict." After another Jakarta informal meeting on September 9–10, the four factions committed themselves to elaborate the framework into a comprehensive political settlement. They also accepted the P-5's judgment that a Supreme National Council should be established "at an early date,"[41] but this proved to be elusive.

Winning the formal acceptance of the framework by the four Cambodian parties within two weeks required maneuvering. Vietnam and the SOC expressed concern over the proposed dominating role of the UN. China made known its rejection of the Tokyo communiqué's two-government formation for the council, even though the framework left that issue up to the Cambodian parties. The three resistance parties, under pressure from the P-5, one by one announced acceptance of the P-5 formula. By August 31, the SOC referred to the P-5 document as "a plan," certain points of which "are worth discussing." The SOC continued to insist on composing the SNC to represent two governments, and on regarding it as a *symbol* of authority, not "the unique source of authority in Cambodia" during the transition period.

The Jakarta informal meeting on Cambodia on September 9–10 generated new tension when Sihanouk resumed the role of reluctant dragon, and Hun Sen matched him step for hesitating step. The diplomatic atmosphere nonetheless was unusually constructive, as China and the USSR, and China and Vietnam (at first secretly), were conferring on the highest level. The United States and Vietnam also conducted private talks in New York City. Under the circumstances, Hun Sen held back his participation so long as Sihanouk withheld his own. The prince eventually pleaded last-minute ill-health, but Hun Sen agreed to attend the Jakarta meeting despite the prince's absence.

The meeting received Sihanouk's five-point peace proposal, of September 8, in which he accepted a Supreme National Council founded on a 6 + 2 + 2 + 2 party representation and suggested that the twelve members

40. "Statement by the Five Permanent Members of the Security Council of the United Nations on Cambodia," Aug. 28, 1990, "Annex," Sections I–V, in ibid., pp. 365–67, 370–77.
41. Ibid.

could elect a thirteenth member as chairman — the position tailored for Sihanouk in the thinking of the P-5.[42] The prince reported that China very much approved of his proposal, abandoning its previous insistence on an SNC composed of four equal parties.[43] This shift may have reflected private Chinese talks with Vietnam. The next day, Hun Sen conveyed to UN Undersecretary Ahmed the SOC's acceptance of the P-5 framework document. France and Indonesia that same day convened a meeting in Jakarta to urged the four Cambodian parties acting individually to adopt the P-5 plan and to create the SNC. In response "the Cambodian parties accepted the framework document . . . in its entirety as the basis for settling the Cambodian conflict,"[44] and agreed to form the SNC (on a 6-2-2-2 basis), which would represent Cambodia at international institutions. Although the SOC had finally prevailed on the makeup of the SNC, it had yielded on language that acknowledged the SNC as "the unique legitimate body and source of authority" during the transitional period which "will delegate to the UN all powers necessary to ensure the implementation of the comprehensive agreement." The final step would be the signing of perfected agreements which the Paris conference co-chairs hoped to achieve by the end of the year, after a short details phase of negotiation.

The three resistance party leaders appealed to Prince Sihanouk to indicate his acceptance of the chair of the SNC, but he turned them down on September 10, announcing that he would be taking a six-month "leave of absence." This familiar device was seen darkly by Phnom Penh as a design to gain more time for the Khmer Rouge to maraud. In the absence of a functioning SNC, Hun Sen hammered again his viewpoint that the framework did not mention dissolution of any government and it limited the UN Transitional Authority in Cambodia (UNTAC) to supervision, *not* administration, of the key ministries.[45]

At long last the SNC held its first meeting on September 17, in the newly renovated Cambodian embassy in Bangkok ("on Cambodian soil"). The six SOC members rejected a proposal to enlarge the council to thirteen members, including a chairman, and insisted on the much-disputed Tokyo joint communiqué of Sihanouk and Hun Sen. A deadline loomed for the SNC to claim its seat at the opening of the UN General Assembly on September 18, by designating a five-person UN delegation and leader, with credentials.

The SOC was unwilling to elect Sihanouk as chairman and thirteenth

42. Ibid., pp. 384–90.
43. Ibid., p. 391.
44. "Joint Statement of the Jakarta Informal Meeting on Cambodia (10 September, 1990)," in ibid., pp. 391–95.
45. Ibid., pp. 396–97, 401.

member of the SNC without making Hun Sen the vice chairman and the head of the delegation to the UN.[46] Therefore the SOC proposed that a fourteenth member be added if Sihanouk became the thirteenth. Such a proposed departure from the Jakarta agreement brought the September 17 meeting to an end, with no designated UN delegation. Sihanouk then announced, from Beijing, his acceptance of a seven and seven formula for the council but did not make his chairmanship conditional on Hun Sen becoming vice chair. The UN Security Council set forth its encouragement to the factions on September 20, with its Resolution 668 (1990), which urged the parties to create the "peaceful climate" required for "a comprehensive political settlement." More than climate was required, however, as Sihanouk's offer of a seventh seat on the SNC if he were elected chairman was rejected by the SOC, because it did not specify a vice-chair post for Hun Sen.[47]

The co-chairs of the Paris Conference on Cambodia stepped into the breach on September 25, by calling (in a joint statement in New York) for a reconvening of the conference by the end of October, since a comprehensive settlement "is again within reach." A memorandum of the three resistance parties accused the SOC of holding up the peace process. The SOC foreign minister, Hor Nam Hong, supported the early reconvening of the SNC, to organize a delegation to the UN, while suggesting a postponement of the chairmanship issue. Yet, if Sihanouk were to be elected chairman, the SOC insisted that Hun Sen be his deputy. The P-5 foreign ministers again expressed their pleasure at the idea of the council electing Sihanouk as chairman, but this seemingly negotiable issue remained deadlocked.

In the end, no Cambodia delegation reached the UN in 1990, although on October 15 the General Assembly unanimously adopted an ASEAN-sponsored resolution on Cambodia awarding its seat to the Supreme National Council and welcoming the enhanced role the UN was about to play in pursuance of the Permanent Five peace plan.[48]

The General Assembly eventually declared the Cambodian seat vacant on October 16, despite the resistance parties' urgent, unrewarded efforts to activate the SNC.[49] China had even gone so far as to speak directly to Hun Sen in its embassy at Jakarta.

46. UN General Assembly, Resolution Adopted by the General Assembly, "The Situation in Cambodia," A/45/15, Oct. 15, 1990, Distr. General, A/RES/45/3. Oct. 16, 1990.

47. Raszelenberg and Schier, *The Cambodian Conflict,* pp. 406–8.

48. United Nations Security Council, S/21800, No. 668 (1990), adopted Sept. 20, 1990; UNGA, Resolution adopted by the GA, "The Situation in Cambodia," A/45/L.5, Oct. 15, 1990; and Haas, *Genocide by Proxy,* pp. 288–91.

49. Haas, *Genocide by Proxy,* pp. 287–90. Sina Than, "Cambodia 1990."

A Comprehensive Framework

The settlement of details in a complex negotiation does not often achieve such a comprehensive formula to work with as the Permanent five had provided in August 1990. The P-5 research groups had fashioned a broad set of arrangements and rules that made agreement on final details appear relatively trouble-free. To be sure, there was room for advantage-seeking in regard to matters such as military disarmament and demobilization, the eligibility and enrollment of voters, the organization of electoral districts and political parties, the principles underlying a new constitution, the timing of election campaigns and voting. All swelled in importance as the prospect of free and fair elections became more real. There was an intricate collection of choices to make before the formula—the P-5 "Framework Document"—could be wrapped together into a binding agreement, to guide and limit the ambitious undertaking to restore peace and stability to the "failed state" of Cambodia. By November 26, 1990, the P-5 had produced a full draft for the Paris Conference on Cambodia to use in negotiating final treaty language covering all the issues. Yet almost another year was expended in achieving the ultimate language of the Paris Agreements on a Comprehensive Political Settlement of the Cambodia Conflict, October 23, 1991.[50]

The framework document presented by the P-5 on August 28, 1990, consisted of 36 articles. After further refinement, the draft agreement presented to the UN secretary-general by the co-chairs of the Paris conference consisted of 32 articles, in 8 pages with 5 annexes. The final instruments agreed to at Paris in October 1991 included the Agreement on a Comprehensive Political Settlement of the Cambodia Conflict, in 32 articles (in 7 pages) with 5 annexes; an Agreement on Sovereignty, Independence, and Neutrality (5 pages); and a Declaration on Rehabilitation and Reconstruction of Cambodia (2 pages). Many key phrases of the framework document survived into the final agreements, speaking well for the thoroughness of the working groups who fashioned them.

The most difficult questions of detail, not surprisingly, related to the definition of political authority during the period of transition to a national election, during which both the Supreme National Council and the United Nations, along with some residual Cambodian government administrations,

---

50. The "draft agreements on a comprehensive political settlement," conveyed to the UN secretary-general by the P-5 on Nov. 26, 1990, became UN document A/46/61, S/22059, Jan. 11, 1991. Cf. Raszelenberg and Schier, *The Cambodian Conflict*, pp. 440–80.

would share responsibility for governing. The struggle for power among the four Cambodian parties was to be rechanneled into a "free and fair election" format, but the details of this arrangement remained laden with political consequence. The questions of the chairmanship of the Supreme National Council and the powers it would delegate to the UN were not settled by the framework, nor were they easily negotiable even with Prince Sihanouk available as a national icon standing for compromise and reconciliation. Military arrangements were clearly of great significance, and especially complex, even assuming—unrealistically—the best of intentions by the rival armed forces. The framework merely identified, without specification, problems such as voter eligibility and enrollment, refugees and displaced persons, voter education, foreign observers, and a code of conduct. Section IV of the framework addressed the need for "special measures" to protect human rights during the election period and beyond, without fully spelling out the form these measures might take. As for safeguarding the independent and neutral State of Cambodia against intervention, the states participating in the Paris Conference on Cambodia were cast by the framework in the role of guarantors, with an obligation to consult in the event of a violation or threat of violation of their commitment. Yet the adequacy of this language was questionable.

So there were multiple areas of detail to be addressed before a draft agreement ready for final signature could be created by the unseen hands of area and legal specialists of the P-5, the UN, and other contributing states. A "Proposed Structure for the Agreements" emerged at the P-5 meeting in Paris, November 23–26, for presentation to the Coordinating Committee of the Paris conference. Momentum was building to the point that Cambodia's diplomatic benefactors were getting well ahead of the parties themselves, which were still hung up on the structure of the SNC.

Surely "the devil was in the details," even though exceptional progress was being made, under the pressure of neighbors and great powers. The barrier to further movement toward a settlement was the headless SNC, about which the P-5's formula provided no clear guidance. The question of a voluntary cease-fire also waited to be resolved; and the Cambodia seat at the UN General Assembly, reserved for the SNC, had no occupant. The SOC even rejected taking a seventh seat in the SNC since it did not include a vice chairman's position for Hun Sen.[51] The P-5 foreign secretaries and the UN secretary-general appealed on September 28 for national reconciliation and the election of Sihanouk as chairman of the SNC.[52] The ASEAN

51. Ibid., p. 408.
52. Ibid., p. 413.

states and the foreign ministers of China and the USSR each called upon the co-chairs of the Paris conference to start drafting a comprehensive settlement agreement.[53]

Phnom Penh spokesmen remained adamant on the twelve-member SNC, but in early November the SOC foreign ministry proposed some compromise formulae such as co-chairs and rotation patterns, and Thailand contrived varieties of vice chairman offices, and deferral of elections.[54] At the same time, the SOC foreign ministry continued to press their position to the Paris conference co-chairs that the two Cambodian governments "will continue to function" since the delegation of powers to UNTAC to exert control or supervision will take place "only regarding free and fair elections." This interpretation clashed with the soon-unveiled draft agreement of the P-5, which made the Supreme National Council the "unique legitimate body and source of authority throughout the transitional period." The issue continued to fester for months to come.

The Next-to-Final Drafts

The November 26, 1990, draft agreements revealed by the P-5 in Paris used the same organization as the August 28 framework version but set forth five "annexes": (1) proposed mandate for UNTAC, (2) withdrawal, cease-fire, and related measures, (3) elections, (4) repatriation of Cambodian refugees and displaced persons, (5) principles for a new constitution. A second draft agreement also covered what the framework document had labeled "international guarantees"; and a nonbinding declaration listed what "should" be done to deal with Cambodia's reconstruction needs. No mention was included of genocide or past violations of human rights, which the PDK had adamantly tried to exclude from the settlement.

The first three annexes of the draft agreements resembled the August 28 framework, while the fifth annex on "principles for a new constitution for Cambodia" covered fully new ground. A fourth annex (of seven paragraphs) covered the repatriation of Cambodian refugees and displaced persons, which the P-5 framework had mentioned only in its introductory statement, which "recalled" the two documents elaborated by the Paris conference on "repatriation of refugees and displaced persons and on reconstruction."[55]

53. Ibid., p. 426. On October 29, Ali Alatas met with representatives of the Paris conference's three committees in preparation for a full meeting within a few months.

54. Ibid., p. 429.

55. "Statement of the Five Permanent Members of the Security Council of the UN on Cambodia," Aug. 28, 1990, in ibid., p. 370. The foresighted "non-papers" of the Paris

The draft also set forth a detailed "proposed mandate for UNTAC" in its annex 1, in place of the framework's more diffused treatment of "transitional arrangements." Appropriate legal language and concepts were certainly available to the parties, yet another eleven months passed before the draft agreements could be perfected and signed in Paris, on October 23, 1991.

1991: Final Steps toward the Paris Agreements

What consumed this tantalizing period of time? For six months, until the spring of 1991, the Persian Gulf crisis absorbed the attention of the great powers, but during the summer of 1991 the Cambodian parties would at last reach the point of negotiating the final details. A compromise on the composition of the Supreme National Council would finally be reached by giving special authority to Sihanouk as chairperson and twelfth member. The disarming of the factions would be stipulated to cover less than 100 percent but to occur *before* the election. The electoral system — i.e., votes applied proportionally to party lists by provinces rather than single-member districts—would be only reluctantly agreed to by the SOC, a month before the final agreement. On the bitter issue of forbidding a return to the "genocide" of the Khmer Rouge period, the language would be much diluted in the face of PDK intransigence. Thus, over time, under pressure from their mentors and regional neighbors, and with the United Nations eager to assist, the Cambodian factions would exhaust the list of disagreements and enter a transitional period of three-legged government—the Supreme National Council, the UN Transitional Authority in Cambodia, and the State of Cambodia.

The SOC initially rejected key sections of the draft agreement, in November 1990, in particular regarding dissolution of the government, disarming of the armed forces, and a "too weak" reference to preventing genocide in the future. Chea Sim reiterated the SOC position that UNTAC's authority would be limited strictly to organizing elections; and Chinese commentaries perceived "the Phnom Penh authorities going back on their word" (i.e., on their acceptance of the framework). To further pressure the SOC, Khieu Samphan declared his party "happy to support and assist the 26th November, 1990 statement." Ranariddh joined the chorus in challenging the SOC for taking back its consent. Hun Sen then proposed a

---

conference's Third Committee on refugees and reconstruction are found in Acharya et al., *Cambodia—The 1989 Paris Peace Conference*, chap. 5.

quadripartite gathering in Bangkok in December, but the Paris conference co-chairs invited the Supreme National Council to meet in Paris instead. On November 26, the Soviet Union announced that it was "giving" no further military assistance to Phnom Penh.[56] The SNC still lacked a designated chairperson, and in the eyes of China it was not regarded as established.

The Explanatory Note

The Paris consultation (December 21–22) of the Paris conference co-chairs and the four Khmer factions produced a three-page Explanatory Note written anonymously in an upbeat tone by UN Undersecretary-General Rafeeuddin Ahmed. Agreement was reached on "most of the fundamental points," and the conferees agreed to submit the current record of negotiations to the Paris conference coordinating committee, with encouragement to further refine it for a possible spring of 1991 reconvening of the conference itself. French Foreign Minister Roland Dumas had warned at the meeting's outset that "the international community cannot indefinitely focus on the fate of Cambodia if the Cambodians do not show the political will to reach a settlement."

The Explanatory Note addressed the issue of transitional-period civil administration, which would be shared by the Supreme National Council ("the unique legitimate body and source of authority"), the UNTAC (to which the SNC would delegate such powers as were necessary for conducting free and fair elections), and "the existing administrative structures." The interaction between UNTAC and these agencies, bodies, and offices would take place at three levels: (1) direct control to ensure neutrality during the election process, (2) lesser control or supervision of bodies that might influence election results, and (3) investigation of complaints. UNTAC's interactions would be limited to those which could directly influence the holding of free and fair elections in "a neutral political environment." Five areas of administration that might directly influence elections had been previously identified in the framework document—foreign affairs, national defense, finance, public security, and information.

The note sought further to clarify the supervisory role of the UNTAC in law enforcement by the existing police, and in the various phases of a cease-fire, which would effectuate the regroupment of armed forces, their cantonment, and their disarming and eventual return to civilian life, by means of full cooperation of all the parties at each phase of the process. The SOC

---

56. Raszelenberg and Schier, *The Cambodian Conflict*, pp. 468–521.

continued to insist that military forces should not be dissolved prior to elections. The three resistance party leaders (backed by Sihanouk) in January 1991 pressed the co-chairs, Dumas and Alatas, for an early reconvening of the Paris conference in view of the recent "attacks" on the framework documents and draft agreements by the "Heng Samrin–Hun Sen party."

Disagreements continued to arise, as the SOC demanded an international tribunal to try the Pol Pot clique for their "genocidal crimes," and reportedly drew up a list of twelve (including Khieu Samphan and Son Sen, who were currently SNC members) to be prohibited from ever returning to Phnom Penh. This demand was partly acted out a year later when Khieu Samphan first came back to Phnom Penh, in November 1991, and faced a nearly fatal pack of demonstrators at his residence. The PDK nonetheless remained adamant against any reference to past atrocities in the draft agreements.

Co-chair Alatas, acting on his persistent optimism, on February 4, 1991, won the consent of the Cambodian National Resistance (CNR, the military elements of the CGDK) to another meeting in Jakarta of the members of the SNC. The CNR representatives reaffirmed their "unconditional acceptance" of the P-5 framework and draft agreement "as the basis for settling the Cambodian conflict." Less positive reports, however, suggested that China, notwithstanding assurances to the United States, had not yet stopped its weapons supply to the Khmer Rouge, and a cease-fire was far from realization. China regarded the cessation of military aid as required once a comprehensive political settlement was actually operating. Hun Sen reiterated his government's absolute refusal to disarm itself until after elections. He also argued that the Khmer Rouge's acceptance of the P-5 draft agreement obliged them to allow inspection of their refugee camps on the Thai border by international organizations.

Assistant Secretary of State Richard Solomon testified to the U.S. Congress that existing administrative structures "will not be dismantled, only politically neutralized." He predicted drastic cutbacks in the estimated $400 million annual Soviet assistance to the SOC, and doubted that the SOC's armed forces could prevail over the Khmer Rouge. Under the circumstances the four Cambodian parties were amenable to a joint plea on April 22, by the Paris conference co-chairs and UN Secretary-General Javier Pérez de Cuéllar, for a voluntary cease-fire to begin May 1, 1991 and last at least until the next SNC meeting. The subsequent unmonitored pause in fighting apparently did not preclude a continuation of military aid to the Khmer Rouge via Thailand, in the belief of the Thai military that they had the right to continue such aid pending a comprehensive political settlement.

Ali Alatas, the dogged Indonesian foreign minister, set up an SNC meeting in Jakarta for June 2–4, to be joined by UN Undersecretary-General Ahmed and General Timothy Dibuama who had just led a three-man UN survey team to Cambodia. The PDK then announced that June 5 was the deadline for Hanoi and Phnom Penh to accept the "Permanent Five peace plan," failing which the PDK would resort to military means. This Khmer Rouge aggressiveness was countered by Hun Sen's threat in the Jakarta press to call for an international trial of the Khmer Rouge leaders. Amendments tabled by the SOC included a clause precluding the "return of the genocidal regime," maintenance of the factions' armed forces, and limitations on the scope of UNTAC's administrative powers. The composition of the SNC itself remained unsettled, but Sihanouk (invited by Alatas) and Hun Sen formally agreed on June 2 to propose the prince as a thirteenth member and chairman of the SNC, with Hun Sen becoming the single vice chair and the SOC obtaining an additional seat (for a total membership of fourteen). The two leaders also agreed to an unlimited extension of the May 1 cease-fire, but Sihanouk failed to get the concurrence of his PDK partners on the SNC-composition question. Khieu Samphan explained in early June that an SOC-designated vice chair of the SNC could constantly disrupt the peace process. Furthermore, his DK party would no longer observe the cease-fire but would continue struggling against the "Vietnamese aggressors." Radio Beijing reported that Son Sann also ordered his forces to resume the attack.

The Supreme National Council Under Way

Some progress was recorded on June 7, nonetheless, in the formal inclusion of Sihanouk as a "simple member" of the SNC in the place of Chausen Coc-sal (the oldest and presiding member), who had asked to retire. The prince immediately called for an "urgent meeting" of the SNC in Thailand, which all four parties approved of, and they fixed Pattaya as the venue, June 24–26 as the dates, and Sihanouk as chairman. China hailed the prince's policy of "national reconciliation." Prior to the SNC meeting, the four factions agreed to an unlimited cease-fire and undertook "to stop receiving foreign military aid." They also established an SNC headquarters, a national flag, and an anthem. During the SNC meeting proper—presided over by Sihanouk as a self-styled "impartial and neutral chairman" who encouraged "as much as possible the spirit of compromise"—Ahmed, representing the UN secretary-general, and the co-chairs of the Paris Conference on Cambodia actively attended. The SNC set up a secretariat in Phnom Penh and empowered Sihanouk to dispatch official communications to various UN agencies. The PDK (with Pol Pot reported to be secretly present in Pattaya) agreed to locate the secretariat in Phnom Penh, so long as the parties were allowed to ensure security within their residences with their own security forces. Another journalistic revelation, by *Le Monde*, reported that Thailand exerted pressure on the Khmer Rouge negotiators by threatening to cut off supplies to their border camps.[57] In a quite constructive fashion the four parties agreed to set up working groups to study electoral laws and principles for the new Constitution of Cambodia.

The concerned states that had worked so long for a Cambodia settlement saw real progress in this meeting. U.S. spokespersons expressed unaccustomed praise for the "wisdom" and "moral influence" exercised by Prince Sihanouk. The other P-5 spokespersons added their congratulations,[58] and Vietnam also welcomed the progress. Sino-Vietnamese relations were clearly on the mend following Vietnam's military exit from Cambodia, and the Khmer Rouge were not immune to Chinese pressure to settle the Cambodia conflict.

The SNC worked with greater urgency to establish itself, with informal talks in Pattaya (June 27–28) and in Beijing in July. The meeting unanimously elected Sihanouk as SNC chairperson, with no vice chair and membership limited to twelve. The new chair promptly requested Secretary-General de Cuellar to send a survey mission to control the cease-fire and suppress military assistance, and he requested UN assistance with the repatriation of refugees and a mine awareness program. The sole remaining areas of disagreement related to procedures for disarming the various forces. The Permanent Five further asserted themselves with a gathering in Beijing that asserted that an end of outside military assistance "must be verified and supervised by the UN," and hoped that neighboring countries (i.e., Thailand and Vietnam) would prohibit the delivery of military equipment to any of the parties from their territory. The ASEAN foreign ministers applauded the Cambodian parties' efforts and decided to accredit representatives to the SNC—which they pointed out was not equivalent to diplomatic recognition, since the SNC was not a government. Notwithstanding, the SNC, as personified by Sihanouk and Hun Sen meeting in Pyongyang, undertook to create a commission to search worldwide for economic and social reconstruction aid.

57. Ibid., pp. 523, 525. Communiqué of the Supreme National Council meeting in Pattaya, June 24–26, 1991, Document 6, in *The United Nations and Cambodia, 1991– 95* (New York: Department of Public Information, United Nations, 1995).

58. Raszelenberg and Schier, *The Cambodian Conflict*, p. 524.

One of the remaining details of a final agreement, the reference to "genocide" under the Khmer Rouge, suddenly dropped out of SOC speech making during August 1991. This constituted a tacit major concession by the SOC, which helped sustain the momentum of final negotiations. Another point of SOC flexibility addressed the storage of weapons under UN control. The SNC worked out a compromise calling for the demobilization of 70 percent of each of the four factions' soldiers and their arms *before* the elections. A disagreement persisted, however, over whether the SOC's security police forces should be covered by these provisions. The PDK favored their inclusion under the term "forces of the parties" (used in the draft), suggesting that they were similar to the Koevoet (security police) set up by South Africa and dismantled by the UN in Namibia.[59] The P-5 and Indonesia proposed to give UNTAC the authority to "identify the civil police necessary to perform law enforcement."

A UN military team led by General Timothy Dibuama arrived in Cambodia on August 23 for an inspection tour, starting in a Khmer Rouge zone. Sihanouk soon requested at least two hundred UN personnel to serve as "observers" of the cease-fire and the halt in military assistance. Khieu Samphan had already demanded that seven hundred UN persons be dispatched. The United States warned, however, that the UN should not commit its resources and prestige before the parties reached a comprehensive agreement.[60] The parties had reached the critical final bargaining over a demobilization of forces. The SOC proposed on August 25 that 60 percent of the forces of the parties be demobilized, including their arms, and 40 percent be regrouped into cantonment areas under UNTAC supervision. The PDK initially rejected the idea, but two days later the parties agreed to a ratio of 70 percent demobilization and 30 percent disarmed regroupment under UNTAC supervision.[61]

The remaining issues, such as election procedures (agreed to on September 19), now seemed manageable, even including a reference to genocide that spoke simply of preventing "the recurrence of human rights abuses."[62] The P-5 and Indonesia thereupon announced that it was "most desirable" that the Paris Conference on Cambodia be reconvened by late October and a comprehensive political settlement be signed before the SNC established itself at Phnom Penh. The new atmosphere of hope was exemplified by Hanoi's invitation to Prince Sihanouk (and Hun Sen) to visit Vietnam—

59. Ibid., p. 548.
60. Ibid. *The United Nations and Cambodia, 1991–1995*, Document 14.
61. Raszelenberg and Schier, *The Cambodian Conflict*, p. 549.
62. Ibid., p. 551.

which Sihanouk agreed to do before 1992. On September 26, he hailed "a new era of peace" and resumed Cambodia's attendance at the UN General Assembly. The next day, the P-5 presented a final draft of the comprehensive political settlement to the SNC. Three weeks later the UN Security Council decided to establish under its authority the United Nations Advanced Mission in Cambodia (UNAMIC) with 268 personnel, immediately after the signing of the Paris Agreements.[63]

At this time he ruling party of the SOC, the Khmer People's Revolutionary Party (KPRP), recast itself into the Cambodian People's Party (CPP) (October 17), with Chea Sim as secretary-general and Hun Sen as vice chairman. The new CPP claimed to be "the leading political party in protecting human rights."[64] They spoke of initiating a national movement to protect human rights—which could be interpreted to mean fighting the Khmer Rouge—and they professed to favor a free market, liberal democracy, and neutrality. At the CPP's constitutive congress the two top leaders spoke out in support of Sihanouk for national president.

The Paris Conference Reaches Agreement

A week later, on October 21, the Paris Conference on Cambodia, at the invitation of France, opened its second session, with the UN secretary-general, the chairman of the SNC, and foreign ministers of nineteen countries attending.[65] The *Final Act of the Paris Conference on Cambodia* was signed on October 23, 1991, as well as the *Agreement on a Comprehensive Political Settlement of the Cambodian Conflict* (with annexes); the *Agreement Concerning the Sovereignty, Independence, Territorial Integrity and Inviolability, Neutrality, and National Unity of Cambodia;* and the *Declaration on the Rehabilitation and Reconstruction of Cambodia.*[66] The UN General Assembly welcomed the accords on November 20 with "deep appreciation" to the Paris conference, the P-5, regional state, and in

63. Ibid., pp. 553–56. Final Communiqué of the Supreme National Council of Cambodia (Pattaya, Aug. 26–29, 1991).

64. Raszelenberg and Schier, pp. 564–65. See *The United Nations and Cambodia*, Document 17 and 18, Report of the Secretary-General on Proposals for a UN Advanced Mission in Cambodia (UNAMIC), Sept. 30, 1991; and Security Council resolution on UNAMIC, Oct. 16, 1991.

65. Australia, Brunei, Canada, People's Republic of China, U.S.A., France, India, Indonesia, Japan, Laos, Malaysia, the Philippines, United Kingdom, Singapore, Thailand, USSR, Vietnam, Yugoslavia, and Zimbabwe. These represent ASEAN, the Non-Aligned Movement (Yugoslavia, Zimbabwe), and neighbors.

66. See summary in Raszelenberg and Schier, *The Cambodian Conflict*, pp. 567–70.

particular Prince Sihanouk, as well as the secretary-general and his staff.[67] The Security Council also welcomed the Paris outcome and immediately requested the secretary-general to report as soon as possible with an implementation plan and cost estimates.[68]

Thus, the "details" consumed a year of serious and persistent effort within the staffs of the foreign ministries of the P-5 plus Indonesia and the United Nations. One unresolved item after another in the final text was settled through patient testing and bargaining. The precise authority of the UNTAC and the SNC, as well as their composition, remained critical to the entire enterprise, since the very idea of transition to free and fair elections depended on it. The cease-fire and procedures for demobilization and cantonment of troops were also critically important to a final settlement. The procedures for registering eligible voters and political parties, and the choice of proportional representation, were also central to the idea of a binding settlement. In many articles of the final agreements the language originally used in the framework document survived into the final text; in other areas the final choice of language came only as the Paris conference was preparing to reconvene. The durability of the earliest drafts and the degree of clarity achieved in the final texts were notable. The three constituent documents were (1) the framework document, August 28, 1990; (2) the draft agreements of November 26, 1990; and (3) the agreement signed in Paris on October 23, 1991, by the states participating in the Paris Conference on Cambodia.

An even earlier source of language for the final agreements was the "Red book" put together by the Australian foreign ministry in February 1990. It set forth the idea of "free and fair elections" and a "transitional period" until the installation of a new government, as well as recommending a special representative of the UN secretary-general. Most importantly, it called for a Supreme National Council[69] in which the "sovereignty of Cambodia would be vested for the duration of the transitional period." The Australian proposal also called for the SNC to occupy the UN seat of Cambodia, and laid out a simple process for moving from an elected constituent assembly to a legislative body that would install a new government. Its general thrust in delegating power to the UN secretary-general was stronger than the SOC was willing to accept, but the SOC could console itself by recalling that the original proposal by Congressman Solarz for a UN interim author-

67. UN General Assembly resolution on the situation in Cambodia, A/RES/46/18 Nov. 20, 1991.
68. UN Security Council resolution on political settlement in Cambodia situation, S/RES/718 (1991), Oct. 31, 1991.
69. "Supplemental Paper B," *Cambodia: An Australian Peace Proposal.*

ity called for the outright dissolution of the People's Republic (the later SOC) — which Hun Sen successfully kept out of the Paris accords.

The drafts fashioned by the P-5, plus Indonesia and the secretary-general's staff, after the pioneering research of Australian experts in early 1990, recorded the settlement of details such as the size of the constituent assembly. Some ideas and language appeared subsequent to the six-page framework document. For example, the principles to guide the writing of a new constitution ("liberal democracy, on the basis of pluralism" and periodic elections) appeared only at the final agreements stage. The extensive program for rehabilitation and reconstruction took original form in a "nonpaper" of the rapporteur of the Paris conference's Third Committee, on August 25, 1990.[70] The text of the Declaration on Rehabilitation and Reconstruction of Cambodia utilized all but one article of the Third Committee's report entitled "Reconstruction."[71] Annex 4 of the Agreement on a Comprehensive Political Settlement, entitled "Repatriation of Cambodian Refugees and Displaced Persons," was drawn from the same Third Committee report as the Declaration on Rehabilitation. Occasionally the phrasing was adjusted, but the Third Committee essentially provided the annex.

The Agreement Concerning the Sovereignty, Independence, Territorial Integrity and Inviolability, Neutrality, and National Unity of Cambodia, consisting of eight articles, was first conceived by the Paris conference's Second Committee in its "communication" circulated to the conference at the request of Sihanouk, Son Sann, and Khieu Samphan of the CNR on August 21, 1989.[72] The only substantial deviation in the final treaty from the Second Committee's draft was the addition of an assurance by Cambodia to respect "human rights and fundamental freedoms embodied in the Universal Declaration of Human Rights" and other relevant international human rights instruments, and a pledge "to take effective measures to ensure that the policies and practices of the past shall never be allowed to return" (art. 15). This was as close as the SOC was able to get in the agreements to excoriating its Khmer Rouge rival.

The work of the conference's First Committee, on a cease-fire and international control mechanism, was not fully resolved at the first Paris conference, and no summary document emerged for use in the final agreements. The First Committee received in August 1989 a number of meticulously

70. Acharya et al., *Cambodia—The 1989 Paris Peace Conference*, provides some key documents produced at the Paris Conference on Cambodia, organized by committees of origin.

71. Letter, Aug. 25, 1989, from the Rapporteur of the Third Committee to the Co-chairmen of the Coordinating Committee, in ibid., pp. 370–76.

72. Ibid., pp. 184–88.

fashioned draft mandates for an international control mechanism, but full agreement in this area was not reached, before adjournment.[73] The implementation of the military provisions of the agreements also proved to be less successful than the other elements of the UNTAC operation. The complexity of the military arrangements can be measured in terms of the number of articles devoted to them in the three constituent documents—over thirty articles devoted to military matters.

A long and twisting road had been traveled to reach the Paris Agreements of October 23, 1991. Each of the Cambodian parties emerged less than fully satisfied, but willing to try out a political settlement (rooted in a cease-fire, free and fair election, and an exercise of authority by the UN during the transition period before the voting). The twelve years of diplomatic maneuver eventually paid off thanks to persistence and imaginative draftsmanship. The waning of the Cold War lowered the stakes for the great powers in Cambodia and made possible an unprecedented Permanent Five cooperation. Nonetheless, some original devices created during the course of diplomatic bargaining deserve special mention.

Bold originality accounted for the creation of a Supreme National Council as the sovereign source of authority in Cambodia, designed to delegate some of its authority to a special transitional United Nations organization (UNTAC) prior to the national election of a constituent assembly. The UN was to carry out the demobilization of about 70 percent of the rival party forces. An atmosphere of political neutrality was to be created by UN "control" or "supervision" over key existing areas of administration; and human rights were singled out for special UN advocacy and monitoring. A major population transfer back from displaced person camps outside Cambodia was authorized, and rehabilitation of the national economy was encouraged with UN help but Cambodian initiative.

Ingenuity was clearly present in the creation of a Supreme National Council by the parties and an UNTAC (by the UN Security Council), as well as the UN leadership posts of special representative of the secretary-general and his military commander. Whether these organizations would fulfill their intended purpose was not certain, but the grand design could encourage hopes if demobilization of the parties' forces by the UN became real, if UN control over the existing administration became effective, if elections remained free of intimidation and fraud, if outside military aid was truly suspended and UN financing was forthcoming, if the election out-

---

73. A definitive legal analysis of the Paris Agreements and their genesis is found in Steven R. Ratner, "The Cambodia Settlement Agreements," *American Journal of International Law,* January 1993.

come was genuinely accepted by all the parties, who could then agree upon a new constitution. So many "ifs" made success far from certain, but the framework for a restoration of Cambodia to constitutional government had been creatively and logically set forth. The logic of the party leaders, however, embraced the pursuit of power without regard to outsiders' rules of democracy.

PART 2

UNTAC

CHAPTER THREE

Implementing the Paris
Agreements, 1991–1993

Translating the Paris accords into a United Nations operation in Cambodia required planning and action of an unprecedented sort, with no exact prototype to follow. The UN mandate for the transitional period in Cambodia was outlined in Annex 1 of the Agreement on a Comprehensive Political Settlement of the Cambodia Conflict, in which separate sections outlined responsibilities in "civil administration" (including "civil police"), "military functions," "elections," and "human rights." Annex 4 dealt with repatriation of refugees and displaced persons, and the Declaration on the Rehabilitation and Reconstruction of Cambodia called for "an international aid effort" and plan. Out of these loosely related indications the Security Council requested the secretary-general of the UN on October 31, 1991 to submit an implementation plan "at the earliest possible date."[1] Thus, at least seven major tasks faced the UN, and these quite naturally shaped the structure of the UN Transitional Authority in Cambodia (UNTAC) devised by the Secretariat. Each task was managed as a "component"; and an information and education "division" (not specified in the Paris accords) was developed in the office of the special representative of the secretary-general.

Even though the 1991 Paris accords on Cambodia grew out of the draft agreement of the previous year and the research efforts of the working committees of the Paris Conference on Cambodia in August 1989, there had been no sustained effort by the UN or the key negotiating states to

1. UN Security Council Res. 718 (1991), Oct. 31, 1991, Doc. 21, in *The United Nations and Cambodia, 1991–1995*, (New York: UN Department of Public Information, 1995), p. 149.

draw up the blueprint for a transitional authority in Cambodia. The prospect of a full agreement by the Cambodian factions, or of a willingness to let the UN supervise or control the governance of Cambodia, or of international readiness to finance a military force to maintain a cease-fire and to launch economic rehabilitation apparently seemed too uncertain to warrant a sustained effort to write the book or detail a plan. The possibilities of obtaining a cease-fire, a national election, and repatriation and rehabilitation were uncertain enough to put off any vigorous effort to design the diverse structures to be required of the UN. Other peacekeeping operations were already under way in Yugoslavia and Angola, whereas a political settlement in Cambodia was not yet fully designated as a UN undertaking.

Yet the UN secretary-general had sent a delegation to the 1989 Paris conference under Rafeeuddin Ahmed, who submitted what the secretary-general characterized as a number of "helpful papers." By February 1990 an intra-secretariat Task Force on Cambodia was established, and the UN sent seven fact-finding missions to Cambodia between 1989 and 1991. These groups studied, among other things, communication and transportation infrastructure, water supply, sanitation and housing, and means of repatriating displaced persons and refugees. The first of these missions, composed of fifteen specialists, was sent with the agreement of the Paris conference under the direction of Norwegian Lieutenant-General Martin Vadset, who had undertaken similar missions in Iran and Iraq. Despite these early initiatives, however, the signing of the Paris accords caught the UN far from ready, even in the more familiar military peacekeeping realms, where key elements like maps, Khmer speakers, or military advisers were lacking.[2] In August 1991, with the concurrence of the Supreme National Council, Secretary-General Javier Pérez de Cuellar sent a twelve-person exploratory mission under his military advisor, Major-General Timothy Dibuama, to assess the modalities for controlling a cease-fire. Three weeks before the signing of the Paris peace accords, the secretary-general recommended to the Security Council that a UN advance mission be deployed to Cambodia to gather information for operational planning and to get the lay of the land.[3] On October 16, a week before the signing of the accords, the Security Council authorized a UN Advance Mission in Cambodia (UNAMIC) to investigate a country that was about to receive unprece-

---

2. Trevor Findlay, *Cambodia: The Legacy and Lessons of UNTAC* (Oxford: Oxford University Press, 1995), pp. 116–19.

3. Report of the Secretary-General on Proposals for a UN Advance Mission in Cambodia (UNAMIC), S/23097, Sept. 30, 1991, Doc. 17, in *The United Nations and Cambodia, 1991–1995*.

dented resources and support.[4] This task force of 268 persons has been characterized as an "afterthought," emerging only after it became apparent that the UNTAC would not be ready for deployment for some time after the signing of the accords.[5]

Not until four months later, in fact, on February 19, 1992, did the secretary-general report back to the Security Council with "his proposed implementation plan for UNTAC, including administrative and financial aspects."[6] On January 9, 1992, the new UN secretary-general, Boutros Boutros-Ghali, had appointed Yasushi Akashi as his special representative for Cambodia. On February 28 UNTAC was formally established by the Security Council at the invitation of the signatories. On March 15 Akashi, now the head of UNTAC, established himself in Phnom Penh. Akashi had been associated with the United Nations since 1957, starting in the political affairs section of the Secretariat, and later posted at the Permanent Mission of Japan to the United Nations in 1974, and since 1987 had served as under-secretary-general for disarmament affairs.

The Security Council had expanded the UNAMIC mandate in January 1992 to initiate a mine clearance program. The UNAMIC meanwhile conducted survey missions relating to military matters, civil administration, police, human rights, and elections. Clearly the UN machinery was engaged, but by the spring of 1992 months of preparation had been used up and vital political momentum had been dissipated in organizing the seven principal tasks and recruiting qualified personnel.

By June 1992 the assessments given to the authors in interviews, both at UN headquarters in New York and UNTAC headquarters in Phnom Penh, were that UNTAC was behind its schedule, but it fully intended to catch up in time for elections (scheduled for the end of April 1993.) If the elections were to be delayed by a month or more they would fall into the mud and stagnation of the rainy season, and the cost of maintaining UNTAC beyond May 1993 would be staggering. The election dates therefore drove UNTAC's efforts, and the array of responsibilities placed upon UNTAC by the Paris accords were very ambitious.

4. UNAMIC was to be established immediately upon the signature of the Paris accords, S/RES/717 (1991), Oct. 16, 1991, Doc. 18, *The United Nations and Cambodia, 1991–1995.*

5. Findlay, *Cambodia: The Legacy and Lessons of UNTAC*, p. 25.

6. Report of the Secretary-General on Cambodia, S/23613, Feb. 19, 1992, Doc. 30, in *The United Nations and Cambodia, 1991–1995.* This lengthy, detailed report and plan were composed in a team effort by a wide variety of Secretariat members. Interview with James Cunningham, U.S. Mission to the UN, New York, May 7, 1992. One of the leading Cambodia specialists within the Secretariat had worked on the issue since 1980, but was moved out of the area in summer 1992 as the UN headquarters was being subjected to reorganization by the new secretary-general, Boutros Boutros-Ghali.

As previously indicated, the tasks assumed by the UN in Cambodia, first via UNAMIC and then through UNTAC and Special Representative Akashi, were assigned to seven organizational components. These were discussed one by one in the secretary-general's implementation plan of February 19 and 26, 1992 (starting with human rights and ending with rehabilitation.) An additional activity called "information and education" was organized as a division within the office of the special representative.[7]

The implementation plan for seven components offers no particular priorities in terms of cost, urgency, interdependency, favorability of conditions, prior experience, or other possible criteria. Some sense of priority might by gleaned from the three survey missions dispatched by the secretary-general in late 1991, to explore (1) elections, (2) military arrangements, and (3) civil administration, police, and human rights. In retrospect it seems clear, even if not conclusively articulated at the time, that conducting a fair and free election was the overriding goal, and a politically neutral, violence-free electoral environment was a prerequisite. Thus, the organization of a military cease-fire and disarmament, the repatriation of displaced persons, the economic rehabilitation effort, and the promotion of human rights and civil police training all interconnected with the overriding goal of a legitimizing election of a constituent and legislative national assembly. To make this tremendous undertaking intelligible and real to the traumatized Khmer nation, the information and education division developed on its own.[8]

It would probably have added heavily to the strain of organizing UNTAC to have centralized the planning in the interest of maximizing the coordination of effort by UNTAC. Rather than applying such a rational approach, each component examined its own functions, procedures, and goals. The result was described by Trevor Findlay as "deploying seven quasi-independent components and trusting them to cooperate in the field once they are deployed." He would have preferred "combined strategic planning" "to determine how each component's mission dovetails with the strategic goals of the operation."[9] In Phnom Penh, however, each component reported to its own headquarters rather than to UNTAC headquarters.

7. In his "second progress report," Sept. 21, 1992 (Doc. 45 in *The United Nations and Cambodia, 1991–1995*), the secretary-general gives full attention to the information/education function but designates it a division, not a component.

8. A civic education program and training were suggested as possible developments under the Electoral and the Human Rights Components of the Secretary-General's implementation plan (Feb. 19, 1992), and they did develop into a much-heralded operation. The story gets rather colloquial telling in Zhou Mei, *Radio UNTAC of Cambodia: Winning Ears, Hearts, and Minds* (Bangkok: White Lotus Co., 1994).

9. Doc. 30, in *The United Nations and Cambodia, 1991–1995*, para. 13, 24b; and Findlay, *Cambodia: The Legacy and Lessons of UNTAC*, p. 126.

The Military Component

After years of civil war in Cambodia, nourished by military assistance from the outside, it was important for UNTAC to focus early on the goals of its Military Component. Without a working cease-fire, no legitimizing election would be possible. The Military Component's functions were fundamental to the entire undertaking. They would clearly require the largest element of personnel, with a goal of 15,900 troops during a transitional period of fifteen months.[10] Their functions were numerous, as well as critical to the achievement of UNTAC's nonmilitary functions.[11]

The Paris agreements on Cambodia created an obligation on the part of all Cambodian parties to observe a comprehensive cease-fire, to be "supervised, monitored, and verified by UNTAC." Upon the signing of the agreements each party was to inform UNTAC of the strength and deployment of its armed forces, police forces, arms, and minefields. UNTAC was pledged in Annex 2 to plan the regroupment and cantonment of the forces of the parties and storage of their weapons in areas holding battalion size or larger. It was surely too much to expect that all parties would report exact numbers to the UNTAC military commander. A mixed military working group chaired by the most senior UN military officer in country was to be established to resolve problems relating to the cease-fire. First, parties were to order all their forces to regroupment areas, within two weeks of the beginning of the UNTAC-supervised cease-fire, and then the Military Component was to escort them to designated cantonment areas with their arms and equipment for storage in the custody of UNTAC.

A second set of functions assigned to the Military Component was weapons control, a process that the authors observed at first hand near Phnom Penh in June 1992. The agreement called for demobilization of at least 70 percent of each party's military forces, prior to the end of the period set for registration for the elections. The remaining mobilized forces, it was hoped, would demobilize soon after the elections and abide by the decisions of the postelection government regarding a new national army. In practice, the process was broadened to permit the departure of soldiers from cantonment (with UNTAC assistance) to provide labor at home or

10. Basic personnel projections, broken down by types of units and functions, are found in the Secretary-General's report, S/23613, Feb. 19, 1992, Doc. 30 in *The United Nations and Cambodia, 1991–1995.*

11. Annex 1, section C, of the Agreement on a Comprehensive Political Settlement of the Cambodia Conflict and Annex 2 (withdrawal, cease-fire, and related measures) list the military functions; and the Secretary-General's implementation plan of Feb. 19, 1992, Doc. 30, section C, adds pages of detail.

reentry into civilian life. The process eventually would be terminated by UNTAC, after several months of noncompliance by the DK armed forces.

A fundamental piece of preparation for elections—which the secretary--general's report discussed first of all—was the verification of withdrawal from Cambodia and nonreturn of all categories of foreign forces. The Vietnamese armed forces had announced their full departure countless times, but the resistance parties just as often voiced their contradictions. UNTAC was authorized by the political settlement agreement to investigate any detailed written information regarding withdrawals,[12] but the issue gradually lost its steam and focused on Vietnamese settlers (many of them seasonal fishing families) who were alleged to include soldiers in disguise. Annex 2 of the agreement called for detailed information in writing with respect to withdrawal of foreign troops, and investigations by UNTAC of any complaints.

The long-established flow of military assistance from outside sources was to be regulated by the agreement of all parties "not to obtain or seek" such aid; and the adjacent states undertook to prevent their territories from being used for providing or storing any form of military assistance. The parties were also to assist UNTAC in investigating any complaints and to provide information about illicit transportation routes. Further, with respect to weapons, each party agreed to provide UNTAC all information at its disposal about caches of weapons and military supplies—which UNTAC was empowered to destroy.

Another effort that rested on extensive optimism was the agreement that "all known minefields" be clearly marked and that mine-clearing teams be organized by UNTAC, to be assisted by the training of Cambodian volunteers and a public education program in the avoidance of explosives.

UNTAC also had a responsibility to help the International Red Cross fulfill its function in promoting the release of prisoners of war. The voluntary repatriation and resettlement of Cambodian refugees and displaced persons was also dependent on the Military Component for mine clearance from the routes and affected areas.

Thus the Military Component handled vital functions relating to ending the conditions of civil war, verifying the departure of foreign troops, precluding further military assistance from the outside, cantoning all military forces and equipment, demobilizing 70 percent of the military forces, demining the countryside, releasing POWs, and destroying weapons caches. To help accomplish these vital tasks a mixed military working group of rep-

---

12. Agreement on a Comprehensive Political Settlement of the Cambodia Conflict, Oct. 23, 1991, Annex 2, Art. VI, Doc. 19, p. 143.

resentatives of all "the Cambodian Parties" was established by UNAMIC and subsequently placed under the chairmanship of the commander of the Military Component of UNTAC. The secretary-general in his implementation plan tried to fix a calendar for the strict unrolling of a four-phased deployment of the Military Component—from preparatory stage, to cantonment and demobilization, to electoral, to postelectoral phases—over a period of twenty months.[13]

The seven components derived from the Paris accords specified no priority of importance, but the observance of a cease-fire and ban on military assistance from the outside clearly merited first attention, as they did in the secretary-general's survey mission two months before the signing of the agreement, and in the formal establishment of UNAMIC under the UN Security Council on October 16, 1991. The Military Component dominated the scene in terms of number of personnel, infrastructure needs, cost, and urgency of installation. Once their demands had been answered, albeit with a damaging delay and ultimate refusal of full cooperation by the DK, the other components worked their way to the forefront. The function to be principally concerned about was holding elections. Here the UNTAC would be plowing new ground for the UN, which had never organized and conducted an election, although they had supervised national elections in Namibia. Also, as the Military Component encountered Khmer Rouge refusal to participate in cantonment and demobilization (phase two), the holding of an election, as free and fair as possible under the circumstances, became, by default, the overriding goal; and the Military Component redefined its role to provide security for election participants.[14] This called for protection of electoral workers, political party offices, and candidates, and altered the original deployment scheme.

The estimated numbers of military personnel in the four Cambodian parties were garnered for the secretary-general's implementation plan from the work of his military survey missions of November–December 1991 and from the observations of UNAMIC. The four parties revealed their regular forces at over 200,000, deployed in some 650 locations. Added to this number were some 250,000 militia, operating in almost all villages, with over 300,000 weapons of all types and some 80 million rounds of ammunition.[15] By agreement with the parties, the militia were not to be physically can-

13. Annex II in Doc. 30, p. 181.

14. Janet E. Heininger, *Peacekeeping in Transition: The United Nations in Cambodia* (New York: 20th Century Fund, 1994), pp. 38–40, discusses priorities of tasks and provides an UNTAC table of organization. Cf. also Findlay, *Cambodia: The Legacy and Lessons of UNTAC*, p. 30.

15. Doc. 30, paras. 65–75.

toned, because of the heavy disruption this would make in local economic and social life. They would, nonetheless, hand over their weapons to UNTAC. The number of cantonment areas was fixed at fifty-two after discussions between the military survey mission and the commanders-in-chief of the four Cambodia parties. Thirty-three cantonments would be for the Cambodian People's Armed Forces (CPAF), and ten for the National Army of Democratic Kampuchea (NADK), six for the KPNLAF, and three for the National Army of Independent Kampuchea (Sihanoukist).

The process of regroupment, followed by cantonment, was to begin shortly after the start of phase two of the cease-fire, in accordance with the timetable drawn up by the military commander of UNTAC. The four parties were to produce for counting all the troops, weapons, ammunition, and equipment they had previously declared. After the UNTAC commander was satisfied that a proper accounting had been made, phase two would begin, with a demobilization according to UNTAC's timetable from June through September 1992.[16] The Military Component would focus on demining and supervising the regroupment and cantonment areas. The numbers of military personnel would be verified in an effort to ensure that all were cantoned and disarmed. The cantonments would be supervised and a phased demobilization of 70 percent (or more, if possible) of the cantoned forces would be carried out during the voter registration period in the fall of 1992.

A heavy cloud hanging over the prospects of a "free and fair election" was the presence in Cambodia of 300,000 weapons, idled but not eliminated by a cease-fire. A combination of prompt investigations of reports of arms caches and rapid seizure and destruction of weapons and military supplies was expected to cope with this threat. The cooperation of neighboring states was to be solicited by UNTAC military liaison officers stationed abroad for the purpose of ending military supply from the outside. Secure facilities would be needed at each cantonment area for the storage of weapons deposited by demobilizing troops.

The authors visited one of the earliest organized cantonment sites (917) on June 28, 1992, at Long Vek in the vicinity of Phnom Penh. A Ghanaian company of ninety-five men in blue berets was supervising the cantonment and disarming of more than 3,000 seasoned troops from the Cambodian People's Armed Forces (CPAF). A feisty thirty-seven-year-old lieutenant general, leader of this SOC force, pointed out that some of their weapons had been retained because of the presence of DK troops in the vicinity. As

---

16. Ibid., paras. 66–79; and Annex II, "Proposed Schedule of Deployment—Military Component of UNTAC."

for large-scale weapons, two dozen Russian tanks with 100 mm guns and five armored troop carriers were neatly parked in the cover of a large army garage, lubricated and ready to go into action at any time, if this camp were to be attacked and UNTAC released them with fuel. Many of the troops in cantonment had been released to nearby villages to engage in farming, but a shortage of housing and sometimes the loss of family connections were said to be delaying such moves by others. A roll call of the cantoned troops was taken twice a week. The CPAF spokesman did not believe at that point, four weeks into phase two of the UNTAC deployment plan, that the DK intended to join the demobilization process. Thailand and China, he said, were the source of arms still coming in for the DK forces by truck to Siem Riep province just a week earlier.

The secretary-general's implementation plan rightly addressed the problems of inadequate infrastructure which faced the Military Component. Obviously the roads, airfields, ports, fuel supply, power supply, communications, warehousing space, personnel accommodations, and repair capacities would require an enormous engineering effort to restore to an adequate working level before the rainy season starting in June. The total UN military personnel needs were set by the secretary-general as 15,900.[17] Infantry was projected at 12 battalions of 850 men each, constituting virtually two-thirds of the total force (10,200). Engineers were the next largest category, at 2,230 (all ranks). Military observers, a signals unit, and a medical unit were planned, each at close to 500 persons. Air support (including 26 helicopters), a naval patrol element (376), and a logistics battalion (872) also found their place in the secretary-general's scheme.

The deployment of these international military personnel, which started with 200 Indonesian soldiers on March 16, 1992, would reach its peak a week prior to the start of phase two (cantonment and demobilization) of the cease-fire, May 1992. The numbers were supposed to decline to approximately 330 military observers and 5,100 infantry soon after the completion of demobilization.[18] As we shall see, the demobilization of the DK was never allowed by its leadership, and UNTAC military personnel shifted their focus to the security aspects of conducting a free and fair election. Prior to the shift the Military Component divided Cambodia into nine sectors, each with infantry and military observers and appropriate support units, and headquarters in Phnom Penh. The main tasks of the infantry elements were the cantonment and disarming process, monitoring the cessation of outside military assistance (with checkpoints along the border), and

17. Doc. 30, paras. 85–90.
18. Ibid., paras. 87–91.

protecting reception centers for refugees and displaced persons. Military observers were to verify the numbers of troops and weapons at cantonment areas. Eventually, personnel from thirty-two countries were enlisted in the Military Component, a broader representation than in previous UN peace-keeping operations. These blue berets were supposed to be fully deployed by the end of May 1992, and 70 percent demobilization was to be completed by the end of September. This was not to be.

The Electoral Component

UNTAC's deployment of 15,900 military personnel was designed to end a nasty, inconclusive civil war, but beyond that noble objective lay the organization and conduct of a free and fair election. For this purpose the Electoral Component was created. The functions of the component were readily derived from the democratic election process known (if not fully honored) worldwide. Half of the estimated population of 8.7 million Cambodians were foreseen as eligible to vote.

To make this possible UNTAC had to establish an electoral law and regulations, after consultation with the Supreme National Council. A code of conduct was also foreseen, which would reinforce the work of the Human Rights Component. The virus of unfair use of money to solicit votes was sure to be lurking down the road. Annex 1 of the political settlement agreement listed 12 worthy functions for the component, and 72 qualified international personnel were to carry them out. Indeed, over 400 UN Volunteers were eventually enlisted for observing the 200 electoral districts. In addition to these tasks the component oversaw the registration of parties and voters, voter education and facilitation of voter participation, ensuring fairness in the use of the media, enrolling foreign observers (in consultation with the SNC), investigating complaints, running the polls and the vote count, and certifying the fairness of the elections.

The secretary-general's implementation plan addressed the mandate laid out in the agreement and suggested sensible adaptations such as establishing radio broadcasts, print facilities, and mobile video units, and providing sophisticated training in election management. First, to *register* voters approximately 800 registration teams (of five persons each) would be needed, with as many local personnel as possible. Second, an additional 200 teams (of two persons each) would *supervise* the 200 electoral districts. In addition, *polling* teams (of seven persons each) would require approximately 8,000 persons. A group of international personnel seconded from governments for two or three weeks in April 1993 was expected to make it possible to have one polling supervisor per polling station. The exact number and location of polling places was to be determined after the registration revealed the size and distribution of the electorate among the 21 provinces. Each province was to have an office staffed by five persons.[19]

As chief electoral officer, Dr. Reginald Austin, a professor of law at the University of Zimbabwe, was to recruit a staff of 72 for the Electoral component headquarters in Phnom Penh. A dozen or more of them were veterans of the recently successful Namibia election, supervised by the United Nations.[20] A big assist in composing an international election staff was given by some 450 UN Volunteers, who were recruited via a program started in 1971 for short-term UN service at subsistence pay.

Thus, the Electoral Component squarely faced the task which the secretary-general called "the focal point of the comprehensive settlement."[21] A sobering number of staff (62,000 Cambodians) was projected, for registering parties and voters, supervising and educating voters, observing the campaigns and conducting the voting itself, and verifying the freedom and fairness of the outcome. This was to be carried out effectively within fourteen months in a country lacking in electoral experience, by an international staff that was woefully short on interpreters and trained personnel.

Civil Administration Component

Throughout the years of seeking the formula for a political settlements, the Phnom Penh regime tenaciously rejected any diminution of its authority. This intransigence cast an awkward shadow on the agreement's provisions for direct UN "supervision or control" of civil administration during the transitional period. The much-heralded Evans (Australia) proposal of February 1990, which included options such as "root and branch replacement" of existing administrations by UN staff, or replacement of about two hundred officials at the ministerial level and three hundred governors and provincial department heads,[22] or other, less obtrusive arrangements, was ultimately passed over as too far-reaching politically, as well as legally dubious in relation to the UN Charter's trusteeship provisions. During the negotiation of a political settlement the SOC weathered all threats to its

19. Ibid., part B, paras. 23–43.

20. The authors interviewed Austin's deputy, Michael Maley, a UN-in-Namibia veteran, July 1, 1992, in Phnom Penh as the Electoral Component was still deploying itself.

21. Doc. 30, part II, B, 3, para. 49.

22. Department of Foreign Affairs and Trade, Commonwealth of Australia, *Cambodia: An Australian Peace Proposal*, Working Paper I and II (Canberra, 1990).

continuation in office. The Paris accords finally addressed the governance issue in terms that the Cambodian People's Party, which occupied the "existing administrative structures," apparently thought they could tolerate without giving away their preelection advantage as the current rulers of the greater part of the nation and the agency of its governmental services and regulation. The Paris peace agreements stopped short of replacing the existing regimes and tried instead to "ensure strict neutrality" in the preelection political environment. The negotiations over this provision even recorded distinctions between different ministries and agencies in their potential for bias and political influence. Thus, a gradation of safeguards made the mandate of UNTAC's Civil Administration Component both complicated and to some extent unrealistic.

The political settlement agreement specified five fields of governmental activity to be delegated by the SNC to United Nations supervision or control. These administrative agencies and offices, which "could directly influence the outcome of elections," were found in the fields of foreign affairs, national defense, finance, public security, and information.[23] The UN special representative was empowered to issue directives to such agencies in exercising such supervision as UNTAC "considers necessary." He was to determine after consultation with the parties how many civil police were necessary for law enforcement in Cambodia—which UNTAC would supervise. In this respect the special representative could, in consultation with the SNC, undertake investigations of complaints and allegations against the existing administration in relation to achieving a comprehensive political settlement. He could also install personnel in the administrative structure "who will have unrestricted access to all administrative operations and information," and he could require the reassignment or removal of any personnel of such administrative organs, an authority that Akashi was loath to utilize.[24]

On paper, then, the agreement and the secretary-general's implementation plan provided sufficient authority for UNTAC, through its Civil Administration Component, to neutralize the impact of governing bodies (and their underlying political parties) on the Cambodian electorate. The actuality was quite different. Two of the parties, the CPP and the PDK, in their areas, were quite determined to maximize rather than neutralize their influence on future voters, and the UN control or supervision structure was seen as an adversary to contend with rather than a mentor to enable or em-

---

23. Agreement on a Comprehensive Political Settlement of the Cambodia Conflict, Oct. 23, 1991, Part I, art. 6; and Annex 1, sec. B, Doc. 19.

24. Ibid., Annex 1, sec. B, para. 4a, b. Cf. also Secretary-General's Report, Feb. 19, 1993, paras. 94ff., Doc. 30.

ulate. The power struggle had shifted from military or negotiation contests to the partisan exercise of administrative authority. The nature of the game for the "existing administrative authorities" (overwhelmingly found in the SOC) was to retain autonomy and privacy as much as possible; and the goal of UNTAC was to exercise "scrutiny" (as the seretary-general characterized the task)[25] as widely and insistently as possible. The PDK, a highly secretive and scarcely visible revolutionary movement, had survived a lifetime of defiance to external influence, and they were provided an excuse for their intransigence by the secret maneuvering of the far more numerous and widespread State of Cambodia bureaucracy. The SOC being more widely established than the DK and the other "resistance" parties provided more instances of partisan behavior than any of its rival parties.

Had UNTAC been able to assume its control or supervision responsibilities promptly after the signing of the Paris accords, they would have confronted a more compliant civil administration than they encountered in October 1992, when the required international staff was finally fully recruited and put in place.[26] The months that had passed without a compelling UNTAC presence in the ministries, or the provinces, permitted the party in power to grow in its conviction both that it not only could but should evade the scrutinizers. Such behavior only bolstered the PDK's charges of unfair use of the "existing administrative structures" by the CPP, which the PDK translated into arguments for their own exemption from the treaty obligation of openness to UN scrutiny. It was, after all, an extraordinary presumption that scarcely 200 international supervisors, desperately short on translators and interpreters, 123 of them operating mostly in the provinces with local employees, could control or supervise 140,000 SOC civil servants. Yet because UNTAC made the effort to provide a neutral administrative atmosphere the CPP was repeatedly unveiled in blatantly illicit and undemocratic actions. This may have weakened the aura of legitimacy that incumbency afforded them in the eyes of many voters, but a backlash against the CPP was by no means guaranteed, even in so flagrant a case of undermining the UN as the reported *order* by the governor of Battambang province (a nephew of the chair of the CPP) that provincial officials *not* obey UNTAC directives.[27] SOC's complaints about the DK's hostility toward UNTAC supervision was readily counterpoised by DK complaints about the CPP's intransigence.

The secretary-general's initial implementation plan discussed the five

25. Ibid., para. 94.
26. Heininger, *Peacekeeping in Transition*, pp. 85–86, makes this point with convincing illustrative cases.
27. Ibid., p. 86.

areas of administrative activity which were to be subjected to "direct control." Two of these (foreign affairs and finance) were scrutinized by the Civil Administration Component exclusively within the two responsible ministries, but in the other three designated areas (national defense, public security, and information) the components and the ministries were intertwined (e.g., human rights and civil police, and elections). A lesser degree of scrutiny called "optional control" was authorized over the areas of education, agriculture, fishing, transport, energy, tourism, mines, and general administration. The UN Security Council agreed on May 26, 1992, to UNTAC's exercising control over these areas. This policy recognized, however, that administrative bodies could derive propaganda value from their activities, and public funds could be expended in a discriminatory fashion, even when intended for humanitarian purposes. The remaining areas of administration were to function free of UN supervision or monitoring, under a dubious presumption of even-handed behavior in the administration of government services.

The secretary-general's implementation plan briefly indicated the tools that UNTAC might rely on. "Codes of conduct and guidelines for management" were to be created for most of the areas, but these were both delayed in creation and strangers to the Cambodian bureaucratic culture. Questions of "ethical conduct" and "measures to counter corruption" were not familiar problems in the authoritarian, political environment of the long-subjugated Khmer people. Cambodian civil servants could play a significant role in the fairness of an election, but time and skilled instructors to keep them neutral were in short supply. Guidelines might eventually be tailored for specific areas of government, and, if needed, UNTAC had the right under the agreement to issue directives binding all Cambodian parties. This power was used most sparingly, however, as was UNTAC's right to remove or reassign personnel. Special Representative Akashi did not wish to push the SOC to the brink of noncooperation. The SOC bureaucracy could operate through "back channels" and informal networks of communication, and they did. Akashi's strategy was to push for genuine administrative control by UNTAC, but not to push the SOC to the point of overt noncooperation. Had UNTAC insisted on making widespread penetrating personnel assignments in all four parties—assuming they could find sufficient persons with the combination of linguistic, cultural, and administrative capabilities to do the job—the entire concept of international supervision/control might have collapsed or, at the least, have delayed the holding of elections. The secretary-general supported Akashi's approach, which fell within the realm of "peacekeeping," not enforcement, and which relied on yet more negotiation and attempted persuasion.

Notwithstanding UNTAC's cautious approach to supervision they did solicit complaints from the general public regarding the misuse of authority. Many Cambodians raised issues with regard to property ownership which the fledgling judicial system was inadequate to handle.[28] More than 140 complaints, mostly concerning land and property disputes, and sometimes evictions, were registered by January 1993 with the Complaints and Investigations Service of the Civil Administration Component. A public statement of June 26, 1992, advertised the people's right to complain to the director of the civil administration office in their province, or to UNTAC police in their province, or to the UNTAC police or electoral personnel at the district level. Satisfaction or rectification was not always forthcoming, but the idea of a right to complain was symbolically important, and the information conveyed by the protests helped UNTAC to keep abreast of the public disposition.[29] An effective response to complaints was more likely to occur in Phnom Penh than in the less tightly administered provinces, where official written orders were not to be found in many instances, and a smaller number of UNTAC personnel were available to direct the search. The Civil Administration Component set up a service for complaints and investigation, and a Specialized Control Service which could supervise areas of administration other than the five designated areas. It also established control teams, reporting strictly to the deputy special representative, which investigated any abuses of the Paris Agreements, particularly in the form of violence. The component set up offices in all twenty-one provinces and deployed more than 800 persons (219 international and 599 local staff) by August 1992.[30] The Specialized Control Service started in January 1993, monitoring the use of administrative authority outside Phnom Penh with a mobile inspection team, which tried without immediate success to inspect all relevant documents. Like most bureaucracies the SOC did not welcome intruders, especially from foreign nations.

The game played out between the thin ranks of the Civil Administration Component and the existing authority structures produced some bizarre cases of bias or evasion. For example, wireless telephones rapidly came into use by government officials for informal transmissions. Another evasion was the transfer of a unit of the Public Security Ministry to the Ministry of

28. Ibid. This account of hidden channels reports the observations of Gerald Pourcel, the director of the Civil Administration Component.

29. This particular problem area was brought to the authors' attention by Serge Durand, deputy director of the Public Security Service of the UNTAC Civil Administration Component, June 30, 1992, in Phnom Penh.

30. Michael W. Doyle, *UN Peacekeeping in Cambodia: UNTAC's Civil Mandate* (London: Lynne Rienner Publishers, 1995), pp. 38–40.

Culture, which was free of UNTAC scrutiny. UNTAC's use of unannounced raids on SOC offices was late in coming and infrequently attempted. The CPP created so-called A-groups, which were centrally run and designed to infiltrate opposition parties and disrupt them with a "structured sabotage effort." This was closely related to the government's widespread use of military or security personnel for politically focused violence.[31] Within the Ministry of Defense no UNTAC supervisors were stationed until August 1992, half a year after the secretary-general's implementation report and ten months after the agreement. In his second progress report (September 21, 1992), the secretary-general rather laconically averred that "inspections and inquiries have revealed a high level of political activity by the CPP within the armed forces of the Phnom Penh authorities."[32] Given the size and weapons of the military this was not a reassuring acknowledgment. Eventually, in January 1993, an UNTAC control team was established, which several months later conducted four effective raids on the SOC police and military offices and garnered written evidence, on the eve of the election, of a CPP campaign of organized violence. Like so many civil administration efforts, however, this exposure was less than, and later than, the component should have achieved.

This is not to say that the Civil Administration Component was a total failure. Contemporary observers of its brief existence have credited it with managing the issuance of currency, the expenditures and revenues of the state budget, and customs controls. Yet beneath the surface the finances of the SOC became intermeshed with those of the CPP. State employees in the police, army, and civil service were found by UNTAC investigators to be geared into the CPP's election campaign.[33] The Civil Administration Component was able to prevent only some of the smuggling along the extensive borders of Cambodia, just as it was able to monitor and ameliorate only some of the miserable conditions of the prisons. The Supreme National Council adopted a penal code in September 1992 and UNTAC disseminated and explained it to police and judges. This may have cautioned some police-state actors, but full restraint was not achieved. More effectively, UNTAC drafted a traffic code and initiated working groups on port authority, health, forestry, and cultural heritage.[34] Supervision of the defense ministry generated approval requirements regarding any sale, rental, or exchange of land, and initiated an inventory of the army's fixed assets.

31. Heininger, *Peacekeeping in Transition*, p. 88.
32. Second progress report of the secretary-general on UNTAC, S/24578, Sept. 21, 1992, para. 33, Doc. 45, in *The United Nations and Cambodia, 1991–1995*.
33. Doyle, *UN Peacekeeping in Cambodia*, pp. 40–42.
34. Heininger, *Peacekeeping in Transition*, p. 89.

Other state assets also became subject to approval requirements after officials started to enrich themselves through private sales. Thus, many steps
in the right direction were undertaken, but the time was woefully short,
and the cultural traditions and political environment were decidedly ad-
verse to the undertaking. The governed, by long tradition, were accustomed to paying extra for the services of governors.

Indicative of the overriding problem was the dispute between the PDK
and the CPP over the nature of the transitional regime, as evidenced by
documents issued by the parties. The PDK's proposal from Khieu Samphan, dated June 27, 1992, on cooperation between UNTAC and the
Supreme National Council, insisted that "there is no government in Cambodia during the transition period." Rather, the SNC—which "is not a government"—was to delegate powers to the UN which were "necessary to
ensure the implementation of the Agreement."[35] The SOC, on the other
hand, found it convenient to continue as long as it could its governmental
services, such as issuing entry visas to Cambodian territory, or distributing
foreign aid addressed to "Cambodia" or "Cambodian authorities," or receiving high foreign guests, or continuing the "existing administrative structures" in the name of SOC rather than the new and nebulous SNC, or the
ambiguous "Phnom Penh authorities," as the special representative referred to them.[36]

The creation of SNC as the repository of Cambodian sovereignty during
the period leading to an election was an adroit device for moving toward a
legitimate national government, but during the transition to an elected government the existing authority structures were needed to perform essential
governmental functions. Administrative structures were bound to garner
electoral influence, or suspicion of political bias. The attempt of UNTAC's
Civil Administration Component to keep the existing administration structures politically neutral was a bold but overextended effort, dictated by the
fundamental compromise negotiated into the agreement. The administrative control that the UN actually achieved was never more than partial and
begrudging, and rarely a priori, in the sense of allowing scrutiny of authoritative actions *before* the fact.[37] The word "control" is really inappropriate.
At best UNTAC achieved a degree of "influence." The political atmosphere

35. Letter dated June 27, 1992, from Khieu Samphan transmitting proposal of the PDK
on cooperation between UNTAC and the SNC, Doc. 38, *The United Nations and Cambodia,
1991–1995.*
36. Second special report of the secretary-general on UNTAC and phase two of the cease-
fire, *The United Nations and Cambodia, 1991–1995,* Doc. 41.
37. The begrudging attitude was attributed by J. A. Schear, in Findlay, *Cambodia: The
Legacy and Lessons of UNTAC,* pp. 60–63.

was never entirely neutral, but a sufficient effort was exerted in pursuit of that goal that a reasonably fair election could be conducted. As Special Representative Akashi put it, "an approximation of fairness" was created by virtue of the attempt, if not the achievement, of evenhanded administration. Without UNTAC's effort to guarantee fairness, there would have been no check at all on the regime's harassment and intimidation of its political opponents. UNTAC did the best they could with limited resources.

The UN mandate, as summed up by Lyndall McLean, deputy director of the Civil Administration Component, "with its demands to monitor all aspects of the media, scrutinize all sources of information, examine and control all financial records, judicial and administrative decisions, let alone deal with the queues of complainants lining up on a daily basis to present their allegations against officials — was totally unrealistic purely from the point of [view of] language skills alone."[38] Under the circumstances, "selective application" of the agreement became necessary (except in the opinion of the PDK), and this compromise was weakened by the delay in deployment of UN personnel.

The Civilian Police

Annex 1 of the Paris Agreement provided that the special representative of the secretary-general would "determine, after consultation with the Cambodian Parties, those civil police necessary to perform law enforcement in Cambodia."[39] Compared to the other functions assigned to UNTAC by the Paris accords, very little guidance was provided regarding civil police duties. All Cambodian civil police would work under UNTAC supervision or control to ensure effective and impartial protection of human rights and fundamental rights, and UNTAC was empowered to supervise law enforcement and the judicial processes nationwide, but the reality was a nation with very little legal system to supervise. Even though the special representative was empowered to undertake investigations of complaints about existing administrative structures, there was little judicial structure with which to work.

UNTAC's civil police were closely tied in purpose to the civil administration unit, but they were made into a separate component. The size of the operation would depend on the needs of the "law and order" situation, as

38. L. McLean, "Civil Administration in Transition: Public Information and Neutral Political/Electoral Environment," quoted in ibid., p. 61.

39. Agreement on a Comprehensive Political Settlement of the Cambodian conflict, Oct. 23, 1991, Annex 1, sec. B, art. 5, Doc. 19.

decided by the special representative, taking into consideration various factors.[40] A "considerable number of weapons" were in nonofficial hands, and troops would be demobilized whose known skills were limited to the use of weapons. The CPP alone reported itself to have 47,000 police personnel, 40,000 of whom operated at the provincial level and below. The civil police force of the PDK was reported as 9,000, mostly in villages in units of twelve to sixty persons. The PDK police personnel were scarcely distinguishable from military forces. The other two parties claimed to field military police numbering 400 in the KPNLF and 150 in the FUNCINPEC.

The number of civil police required during the transitional period was for the secretary-general to determine, and his initial plan called for a total of 50,000. These were to be allocated as follows: 1,700 men in the FUNCINPEC areas, 1,000 in the KPNLF locations, and about 5,000 for PDK areas, leaving a dominating 42,300 for the CPP areas. Thus, the secretary-general called for a reduction in strength and reconstitution of the PDK forces, and an augmentation of the Sihanouk party's and the KPNLF's. These levels were to be reassessed after UNTAC gained access to survey the situation on the ground.

To supervise this number of civil police the secretary-general proposed to organize at three levels: headquarters (1), provinces (21), and districts (200). There were an estimated 1,500 police posts or stations in the country, to each of which a mobile team of two UNTAC police monitors would be assigned. Thus, 3,000 police monitors would be required for touring the districts and visiting their assigned police stations, in an effort to reassure the populace regarding impartial maintenance of law and order. The total complement of UNTAC civilian police (CivPol) was expected to reach 3,600. The United Nations planners solicited forty-seven nations[41] for police personnel and received contributions from thirty-two, not all of whom amounted to a positive contribution to the CivPol effort. Only twelve of the contributing countries could qualify as having long-standing democratic governments, and of the fourteen states contributing more than one hundred civilian police personnel, thirteen were developing countries.[42] Complaints of child molestation and rape, which might not seem improbable in regard to some UNTAC military personnel, were more dismaying and degrading when leveled against the UN civilian police.

The mobile teams were expected to "tour their jurisdictions continu-

40. Report of the secretary-general on Cambodia, Feb. 26, 1992, part II, E, para. 112–31, Doc. 30.

41. Authors' interview with General Klaas Roos, director of UNTAC Civilian Police Component, June 30, 1992, in Phnom Penh.

42. Findlay, *Cambodia: The Legacy and Lessons of UNTAC*, pp. 144–45.

ously" to build confidence in the populace and foster an atmosphere conducive to free and fair elections. A by-product of such touring would be information about the law and order situation in the villages and communes. Here again, as with civil administration, codes of conduct and training courses (especially regarding human rights) were in order. As the time for elections approached the civil police were called upon to provide security for UNTAC personnel and the voting process in general. It was expected that areas where refugees and displaced persons were resettled would need priority attention in reassuring people about public order. In fact, as preparation for the election moved forward without the cooperation of the PDK, the provision of security for the process took on greater and greater importance. The two hundred district-level UNTAC units would each contain a mobile team of two UNTAC police officials ready to monitor local police activity. For every UNTAC police monitor there would be an estimated fifteen local police.[43]

The performance of the civil police was probably the greatest shortfall of the UNTAC operation, notwithstanding its spirited director, General Klaas Roos, who had conducted a quite successful police mission in Namibia in 1989. The difficulties in Cambodia stemmed in large part from the very tardy deployment of UNTAC civil police, political diversity among their international personnel, and Cambodia's lack of law-and-order structure and traditions. As one observer summed up his criticism, CivPol was "neither a deterrent nor an enforcement mechanism."[44] Notwithstanding the enlistment of some experienced police who had served effectively in Namibia during the UN-supervised election of 1989, the UNTAC Civilian Police Component suffered from a surfeit of personnel ill-prepared for assisting in a democratic election, since their own countries did not fully practice democratic politics. Worse yet, the various police contributions to UNTAC were not only very late in arriving but often poorly disciplined and prone to corrupt behavior (such as smuggling).[45] The local population, particularly women, were harassed and deceived (with talk of marriage) and abused by UN civilian police in a manner that was often racist and demeaning. The sexual license realized by some UNTAC personnel, away from their own tightly restraining cultures, sometimes led to abusive behavior that pro-

43. Report of the secretary-general on the situation in Cambodia, Feb. 26, 1992, II, E, 2, Doc. 30.

44. Findlay, *Cambodia: The Legacy and Lessons of UNTAC*, p. 144, puts it more starkly: "The UNTAC Civilian Police Component was . . . widely perceived as disastrous." Findlay himself acknowledges that some aspects of the job were not in CivPol's hands but "they could have done better." Cf. also p. 106.

45. Ibid., pp. 33, 46.

voked local male revenge and discredited UNTAC's standing.[46] In one such case the violence committed by a vengeful defender of a Cambodian woman against an UNTAC rival was wrongly reported as a Khmer Rouge terrorist action.

By the end of 1992, at a time when CivPol had still not attained full deployment, law and order in Cambodia went into a decline as local bandits and criminals perceived a gap between the SOC and the UNTAC enforcement efforts. The CivPol effort was limited by their lack of firearms and power of arrest (until January 1993).[47] Some civilian police were reported to have purchased arms on their own. The UN civilian police during the Namibia election had served unarmed, but a case could be made that guns were needed in the chaotic, grim aftermath of civil war in Cambodia. Also lacking as late as December was ready communication between headquarters and provincial offices.

An ideal operation in civilian police would insist upon selecting out any personnel who lacked a capability in either of the official languages or in automobile driving.[48] It would also require training courses such as Singapore provided for eight weeks for its exemplary seventy-five-man police contingent. This unit arrived with at least six years' police experience and expert training in mental stress awareness, physical conditioning, intercultural communication, and leadership. There must also be realistic numbers of police personnel to cover the responsibilities—which included monitoring local police, investigating human rights complaints, guarding political party offices in the provinces, and guarding voter registration sites. CivPol also helped at border checkpoints and instructed urban police in traffic control. The UNTAC police tried to carry more burdens than they were able to handle with the available personnel, and they were unable to rely on the SOC to follow through on CivPol investigative work. Generally the SOC did nothing in response to investigations and CivPol lacked the power of arrest (until January 1993) and incarceration of culprits.

In December 1992 attacks with hand grenades and automatic weapons against the newly forming offices of the emerging political parties rose sharply. This was recorded by the secretary-general in his fourth progress report without specifying the origin of the terror.[49] A journalistic look at the

46. Interview with UN Volunteer who had been stationed in Seam Reap, Dec. 12, 1993.
47. General Klaas Roos, in an interview in Phnom Penh, June 30, 1992, during the early days of deployment, argued that side arms would only invite earlier resort to weapons by the persons opposing police control.
48. Some civilian police spoke neither English nor French and could not drive a car.
49. Fourth progress report of the Secretary-General on UNTAC, S/25719, May 3, 1993, II, G, Para. 80, Doc. 79, in *The United Nations and Cambodia, 1991–1995.*

situation, however, revealed a concerted campaign by the CPP to intimidate its rivals. This news account grew out of a confidential UNTAC report
January 18, 1993) that noted "a very serious erosion of public confidence in
UNTAC" and a public belief that SOC/CPP had undertaken a full-fledged
campaign of violent repression, making it impossible for other provisionally
registered political parties to seriously conduct legitimate political activities.[50] What was also disturbing was the readiness of the SOC to break the
cease-fire in February 1993 as it launched offensives against the Khmer
Rouge which exceeded the bounds of self-defense.

To counter this slide into political violence, the civilian police patrols
were initially put on a twenty-four-hour schedule for checking all political
party offices, which eventually numbered six hundred. To cope with the
load, a list of sixty party offices thought to be the most at risk was eventually
settled upon for protection every night. By February 1993 attacks had
ceased at the specially protected offices, and the incidents at other offices
declined sharply into March until a growing number of village-level offices
brought a larger number of attacks. A related, evolving responsibility of
CivPol was the monitoring of political rallies and meetings during the election campaign starting April 7, 1993. Here the going was much smoother.
In the first four weeks, at the two-hundred-odd rallies not a single case of
harassment or disruption of a meeting was reported.[51]

Human Rights

The Human Rights Component of UNTAC started modestly but grew in
size and scope in the course of its brief existence. Dennis MacNamara,
New Zealand lawyer with some experience in relief work in Cambodia,
served as its director. It became the most politically intrusive operation of
its kind in United Nations peacekeeping history. Unlike the other UNTAC
components, it was able to leave behind a legacy in the form of a special
representative authorized by the United Nations Commission on Human
Rights. To this office was appointed in November 1993 Justice Michael
Kirby of Australia, who continued after UNTAC's departure, encouraging
several nongovernmental organizations dedicated to promoting human

50. N. Thayer and N. Chanda, "Cambodia: Shattered Peace," *Far Eastern Economic Review,* Feb. 11, 1993, p. 11. The Secretary-General in his fourth progress report on UNTAC,
May 3, 1993, pinpoints SOC for having organized or condoned violent attacks on the offices
of FUNCINPEC and the KPNLF, for which "only a handful of arrests were made."
51. Fourth progress report of the secretary-general on UNTAC, S/25719, May 3, 1993, I,
A, 5, paras. 80–81, Doc. 79, in *The United Nations and Cambodia, 1991–1995.*

rights, but not receiving permission to investigate and report of because of objections by China and ASEAN.

This unique effort in behalf of human rights was in good part a residue of the earlier diplomatic effort by the CPP to condemn and exclude the Khmer Rouge from participation in the governing of Cambodia. In the course of negotiating the comprehensive political settlement, CPP proposals of condemnation of the KR's record of atrocity were continually rejected or watered down by the PDK. The framework document proposed by the P-5 in August 1990 included section 4 ("Human rights protection"), paragraph 24, which read: "Cambodia's tragic recent history requires special measures to assure protection of human rights." The section went on to outline these special measures in somewhat more detail than is found in the subsequent draft agreement of December 23, 1990, or the Agreement on a Comprehensive Political Settlement of October 23, 1991 (art. 15 and 16). The oblique language of this final agreement commits Cambodia simply to "take effective measures to ensure that the policies and practices of the past shall never be allowed to return."

This tepid condemnation of the Pol Pot period was coupled, however, with an obligation for Cambodia to adhere to relevant international human rights instruments such as the Universal Declaration of Human Rights, which the SNC took pains to do. In addition, Annex 1, section E of the agreement spelled out a mandate for UNTAC in regard to human rights, resting on three activities: education and promotion, oversight during the transitional period, and investigation and corrective action.

Institutional structures of human rights were just about totally lacking in Cambodia. The war-ravaged nation lacked a legal system of any consequence in regulating governmental or individual behavior. The three resistance factions effectively governed their particular areas or followers under martial law, or military justice. The State of Cambodia, the largest of the four "governments," almost wholly lacked judicial structures and personnel. Their few existing courts (rather dubiously established under the 1989 constitution of the SOC) operated with clearly expected deference to the executive branch. The Supreme Court was not required to give any reasons for reversing a provincial court's action, since trained judges were severely lacking and the Ministry of Justice felt obliged to ensure that courts reached "correct" decisions. The minister explained to Human Rights Component officers that a judge who did not follow his instructions "disobeyed the law and must be punished."[52] Yet, not only was the judicial structure and modus operandi heavily politicized, but also the supporting

52. UNTAC, *Human Rights Component Final Report* (Phnom Penh, Sept. 1993), p. 16.

institutions of a civil society, such as a nonpolitical civil service, professional police, and a free press, were lacking. Very limited time existed for the UN transitional authority to play a role in promoting fundamental rights during the run-up to national elections and full sovereignty.[53] Yet, moving pragmatically, the Human Rights Component adapted creatively to the almost lawless condition of Cambodian civil society during its fifteen months of preparing a free and neutral environment for the election.

The early expectation that the Human Rights Component would center itself in Phnom Penh, with ten professionals, to coordinate the work of UNTAC components whose duties touched on human rights, proved to be woefully insufficient. No staff devoted exclusively to human rights had been foreseen outside of Phnom Penh, but soon after the arrival of the first professional staff in early 1992 it became apparent that grievances abounded in the countryside, which UNTAC professionals could station themselves to deal with at the province level. Twenty-one additional personnel slots were granted for the provinces, and ten more were granted for headquarters in January 1993.[54] To further catch up with the pent-up demand in this domain, Special Representative Akashi made a special appeal to some eighteen governments in October 1992, which resulted in a Trust Fund for a Human Rights Education Program in Cambodia, and $1.85 million. An initial nine projects in human rights were undertaken with non-governmental organizations, dealing with such problems as teacher training, election monitoring, training of health professionals, and training regarding womens' rights.

This first or "cornerstone" element of UNTAC's human rights activity, education, brought to bear a variety of media, sometimes in collaboration with the information and education division of the special representative's office. These included printed materials, cultural events and presentations (carefully developed in a culturally sensitive and "accessible" manner), radio and television, videocassettes, and mobile teaching units.[55] Existing media of communication, such as schools, training programs, and community gatherings, were encouraged to adopt curricular materials worked up by human rights staff. With help from UNESCO, a team of traditional

53. The authors visited the office of the Human Rights Component on June 29, 1992, and found a staff of 6, of whom two were lawyers. Seven more staff had reached the provinces, but even by September this level was not fully staffed. The director, Dennis McNamara, had served previously as coordinator for humanitarian assistance to Cambodia.

54. UNTAC, *Human Rights Component Final Report*, pp. 8, 31, 50.

55. Report of the Secretary-General on Cambodia, S/23613, Feb. 19, 1992, II, A, 13, Doc. 30.

singers toured the provinces conveying a human rights message.[56] Indigenous human rights associations were assisted in cultivating solidarity in very
barren soil. An atmosphere of civic freedom and fairness was crucial not
only for the holding of elections but also for the sustaining of democratic
elections as a method of governance in Cambodia. This would obviously require decades of shaky practice, but the human rights staff tried to see to its
inauguration.

In addition to lacking a civil legal system, the SOC showed little cooperation in efforts to rectify patent injustices, such as the imprisonment of political opponents. The Human Rights Component campaigned hard to end
the use of shackles in SOC prisons. The agreement's insistence on
Cambodia's adherence to appropriate international human rights instruments, such as the Covenant on Civil and Political Rights, provided legitimacy for an UNTAC review of prison conditions and treatment of
offenders. The SNC on September 19, 1992, adopted a new Transitional
Criminal Law based on international instruments, which insisted on an independent judiciary, the rights of women, children, and refugees, and the
prohibition of torture; but no serious attempt was made to implement it.[57]
By August a total of 258 political prisoners, held for many months without
trial by the SOC, had been released after human rights staff investigation.[58]

The larger legal issue of genocide, which had long been raised by Western lawyers and politicians, was studiously not picked up by the Human
Rights Component. As the director indicated in an interview with the authors in June 1992 (see note 57), the agreement did not lay out any mandate for human rights staff involvement in rectifying the genocidal actions
of the Khmer Rouge period, and the matter had not been raised with the
Human Rights Component at their level of operations. The staff in Phnom
Penh did receive 599 allegations of human rights violations; and 701 more
reached them in the provinces. Local human rights associations and political parties and the UNTAC Civil Police also registered complaints. The
CivPol moved more and more into the task of investigation. The earliest
complaints related to property rights, often denied to citizens by the SOC
(and earlier the Khmer Rouge), in accordance with the abolition of private

56. Third progress report of the secretary-general on UNTAC, S/25/54, Jan. 25, 1993, I,
19, Doc. 65, in *The United Nations and Cambodia, 1991–1995.*

57. Authors' interview with Dennis McNamara, 29 June 1992. McNamara at this time saw
the SOC making a high-level decision to look good by cooperating with the release of prisoners. Later its position became less commendable.

58. Heininger, *Peacekeeping in Transition*, p. 94; and UNTAC, *Human Rights Component
Final Report*, p. 16.

title. Serious violations of another type were growing as well, in the form of violence against political opponents, ethnic minorities, the civilian population, and prisoners (by means of executions and torture).[59]

Under the political violence category, members of the KPNLF/Buddhist Liberal Democratic Party (BLDP) front alleged that political assassinations occurred shortly prior to their formative party conference in June 1992. UNTAC was not yet sufficiently deployed to investigate many of these very serious charges. As the election approached, attacks expanded to include political party officers and activists. Many of these attacks were traced by investigation to CPP armed forces and the SOC police. Between November 1992 and January 1993, ninety-six FUNCINPEC and BLDP members were killed or wounded in apparently politically motivated attacks, many attributed to the SOC. As the election crept closer, however, an UNTAC Special Prosecutor's Office to prosecute human rights violators, and UNTAC military and civil police patrols to guard party offices, considerably improved the situation. Special Representative Akashi announced sternly to the SNC that "any politically motivated act of violence, especially if it results in death, is unacceptable."[60]

Politically inspired attacks subsided briefly in March 1993, but SOC officials continued to kill and injure opponents at an increasing rate up to the election—which was judged, nonetheless, to have met minimal standards of fairness. The record of violence was further marred by the refusal of the DK and its "national army" (NADK) to enter the electoral contest and by its violent assaults against local officials of the SOC and ethnic Vietnamese. In the end, UNTAC personnel were also targeted by the NADK, with eleven killings and forty-two acts of anti-UNTAC violence recorded.[61] The SOC, on the other hand, indulged in harassment and intimidation of its party rivals in 121 cases, made political threats of violence in 49 cases, and used illegal arrest and detention for political reasons 30 times. The NADK, lacking public office from which to use such corrupt tactics, fell well short of the SOC in these Human Rights Component tallies of antidemocratic behavior.

The Human Rights Component not only monitored the condition of human rights, while preaching a new faith in democratic and humane behavior, but also had a mandate to take "corrective action." Here its record

59. The typology of violence and the data that follow are found in UNTAC, *Human Rights Component Final Report*, chap. 2.
60. Ibid., p. 29.
61. Ibid., Appendix 3, Investigations Statistics.

has received less indulgent evaluation than in regard to its promotion and investigation efforts. Yet some tangible remedies were registered for the pitiful conditions of provincial prisons under SOC. In June 1992, about four hundred prisoners languished in Phnom Penh jails, and all but twenty of them had never been taken before a court. In August, 140 were released outright in Phnom Penh and 90 more in the provinces.

The CivPol visited these sites under rules worked out with the SOC which sought to protect prisoners from reprisals. The Human Rights Component adopted guidelines for prison monitoring which sought to bring the physical conditions up to international standards, and to release political prisoners and those requiring serious medical treatment. In pursuit of these goals the commonplace but painful practice of shackling prisoners was officially banned by the Ministry of National Security, even though it surreptitiously survived in some areas. The use of solitary confinement and withholding of exercise also persisted, and the component authorized its officers in February 1993 to physically remove any shackling irons they encountered and to release any prisoners from dark isolation cells.[62]

The second most important work of the component in the prisons was to ensure due process. This was tackled by a SOC-appointed Prisons Commission in regard to detention without trial. Yet, even though 230 prisoners were released outright, and 73 were finally referred to the Phnom Penh People's Tribunal for trial, sad to say, the trials never took place, and the prisons soon filled up again. The survey of prisons had to be repeated in July 1993. In the absence of a functioning legal system, prison officials treated prisoners without supervision, were susceptible to bribes, indifferent to inhuman deprivation and ill health, and oblivious to concepts of due process. The indifference and ineptness of the court system pushed the component to set up its own prison for detaining (in questionable compliance with due process) persons arrested by UNTAC. It was clearly appropriate that the Human Rights Component was authorized to continue its work after the departure of all other elements of UNTAC.

The hapless state of the courts of the SOC, and their total absence in the areas controlled by the other factions, made clear the value of training courses generated by the Human Rights Component. The component provided special training, a two-day symposium, and considerable coaching of potential communicators such as teachers and police in the task of educating a nation to internationally endorsed standards of civic behavior. Radio and TV dialogues, radio spots, and pamphlets (for 500,000 persons) were

62. Ibid., pp. 16, 19–20.

created to educate an ignorant public about human rights. Yet, simultaneous with the campaign to educate regarding human rights, glaring cases calling for "corrective action" caught the eye.

Even though the agreement authorized UNTAC to investigate complaints of human rights abuses and, "as appropriate," to take "corrective action," the exact dimensions of such activity were not detailed. This enabled the Cambodian parties regularly to contest UNTAC's investigations and proposed remedies for complaints. The issue was further complicated by Special Representative Akashi's desire to rely on persuasion rather than coercion of relevant Cambodian authorities "to meet their responsibilities" to maintain law and order and human rights.[63] UNTAC held potential sanctions in its hands, such as job transfers or dismissal, or legal prosecution against delinquent officials, but their application depended on the cooperation of Cambodian officials. As the component later reported, it quickly became "clear that the Cambodian Parties, particularly SOC, were reluctant to allow direct control in the manner envisaged by the Paris Agreements."[64] Charges against a SOC policeman were declared by SOC to be false, and requests for removal or demotion of officials were firmly refused. No SOC or DK official encountered any corrective action, and even when UNTAC managed to arrest four individuals on its own authority it had to build its own detention facility to avoid the inhumane conditions of the existing SOC prison. Two of the four, accused of assassination, escaped before they could be transferred to the UNTAC facility. Even when UNTAC decided to create its own special prosecutor, Mark Plunket of Australia, it lacked a competent court or a safe house to protect witnesses for the prosecution. The idea of importing foreign judges as an interim measure was rejected as bearing the taint of colonialism.[65]

In the end, the Human Rights Component deserves credit for trying to overhaul a lawless society, and its efforts earned the rating "modest success" by the Twentieth Century Fund analyst Janet Heininger, even though *Asia Watch* called it a "poor model" for the post-UNTAC government which "encouraged grave abuses in the future."[66] Violations of human rights have surely continued since UNTAC's withdrawal of all but its special representative for human rights, but a growing segment of the nation's citizenry has become aware of a modern conception of the rights of individuals in relation to governments. Up to week-long training courses for government offi-

---

63. Ibid., p. 39.
64. Ibid., p. 40.
65. Ibid., p. 46, and Findlay, *Cambodia: The Legacy and Lessons of UNTAC*, p. 149.
66. Heininger, *Peacekeeping in Transition*, pp. 100, 96.

cials and sessions for ninety thousand students were conducted; and syllabi for human rights courses at the university, particularly the law school, were conceived and polished. A variety of media were used to reach tens of thousands of ordinary people, from monks to policemen, in the countryside. Yet the continuing abuses cannot help but discourage those who hold Cambodia to the highest standards. Such expectations, however, after a history of political repression are unreasonable and misleading.

A few solid steps have been made toward a steady public sensitivity to the rights of human beings. A Center for Human Rights and indigenous support groups with up to fifty thousand members have been created, and a special trust fund for teaching projects has been launched.[67] The soil for such undertakings is clearly poor, but seeds have been sown, and the regenerating Cambodian civil society must seek continuing generosity from outside and growing decency from within to bring the fragile plant to full growth.

Repatriation Component

Unlike the other UNTAC operations, the Repatriation Component started with preexisting structures and seasoned personnel. It also benefited from a basic document of instruction, Annex 4 of the Paris Agreement, which built on the work of the Third Committee of the 1989 Paris Conference on Cambodia. Annex 4, which follows (sometimes word-for-word) the Third Committee's report of August 25, 1990, calls for the "voluntary return of all Cambodian refugees and displaced persons in a peaceful and orderly manner." Some of them were expected "to return spontaneously to their homeland," which they did. Mass repatriation was "to be completed as soon as possible," to ensure participation in the election. Repatriation should be voluntary and the decision to return "should be taken in full possession of the facts." "The international community should contribute generously to the financial requirements of the repatriation operation."[68] This was estimated to cost $92.5 million, and UNTAC was supposed to cost $1.6 billion.

The office of the United Nations High Commissioner for Refugees (UNHCR)was designated in July 1989 by the UN secretary-general as the "lead agency," under Sergio Vieira de Mello as director. A memorandum of

67. A detailed resume of the Human Rights Component's accomplishments is found in *Human Rights Component Final Report*, chap. 3.

68. Annex 4, "Repatriation of Cambodian Refugees and Displaced Persons," Agreement on a Comprehensive Political Settlement of the Cambodia Conflict, Paris, Oct. 23, 1991.

understanding was negotiated in November 1991 between the UNHCR, the Royal Thai Government and the SNC. Contingency planning and a population survey had been started already in 1989, with the support of the Ford Foundation. The UN secretary-general presented to the Paris conference in August 1989 a useful ten-page note, "Requirements for Planning of the Repatriation of the Cambodian Refugees and Displaced Persons in Thailand."[69] The UN Border Relief Organization (UNBRO), created in 1982, had been coordinating a score of relief agencies in the refugee camps along the Thai-Cambodian border. In 1990, the UNHCR organized workshops for fifteen international organizations and twenty-seven NGOs, such as Catholic Relief Services, Medécins sans frontières France, the International Rescue Committee, and UN-affiliated agencies such as the UN Development Program, UNICEF, the World Food Program, and the International Committee of the Red Cross. These agencies had acquired years of experience with the border camp population and were more than ready to see the operation ended by the total resettlement of their beneficiaries. Thus, the repatriation and resettlement of more than 360,000 Cambodians residing in 1992 almost astride the border could realistically be scheduled to occur prior to the election, with every intention of seeing the returning population vote. In the end, the spontaneous repatriation of thousands of eligible refugees helped to make the timetable work.

Given its advantage in experience, it is not surprising that the Repatriation Component was considered "one of the most successful aspects" of UNTAC.[70] Even higher praise came from the former Australian diplomat Trevor Findlay, who considered the operation "particularly impressive."[71] Such praise is well warranted when one considers the dimensions of the undertaking and the striking fact that not a single fatality occurred during this immense population transfer. Some 362,209 persons were moved to their homeland in time for the adults to vote in May 1993.

The Cambodian border population grew out of the Vietnamese invasion of December 1978, which uprooted the oppressive Khmer Rouge social structure and caused thousands of Cambodians to flee the invaders or seek out either their former villages or new opportunities in western provinces. The winter rice harvest and spring planting were widely neglected, and by April 1979 a serious food shortage manifested itself, worsened by the added

69. Amitav Acharya et al., eds., *Cambodia—The 1989 Paris Peace Conference: Background Analysis and Documents* (Toronto: Centre for International and Strategic Studies, 1991), pp. 206–16.

70. Peter Utting, ed., *Between Hope and Insecurity: The Social Consequences of the Cambodian Peace Process* (Geneva: UN Research Institute for Social Development, 1994), p. 186.

71. Findlay, *Cambodia: The Legacy and Lessons of UNTAC*, chap.4.

demand of 200,000 invading Vietnamese troops. As the wave of displaced farmers, aspiring tradesmen, and routed Khmer Rouge soldiers and their families reached the western border, the Thai were unwilling to admit them, and the Cambodians were fearful of turning back. A second wave of hungry, exhausted migrants seeking food, medicine, and shelter reached the border in the fall of 1979, posing an international dilemma. Thailand was unwilling to settle the Khmer refugees on its soil even though it was willing to have international donors finance the sustenance of over 300,000 border camp dwellers, many of them resistance soldiers, sitting as a buffer between Vietnamese forces and Thailand. International aid also extended to Thai farmers of the border region who were compensated for the disruption by the newcomers to their local economy.[72] In October 1979, Thailand agreed to create "holding centers" inside its borders, financed by international donations, for what it called "illegal immigrants."

Worldwide sympathy for the suffering migrants generated by televised reportage of very undernourished Cambodian children eventually inspired extensive international relief operations late in 1979, as the second wave of arrivals at the border desperately sought food and medicine. Supply and distribution by such groups as Oxfam, the World Food Program, the International Committee of the Red Cross, and UNICEF were organized, at first on an emergency basis, via both Thailand and Phnom Penh. There was, however, no willingness to reduce the problem through large-scale resettlement abroad. The number of genuine political refugees, with a well-grounded fear of persecution should they return home, was not extensive, except among the Khmer Rouge—who were not interested in emigration. So, more than 350,000 displaced Cambodians eventually settled into camps along the border, confined by Thai military authorities, administered by the resistance parties and military chiefs, and supplied with basic human needs by international organizations, even though guerrilla soldiers were not supposed to receive aid (but did by means of vast inflation of camp population figures). For ordinary camp dwellers life was defined by waiting for the civil war in Cambodia to end, at which time they might care to return home, a few with economic assets acquired from smuggling and local trading, but most with their personal possessions in a few plastic sacks.

---

72. These intricacies are traced in Linda Mason and Roger Brown, *Race, Rivalry, and Politics: Managing Cambodian Relief* (Notre Dame, Ind.: University of Notre Dame Press, 1983), chap. 2. William Shawcross reveals the exaggerated forecasts of starvation that helped to generate the international relief effort in 1979 in *The Quality of Mercy: Cambodia, Holocaust, and Modern Conscience* (New York: Simon and Schuster, 1984), chap. 18. See also Asia Watch, *Political Control, Human Rights, and the UN Mission in Cambodia* (Washington, D.C.: Human Rights Watch, 1992).

The Repatriation Component clearly benefited from the cooperation of the factions, including the Khmer Rouge. The self-interest of the factions and UNTAC coincided in regard to getting Cambodians out of the camps and into Cambodia, to enter a new phase of political struggle. The Paris Agreement laid down the principle of a free choice of place for resettlement and mode of assistance upon reentering Cambodia. This was not opposed by the Khmer Rouge even though they had long isolated their seventy-five thousand followers in KR-administered border camps. The working principle of the repatriation operation was free choice by individuals, with encouragement for family units. With the advent of the cease-fire in 1991, the military struggle of the resistance factions no longer depended on maintaining the border camps as home bases for their guerrilla units.

Notwithstanding its overall success, the repatriation operation started poorly with an expensive aerial survey looking for mine-free land for distribution to the predominantly farmer population of the border camps. Such land, and acquiring title to it, proved to be far less attainable than planned for, so the component shifted its course to attract the returnees to other options, particularly cash start-up transfers. Eighty-eight percent eventually chose cash and only 3 percent chose land, while 7 percent chose a housing plot.[73] The camp population was young—90 percent under the age of forty-five, and almost half under fifteen. Even though farming was the predominant pre-camp occupation, few had practiced it in the preceding decade. Eventually the cash option proved to be far more attractive to the former farmers; but the clearing of mines from agricultural land limped slowly along. The returning camp population redistributed themselves primarily in the western provinces whence most of them originated (57 percent from Battambang province), and where they could retain an escape route toward Thailand.

The process of guaranteeing a free choice of destination proved to be less complicated than anticipated. The initial scheme was to bring all migrants to a neutral staging camp, where they could choose their final destination privately and independently of the faction camp in which they had been living. This proved to be too complicated and unnecessary. The families made their choice without coercion by faction camp cohorts. Miscalculation also marred the proposed timetable of only six months to complete the resettlement, but the camps did close in a year's time, before the election.

The new options devised by the Repatriation Component were announced in May 1992, to supplement the basic choice of two hectares of agricultural land in a chosen place, with materials for a house. A new possi-

---

73. *The United Nations and Cambodia, 1991–1995*, p. 33.

bility was land and materials for a house, plus a cash allotment of $20; or cash only ($50 per adult and $25 per child below twelve years); or a kit with tools for a rural, nonagricultural business such as carpentry, electrical work, or bicycle repair, or a "kit for women." Each of these options would include a household kit of tools and food for twelve months (only six months for persons going to Phnom Penh).[74] In the end, more than 80 percent of the returnees chose the cash-only option, in some cases after they had preferred a land-based option but found it unavailable. The displaced Cambodians chose to fend for themselves more readily than their longtime benefactors and supervisors had anticipated.

Thus the advent to power of the Khmer Rouge, which began in 1975 with a brutal, doctrinaire evacuation of the cities in order to establish harsh communal farming in the countryside, was put to further shame seventeen years later, by a carefully planned and safely executed transfer of population based on free choice of destination and worldwide economic and managerial support.

The atmosphere of the repatriation could not have been more different from that of the Khmer Rogue evacuation. In March 1992 the first truck and bus caravans set out from staging camps in Thailand to reception centers in Cambodia. The first full use of railroad, which the authors attended, occurred three months later. Each family, long accustomed to dependency and little privacy, waited patiently at the reception grounds to pick up their few belongings, wrapped, except perhaps for a child's tricycle, in blue plastic waterproof sheets or sacks. Then they proceeded to the bamboo thatch huts to which they were assigned for a day or two before moving on to their chosen destination. So many of these people had never stood in their home country before. The self-discipline and patience these day-long travelers displayed, waiting for the crowd to thin out in the direction of their huts, as the Cambodian Red Cross personnel prepared an evening meal for the weary families, was quite awesome. Within a week they would be coping with independent life, sustained in many cases by family, but often with no close relatives alive to receive them. The cash grant, or the kit of tools and supplies for farmers, would be theirs to manage, after living more than a decade as inmates in teeming and precarious camps, dependent on charitable organizations for daily water trucks, bamboo thatch shelters dirt road maintenance, basic sanitation, medical attention, and hope. The longed-for self-sustaining life with surviving family was about to be realized.

---

74. Asia Watch, *Political Control*, p. 51.

Rehabilitation and Reconstruction

The task of rebuilding Cambodia economically was bolstered by a separate document signed at the Paris peace conference the Declaration on the Rehabilitation and Reconstruction of Cambodia. This agreement, containing thirteen brief paragraphs, was derived almost word for word from the report of the Third Committee of the Paris Conference on Cambodia on August 25, 1989 (two years before the final Paris conference), and it set forth prudent principles to observe in reconstructing the nation. Warning notes resounded concerning fair distribution of aid, respect for human rights, coordination of sources, immediate versus long-term needs, private entrepreneurship, and consultation among donors. Rehabilitation of the impoverished, war-racked country was expected to focus on immediate needs in food, security, health, housing, training, education, transportation, and restoration of basic infrastructure (especially roads) and public utilities—a staggering challenge, given the lack of investment capital and the fragile coalition governance to be provided via SNC and UNTAC. After the election, the declaration proclaimed, a longer-term international development plan should be initiated by the new government. The United Nations system was to help set up an International Committee on the Reconstruction of Cambodia, open to potential donors and "other relevant parties," and charged with achieving a smooth transition from rehabilitation to reconstruction after the election. Fact-finding missions from the United Nations system were expected soon to visit the scene of economic desperation.

Notwithstanding this special emphasis, and the triumphant record level of aid pledged by the international ministerial conference for aid to Cambodia, held in Tokyo on June 22, 1992, the Rehabilitation Component did not turn out to be as effective as its mandate warranted. Michael Doyle judged it "one of the least effective parts of UNTAC."[75] At Tokyo, thirty-three nations pledged $880 million, well above the secretary-general's target figure for dealing with rural development and refugee resettlement, infrastructure renewal, and budget support. Actual disbursal lagged far behind. The component lost two directors, through resignation or dismissal,[76] and finally was placed under the economic adviser to the special representative, an American, Roger Lawrence. The component's task, unlike those of the other components, was the planning and coordinating of funds and

75. Doyle, in *Peacekeeping in Cambodia*, p. 58. It "fell far short of its goals," p. 50.
76. Ibid., p. 51.

projects made available and administered by international donors. Its staff was only a dozen or more economic specialists.

During the ten months before the election, only $100 million was actually disbursed, in quick-impact projects, much of it for refugee resettlement. These projects, initiated by the UNHCR, included road and bridge repair, mine clearance, agricultural development, digging of wells and ponds, and construction of health and sanitation facilities. A major cause of the implementation lag was the objections raised particularly by the PDK with respect to political neutrality in the distribution of rehabilitation projects. The Khmer Rouge initially withheld its approval in the SNC of projects for which the SOC might gain credit and support as the administering authority. The same way of thinking delayed the SNC from reaching agreement to accept a World Bank loan to cover the current budget deficit of the SOC. Such assistance the PDK considered to be un-neutral, and the final decision to accept it was made by SNC President Sihanouk, in accordance with his powers under the Paris Agreements. The issue continued to raise conflict and cause delays up to the election, despite earnest efforts by the component to work out a statement at the Tokyo Conference that "Cambodia" refers "to the whole territory of Cambodia or to the administrations of all Cambodian parties."[77] The international banks were not always sensitive to the political fallout of dealing directly with the SOC, rather than with the SNC, which was created to represent all four parties.[78]

The economy of Cambodia was not only frightfully weakened by the long civil war but also historically unbalanced, and the UNTAC presence and economic demand both stimulated and distorted it. Agriculture constituted the overwhelming element of Cambodia's economy, engaging 80 percent of the labor force and about half of the gross domestic product (GDP). Industry contributed only 19 percent of GDP, most of it very small-scale. Mining activity was also limited but politically significant. The foreign economic planners recruited by UNTAC to struggle with both immediate and long-term development needs found precious few Cambodian economic technicians to work with, and far from a consensus on priorities, projects, and programs. Even though foreign donor and business interests were sympathetic to humanitarian needs, they were quite averse to the risks regarding investment ventures. To further complicate the prob-

77. "Second Progress Report of the Secretary-General" on UNTAC, Sep. 21, 1992, in *The United Nations and Cambodia, 1991–1995*, Doc. 45, p. 21. Some twenty three project proposals were at risk.

78. Steven R. Ratner, *The New UN Peacekeeping: Building Peace in Lands of Conflict after the Cold War* (New York: St. Martin's, 1995), chap. 7, p. 183.

lem, the UNTAC presence itself skewed the economy toward service sector activities, such as restaurants, banks, hotels, and transportation, and toward urban needs.[79] Attention to long-term development programs was not easily maintained, as commercial activity surged. The export of timber and gems to Thailand, however, became the major source of income for the Khmer Rouge. It also threatened the prudent management of the nation's precious stock of timber.

The SNC's Technical Advisory Committee on natural resource exploitation prepared a directive in September 1992 banning the export of logs and later of gems, which made sense as natural resource management but also aimed, ineffectually, at shutting down the illicit revenue garnered by the Khmer Rouge from their timber and mining areas' assets. A true shutdown of this lucrative commerce would have required cooperation by the Thai military along the border, which did not occur during UNTAC's lifetime. The UN Security Council recommended to the SNC that it impose a moratorium starting December 31, 1992, on the export of logs; and the SNC added a ban on oil sales to Khmer Rouge areas for good measure. Another conservation measure approved by the SNC in 1993 was the establishment of a National Heritage Protection Authority of Cambodia to coordinate, with UNESCO's help, the restoration of world-renowned Angkor Wat and other cultural monuments.

Notwithstanding the PDK's objections to letting international financial institutions deal with the SOC rather than the SNC, international nongovernmental organizations made welcome progress by funding over forty modest quick-impact projects (by January 1993), many outside Phnom Penh. These included job training for health care, rural development, road and bridge repair, sanitation projects, and air traffic control. The long-term development needs of Cambodia remained awesome, however, and outside donors remained wary of trying to work in so broken-down an economic system. The Rehabilitation Component helped to coordinate quick-impact, immediate-need reconstruction projects, but in a time span of only a year and a half it could not make a dent on the long-term development priorities of a seriously crippled economy.

79. William Shawcross, *Cambodia's New Deal* (Washington, D.C.: Carnegie Endowment for International Peace, 1994), chap. 4; and the World Bank, East Asia Pacific Region, *Cambodia: Rehabilitation Program: Implementation*, February 1995, pp. I–VII.

Information/Education

The most surprising performance among the elements of UNTAC was registered by the Information and Education Division. These specialists, concerned with informing the Khmer nation and providing massive civic education about the elections and human rights (as well as mine awareness), were assigned to Akashi's office under the leadership of Tim Carney, a veteran U.S. Foreign Service officer on loan to the UN. American researcher Steve Heder, another Khmer speaker, previously with Amnesty International, helped to validate translations of UNTAC announcements and documents, and to avoid linguistic and cultural mistakes and malapropisms that most of their dedicated Cambodian staff writers were bound to make from time to time. The total staff allowed to this division was to be thirty-two, but by June 1992 only ten had been found and taken aboard.[80] Finding personnel who possessed both language and communications skills in radio, press, video, leaflets, and computer was a continuing adventure throughout the short happy life of the Information and Education Division. Some of its remarkably dedicated workers were virtual "walk-ons," travelers off the streets of Phnom Penh.

The radio facilities existing at the outset, under the control of the SOC, reached barely half the country, and not until April 1993 was Radio UNTAC able, with its own equipment, to cover the entire Cambodian population. The SOC was not willing at first to share its own transmitter, a Russian aid relic of former times. Eventually UNTAC obtained its own facility, which was very closely guarded by Ghanaian troops. Until that point they depended on the help of the Voice of America in Thailand, which rented hours of use twice a day for reaching the Thai-Cambodia border area. Secretary-General Boutros-Ghali was initially opposed to creating a centralized broadcasting outlet, but in the end the voice of UNTAC fully vindicated its resourceful struggle and earned a rating as "one of the most successful components" in Cambodia, even as "UNTAC's most unqualified success," by William Shawcross.[81]

The most important feature of the information/education effort was not only its daily radio broadcasting, which grew to fifteen hours per day in

---

80. Authors' interview with Steve Heder, June 25, 1992, Phnom Penh.

81. Shawcross, p. 18; and Heininger, *Peacekeeping in Transition*, p. 116. Steven R. Ratner, *The New UN Peacekeeping*, p. 184, hailed the division as a "major success." Doyle, *UN Peacekeeping in Cambodia*, described the division as "one of the stars of UNTAC." A somewhat playful account of the bureaucratic struggles and adaptability of the improvising staff at Radio UNTAC is found in Zhou Mei, *Radio UNTAC of Cambodia*.

April 1993, but its ability to inform the potential electorate that an honest election was being prepared and that the ballot would remain secret at every polling station. The donation of radios (and one thousand cassette recorders) by the Japanese government and NGOs, which eventually, reached a totaled 347,804, played a special role in reaching the brooding electorate. The major political parties utilized their own broadcasting facilities on a partisan basis, even though it required the strong intervention of UNTAC to get the SOC to release TV broadcasting equipment already imported by FUNCINPEC.[82] UNTAC radio tried to build its credibility by scrupulous neutrality and accuracy. It guaranteed the "right of response" to any candidate or political party that believed itself to be a victim of unfair attack or misrepresentation of its public statements. Interviews with UNTAC officials were used to help popularize its intrusive mission. Eventually, round-table discussions including representatives of the twenty political parties contesting the election were shown on television in Phnom Penh and distributed to the provinces where "video parlors" served as TV program sponsors. UNTAC advertised the upcoming election with billboards, banners, and posters for all the parties, and this surely helped in inspiring 95 percent of the eligible electorate to register.

The PDK Radio, however, grew hostile to the election during 1992 and refused to broadcast Radio UNTAC information and public awareness materials.[83] The goal of fair media access, even though translated into "Media Guidelines" for all the political parties, was not attainable. The SOC, as well as the PDK, rejected any attempt by UNTAC to exercise a priori editorial control of their TV broadcasts or newspapers.[84] The SOC also refused for some months to allow UNTAC to use the SOC TV transmitter for broadcasting neutral information concerning the coming election.

The challenges of communicating with the largely illiterate Cambodian nation were met not only with broadcasting and video, but also with simple cartoon-form flyers with as few as six scenes depicting the process of military regroupment, disarming, reeducation, graduation, and reunion with family. These were addressed to all four parties, which were distinguished in the cartoon scenes by their distinctive military uniform caps. Radio skits and dialogues between "Aunt and Uncle" were equally bare-bones and

82. *The United Nations and Cambodia, 1991–1995*, p. 39. A similar attitude toward an independent radio, offering propaganda-free news to the populace during an election period, was found in Bosnia in August 1996, where the government refused to issue frequencies to nongovernment broadcasters and opposed the idea of "free media." *New York Times*, Aug. 23, 1996.

83. *The United Nations and Cambodia, 1991–1995*, "Overview," p. 39.

84. Doyle, *UN Peacekeeping in Cambodia*, pp. 54–55.

homely, with careful scripting conveying a message of hope for a new era. Such programs helped to explain how to register and vote.

A function associated with educating and training the electorate was the monitoring of public opinion, which Heder was able to supervise in the interests of knowing what Radio UNTAC's audience was thinking. The effort created a sort of UNTAC political intelligence unit (in the office of the UN special representative) capable of producing systematic reports on the activities of the parties in the key provinces.[85] Such measurement of popular opinion, even though less reliable than voter surveys in Western democracies, was surely helpful to the special representative's office as well as the Election Component, and it will doubtless merit reenactment in future peacekeeping operations.

Thus, the essential functions required of UNTAC by the Paris Agreements were addressed with a workable organizational design and widespread institutional zeal. The tasks so hopefully set by the Paris Agreements were not equally achievable, but lasting evidence of UNTAC's impact was recorded in the holding of a national election and the working of a constituent assembly and interim administration, followed by the promulgation of a constitution and the installation of a national coalition government. The departure of UNTAC by the end of 1993 would launch the "failed state" into a new era, with sole responsibility for its domestic reconstruction and its international relations.

How effectively would the new state meet the challenge?

85. Ibid., p. 55. Steve Heder (June 25, 1992, interview in Phnom Penh) preferred to call these reports "local snapshots," not opinion surveys. A sample report is found in Utting, *Between Hope and Insecurity*, pp. 174–78.

CHAPTER FOUR

Conducting the Election, 1992–1993

In Cambodia the UN, for the first time, assumed responsibility for directly conducting an election. In other countries, including Namibia and Nicaragua, the UN had served as monitor or observer. In Cambodia, UNTAC was responsible for initiating and administering an election, an undertaking that turned out to be *the* centerpiece of the UN effort at peacemaking.

The Paris Agreements of 1991 proclaimed that the Cambodian people had a right to determine their own political future through a "free and fair" election of a Constituent Assembly. The assembly would draft and approve a constitution, and then transform itself into a legislative assembly, which would create the new Cambodian government. UNTAC was charged with creating a "neutral political environment" for the election and with maintaining "full respect for the national sovereignty of Cambodia." The signatories to the agreements committed themselves to respect the results of the election, once it was certified by the UN as "free and fair."[1]

The agreements set forth instructions for UNTAC to follow in conducting the elections. UNTAC was to "consult with" the Supreme National Council (SNC) in many of its tasks, but responsibility for the final decisions lay with UNTAC. UNTAC was invested with authority to carry out the following tasks in organizing the electoral process:

- create an electoral law and a code of conduct regulating participation in the election;

1. Agreement on a Comprehensive Political Settlement of the Cambodia Conflict, Paris, Oct. 23, 1991, Part II, art. 12–14.

- design a voter education program; design a voter registration program;
- design a program for registering political parties;
- ensure fair access to the media for all political parties contesting the election;
- facilitate the participation of Cambodians in the electoral process;
- design balloting procedures;
- make arrangements for foreign observation of the campaign and voting;
- direct the polling and vote count;
- deal with complaints of electoral irregularities;
- determine whether the election was free and fair, and certify those candidates who were elected.

In carrying out these tasks, UNTAC was instructed to take measures to guard against fraud and to set up mechanisms for dealing with complaints. UNTAC was to establish a timetable for the various phases of the electoral process, ensuring that it would be completed within nine months from the commencement of voter registration. Finally, UNTAC was admonished to see that the electoral procedures would be impartial and that the administration of them would be simple and efficient.[2]

In Annex 3, devoted exclusively to elections, the agreement provided additional guidance concerning the electoral process. The Constituent Assembly, which would consist of 120 members, was to draft and adopt the new constitution within three months of the election and, as noted above, transform itself into a legislative assembly which would form the new government. The electoral law (discussed below) was to provide for a provincially based system of proportional representation with a list of candidates proposed by political parties. All Cambodians, including refugees and displaced persons, were to have the same rights and opportunities to take part in the electoral process. Any group of five thousand registered voters could form a political party, provided that its platform was consistent with the principles of the agreement. All candidates were required to have a party affiliation and to appear on the list of registered voters that the parties were obliged to submit to UNTAC. UNTAC was to confirm that the parties and candidates met the criteria for participation in the election. Further, UNTAC, in consultation with the SNC, would establish a code of conduct to which all participants must adhere. Voting would be by secret ballot. Finally, freedom of speech, assembly, and movement were to be respected and all parties were to enjoy fair access to the media.[3]

2. Ibid., Annex 1, Section D.
3. Ibid., Annex 3.

Implementing the Electoral Mandate

An election in Cambodia presented UNTAC with major challenges. Very few UN personnel knew the language, culture, and customs of Cambodia, and technical expertise in election management was also scarce. Limited time was available to recruit, train, and deploy the necessary personnel. Cambodians had little experience with free elections. In a country wracked by political turbulence in the preceding decades, the potential for factional and ethnic violence, political intimidation, and cease-fire violations remained high. The electoral process had to be coordinated with other complicated activities, including the return of refugees and displaced persons and the disarming, cantoning, and demobilizing of the factional armies.

Members of the UNTAC Electoral Component understood the importance that their operation played in the larger peace process. A high official of the Electoral Component, in Phnom Penh in July 1992, readily averred that the test of the election would be to bring forth a "functioning, legitimate government, accepted by the previous warring parties." That was the aim of the Paris Agreements, he noted. Yet the "UN is *not* an imperial body creating a new government. Whether it succeeds depends upon the role of Cambodians."[4] Success for this enterprise was far from certain.

The Electoral Law

Drawing on UN experience in Namibia, the Electoral Component prepared a draft law.[5] It outlined the administration of the election, listed requirements for the registration of political parties and of voters, allocated seats according to provinces, regulated the campaign activity, provided instructions for the polling and tabulation of the election result, and prescribed a code of conduct for all participants. At least five or six UNTAC officials in the Electoral Component, including the deputy director, had served in the UN-guided election in Namibia.[6] The director of the Electoral Component, Reginald Austin, a respected professor of law from the University of Zimbabwe, had closely followed the Namibia election from Zambia, a front-line state. Trevor Findlay, analyzing the UNTAC performance, commented on the electoral process that "this is one case where the

4. Interview by the authors with Michael Maley, deputy director of UNTAC Electoral Component, Phnom Penh, July 1, 1992.
5. United Nations Electoral Law for the Conduct of a Free and Fair Election of a Constituent Assembly for Cambodia, 1992, dated March 31, 1992 (56 pages, single-spaced).
6. Interview with Michael Maley.

UN learned from previous experience, something that cannot be said for other aspects of the Cambodian operation."[7]

Between the time that UNTAC introduced the draft electoral law, on April 1, 1992, and its adoption by the SNC on August 5, 1992, the Cambodian factions debated some of its provisions. Particularly salient were the definition of eligibility to vote and permission for Cambodians overseas to vote.[8] Regarding voting eligibility, the Paris Agreement had stipulated that "Every person who has reached the age of eighteen . . . and who either was born in Cambodia or is the child of a person born in Cambodia, will be eligible to vote in the election."[9]

A contentious debate ensued which raised the question as to whether ethnic Vietnamese, particularly those who had lived in Cambodia for several generations, would be entitled to vote. The PDK were vehemently opposed to eligibility for possible ethnic Vietnamese voters. The FUNCINPEC and BLDP were not far behind the PDK in expressing their hostility to the "danger" of Vietnamese voting. The CPP showed themselves to be more indulgent on the issue, probably with the expectation that they would benefit from an ethnic Vietnamese vote. Yasushi Akashi, the special representative of the UN secretary-general supported the SNC enactment that the franchise be resticted to "Cambodian persons" (i.e., non-Vietnamese) who were born in Cambodia *and* had at least one parent born in Cambodia.[10]

On the issue of voting by Cambodians living abroad, the FUNCINPEC and BLDP, who had reason to expect to gain from this voting group, proposed that all Cambodians should be permitted to both register and vote at designated polling stations abroad. The electoral law adopted by the SNC on August 5, 1992, permitted Cambodians living overseas to vote at one polling station in Europe, one in North America, and one in Australia, provided that they had personally registered in Cambodia.[11]

Another controversial issue relevant to the electoral law had been debated and submitted to compromise in the fall of 1991, even before the draft law was formally presented to the SNC. The CPP, calculating that it had the best chance to command a majority vote in most districts, called for

7. Trevor Findlay, *Cambodia: The Legacy and Lessons of UNTAC*, Stockholm International Peace Research Institute Report No. 9 (Oxford: Oxford University Press, 1995), p. 56.

8. *The United Nations and Cambodia, 1991–1995*, with an introduction by Boutros Boutros-Ghali, Secretary-General of the United Nations (New York: UN Department of Public Information, 1995), p. 28.

9. Agreement on a Comprehensive Political Settlement of the Cambodia Conflict, Annex 3, para. 4.

10. *The United Nations and Cambodia, 1991–1995*, p. 28.

11. Ibid.

a single-member district constituency. The former CGDK factions, judging that they would fare poorly in such an electoral process, supported the UN plan for proportional representation. As we have seen, this issue reached a compromise in September 1991, during a meeting at the UN General Assembly, when the four factions agreed to a cluster of arrangements. Hun Sen dropped the CPP's insistence on a reference to genocide in the constitution, settling for a guarantee of the protection of human rights. Searching for credibility in the international community, he agreed to voting by proportional representation, with each of the twenty provinces receiving a portion of the assembly seats, in accordance with their number of registered voters. Each party was to submit a list of candidates, and the province's seats were to be awarded to the parties in proportion to their total vote in the province, distributed in order of their ranking on their party's list.

As events unfolded, parties listed far more candidates in every province than there were seats to win. This was to make certain that there would be enough registered candidates left, as Michael Vickery writes, "if some resigned, switched sides, or met an untimely end."[12] FUNCINPEC and the BLDP followed the procedure of appointing candidates to the assembly in order of their placement on the province list. After the announcement of the election outcome but before UNTAC's designation of the winning candidates, thirty-two of the CPP candidates whose placement on the list made them winners resigned, making way for candidates further down on the list to take seats. It appears that the CPP had expected to fare better in the voting, and the postelection juggling was conducted to meet factional political obligations.

The UNTAC Electoral Component gave primary importance to the requirement that the vote be secret. The deputy director, Michael Maley, in an interview in July 1992, emphasized the signal effort that UNTAC would make to get the message to voters that their vote was secret. (Widespread commentary by international observers after the election confirmed that UNTAC had effectively conveyed this message.) Enormous logistical problems confronted the Electoral Component. These included meshing into the complicated timetable, which all components faced. Further, the electoral staff had to "hack its way through the UN bureaucracy, not designed to move fast." It needed computers to compose voter lists and registration cards. In countries accustomed to elections, there are personnel who have served at the polls and can be given refresher training. All of the more than

---

12. Michael Vickery, "The Cambodian People's Party: Where Has It Come from, Where Is It Going?" in *Southeast Asian Affairs, 1994* (Singapore: Institute of Southeast Asian Studies, 1994), p. 111.

fifty thousand Cambodians who were to be recruited as election officials had to be provided initial training.

The Phased Implementation

As previously discussed, the election was part of an intricate phasing process laid out for UNTAC by the secretary-general's plan. Phase I, (preparation), from November 1991 to June 1992, was carried out by the UN Advance Mission in Cambodia (UNAMIC). Phase II, from June to September 1992, was to effect the disarmament, cantonment, and demobilization of 70 percent of the military forces of the four factions and the cantonment of the remaining 30 percent. Their arms were to be surrendered to UNTAC's military units.

The electoral process was to be conducted as Phase III, from October 1992 through April 1993. (Elections were actually held May 23–28, 1993.) During this period, UNTAC's tasks were to resettle more than 350,000 refugees, register eligible voters and political parties, oversee the electoral campaign, train Cambodian election workers, recruit and deploy UN Volunteers to assist in the election, conduct the polling, count the ballots, and certify the outcome.

Voter Registration

From October 5, 1992, until January 31, 1993, the Advance Election Planning Unit (AEPU) undertook a remarkably effective voter registration campaign. They succeeded in registering some 4.6 million potential voters, representing nearly all of the estimated eligible voters to whom UNTAC had territorial access.[13] The AEPU managed to penetrate some Khmer Rouge–controlled areas and even registered some KR soldiers and their commanders, despite the KR's opposition to the election.[14] The AEPU created a Cambodian-language computer system that could store as many as 5.2 million voter registration records. The electoral unit prepared laminated voter identity cards that contained a color photograph and fingerprint of the prospective voter. UN Volunteers and UNTAC staff reported that

13. *The United Nation and Cambodia, 1991–1995*, p. 29.
14. Findlay, *Cambodia: The Legacy and Lessons of UNTAC*, p. 55.

the process of getting one's photograph and displaying the voting card was a source of freely expressed pride to great numbers of Cambodians.[15]

Information and Education

The Information and Education Division set up in the Office of the Special Representative of the Secretary-General faced special challenges in preparing Cambodians for the election, informing them about UNTAC and the Paris Agreements, and educating them about the public's rights and responsibilities. The level of literacy of Cambodians who had survived the "Pol Pot period" was low. Their knowledge about "free and fair" elections and about campaigning by competitive political parties was limited. They had reason to fear violence and intimidation during the electoral process. Nevertheless, after the election international observers would join in widespread acclaim for the way that the Information and Education Division had met the challenges.[16]

The programs covered a variety of forms, including comic dialogues between uncle and nephew, so-called "oxcart conversation" relevant to a rural audience. As we have seen, UNTAC had by January 1993 distributed thousands of radios contributed by Japanese nongovernmental organizations.[17] Videos for TV screening, comic books with clear messages, posters, and banners for public display were thoroughly distributed. Mobile information units penetrated the countryside with traveling troupes performing skits, loudspeakers, video monitors, film strips, and movies. The UNTAC presentations conveyed the important messages that the vote would be secret and that voters could freely select the party of their choice. Human rights themes were intermixed with messages about the upcoming "fair and free election." During the election campaign itself, UNTAC made broadcast time available to the political parties. It arranged for public rallies and debates among candidates. Only the PDK did not avail themselves of the opportunity to participate in these campaign activities.

UNTAC did not play a role in developing democratic political structures for the contending political parties.[18] This task was undertaken, in part, by organizations funded by the two major American political parties, the Na-

15. Interviews by Joseph J. Zasloff with UNTAC staff and UN Volunteers, in Washington, D.C., 1995.

16. See also Janet E. Heininger, *Peacekeeping in Transition: The United Nations in Cambodia* Report (New York: Twentieth Century Fund, 1994), pp. 109–11.

17. Third Progress Report of the Secretary-General on the United Nations Transitional Authority in Cambodia, paras. 19, 91, 93, in *The United Nations and Cambodia, 1991–1995.*

18. *The United Nation and Cambodia, 1991–1995,* p. 32.

tional Democratic Institute and the International Republican Institute. These institutes sent several staffers to conduct seminars and workshops on party-related issues, to any of the twenty parties competing in the election who wished to send trainees. The PDK, which did not compete in the election, did not participate in these sessions.

Political Environment of the Election

A premise of the Paris Agreements was that a neutral political environment would be created in Cambodia to permit voters to exercise their franchise free from threats of violence and intimidation. The parties that signed the agreements were committed to cooperate in implementing them, including to respect the cease-fire and fulfill the measures designed to increase security. Most important among these were the disarming, cantonment, and demobilization of the factional armies. Many of the requirements for the creation of a neutral environment remained unfulfilled during the run-up to the election. A multitude of serious problems confronted UNTAC. Among the most challenging were the withdrawal of PDK cooperation, the violence and intimidation provoked by the CPP, the general breakdown of law and order in the civil society, and doubts raised by Prince Sihanouk and FUNCINPEC about continuing to cooperate in the electoral process in the face of these conditions. Indeed, until the day of the election, doubts remained about whether UNTAC could or should persist in conducting the election.

PDK Withdrawal of Cooperation

Although the PDK had signed the Paris Agreements and pledged its cooperation in their implementation, by June 1992, when UNTAC was to conduct the regroupment and cantonment of Phase II, the PDK refused to take part, contending that Vietnamese forces remained in Cambodia.[19] The UNTAC special representative, Yasushi Akashi, and the UNTAC military commander, General John Sanderson, issued assurances that their intelligence showed that the Vietnamese forces had withdrawn, and diplomatic representatives of the Permanent Five confirmed the judgment. But when the PDK persisted in its noncompliance with the elements of Phase II, the other parties, with UNTAC's agreement, reduced their own fulfillment of

19. See letter dated Sept. 29, 1992, from Khieu Samphan, member of the Supreme National Council, to the secretary-general referring to "Cambodia: Next Steps," Australian paper, in *The United Nations and Cambodia, 1991–1995*, pp. 222–24.

the regroupment and cantonment. UNTAC attempted to bring diplomatic pressure to bear on the PDK, organizing a meeting in Beijing on November 7–8, 1992, with members of the SNC, Permanent Five representatives, and representatives from Australia, Germany, Japan, and Thailand, but the PDK refused to comply with Phase II. In fact, according to the UN secretary-general's report, "the PDK had stiffened its position in Beijing, saying it would not take part in the electoral process or the elections as long as it felt that a neutral political environment had not been created."[20]

Besides its claim about the continued presence of Vietnamese troops in Cambodia, the PDK contended that UNTAC, in violation of the Paris Agreements, was permitting the SOC/CPP to continue governing the country. On July 12, 1992, the PDK put forth a formal proposal to UNTAC linking its future regrouping and cantonment with a dismantling of the Phnom Penh government.[21] Although the PDK charge was exaggerated, it was true that UNTAC had been unable to exercise full supervisory control over SOC administration. Few persons in UNTAC could speak Khmer, or were familiar with Cambodia's culture and intricate administrative politics. It seemed inevitable that SOC officeholders, closely linked to the CPP, would continue to exercise influence.

While the PDK gave lip service to adhering to the Paris Agreements, if properly implemented, it actively sought to sabotage their implementation through obstruction, intimidation, and violence. PDK authorities prohibited UNTAC key administrative and military personnel from entering their zones of control. When Special Representative Akashi and General Sanderson attempted to penetrate the PDK-controlled zone near Pailin in western Cambodia, on May 30, 1992, Khmer Rouge soldiers used a simple bamboo pole to bar their entry. General Sanderson's deputy at the time, General Jean-Michel Loridon of France, was said to favor calling the KR's bluff by sending UNTAC troops to the KR area, which was not heavily defended. General Sanderson judged that this might result in wider warfare, and it did not appear that the countries that had contributed forces to UNTAC would support committing them to fight the Khmer Rouge. This issue was a source of heated debate about UNTAC's actions.[22]

A variety of violent acts by the Khmer Rouge created a climate of tension and malaise. Khmer Rouge military forces frequently breached the cease-

20. *The United Nation and Cambodia, 1991–1995*, p. 25.

21. See *Proposal Dated 12 July 1992 of the PDK on the Implementation of Phase II of the Cease-Fire and the Regroupment and Cantonment of the Forces of the PDK*, in *The United Nations and Cambodia, 1991–1995*, pp. 200–201.

22. See William Shawcross, *Cambodia's New Deal* (Washington, D.C.: Carnegie Endowment, 1994), p. 14.

fire. In December 1992, for example, sustained shelling in the Bavel area of Battambang Province forced some fifteen thousand people to flee their homes. In the same month, PDK forces detained UNTAC personnel on several occasions, charging that they had entered the PDK zone without permission.[23] In April 1993, a Japanese district electoral supervisor and his Cambodian interpreter were killed, followed in early May by the killing of a Japanese civil police officer, all attributed by the press to the Khmer Rouge (although, in the climate of violence then prevailing in Cambodia, the true culprits in each case were not always known). The Japanese deaths created a crisis in Japan, and the political debate in Tokyo raised the possibility, which was not carried out, that Japan might withdraw its personnel from UNTAC. Seven UN workers were killed during a two-week period.[24] Military clashes between State of Cambodia and Khmer Rouge forces increased in early 1993. In February 1993, for example, the PDK deployed its forces to consolidate its influence over areas in the northwest of the country. SOC forces responded with attacks on the PDK in a number of districts, sparking the worst fighting since the signing of the Paris Agreements.[25]

Perhaps the most brutal activities were the PDK assaults on ethnic Vietnamese residents of Cambodia. PDK attacks in December 1992 stirred thousands of Vietnamese civilians, mainly fishermen and their families living along the Tonle Sap (Great Lake), to flee toward Vietnam. Vietnam's minister of foreign affairs condemned, in a letter to the UN secretary-general on December 30, 1992, what he called the PDK's "barbarous acts of terrorism" against ethnic Vietnamese.[26] Vietnam again protested another outrage, on March 10, 1993, in which thirty-three ethnic Vietnamese were massacred. UNTAC investigators concluded that the murders were committed by PDK soldiers.[27]

The PDK ignored the ban on the export of logs and gems from Cambodian mines which UNTAC had imposed in 1992. (SOC and FUNCINPEC were also guilty of violating the ban, although their trade was minor compared with that of the PDK.) Income from illegal logging and gem sales to Thai entrepreneurs, reported to be in league with the Thai military pa-

23. *The United Nations and Cambodia, 1991–1995*, p. 34.
24. See Heininger, *Peacekeeping in Transition*, pp. 108–9.
25. *The United Nations and Cambodia, 1991–1995*, p. 34.
26. Letter dated Dec. 30, 1992, from Nguyen Man Cam, minister of foreign affairs of Vietnam, to the secretary-general concerning violence against Vietnamese residents of Cambodia, in *The United Nations and Cambodia, 1991–1995*, pp. 248–49.
27. Introduction by Secretary-General, *The United Nations and Cambodia, 1991–1995*, p. 34.

trolling the border areas, was an important source of PDK revenue.[28] One estimate of PDK earnings from gem mining and logging put the figure in October 1991 at $100 million per year.[29]

The PDK refused cooperation with the electoral process. PDK authorities did not register their party with UNTAC to compete in the election, nor did they campaign. They prohibited UNTAC agents from conducting registration in their zones, although some personnel managed to penetrate certain areas partially dominated by the PDK to register voters, among them (as noted above) some Khmer Rouge soldiers and their officers. On April 5, 1993, three days before the formal opening of the election campaign, Khieu Samphan announced to the SNC that the PDK would take part in the election "only when the Paris Agreement has been respected and implemented." He contended that Vietnamese forces remained in Cambodia and that "Vietnam's Phnom Penh puppets, . . . too, are getting more and more insolent, like their masters." He asserted that "UNTAC's election is just a theatrical farce to hand over Cambodia to Vietnam, the aggressor. It is simply a farce to legitimize the puppets Vietnam installed in Phnom Penh since 1979."[30]

A week later, the PDK staff abruptly loaded baggage from their headquarters in Phnom Penh onto trucks, and departed by convoy to the airport for Bangkok, informing Special Representative Akashi that security for them in the capital was inadequate. Akashi, still outraged by the killing of seven UNTAC officials in the previous days, recognized the seriousness of the PDK withdrawal and responded in the strongest terms he had yet used in communicating with the recalcitrant PDK:

> The Party of the DK risks stripping itself of the legitimacy it regained by signing those [Paris peace] agreements and has taken a dangerous step toward outlaw status. Let us be clear what this means: nothing less than internal and international isolation. The world will not forgive the party of DK for disrupting the Cambodian elections. There should be no more sanctuaries for that party, and no more chances . . . that party still has the choice of allowing the elections to proceed without further attacks and making such accommodation it can with the new government.[31]

28. Ibid., p. 35.
29. *Economist*, October 5, 1991.
30. Voice of the Great National Union Front of Cambodia, in Cambodian, April 5, 1993, in *FBIS-EAS*, April 6, 1993.
31. Cited in Nate Thayer, "Khmer Rouge: Will They be Back?" *Phnom Penh Post*, April 23–May 6, 1993.

If the PDK had intended to abide by the Paris Agreements in October 1991, it was now clear that they would oppose their full implementation.

Why had the PDK entered into the Paris Agreements? By the time of the second Paris Conference on Cambodia in 1991, the shift in the balance of forces, both internal and external, made it prudent for the PDK to appear ready for compromise. They were under pressure from China, their former key supporter, which was now a cooperative member of the Permanent Five peace effort. Their factional allies within the CGDK, most importantly Prince Sihanouk, and also Son Sann and his KPNLF, were committed to the settlement worked out by the Permanent Five. The UNTAC-directed peace process, they seem to have calculated, could provide the opportunity for expelling from power their despised enemy, the Vietnamese-dominated SOC. After the election, they apparently believed, the greed and corruption of their competitors, juxtaposed against their own superior political organization and military strength, would allow them to achieve power again, once the UN had departed.

To what extent did the PDK intend to cooperate in the implementation of the Paris Agreements? One answer is that "at the time it signed the Paris Agreements, the PDK intended both to demobilize the NADK [National Army of Democratic Kampuchea] and to set up a political party to participate in the elections." Stephen Heder, drawing upon interviews with former Khmer Rouge cadres, public statements by PDK leaders, as well as captured internal documents and internal reports of UNTAC (in which he served), reached this conclusion. He believed, however, that the PDK did not intend to respect the Paris Agreements as a whole. Rather, they planned to overthrow the SOC by penetration at the rice roots level, believing that the Paris Agreements would provide the opportunity to do so.[32]

Heder cites a speech by Pol Pot in December 1991 to a "leadership team" which revealed the PDK strategy of attempting to consolidate power at the village level. Pol Pot announced the launching of "a strategic offensive in the countryside." His speech called for doubling the number of villages under PDK control between February and March 1992. A PDK directive of February 1992 said: "There must be no let-up in consecutive storming breakthrough attacks. . . . Only by dissolving the village political administration of the contemptible Yuon [derogatory term for Vietnamese] enemy . . . can we consolidate and expand liberated villages . . . sub-district National Councils . . . which is to say consolidate and expand our

---

32. See Stephen Heder in two-part article in the *Phnom Penh Post*, March 24–April 6, and April 7–20, 1995.

strength . . . and make the contemptible Yuon enemy and its lackeys disappear in domain after domain."[33]

A PDK strategy of giving lip service to the implementation of the Paris Agreements while at the same time building secret bases and spreading PDK control throughout the countryside was also perceived by Nayan Chanda, another veteran analyst of Khmer Rouge behavior. Chanda quoted a PDK directive, dated January 10, 1992, which outlines the necessary steps to implement this strategy.[34] "We must concentrate first on accelerating the infiltration of category one forces in order gradually to establish in advance the pre-requisites [for military activity] *sur place*. Category two forces can be infiltrated thereafter, and eventually category three forces can also be infiltrated one after the other. . . . Things must be thought through, particularly the routes by which they will walk, in order to protect our strength."

However, the PDK's plans to overthrow the SOC from below were frustrated even before the arrival of UNTAC, Heder points out. In the month following the signing of the Paris Agreements, Prince Sihanouk, whose cooperation the PDK had been hoping to secure, called for the PDK leadership to be tried for genocide. Further, he proposed that the SOC should be regarded as the de facto government and called for direct economic assistance to it. He endorsed an alliance between FUNCINPEC, whose cooperation the PDK wished to lure, and the SOC, which the PDK regarded as a traitorous abomination. Sihanouk even proposed the formation of a coalition government that would include the SOC. As for the hated Vietnam, Sihanouk said he regarded it as Cambodia's friend. He contended that there were no Vietnamese troops in Cambodia and that Vietnamese residents should be protected, not expelled.[35]

Around the same time, just one month after the signing of the Paris Agreements, the PDK received another jolt when Khieu Samphan returned to Phnom Penh to establish PDK headquarters for the implementation of the peace plan. He was brutally attacked by a crowd at his residence and narrowly escaped with his life. Rumors pervaded the capital that the SOC had set up an anti-Khmer Rouge demonstration which then got out of control. Another blow to the PDK came at the SNC meeting of January 26,

---

33. Cited in ibid.

34. "Decisions of the meeting of 1001 Leading Cadre, 10 January 1992. Document for study in every location. This document elaborates on the leadership team's Decision Document of 13 December 1991." Cited in Nayan Chanda, "Cambodia: In Search of an Elusive Peace," in *The American-Vietnamese Dialogue* 8, no. 2 (Feb. 8–11, 1993) (Queenstown, Md. Aspen Institute), p. 24.

35. Heder, *Phnom Penh Post*.

1992, when Sihanouk declared that the PDK had no right to set up local councils (which the Khmer Rouge were labeling "national councils") or otherwise extend their territorial control. It appeared that Pol Pot was still weighing the advantages and risks of cooperating with UNTAC when he declared on February 6, 1992, that "the contents of the [Paris] Agreements are to our advantage." However, he warned, "if the Agreements are incorrectly implemented we are dead, but if they are correctly implemented then we will win."[36] In the PDK view, a critical requirement of the implementation was that the SOC be dismantled. By May 1992, Pol Pot had come to the conclusion, according to Chanda, that the imperfect implementation of the peace accords was damaging PDK interests. The SOC was not being dismantled, but rather its political structure and military forces were still intact. Disarming Khmer Rouge forces and opening their zones to UNTAC would threaten the morale of Khmer Rouge fighters and expose the people under their control to hostile influences.

Another interpretation of these events is that the PDK never intended to comply with the Paris Agreements. This viewpoint is held by historian Ben Kiernan, who asserts that the Khmer Rouge went along with the agreements expecting they would serve their quest for power. As of early 1993, their strategy seemed to be working out well for them, Kiernan argues. They had gained a solid base from which to attempt their return to power "if their long-time allies won a plurality or majority of seats in the election." In the atmosphere of political paralysis which they anticipated, they could continue their military offenses and civilian massacres, or bide their time until the UN forces would withdraw. The PDK were in a strategic position to subvert the agreement.[37] In a synthesis of the benefits he believes the PDK gained from their venture into the peace process, Kiernan writes:

> The Khmer Rouge withdrew from the peace process with the gains they had made from it. They had quadrupled the territory and population under their control, increased their regular forces from ten thousand to fifteen thousand in the past year, and doubled their annual income, to US$250 million through trade with Thailand. What distinguished the proponents of the UN plan from its critics was the proponents' insistence on including the Khmer Rouge in the

36. Minutes of speech, "Clarification of Certain Principled Views to Act as the Basis of Our Views and Stance," Feb. 6, 1992. Cited in Chanda, "Cambodia: In Search of an Elusive Peace."

37. Ben Kiernan, "The Inclusion of the Khmer Rouge in the Cambodian Peace Process: Causes and Consequences," in Kiernan, ed., *Genocide and Democracy in Cambodia* (New Haven: Yale University Southeast Asian Studies, 1993), p. 233.

peace settlement and elections. That strategy foundered badly—especially if it was an attempt to undermine Khmer Rouge power.[38]

In a highly critical review of Kiernan's thesis, Stephen Heder charges that this interpretation seems to ignore numerous indications that, even though the PDK intended to cheat on the demobilization process, it was prepared to go along with it to a significant extent, and had even conducted a major troop cut on its own. Further, the Kiernan thesis ignores evidence that, while the PDK was hostile to "bourgeois democracy," Pol Pot and other PDK leaders advocated playing the "parliamentary game." Heder asserts that Pol Pot intended to convert PDK military strength into a strong political movement, a factor Kiernan ignores. The course of events after October 1991, as explained above, led the PDK to change its mind about cooperation in the peace process, Heder concludes.[39]

Special Representative Akashi has speculated that the PDK, like the Hun Sen government, signed the accords hoping the peace process might work to its advantage but remained ready to resume fighting if it did not. His analysis of PDK behavior supports this conclusion:

> In late 1991 and early 1992 the KR was pressing strongly for the full and rapid deployment of UNTAC. When UNTAC was finally deployed, the KR initially adopted a posture of cautious cooperation, despite engaging in numerous cease-fire violations. It was represented actively at SNC meetings in Phnom Penh by Khieu Samphan, its nominal president, it accepted UNHCR's repatriation program and the presence of UNTAC civilians in contested areas, concurred in the SNC's accession to international human rights instruments and it joined UNTAC's police training programme. It even allowed a small number of UN military observers into its territory to reconnoitre regroupment and cantonment areas—although 'circumscribing their movements so closely that at times they seemed to be more hostages than monitors.'[40]

From the indicators noted above, Akashi retained his "optimism," (as he told the authors in June 1992) that the PDK might cooperate. Evidence now appears to indicate that a debate took place within PDK leadership circles in early 1992 over whether the PDK should continue to cooperate in

38. Ibid., p. 21.

39. Stephen Heder, review of Ben Kiernan, ed., *Genocide and Democracy in Cambodia*, in *Phnom Penh Post*, June 16–29, 1995.

40. Findlay, *Cambodia: The Legacy and Lessons of UNTAC*, p. 51.

the peace process.[41] Some PDK leaders were adamant that they must prevent UNTAC access to their zones and that they could not afford to demobilize their military forces, which were their primary source of protection from their enemies, including most of the external powers involved in the UNTAC operation. By contrast, according to Nate Thayer, General Son Sen, a PDK member of the SNC along with Khieu Samphan, argued that the PDK should enter into Phase II of the peace plan, which called for demobilization of the factional armies. Thayer writes:

> Son Sen argued, during April and May 1992, that the KR's future also depended on remaining sincere in the eyes of the world for desiring a peaceful, political solution to Cambodia's conflict and participating in a democratically elected coalition government. To pull out would undermine the group's already rock bottom credibility both domestically and internationally which the KR continue to see as vital to reestablishing their ability to play a role in future Cambodian affairs.[42]

Son Sen lost the argument during PDK leadership meetings in May 1992 and appeared to have been purged, assigned to "reeducation," from June to December 1992, during which he is said to have confessed to error in his earlier views.[43]

Unless Pol Pot and other PDK leaders publish their memoirs, we may never know definitively whether the PDK intended to cooperate in the implementation of the Paris Agreements. However, it appears, as we will later show, that (contrary to Kiernan's assessment of PDK gains), the PDK lost ground in distancing itself from the UN-directed peace plan.

It is also relevant to examine the rationale for UNTAC policies regarding PDK obstruction of the peace process. In June 1992, Special Representative Akashi told the authors, in an interview in Phnom Penh, that he was disappointed by the PDK's refusal to honor its commitment to abide by the Paris Agreements. Its noncooperation was creating serious problems in the implementation of the intricate time table he was obliged to carry out. However, while keeping the door open for the restoration of PDK cooperation, he expressed determination to continue with preparations to conduct the election. This policy, endorsed by intermittent Security Council resolutions and affirmed by the secretary-general, persisted until the election took place in May 1993. As for military options, General Sanderson pointed

41. Based on a report by Nate Thayer, "Shakeup in KR Hierarchy," *Phnom Penh Post*, Jan. 28–Feb. 10, 1994.
42. Ibid.
43. Ibid.

out to the authors, in Phnom Penh in June 1992, that he was required to operate within the standard operating procedures that the Security Council had established for "peace-keeping," *not* "peace-enforcing," missions.[44] The rules of engagement limited military activities to self-defense. Going beyond those rules was a political question, not in the general's province to address. These Security Council–determined procedures persisted throughout the period of the UNTAC mission.

SOC Intimidation and Violence during the Electoral Campaign

Threats to public order in Cambodia were classified, as indicated in the UN secretary-general's report of February 13, 1993, in three categories: politically motivated attacks on political party offices and staff, attributed to soldiers, police, or supporters of the SOC; attacks on ethnic Vietnamese, attributed to PDK elements; and killings that seemed to have no particular political motivation.[45] SOC intimidation and violence, in many ways similar to that of the PDK, was aimed primarily against FUNCINPEC and, to a lesser extent, the BLDP. These SOC-created threats amplified the breakdown of public order as UNTAC prepared the election. The SOC-sponsored campaign of violence, which included murder, began in September 1992 and reached a peak in December as the opposition parties set up offices in the provinces. The campaign continued into 1993, when UNTAC's Human Rights Component listed fifty incidents of harassment or of violence, including murder, from March 1 to May 14, 1993. Convincing evidence that the campaign had SOC inspiration was the failure by SOC authorities to prosecute any of the perpetrators.

In addition to other violence and intimidation (described below), the SOC undertook a propaganda campaign against UNTAC through television, radio, and party newspaper. The secretary-general's report attributes these attacks to the SOC's intention to "spread the message that only SOC can defend the country against PDK and so deserves electoral support, while UNTAC cannot be trusted to protect Cambodians."[46] Timothy Carney, who headed UNTAC's Information and Education Division, made a

44. Interview with Lt. General John Sanderson, June 1992, Phnom Penh.
45. Report of the Secretary-General on the Implementation of Security Council Resolution 792 (1992) S/25289, Feb. 13, 1993, in *The United Nations and Cambodia, 1991–1995*, pp. 270–71.
46. "Incidents of Political Violence, Harassment, and Intimidation: 1 March 1993 to 14 May 1993," UNTAC release, quoted in Timothy Carney and Tan Lain Choo, *Whither Cambodia? Beyond the Election* (Singapore: ISEAS, 1993), pp. 4–6.

similar judgment, describing the SOC electoral strategy as intended to "remind the voters that the CPP was the only bulwark against the hated Khmer Rouge; and that FUNCINPEC was an old and probably future ally of the genocidal Red Khmer."[47] Carney describes the clandestine effort of the CPP, begun in 1992, to undermine its political opposition. The CPP sent secret police groups "to identify 'targets' and to engage in dirty tricks, including fomenting louts to harass opposition parties," while spreading propaganda in an attempt to legitimize their repugnant behavior.

William Shawcross, a British journalist who witnessed part of the electoral campaign, notes that the SOC employed "what it called 'reaction forces' and 'A-groups'—often vigilante thugs." He adds that "SOC security forces hand-picked trouble makers in the local communities to carry out attacks. One district-level document recorded the instruction, 'in the work of fashioning reaction forces, aim at getting persons with foul mouths.' The police were told to view all other political parties as 'targets' but at the same time to ' keep their hands clean'—not get caught."[48]

Violence was pervasive up to election time. Just prior to the election in May 1993, UNTAC published a report estimating that since March 1 there had been 200 deaths, 338 injuries, and 144 abductions as a result of pre-election violence. Among the principal victims were UNTAC personnel, ethnic Vietnamese, Cambodian civilians, and political party members. The Khmer Rouge were blamed for 131 deaths, 250 injuries, and 53 abductions. Twenty serious attacks against other political parties were attributed to the SOC. The head of the Human Rights Component pointed out that these figures did not account for all of the political violence, but only for cases in which UNTAC had been able to identify the culprits.[49]

In addition to the SOC intimidation and violence, corruption within SOC ranks reached enormous levels as the election approached. Besides selling timber resources, already mentioned, SOC incumbents engaged in the brazen sale of government assets such as machinery, vehicles, and even entire government buildings to the highest bidder for personal profit. Seizing opportunities for enrichment as authority and control were collapsing, probably sensing that their party might lose or have to share power, certain political operatives shamelessly sold off the national patrimony. Such blatant corruption was an indication of how far the civic order had declined in this failed state.

47. Carney and Choo, *Whither Cambodia?* pp. 4–6.
48. Shawcross, *Cambodia's New Deal*, p. 18.
49. Findlay, *Cambodia: The Legacy and Lessons of UNTAC*, pp. 81–82, quoting *Bangkok Post*, May 24, 1993.

FUNCINPEC and Electoral Violence

FUNCINPEC, lacking the large army and security units controlled by both the SOC and the PDK, was more often victim than assailant in the climate of violence in the run-up to the election. There were significantly fewer UNTAC charges of threats and intimidation against FUNCINPEC, a relative newcomer in the Cambodian political scene, than against its two more entrenched political rivals. There was widespread fear of SOC-inspired violence among FUNCINPEC political cadres, particularly in the provinces.

However, FUNCINPEC vied with its competitors in inflammatory rhetoric against the ethnic Vietnamese, sensing that there were political gains to be made in appealing to historic Khmer suspicions of their more powerful neighbor.

FUNCINPEC shamelessly appropriated the charges against ethnic Vietnamese, tailoring them to their own purposes.[50] UNTAC information and education chief Timothy Carney characterized FUNCINPEC's approach to the ethnic Vietnamese issue:

> FUNCINPEC media crossed the line to incitement to racial hatred in an effort to woo voters, traditionally suspicious of Vietnamese activities and intentions toward Cambodia. A cartoon in the Party youth magazine viciously recalled one of the popular memories of the nineteenth century when Vietnamese forces would bury three Cambodians up to their necks, light a fire to boil water for tea, and urge the victims not to shake the kettle. UNTAC Information/Education Division required a senior FUNCINPEC official to re-record a video political statement that risked incitement in its language excesses referring to the CPP debt to the Vietnamese. (He then complained to the press about UNTAC censorship.)[51]

In a letter on January 4, 1993, Prince Sihanouk informed UNTAC chief Akashi that the persistent violent attacks on FUNCINPEC offices and staff obliged him to cease cooperation with UNTAC. On the following day,

---

50. It appeared that even moderate, educated FUNCINPEC political leaders were not immune to raising the specter of Vietnamese aggression for political purposes. In an interview with the authors, the younger half-brother of Prince Sihanouk who was to become foreign minister at the outset of the new government, Prince Norodom Sirivuddh, contended that even the Vietnamese artisans he had employed to remodel his villa, and who were hammering on the wall during our conversation, could well be Vietnamese soldiers. His assertion was almost surely sham. Interview with the authors in Phnom Penh, June 25, 1992.

51. Carney and Choo, *Whither Cambodia?* p. 6.

Prince Ranariddh also wrote to the UN secretary-general, asserting that "politically motivated terrorist attacks" on FUNCINPEC had become "intolerable." He noted that since November 1992, "because of UNTAC's weakness," eighteen attacks had been made on FUNCINPEC party members, with eighteen dead and twenty-two wounded. Ranariddh declared that he would suspend working relations with UNTAC until effective measures were taken to put an end to the violence.[52] The secretary-general responded with assurances that UNTAC would do its utmost to improve security and work toward creating a neutral political environment. Princes Sihanouk and Ranariddh subsequently agreed to cooperate with UNTAC's efforts.[53]

Despite calls from a variety of sources to suspend the election, the special representative, supported by the secretary-general, persisted in his determination to conduct it. The UN officials recognized the absence of a fully "neutral political environment." But, as the secretary-general explained in his report to the Security Council, the United Nations was obligated to carry out the election as planned. He added:

> I argued that to do otherwise would in effect give a veto over peace to one armed faction in Cambodia, and to let down the Cambodian people and the international community who entrusted the United Nations with the task of peace-building in Cambodia. I also suggested that perhaps the international community had maintained unreasonable standards for a neutral election environment in Cambodia, given the country's internal divisions and traumatized population. The fact that ideal conditions did not exist in Cambodia was not sufficient reason to prevent elections from taking place; after all, I stated, this was only the beginning of Cambodia's renewal, not its end.[54]

The Security Council, in a resolution on March 8, 1993, while "deploring" the PDK cease-fire violations and "expressing strong concern" about the threats, intimidation, and violence surrounding the electoral campaign, endorsed the recommendation to carry on with the election.[55]

---

52. "Letter dated 5 January from Prince Norodom Ranariddh, member of the Supreme National Council, to the Secretary-General concerning the political situation in Cambodia," in *The United Nations and Cambodia, 1991–1995*, pp. 251–52.

53. *The United Nations and Cambodia, 1991–1995*, pp. 36–37.

54. Ibid., p. 43. See also Report of the Secretary-General in pursuance of paragraph 6 of Security Council resolution 810 (1993) on preparations for the election for the constituent assembly in Cambodia, S/25784, May 15, 1993.

55. Security Council resolution on the election for the constituent assembly, S/RES/810 (1993), March 8, 1993, in ibid., pp. 278–79.

The Electoral Campaign

The formal political campaign was designated by UNTAC's calendar to begin on April 7, 1993, although the contest for power via the ballot box actually began with the signing of the Paris Agreements, which designated elections as the key to who would rule in Cambodia. During the six weeks before the balloting began on May 23, hundreds of meetings and political rallies took place throughout the country, many with protection by UNTAC civilian police. UNTAC conducted training for 900 international polling station officers from 44 countries and the Inter-Parliamentary Union, 130 from the UN Secretariat, and 370 from UNTAC. UNTAC recruited and trained 50,000 Cambodian electoral staff. Radio UNTAC gave daily assurances that the ballot would be secret. Each political party was offered weekly time to broadcast its messages and was accorded a right of response if it believed it had been unfairly attacked by opponents. The UNTAC Information and Education Division prepared TV videos that included round-table discussions for distribution throughout the country. It mounted billboards, posters, and banners with electoral materials. It assisted in the organization of political rallies, transporting candidates and equipment to remote areas.[56]

A total of twenty parties registered for the election. The most important were the Cambodian People's Party (CPP), which was the political foundation of the State of Cambodia (SOC), led by Hun Sen; FUNCINPEC (United National Front for an Independent, Neutral, Peaceful, and Cooperative Cambodia), led by Prince Ranariddh (and closely associated with his father, Prince Sihanouk); and the offshoots of the KPNLF (Khmer People's National Liberation Front) which had split into two quarreling factions, the Buddhist Liberal Democratic Party (BLDP), led by Son Sann (and his son, Son Soubert), and the Liberal Democratic Party, led by General Sak Sutsakhan (who died on April 29, 1994). The Party of Democratic Kampuchea (PDK) did not compete in the election.

Campaign Issues

The six-week political campaign revealed critical issues that the parties believed would resonate with the Cambodian public. Frederick Z. Brown synthesized these election issues as essentially a referendum on three negative

---

56. *The United Nations and Cambodia, 1991–1995*, pp. 38–40.

attitudes, plus one vague positive issue. The three negatives were anti–Khmer Rouge, anti-CPP/SOC and anti-Vietnam. The vague positive issue was war-weariness.[57]

The CPP presented itself as the party responsible for ousting the hated Khmer Rouge (which CPP spokesmen typically referred to as the "Pol Pot regime," using rhetorical techniques to avoid reminding voters that their own leaders had once participated in that revolutionary movement). The lunar New Year's message delivered by Heng Samrin, honorary chairman of the CPP's Central Committee, carried the central theme that the CPP would be the country's savior from the ever-present Khmer Rouge threat:

> One ballot can decide the fate of us all. It is a ballot to decide the life or death of our motherland. Therefore, the ballots that our people will cast for the CPP are ballots to save our lives. This is because it was the CPP that toppled the brutal genocidal Pol Pot regime, revived our nation, and prevented the return of the Polpotists over the past more than 14 years. Electing the CPP means selecting the group than can prevent the return of the genocidal Pol Pot regime, that can ensure the ownership and achievements made in the past 14 years, and that can lead us toward progress.[58]

Political opponents frequently charged that the CPP had been created by Vietnam with its invasion in 1979, and that the CPP remained subservient to its Vietnamese masters. The responses of Hun Sen, the CPP's master orator,[59] gave the flavor of the CPP response to this charge, which carried great weight in the Cambodian political arena. In a campaign speech in Kandal Province, Hun Sen reminded his audience that Cambodia had been dominated by the "genocidal Pol Pot regime" from 1975 to 1979. "In 1979, if we did not ask for help from Vietnam," he queried, "could we have liberated our country?" "Had we not relied on Vietnamese liberating troops, we would have never survived to this day," he asserted. Responding to the criticism that Vietnam stayed too long—a full ten years —in Cambodia, Hun Sen continued, "Vietnam's initial idea was to stay only one year in Cambodia: attack Pol Pot in 1979 and withdraw in 1980. I my-

---

57. Frederick Z. Brown, "Cambodia in Crisis: The 1983 Elections and the United Nations," Asian update (New York: The Asia Society, May 1993).

58. Phnom Penh Samleng Pracheachon Kampuchea Radio Network in Cambodian, April 13, 1993, in *FBIS-EAS*, April 14, 1993.

59. Timothy Carney has pointed out the CPP's heavy reliance on the speeches of Hun Sen. He noted that Chea Sim, the chairman of the CPP, "included heavy reference to Hun Sen's own speechmaking." See Carney and Choo, *Whither Cambodia?* pp. 4–6.

self went to see Le Duc Tho. . . . I said you cannot withdraw your troops because Cambodia does not have sufficient strength; if you withdraw, Pol Pot would come back."[60]

Hun Sen invoked the name of Prince Sihanouk, a tactic used by a variety of Cambodian politicians who recognized the widespread appeal of the prince, to justify his military service with the Khmer Rouge–led revolutionary movement: "The parties . . . shout insults at me. . . . They call me one-eyed jack. This does not upset me because actually I am one-eyed. . . . If there was no war and no appeal from His Royal Highness Prince Norodom Sihanouk, I would still have my eye to earn my living as a farmer. I have become one-eyed because . . . [I] joined his front after his appeal."[61] In one of his rhetorical counterattacks, Hun Sen charged that FUNCINPEC and the KPNLF had been in league with the Khmer Rouge, while the CPP/SOC was fighting against Khmer Rouge aggression. A FUNCINPEC victory, he implied, would bring the Khmer Rouge back into the government.

FUNCINPEC, recognizing the war-weariness abroad among the Cambodian populace, portrayed itself as the party of peace, while warning that a CPP victory would mean continued war. In a campaign speech in Prey Veng Province, Prince Ranariddh said, "If the CPP win the elections, they will fight [with the Khmer Rouge]. Fighting means war and suffering again. If there is war, it will not only mean suffering but also foreign troops [alluding to the possible return of Vietnamese soldiers]."[62] Using the strongest campaign appeal in the FUNCINPEC inventory, Ranariddh added that a vote for FUNCINPEC was a vote for his father, Prince Sihanouk, who was the only person capable of restoring peace, territorial integrity, and the economic bounty that the people had enjoyed during his revered period in power. When Ranariddh asked his supporters at the rally if life was better during Prince Sihanouk's rule, the crowd responded each time with an exuberant "yes." He emphasized that a FUNCINPEC victory would remove the Khmer Rouge pretext for struggle, since a new democratic government would be made up of Cambodians, not Vietnamese, and would be recognized internationally.[63]

---

60. Phnom Penh Samleng Pracheachon Kampuchea Radio Network in Cambodian, April 22, 1993, in *FBIS-EAS*, April 29, 1993.

61. Ibid.

62. *The Nation*, Bangkok, in English May 7, 1993, quoted in *FBIS-EAS*, 93-087, May 7, 1993.

63. Ibid.

Prince Sihanouk and the Electoral Campaign

Prince Sihanouk played an important, if volatile—as always—role in the electoral process. Sihanouk was closely associated with FUNCINPEC, the so-called royalist party, which he had founded and which was now led by his son, Prince Ranariddh. However, upon assuming the chairmanship of the SNC, as the titular "chief of state" Sihanouk shifted into official political neutrality, even though he was still connected in the minds of many with FUNCINPEC. He positioned himself as the "father of his country," who might bring harmony and reconciliation among the contesting factions. Prince Sihanouk—former "God King"—was almost worshipped by many of the Cambodian traditional folk. At the same time some Cambodians, particularly among the political elite and in educated circles, mistrusted him. Some remembered his rule from 1953 to 1970 as peremptory, arrogant, personalistic, and destructive. Some held him responsible for having contributed to the disastrous events following his overthrow: the terrible war from 1970 to 1975 and the brutal Khmer Rouge rule from 1975 to 1979. They deeply resented his alliance with the Khmer Rouge from 1970 to 1975, and were later uneasy with his collaboration with them during Vietnamese-dominated PRK/SOC rule after 1979. His vacillating pronouncements and his frequent absences continued to raise concern in sophisticated political circles.

During the campaign period Prince Sihanouk spent most of his time in Pyongyang or Beijing. Several SNC meetings were conducted in Beijing, in order to accommodate his schedule while also heightening the influence of China. From his headquarters in Beijing, Sihanouk issued a stream of statements and faxes, some describing his poor health, which he said required his stay in Beijing, and others propounding his views on a variety of issues. Sihanouk appeared unrestrained in his criticism of all parties and organizations, and of his son Ranariddh—although his focus of criticism appeared to change with his mood, and a target of criticism one day might become an object of praise another. From time to time he threatened to withdraw from the chairmanship of the SNC but was persuaded by Akashi to stay on. Several times he withdrew his cooperation with UNTAC, only to return after the urging of a variety of voices.

PDK leaders tried to persuade him to sit out the election in China and at times he gave the impression he might do so. In the week prior to the election, both the UN secretary-general and the president of France urged him to return. President François Mitterrand, whose letter is said to have made a strong impression on the prince, reminded him that the world had invested much, including UNTAC lives, in the peace process in Cambodia, and no one would understand if he failed to go home and support the election.[64]

In February 1993, in a frank interview with journalist Nayan Chanda in Beijing, Sihanouk had denounced the failure of UNTAC and the violence, corruption, and chicanery of all of the Cambodian factions. He spoke pessimistically about the forthcoming election, noting that "UNTAC is going to have an election despite the fact none of the conditions for the election have been met. None. It is a hideous comedy. You can write that." He revealed that he and Hun Sen had suggested that "they allow me to be elected by my people in January or February in order to give me five or six months to improve the situation. I was sure that I would be able to perform much better than UNTAC. But UNTAC, especially the Americans and the British, don't want it."[65] This observation referred to an effort by Sihanouk in early January 1993 to promote the staging of a presidential election—obviously to elect Sihanouk as president—either before, during, or after the elections for the Constituent Assembly. Some external powers[66] had proposed a presidential election before the general election to permit Sihanouk to unify the country under a quadripartite interim government.[67] Some appeared to favor a presidential election simultaneously with the general election. The United States and Great Britain opposed such an election on the grounds that it had not been provided for in the Paris Agreements.[68] Sihanouk then abandoned his quest until the adoption of the new constitution.

The PDK and the Electoral Campaign

Throughout the electoral campaign, as already pointed out, the PDK referred to the electoral process as a "theatrical farce" and continued with their efforts to disrupt it. At the same time, they retained a respectful public posture toward Prince Sihanouk. They persisted in their statements that

64. Shawcross, *Cambodia's New Deal*, p. 20.
65. *Far Eastern Economic Review*, Feb. 4, 1993, p. 21.
66. ASEAN, China, and Japan, according to reports in *The Nation* (Bangkok), Jan. 16 and 22, 1993, and also France, according to Shawcross, *Cambodia's New Deal*, p. 16.
67. Findlay, *Cambodia: The Legacy and Lessons of UNTAC*, pp. 56–57.
68. Interviews by the authors at the U.S. Embassy, June 1992. See also *The United Nations and Cambodia, 1991–1995*, p. 31; and "Letter dated 1 February 1993 from the Secretary-General address to the President of the Security Council concerning the holding of a presidential election in Cambodia," S/25273, Feb. 10, 1993, in *The United Nations and Cambodia, 1991–1995*, p. 269.

they were willing to abide by the Paris Agreements, but they denounced UNTAC for ignoring the presence of Vietnamese troops in Cambodia and for permitting the SOC to govern the country. Their most virulent denunciations were aimed at the "CPP puppets and their Vietnamese (Yuon) masters."

The PDK appeared to believe that there was a conspiracy abroad to ensure an electoral victory for the CPP. As late as a week prior to the election, Khieu Samphan, in a radio broadcast, predicted an overwhelming CPP victory: "As for the results of the election, it has been predetermined that Vietnam's puppets will get between 70 and 80 percent of the votes, with the remaining votes distributed among the various parties. This will be paraded as democracy, freedom and so on. The PDK, like the entire Cambodian nation and people, categorically rejects this theatrical farce to destroy the Cambodian nation and also categorically rejects the predetermined result of this election."[69]

The Election

The turnout of Cambodian voters for the election, beginning on May 23, 1993, was remarkable, beyond the most optimistic expectations of UNTAC election officials. Some 46 percent of the registered voters, or 2.2 million, voted on the first day, and by the end almost 90 percent of the registered voters had turned out to vote. Except for a few incidents of violence and the death of one Cambodian civilian from mortar rounds in Kampong Cham Province, there was relative calm on voting day.[70]

UN Volunteers reported that many Cambodian voters came in their best clothes and offered flowers to the international poll watchers. Some walked for miles, at times through heavy downpour (for the rainy season had begun) to reach the polls. In some regions, voters stood in line in the sun to cast their ballots. Observers consistently reported the exhilaration that so many Cambodians felt at the opportunity to make a political choice in a "fair and free" election. William Shawcross wrote that he had "rarely seen anything so moving as the joy with which ordinary Cambodians defied violence and intimidation and grabbed the opportunity the world gave them to express their wishes."[71]

Voters voted in more than 1,400 fixed polling places, and at some 200

69. Voice of the Great National Union Front in Cambodia in Cambodian, May 13, 1993, in FBIS-EAS, May 14, 1993.
70. *The United Nations and Cambodia, 1991–1995*, p. 44.
71. Shawcross, *Cambodia's New Deal*, p. 20.

mobile units for reaching people in remote areas. Some 400 stations were closed prior to the voting because of threats to security. Yet during the voting only a few technical difficulties arose, including the rupture of several plastic and padlock seals on the ballot boxes in transit over rough roads.[72] (These broken seals were later used as part of a pretext by the CPP, discussed below, to call for a revote in seven provinces.) UNTAC took great care to ensure the secrecy of the ballot. Since the majority of the voters were illiterate, voters made their selection by checking the party symbol on the ballot. Ballots from a number of villages in a province were intermixed in order to disguise the pattern of local voting and reduce the risk of reprisal. Counting was conducted at the province level, and results were transmitted to Phnom Penh. The challenging of votes was permitted at the polling place by rival parties. A challenged vote was classified as "tendered," and a procedure for verifying it was undertaken.

The political opponents of the Cambodian People's Party feared that the CPP would use the assets of incumbency to haul people to the polls and intimidate them into voting for their party. The CPP, the backbone of the SOC, had access for their political activities to ready-made offices in the SOC provincial administration compounds. SOC officials served as CPP political "ward heelers" and on voting day mobilized people to vote. An example from Kampong Cham, where Hun Sen was a candidate and his brother was the "notably corrupt" governor, offers insights into events during voting week.[73] SOC cadres there carried out an intricate campaign to get people to the polls. A cadre was assigned to a group of ten villagers and given responsibility to get them to voting stations, instruct them how to vote, and quiz them as they came out. The big surprise was that thousands of people who had been dragooned in this manner actually voted for FUNCINPEC, as they did in Kampong Cham, where FUNCINPEC won ten seats, BLDP won one, Molinaka won one, and the CPP won only six.

Khmer Rouge behavior at election time still remains a puzzle. The Khmer Rouge had denounced the election and advised people not to vote, and their cadres in certain regions warned that to vote would be to commit suicide. PDK radio frequently repeated Khieu Samphan's labeling of the election as a "theatrical farce." A few days prior to the beginning of the balloting, the PDK predicted a low voter turnout. In a broadcast on May 17, 1993, a long diatribe against UNTAC's organization of the elections ended with this pronouncement:

72. *The United Nations and Cambodia, 1991–1995*, p. 44.
73. Described by Shawcross in *Cambodia's New Deal*, p. 21.

UNTAC only wants to hold the election and then renew the war in Cambodia. UNTAC is not here to extinguish the flames of the Vietnamese war of aggression in Cambodia. This clearly attests that UNTAC is the offender. Thus, it deserves heavy punishment before the Cambodian people, Cambodian history, and Cambodian People's Tribunal. UNTAC must be held responsible for all the consequences that arise in Cambodia. It cannot put the blame on others. As for UNTAC's electoral offices they all exist only on paper. In fact, there are electoral offices only in villages, communes, and districts only 10 and not more than 30 percent of the eligible voters have been registered.[74]

On the third day of the balloting, a PDK announcer read a statement entitled "The Cambodian people categorically reject the elections organized by UNTAC for the purpose of decimating the Cambodian nation, people and race." He charged that "Akashi and other UNTAC chieftains are, in collaboration with the Yuon aggressors and their puppets, destroying the Cambodian nation, people and race through the polls. He added that the "Yuon puppets plan to oppress, to intimidate, and to threaten to shoot to death those who will turn up to vote."[75]

Yet, these radio broadcasts notwithstanding, reports appeared that some local PDK commanders, particularly in western and northwestern areas, sent hundreds of people to the polls to vote for FUNCINPEC,[76] after concluding that the hated CPP was not sure to win.

A variety of explanations has been offered to explain the puzzling PDK behavior at election time. The UN secretary-general noted that "there are several theories attempting to explain the PDK's failure to disrupt the election, from the suggestion of some kind of eleventh hour intervention to reports by deserters from PDK forces of a general unwillingness or inability to attack the polling sites."[77] General Sanderson believed that UNTAC units and the SOC military had driven the Khmer Rouge out of the main population areas.[78] Trevor Findlay, surveying reports on the election, extracts four hypotheses as to why the PDK did not try to disrupt the election:

74. Voice of the Great National Union Front of Cambodia in Cambodian, May 17, 1993, in *FBIS-EAS*, 93-094, May 18, 1993.
75. Voice of the Great National Union Front of Cambodia in Cambodian, May 25, 1993, in *FBIS-EAS*-93-100, May 26, 1993.
76. *Bangkok Post*, May 27, 1993.
77. *The United Nations and Cambodia, 1991–1995*, p. 44.
78. Shawcross, *Cambodia's New Deal*, p. 21.

1. They may have been incapable of causing major disruption.
2. The Khmer Rouge had already infiltrated FUNCINPEC and were therefore quite willing to encourage a vote for it.
3. Outside pressure on the PDK, particularly by China, but also pressure by Japan, the U.S., and other Western countries on Thailand to sever its ties with the PDK, may have had a dampening effect on the PDK's inclination to disrupt the election.
4. The PDK had no plan but was simply muddling through in a new situation. Perhaps the leadership was divided, or lacked central control. In the absence of firm guidance, local commanders acted in ways they thought would please the hierarchy in some cases assisting the voting, in others attacking it, in still others just doing nothing.

Findlay sees the fourth hypothesis, combined with pressure from China, as the most likely explanation for PDK behavior at election time.[79]

The Election Results

According to the report of the UNTAC Electoral Component, 3,767,412 valid ordinary votes were cast (see Table 1).[80] In addition, 244,219 valid "tendered" (those that had been challenged) votes were cast, bringing the total of valid votes to more than 4 million. Ordinary votes that were declared invalid totaled 112,761. Slightly over half of the tendered votes were rejected after the records were checked, and 5,984 tendered votes were declared invalid. In summary, 4,267,192 votes were cast, amounting to 89.56 percent of the registered voters. (UNTAC estimated the Cambodian population to be 8,831,296.) The turnout would have been noteworthy in any democratic country. It was all the more remarkable in a country with a history of unending strife, with little experience in free elections, with rugged roads often mired in mud, and with an election conducted by an international agency.

The results by party show that FUNCINPEC garnered 45.47 percent of the votes and was awarded 58 seats in the 120-member Constituent Assembly, or 48.3 percent of the seats. The CPP won 38.22 percent of the votes and gained 51 seats, or 42.5 percent of the seats (about 7 percent more than the proportion of their votes). The BLDP won 3.81 percent of the votes and gained 10 seats (or 8.3 percent of the seats). Molinaka won 1.37 percent of the votes and was awarded 1 seat (or .8 percent of the seats).

79. Findlay, *Cambodia: The Legacy and Lessons of UNTAC*, pp. 87–88.
80. Electoral Component report.

Table 1. Cambodian election, May 23–28, 1993

Number of valid ordinary votes	3,767,412		
Number of valid tendered votes	244,219		
Total number of valid votes	4,011,631		
Number of invalid ordinary votes	112,761		
Number of tendered votes rejected after checking of records	136,816		
Number of invalid tendered votes	5,984		
Total number of votes cast	4,267,192		
% of registered voters who voted	89.56		

Party	Number of valid votes received	% of total valid votes	Number of seats won
FUNCINPEC	1,824,188	45.47	58
CPP	1,533,471	38.22	51
BLDP	152,764	3.81	10
MOLINAKA	55,107	1.37	1
Others	466,101	11.12	0

Source: Electoral component, UNTAC, June 10, 1993

The other 16 parties won a total of 11.12 percent of the vote, but gained no seats. Most of these parties earned less than 1 percent of the votes. The largest vote of any of these 16 was won by the LDP, which earned a total of 62,698 votes throughout the country, or 1.56 percent of the vote, slightly more than MOLINAKA's 55,107 votes, but not enough in a single province to win a seat.

The remarkable turnout of voters could be attributed to a variety of factors. Two of the UNTAC components made a special contribution, the Electoral Component and the Information and Education Division. The logistics of the electoral planning, already described, worked out remarkably well. The UN secretary-general singled out for praise the young UN Volunteers "from all over the world who risked their personal safety in many cases to reach potential voters in remote and contested districts." The secretary-general, as well as other observers, commended them for "commitment, integrity and enthusiasm for the democratic process."[81] Radio UNTAC made a signal contribution to voter awareness of the election. The UNTAC voter education campaign, especially the theme that the vote would be secret, was well received and made credible to the Cambodian

81. *The United Nations and Cambodia, 1991–1995*, p. 45.

audience. The well-advertised support of the international community for a "free fair and" election was reassuring to prospective voters. Prince Sihanouk's triumphant return to Phnom Penh from Beijing on the eve of the first day of election, and his appeal for calm during the voting process, added a drama that contributed to the large turnout. Most important was the sense of excitement that so many Cambodians felt at this rare opportunity to express their opinion about their own political future. A stirring sense of pride and enthusiasm expressed itself among Cambodians who waited so patiently to cast their ballots. Tens of thousands of Cambodians had been involved in the electoral process, assisting in registration, participating in the campaign, working at the polling stations, some at risk to their lives or the well-being of their families. Those involved in the electoral process helped to convince others of the election's importance. For many, the vote was a unique opportunity to express their disgust with both the incumbent regime and the Khmer Rouge, and to record their desire for change.[82]

Although no postelection survey was conducted to provide data to interpret the results, certain conclusions about the outcome appear evident. The FUNCINPEC lead, despite the organizational assets enjoyed by the CPP, must be attributed in good part to the popularity of Prince Sihanouk. A high-level observer at the U.S. Embassy told us that many Cambodians, when asked why they voted as they did, responded, "We voted for the king."[83] Sihanouk remained revered—despite his vacillation and former alignment with questionable allies—by great numbers of simple folk. His return to Phnom Penh on the day before the election helped the FUNCINPEC cause.[84] As part of this positive choice many, especially older people, appeared to vote their hope for a return to the calmer, more prosperous pre-1970 days of Sihanouk's rule. This attachment to Sihanouk was transferred to his son, Prince Ranariddh, who much resembled his father in voice and manner, and to the "royalist" FUNCINPEC party.

As for the negative sentiments expressed by the vote, clearly an important expression of revulsion was registered against the CPP. Their venality and corruption, particularly as these reached monumental proportions during the run-up to the election, were a source of voter disgust. Further, campaign rhetoric by FUNCINPEC and the PDK countered the CPP's efforts to shake the taint of past association with Vietnamese mentors. Cambodians were aware that most of the CPP leaders had been dissident Khmer Rouge

82. Interview by the authors at U.S. Embassy, Phnom Penh, Dec. 14, 1993.
83. Ibid.
84. Ibid., Dec. 16, 1993.

revolutionaries who had fled to Vietnam in 1977 and 1978 and had followed Vietnamese tanks into Phnom Penh in 1979 to form the government that had ruled until the election. In rejecting the CPP and choosing FUNCIN-PEC, voters were opting for change.

Of course, the CPP had its adherents, including those who worked for the SOC and their families and other dependents. There were undoubtedly those, too, who were bribed or intimidated by the incumbents and did as they were instructed. (Although the CPP must have benefited from its power to coerce, in certain cases the coercion appeared to cause a courageous backlash against them.) The poor showing of the BLDP and LDP came as a surprise to many observers, particularly Westerners. The KPNLF, split into electoral factions, and turned out to be "its own worst enemy."[85] Further, it was noted, people thought it necessary to beat the CPP. The profusion of small parties confused people, and they gained relatively few votes.

Following the final day of voting, but before the votes had been counted, Special Representative Akashi told reporters on a tour of polling stations in northwest Cambodia that the election had not been held in an ideal situation, but nevertheless it met the yardstick for a realistic standard of "free and fair elections." On May 29, Akashi made a formal declaration to the Supreme National Council that the conduct of the election had been free and fair. The UN Security Council endorsed this declaration on June 2, thus providing an international imprimatur for the election process.[86]

85. *New York Times*, May 26, 1993.
86. Security Council Resolution on the completion of the election in Cambodia, S/RES/835 (1993), June 2, 1993, in *The United Nations and Cambodia, 1991–1995*, pp. 311–12.

PART 3

THE NEW STATE

CHAPTER FIVE

Maneuvering for Position, June–September 1993

Due to slow UNTAC vote-counting procedures, it was not until June 10, 1993, that the final tally of the May 28 voting was announced. Interim reports had shown FUNCINPEC in the lead and prompted signs that the Cambodian People's Party were unlikely to be sporting losers. CPP politicians sent out a cry that there had been irregularities and fraud in the voting, and called upon UNTAC to hold new elections in four provinces, including Phnom Penh. Special Representative Akashi stood firm, with an announcement on June 10 that the election results fairly and accurately reflect the will of the Cambodian people and must be respected.[1]

The UN secretary-general, Boutros Boutros-Ghali, in a report to the Security Council on same day, endorsed this judgment. He noted that "we were not satisfied that a neutral political environment" had prevailed during the campaign period and he expressed concern that violence and intimidation continued throughout the country. But he justified pressing ahead with the election "in the firm belief that the Cambodian people wanted an election." The massive turnout in a "festive atmosphere of joy and hope for the future," he noted, was testimony to their courage and determination.[2] The secretary-general added that the first task of the newly elected assembly would be to approve a constitution and create a government. He made

1. *The United Nations and Cambodia, 1991–1995*, with an introduction by Boutros Boutros-Ghali, Secretary-General of the United Nations (New York: UN Department of Public Information, 1995), p. 46.

2. Report of the Secretary-General on the conduct and results of the election in Cambodia, S/25913, June 10, 1993.

a special plea to all parties "to bury the hatchet of yesterday, to cease mutual recriminations forthwith and to concentrate from now on upon building a new Cambodia, based on genuine fraternity and concord."

Major obstacles loomed ahead for the new task of mending a failed state. The Khmer Rouge remained unreconstructed obstructionists. It seemed unlikely at the time that a new, fragile regime would have the capability—at least in the short run—of eliminating the Khmer Rouge threat. In addition, the CPP immediately entered a protest about the election results, and some of its leaders were threatening secession of certain provinces. There was even a hint of a military coup.[3] Trouble from the CPP was surely to be faced in attempting to form a government that would separate the CPP from power.

Resistance by the CPP and the Khmer Rouge to the fulfillment of the new tasks reflected Cambodia's fractured society. To begin the process of reconciliation was the greatest challenge. Cambodian society had been decimated by a civil war from 1970 to 1975, followed by the brutal Khmer Rouge regime from 1975 to 1979. The fourteen years of the State of Cambodia regime, which had been installed by an invading Vietnam, created new divisions. The incumbent SOC was riddled by corruption, and few persons with experience, education, and energy were available to manage an effective new government. There was reason to doubt SOC willingness to accept a minority position in a newly elected government. UNTAC, which had provided vital administrative and material support, was to terminate its mandate as soon as the new government took power in September 1993.

Although the obstacles were formidable, Cambodia possessed some assets for the task of rebuilding the failed state. A major one, despite his volatility, changeability, and undependability, was Prince Sihanouk. The prince still commanded great devotion, even awe, among a large segment of Cambodian society, especially among the peasantry. He was accepted as a leader, or at least a legitimate mediator, by each of the competing political factions. He also retained his standing as an interlocutor of Cambodian national interests among the international community. Sihanouk was to play a vital role—even though he was to be predictably unpredictable—in the formation of a new government.

Another important asset was the relative homogeneity of Cambodian society. Unlike many failed states, including Yugoslavia, Somalia, and Rwanda, Cambodia was not divided into competing ethnic groups. At least

---

3. Trevor Findlay, *Cambodia: The Legacy and Lessons of UNTAC* (Oxford: Oxford University Press, 1995), p. 91. Nate Thayer, "Sihanouk Back at the Helm," *Phnom Penh Post*, June 18–July 1, 1993.

90% of the population are ethnic Khmer, Theravada Buddhists, who share a common language, culture, and sense of history. (A Vietnamese ethnic minority, it must be noted, has been a source of conflict.) There is, therefore, a good potential for national unity within Khmer society. Further, the impressive turnout for the election, in spite of threats, danger, and inconvenience, suggested a strong popular yearning for a new political era. Cambodians were exhausted by the turbulence of the previous two decades and eager for a fresh start. They were encouraged by the consensus among the Great Powers to support the peace process, significantly different from the earlier decades when Cambodia was a "sideshow" of the competition among these powers. The regional powers, too—Vietnam and Thailand, in particular—appeared ready to accept the emergence of an independent Cambodian government.

In the first half of June 1993, political tumult raised questions as to whether the plan of the Paris Agreements could be fully implemented. The CPP challenged the election and, as noted above, called for a repeated vote in four provinces. A group of CPP dissidents, led by Prince Chakrapong (son of Prince Sihanouk, half-brother of Prince Ranariddh, and a vice prime minister in the SOC), attempted to break away seven provinces from Cambodia. Prince Sihanouk himself launched an effort to form a government that ignored the outcome of the election. Nevertheless, during this tumult, the Constituent Assembly would meet for its inaugural session and choose Prince Sihanouk as head of state. Finally, the new head of state would succeed in forming an interim government.

CPP Challenge of the Election Results

Shortly after the polls closed, when the SOC television network interrupted, symbolically, a Charlie Chaplin film to announce that it would stop releasing preliminary election results which showed FUNCINPEC in the lead, UNTAC refused to withhold results. Its press spokesman, Eric Falt, insisted that UNTAC was committed to "openness and transparency in the conduct of elections."[4] Chea Sim, hard-line president of the CPP, followed up an earlier protest with a letter to UNTAC declaring that the CPP could not accept the electoral process. New elections would have to be held in the provinces at issue, he declared.[5] The normally reclusive Chea Sim met

4. *New York Times*, June 1, 1993. Postelection developments from an UNTAC perspective are described in Timothy Carney and Tan Lian Choo, *Whither Cambodia? Beyond the Election* (Singapore: Institute of East Asian Studies, 1993), pp. 1–28.

5. *New York Times*, June 2, 1993.

with Akashi—the only other time he had called upon Akashi was the day before the election, when the CPP threatened to withdraw itself—to insist that the CPP would not accept the election results unless there was a rerun of the voting in four provinces (Phnom Penh, Battambang, Kompon Chhnang, and Prey Veng).[6] The CPP protests were accompanied by slightly veiled threats that "insurrections and riots" might take place if UNTAC refused to reopen the voting. Khieu Kanharith, chief SOC spokesman, warned at a news conference that "soldiers will riot . . . when hearing the results of the election," although he maintained that the SOC was trying to prevent such violence.[7] Although he did not take the threat lightly, UNTAC chief Akashi was undeterred in maintaining that the election had been free and fair. He told a reporter, "I don't believe the predictions of major unrest have any basis in reality."[8]

Sihanouk's Abortive Attempt to Name a Government

In the few days following the CPP rejection of the election results in at least four provinces, Prince Sihanouk surprised UNTAC by announcing, on June 3, the formation of a new national government. It appears that Japan, France, and Russia had encouraged Sihanouk to create an interim government after the election, in which he would exercise a dominant position.[9] However, the United States, China, Great Britain, and Australia opposed the prince's initiative.[10] In his announcement, Sihanouk designated himself prime minister and supreme military commander and retained his title as chief of state. He named as joint deputy prime ministers his son Ranariddh, leader of FUNCINPEC, and Hun Sen, leader of the CPP. Few details were provided about the makeup of the rest of the government.

The CPP accepted this new arrangement with alacrity, and their opposition to the election results appeared to evaporate.[11] Spokesmen for Hun Sen said the new government would lead Cambodia only until the National Assembly was seated in the summer, but Prince Sihanouk's announcement of the new government had made no mention of being temporary or provisional. A spokesman for Hun Sen claimed that the negotiations for the creation of the coalition government were "very smooth and very friendly."

FUNCINPEC spokesmen, on the other hand, appeared confused by this

6. UPI, June 1, 1993.
7. *New York Times*, June 2, 1993.
8. Ibid.
9. Reuter, June 5, 1993. Carney and Choo, *Whither Cambodia?* p. 8.
10. *Pnom Penh Post*, June 18–July 1, 1993.
11. *New York Times*, June 4, 1993.

unanticipated turn of events. A senior FUNCINPEC official said that the coalition was "the work of Prince Sihanouk" and that "while some people aren't happy with this arrangement, we have to accept it because Prince Sihanouk is the father of the nation."[12] A senior source in FUNCINPEC, who often echoed Prince Sihanouk's views, told reporters that "Prince Ranariddh always said during his election campaign that he would bring the Khmer Rouge back to the Cambodian community and if we give them a chance the Khmer Rouge will make peace. The key problem now is how to bring SOC and the KR to compromise as some SOC elements do not accept the KR."[13] But Prince Ranariddh was angered by his father's peremptory maneuver and he rejected the new coalition. Formation of a coalition government with equal representation by FUNCINPEC and the CPP, led by Sihanouk, ignored the outcome of the election.

Ranariddh's displeasure was matched by that of UNTAC and important members of the international community. A "senior" UNTAC official was quoted as saying, "We've been presented with a *fait accompli*. After spending $2 billion to save this country, the United Nations was shut out of this process. You have to wonder what the Prince is up to."[14] The U.S. expressed its opposition to Sihanouk's surprise announcement that he intended to lead an "interim coalition government." The United States was particularly concerned about reports that Prince Sihanouk had invited the PDK to join this new coalition in an "advisory" role. The U.S. Embassy in Phnom Penh made public its position the same day as Sihanouk's announcement, June 3, in a so-called non-paper:

> The U.S. is concerned about recent discussions among the Cambodian parties concerning the immediate formation of an interim coalition government in Cambodia [that] may lead to a violation of the Paris Accords and the spirit of the successful election. . . . We thus want to underscore the importance of ensuring that any attempts to forge a coalition among the parties which participated in the elections to create a new government adhere strictly to the process laid down by the Paris Agreements. In particular the constituent assembly must be permitted to carry out fully its responsibility to draft a new constitution and form the new government in Cambodia.[15]

As hurriedly as he had proclaimed the formation of this new government, Prince Sihanouk, on the next day, announced its abandonment. In a message to the people of Cambodia, Sihanouk pleaded, "I ask you to please

12. Ibid.
13. Reuter, June 5, 1993.
14. *New York Times*, June 4, 1993.
15. *Phnom Penh Post*, June 18–July 1, 1993.

forgive me—I have to renounce forming a national government." He alluded to UNTAC's and other international criticism of his move. "A number of Cambodians and foreigners are saying this national government was formed of a constitutional coup. I renounce to form it."[16]

The prince was said to have been outraged by the U.S. position. In a nationwide radio broadcast on June 8, he announced that he had abandoned the idea largely because of U.S. opposition. Prince Sihanouk's anger was not assuaged by the announcement in Phnom Penh on June 22 by the visiting American deputy secretary of state, Clifton Wharton, that though the United States acknowledged that it was the task of the Cambodian people to form their own government, the U.S. would not provide any economic assistance to a coalition that included the Khmer Rouge.[17]

Sihanouk's motives in announcing the coalition government were, as always, difficult to discern. A benevolent interpretation would hold that Sihanouk's primary impulse was to achieve peaceful national reconciliation. Bringing the CPP into a coalition with FUNCINPEC might have been calculated, it could be argued, to end the CPP's challenge to the results of the UNTAC-led election. Since the CPP retained an army, an organized party, and a major portion of national civil service, they were a powerful force that had to be accommodated. Offering them an equal share of political power with FUNCINPEC would encourage them to cooperate, rather than to sabotage a new government. Sihanouk may have believed that, with the Khmer Rouge in an "advisory" role, he could entice them to cooperate with the interim government. In announcing his new government, Sihanouk made conciliatory remarks to the Khmer Rouge, asking them to take part in "national reconciliation and national union" and offering "official recognition" to their two nominal leaders, Khieu Samphan and Son Sen.[18] As for FUNCINPEC, even though they might be disappointed not to lead the nation after an electoral victory, their leader Ranariddh would accept the judgment of the "father of the nation" (and his own father) as to the best course to pursue in the quest for peace and reconciliation.

A less flattering interpretation might add that Sihanouk saw the opportunity to resume his role as Cambodia's primary political leader. He could easily persuade himself that only he possessed the wisdom, courage, and cunning to lead his nation. He would enjoy exercising dominant political power.

Ranariddh's rejection of his father's proposal added strain to a family re-

16. UPI, June 4, 1993.
17. AFP in English, June 23, 1993, in *FBIS-EAS*, June 23, 1993.
18. *New York Times*, June 4, 1993.

lationship that was already fraught with tension. Earlier reports of serious divisions between father and son had surfaced, but now their discord emerged into the open. Their letters to one another showed up in Phnom Penh. In a letter to Ranariddh, Sihanouk wrote that he had organized the interim government only to "avoid a bloody conflict" that might result from the elections. He further asserted that the parties led by Ranariddh and Hun Sen would now be responsible for any "bloodshed or tragedy that befalls our unfortunate country and our unhappy people."[19] Ranariddh, in his letter to his "very venerated papa," noted that he accepted the concept of national reconciliation, but he was caustic in his assertion that he could not work with "killers" in the CPP who had been responsible for the assassination of FUNCINPEC members during the election campaign. He alluded to another source of family tension in noting that he could not work with his estranged half-brother, Prince Norodom Chakrapong, who had crossed over to become a key official in the CPP and a deputy prime minister in the SOC. Ranariddh asked in the letter, "How could I work with Prince Chakrapong, whose aim is to want to see me destroyed—or even killed?"[20]

Prince Chakrapong was commonly described by Cambodians as the *kon chloy* or wayward son of Prince Sihanouk.[21] His reputation among the Western diplomatic community was one of political opportunism and doubtful reliability. Appointed by the SOC to run the civil aviation authority, he was accused by FUNCINPEC of using his official position to prevent aircraft chartered by their party from landing at Cambodian airports. UNTAC imposed a $5,000 fine on him for violating the electoral law. In an obvious show of contempt for UNTAC, he paid the fine with a sack of Cambodian notes of small denomination. Chakrapong was thought to be estranged from his father and his half-brother.[22] There was, therefore, astonishment in Phnom Penh when Prince Chakrapong appeared on the balcony of the Royal Palace, where he listened to his father give a speech denouncing FUNCINPEC for standing in the way of a new government.[23] Hundreds of citizens gathered outside, including truckloads of supporters brought in by the CPP, who cheered Prince Sihanouk's denunciations of FUNCINPEC and called for him to take power.[24]

Still angered by Ranariddh's rejection of the new government, Prince Si-

19. Ibid., June 5.
20. Ibid.
21. Ibid., June 16.
22. Ibid., June 5.
23. Ibid., June 7.
24. AP, June 6, 1993; *New York Times*, June 7, 1993.

hanouk asserted, on June 6, that a new government would have to wait until later in the year, when the heavens would be aligned properly. He noted that "astrologers have advised me not to pressure for a new government because I won't succeed until my birthday next October."[25]

The Abortive Secessionist Movement

A few days after he had appeared on the balcony with his father, Prince Chakrapong surfaced, on June 12, in Prey Veng, thirty miles east of Phnom Penh, where he issued a statement warning that UN vehicles should not cross the Mekong River into that province, and that UN aircraft were prohibited from flying over "security areas." These pronouncements were made at the same time that SOC government and army officials in three eastern provinces (Kampong Cham, Prey Veng, and Svay Rieng) were preventing UN peacekeepers from operating.[26] Chakrapong labeled these eastern breakaway provinces (later said to total seven of Cambodia's twenty one provinces), located along the borders with Vietnam and Laos, the "King Father Autonomous Zone," referring obviously to Sihanouk. Chakrapong told a rally of about three thousand people in Svay Rieng that he formed the zone in response to charges of irregularities in the election.[27]

The secessionist movement did not last long. Hun Sen traveled by speedboat to Kampong Cham town on June 13, where he met with his brother, Hun Neng, the provincial governor who had earlier ordered UNTAC to leave the province. A spokesman for Hun Sen declared that "Kampong Cham is no longer an autonomous zone." He added that Hun Sen was "trying to persuade other provinces to break away from the dissident groups."[28] By June 15, the secessionist movement had collapsed, as Prince Chakrapong fled into Vietnam in a convoy of about twenty vehicles and turned over a cache of weapons to startled Vietnamese guards. Akashi announced on June 15 that Hun Sen had informed him that "he has been successful in calming down the situation in the eastern provinces." Prince Chakrapong was awarded amnesty by his father and returned from Vietnam to Phnom Penh. Chakrapong met with his father, and Prince Sihanouk announced that all was forgiven. He added that the "patriotism" of Prince Chakrapong "makes me embrace you with all my profound affection."

25. Ibid.
26. UPI, June 12, 1993.
27. AP, June 12, 1993.
28. UPI, June 14, 1993.

Chakrapong, in a handwritten letter, responded, "I volunteer to serve your royal policy forever, without conditions." [29]

It is not clear what induced Prince Chakrapong to lead a secessionist movement. He may have believed he could succeed. He may have thought he had the support of Hun Sen or even of Prince Sihanouk. He may have calculated that his action would inspire support from neighboring Vietnam. Perhaps he believed he could intimidate FUNCINPEC into accepting a power-sharing arrangement with the CPP. It is possible, of course, that this adventuresome, wayward son was acting brashly under others' manipulation.

Not surprisingly, Chakrapong's coupette stirred a torrent of speculation in Phnom Penh. One widely circulated rumor was that the creation of the "autonomous zone" was a ploy intended to put pressure on Prince Ranariddh to agree to a coalition government. The *New York Times* correspondent in Phnom Penh wrote, "If it was a ploy, it worked." He noted that on June 17, Prince Ranariddh had agreed to an interim coalition government with Hun Sen, only a week after he had rejected a similar proposition. [30] The Reuters correspondent reported, "Diplomats say the move [Chakrapong's secession] is a negotiating ploy by the former communist government to cling onto as much power as possible in some form of coalition with Ranariddh." [31] Many believed that, despite his efforts to curb the secession, Hun Sen had initially encouraged it. There was even speculation, less widely believed (but even curious convolutions must be considered in Cambodian politics), that Prince Sihanouk had a hand in inspiring his devious son's maneuver, to create the dynamics for acceptance of a coalition government.

When he fled to Vietnam and abandoned the secessionist movement, Prince Chakrapong could claim that one of his central demands—the appointment of his father as chief of state—had been met. Further, Sihanouk, Ranariddh, and Hun Sen had agreed in principle that a coalition would be formed to include the CPP and FUNCINPEC in a new interim government.

Inaugural Session of the Constituent Assembly

The newly elected Constituent Assembly convened for its inaugural session on June 14, 1993. A UN helicopter hovered above the National Assembly

29. *New York Times*, June 18, 1993; UPI, June 14, 1993.
30. *New York Times*, June 18, 1993.
31. Reuter, June 14, 1993.

building, located next to the Grand Palace on Lenin Boulevard, and UN security guards stood at the alert, as Prince Sihanouk and UNTAC chief Akashi arrived. Prince Ranariddh introduced a motion, approved unanimously, to "render null and void the unconstitutional coup d'etat in 1970." Thus, as announced by the general secretary of the Constituent Assembly, Lt. General Tol Lah, the status of Prince Sihanouk as chief of state "since before 1970" was declared to have been uninterrupted.[32] In reaffirming Prince Sihanouk as the head of state, "The members . . . decided on behalf of the entire Khmer people to once again vest . . . Sihanouk with the full and special powers inherent in his capacity and duties as head of state in order that he may save our nation and lead it on the path towards progress and prosperity."[33] Addressing the assembly, Sihanouk pledged to "inaugurate a new era of liberal democracy." Akashi told the legislators that he was confident they would be able to work together to write a constitution and then form a new government. He added an admonition that "the willingness of governments and private investors to commit funds to Cambodia will largely depend on the degree of political stability that they can see here."[34]

The timetable established by the Paris Agreements provided for the Constituent Assembly to draft and promulgate a new constitution within ninety days, transform itself into the National Assembly, and choose a permanent government. UNTAC would then withdraw. Despite the turbulence over the formation of an interim government, the initial refusal of the CPP to accept the election results, and the secessionist threat of the Prince Chakrapong group, the assembly carried out its required tasks.

Formation of an Interim Government

On June 16, the newly reaffirmed chief of state proposed the formation of an Interim Joint Administration with Prince Ranariddh and Hun Sen as the co-chairmen of a Council of Ministers. The appointment of an interim government following the election but prior to the promulgation of a constitution had not been envisaged in the Paris Agreements.[35] Its formation appeared to emerge from the maneuvers of Prince Sihanouk and, according to Trevor Findlay, from "delicate statecraft and diplomatic pressure, in-

32. *Phnom Penh Post*, July 16–29, 1993.
33. Reuter, June 14, 1993.
34. Ibid.
35. *The United Nations and Cambodia, 1991–1995*, p. 47.

volving UNTAC and key foreign parties to the Paris Accord."[36] The UN secretary-general reported that its establishment "proved to be a stabilizing mechanism in the Cambodian polity."[37] Special Representative Akashi, in a retrospective speech at Columbia University, commented on the formation of this interim government, which had not been anticipated by the Permanent Five: "We had to admit the practical wisdom of combining the 'new wind,' represented by the victorious FUNCINPEC, consisting mostly of upper and middle class intellectuals aspiring to the restoration of the monarchy, with the experience and power of CPP, which is authoritarian but has 14 years of administrative experience, with much of the army and police under its control."[38]

In light of the coup d'état of Hun Sen in July 1997 (discussed in Chapter 8), the wisdom of creating two prime ministers to govern following the election but prior to the promulgation of the constitution is not self-evident. The more usual parliamentary practice of naming a single prime minister from the party winning the most votes (FUNCINPEC) and inviting leaders from other parties garnering substantial votes (CPP, BLDP) to take cabinet posts in a coalition government might have reduced Hun Sen's tendency to think in July 1997 that he had a right to overthrow the "first" (but not superior) prime minister.

At the same time that he announced the formation of the new Interim Joint Administration, Prince Sihanouk proclaimed the "official" end of the secessionist movement. A statement issued by Sihanouk declared that "the head of state thanks all the secessionists who obeyed the order to bring a complete end of the secession for the safeguard of national, political and territorial unity of the country."[39]

During the ensuing week, intense negotiations took place among the key actors regarding the structure of the future government coalition. On June 24, the newly nominated joint presidents (as Prince Ranariddh and Hun Sen were referred to in UNTAC parlance), after a four-hour session of negotiations, met with reporters to announce the composition of a provisional government. Ranariddh and Hun Sen confirmed that they would be co-

---

36. Findlay, *Cambodia: The Legacy and Lessons of UNTAC*, p. 92.

37. Report by the Secretary-General pursuant to paragraph 7 of resolution 840 (1993) on the possible role of the United Nations and its agencies after the end of the UNTAC mandate according to the Paris Agreements, S/26090, July 16, 1993, in *The United Nations and Cambodia, 1991–1995*, p. 321.

38. Yasushi Akashi, "The Challenges of Peace-Keeping in Cambodia: Lessons to Be Learned." Paper presented to School of International and Public Affairs, Columbia University, New York, Nov. 29, 1993, p. 7. Quoted in Findlay, *Cambodia: The Legacy and Lessons of UNTAC*, p. 93.

39. UPI, June 17, 1993.

presidents of the provisional government and co-ministers of the defense and interior ministries. FUNCINPEC and the CPP would each lead ten other ministries, the BLDP would run three ministries, and MOLINAKA one.[40]

Ranariddh was apparently persuaded to accept the joint "chairmanship" of the Council of Ministers by agreement that he would be designated as the "first president" and Hun Sen as the "second" in the provisional government. In each ministry, it was agreed that a member of the other party would hold the second post. FUNCINPEC governors would be appointed in one-half of the provinces. Further, a governor of one party would have a deputy governor of the other in each province.

On June 26, the makeup of the new provisional government was announced. FUNCINPEC appointed Prince Norodom Sirivuddh, a half-brother of Sihanouk, as foreign minister. The CPP named the former SOC foreign minister, Hor Nam Hong, as minister of state in the foreign ministry. Co-vice-chairmen of the new government were a CPP appointee, Keat Chhon, a former consultant to the UN Development Program (UNDP), and Ung Phan, a FUNCINPEC nominee, who had once served in Hun Sen's cabinet (but broke with Hun Sen and joined FUNCINPEC during the civil war). Minister for post and telecommunications was Ung Huot, a veteran political adviser to Ranariddh (who later joined Hun Sen in July 1997 as his designated first prime minister). Information minister was an intellectual and former editor, Khieu Kanharith, a close adviser to Hun Sen. Agricultural minister was a CPP appointee, Kong Sam Ol, an agronomist educated at the University of Texas. The BLDP was assigned three ministers, and MOLINAKA one. On July 1, the Constituent Assembly unanimously approved this intricately balanced government.[41]

The new FUNCINPEC ministers would soon encounter resistance from incumbent SOC/CPP cadres, some of whom had served since the installation of the Khmer People's Republic in 1979. For example, Sin Song, SOC minister of national security, who had collaborated with Prince Chakrapong in the abortive secession attempt, had announced that he would not give up his post unless compelled to do so by a two-thirds vote of the Constituent Assembly. Large areas of Phnom Penh had been without electricity for a week because of insufficient fuel to run aged generators. Civil servants had not been paid for weeks. Corruption was rampant in the crumbling public service. There were widespread reports that civil servants were selling furniture, office supplies—indeed anything available to them.

40. Reuter, June 18, 1993; UPI, June 21, 1993; DPA, June 25, 1993.
41. Reuter, June 25, 1993; UPI, July 1, 1993.

Along with the negotiations for the formation of a coalition government, talks proceeded about unifying the armies of the formerly disputing factions. The CPP/SOC was estimated to control 45,000 regular troops and provincial militia numbering near 100,000. FUNCINPEC and the KPNLF were estimated at 10,000. The Khmer Rouge were said by UNTAC sources to have 15,000.[42] The military leaders of FUNCINPEC, the KPNLF, and the SOC had agreed on June 10 to work together to set up a single army to be known as the Cambodian Armed Forces (CAF).[43]

The coalition elements of the new provisional government were not a great deal different from the ones that Sihanouk had first proposed, although, significantly, Sihanouk was not assigned the central executive role. Yet Sihanouk had pushed for the coalition arrangement and he had the important support of UNTAC and the external powers. A measure of political stability appeared to emerge from this new coalition and it helped the economy, encouraging international support, foreign aid donors, and investors.[44] It also contributed to further isolation of the Khmer Rouge. Although this curious coalition raised hopes, during its first three years, that it would survive until the 1998 elections, by the middle of its fourth year tensions were severe and Hun Sen fundamentally altered the negotiated arrangement.

The Interim Government's Negotiations with the PDK

The greatest threat confronting the new interim government, it appeared at the time, was the hostility of the PDK. (It later developed that the greater threat to the stability of the fragile new quasi-democracy was the tensions between Hun Sen and Ranariddh.) Finding an appropriate formula for interacting with the PDK was a primary challenge to the government. The Paris Agreements had reflected the premise that political reconciliation would emerge from the peace process, with elections substituting for armed combat. But the PDK had withdrawn from participation in the election, and low-level violence, much of it initiated by the PDK, continued in the countryside. The question for the interim government, therefore, was what to do about the PDK. The dominant approach, particularly by chief of state Sihanouk, was to strive for political reconciliation by negotiation.

A positive sign that might be thought to favor reconciliation was the initial progress in working together made by FUNCINPEC and the CPP.

42. Reuter, June 23, 1993.
43. *The United Nations and Cambodia, 1991–1995*, p. 47.
44. Findlay, *Cambodia: The Legacy and Lessons of UNTAC*, p. 94.

FUNCINPEC, a royalist movement, and the CPP, a communist movement formerly dominated by Vietnam, had evolved from bitter enemies engaged in armed combat, into suspicious electoral adversaries angrily denouncing each other, and subsequently into wary partners cooperating tentatively in a fragile new coalition, with Co-Presidents Ranariddh and Hun Sen scheduled to work in tandem. Could the arrangement be broadened somehow to include the Khmer Rouge? There were differing perspectives on this question among the major political actors.

Approaches to Negotiations by Sihanouk, Ranariddh and Hun Sen

Prince Sihanouk saw himself as the great unifier and defined his mission to be a search for peaceful reconciliation. He held the hope and belief that he could successfully bring the PDK into the national fold. Sihanouk was not a newcomer to cooperation with the Khmer Rouge. As previously related, twenty-three years earlier, following his ouster by the coup of General Lon Nol in 1970, Sihanouk had thrown in his lot with the Khmer Rouge. He accepted their appointment as the (figurehead) "chief of state" of the "government in exile," the GRUNK (gouvernement royal unifié national khmer), even though he confided to a journalist that he knew they would "spit me out like a cherry pit" when they no longer had use for him. He made his base in Beijing during Lon Nol's rule, from 1970 to 1975, with occasional KR-guided visits to their zones of control. Sihanouk's Chinese friends had encouraged his cooperation with the Khmer Rouge. During the full-scale Khmer Rouge rule of Cambodia, from 1975 to 1979, Sihanouk lived at the isolated palace in an almost empty Phnom Penh, under virtual house arrest. The Khmer Rouge recognized Sihanouk's symbolic appeal to the Cambodian peasantry and did not harm him or his wife, although some thirteen of his children and grandchildren perished under their brutal rule.

It is not clear what impact the experience of cooperating with the Khmer Rouge during this turbulent decade from 1970 to 1979 made upon the prince. Whatever ambivalent sentiments he may have felt, he professed to see a greater danger to his beloved Cambodia from Vietnamese domination than from the Khmer Rouge, and he agreed to resume his cooperation with them in 1979 at the United Nations Security Council debate on Cambodia, and in 1982 when he assumed the post of titular head of the Coalition Government of Democratic Kampuchea (CGDK). This long experience of cooperating with the Khmer Rouge may well have left Sihanouk with the conviction that they could be brought into the national community. He was certainly dedicated to the premise that he should reign over a reunified nation, and that he must make a majestic effort to bring them in. Perhaps he believed he could outmaneuver them.

Prince Ranariddh approached the prospect of reconciliation with the Khmer Rouge with greater skepticism than his father. Ranariddh had been a dutiful son and had generally followed the political guidance of his father. During the Khmer Rouge rule from 1975 to 1979, he had lived quietly in France at Aix-en-Provence, teaching at the Faculty of Law, and so had not experienced his father's deep immersion with the Khmer Rouge. At his father's behest in the early 1980s, he took up leadership of the FUNCINPEC faction in the camps along the Thai border. Ranariddh had, of course, cooperated with the Khmer Rouge within the CGDK in the struggle against the PRK/SOC, but it was an arm's length relationship.

The success of Ranariddh's party in the election was due significantly to its identification with Prince Sihanouk. Thus, Ranariddh's political career had been heavily dependent on his identification with his father, and his natural inclination was to follow his father's counsel. Nevertheless, during the postelection period Ranariddh had shown himself willing to disagree publicly with his father's political proposals. On the issue of bringing the PDK into a participatory role in the new government, Ranariddh initially supported his father's attempts at reconciliation, but by 1994, when efforts to achieve PDK cooperation had proved fruitless, he advocated outlawing the PDK, in public opposition to the king's position.

Ranariddh had been the peace candidate, running on a platform suggesting that FUNCINPEC could end the fighting and achieve peace, while the CPP could not. When asked during the electoral campaign if he would be willing to share power with the PDK, he responded that he would have no objection to inviting the PDK's young intellectuals into a government of national reconciliation if it would avoid war. He said he would not be willing to share power with the PDK's old leadership—Khieu Samphan, for example, "is not a young intellectual."[45] When asked about a role for the PDK later in the campaign, Ranariddh said that it would be up to his father to bring them back into the political fold, adding that the PDK "should not feel they are excluded from the national community."[46]

In the immediate postelection period, Prince Ranariddh offered guarded endorsement of his father's appeal to the PDK to negotiate peacefully for a role in the government and to bring their soldiers into a single national military force. Ranariddh was willing to accept the PDK into some sort of advisory role in government, or even in middle-level posts, below that of

45. AFP in English, April 6, 1993, in *FBIS-EAS*, April 7, 1993.
46. Ibid., May 23, 1993, in *FBIS-EAS*, May 24, 1993.

minister or deputy minister. But the new constitution, in September 1993, expressly prohibited the appointment of members of a party that had not participated in the election to ministerial posts. As the attempts to reach an accommodation with the PDK failed to bear fruit in 1993, Ranariddh moved closer to the rejectionist position of his co-president, Hun Sen.

Hun Sen and other leaders of the CPP were essentially opposed to any role for the PDK in the new government. For tactical political reasons, Hun Sen sometimes publicly endorsed Sihanouk's search for an accommodation with the PDK. But these endorsements scarcely hid the loathing, and probably fear, that Hun Sen and his colleagues held for most of the PDK leaders. The CPP leaders had been members of the Khmer Rouge movement, defecting and fleeing to Vietnam in 1977 or 1978, during a period of internecine warfare and purges in the revolutionary organization. The PDK leaders regarded them as renegades who had thrown in their lot with the hated Vietnamese, and considered them traitors. Hun Sen and his colleagues had reason to fear the PDK. If the PDK were successful in seizing power, or even if they arranged only to share power, would they be inhibited from settling scores by violence against CPP leaders? During the election campaign, the PDK radio had announced with approval that "people" were calling for Phnom Penh leaders to be condemned to death:

> During the 13 years of the Yuon war of aggression, Hun Sen, Chea Sim, Heng Samrin, Tie Banh, Hor Nam Hong, Pol Saroeun have served the Yuon policy of invading, annexing, and swallowing Cambodia's territory. They have in connivance with the Yuon aggressors, systematically massacred the Cambodian people. They have given the Yuon a free hand to cut off Cambodia's terrestrial and maritime territory and allowed the influx of millions of ethnic Yuon into Cambodia in order to plunder houses, farmland, lakes, and rivers of the Cambodian people in accordance with the Yuon's Indochinese strategy.[47]

Hun Sen and his colleagues had issued similar denunciations of the PDK. For example, at a meeting of the SNC in April 1993 attended by Secretary-General Boutros Boutros-Ghali, Hun Sen presented a memo enumerating the violations of the Paris Agreements and human rights by the PDK which included the following clause: "We demand that the Khmer Rouge ringleaders be tried before an International Tribunal for their past genocidal crimes committed from 1975 to 1979 and for their crimes committed barbarously against mankind after the signing of the Paris Agree-

---

47. Voice of the Great National Union Front of Cambodia in Cambodian, April 23, 1993, in *FBIS-EAS*, April 29, 1993.

ment, crimes similar to those that have taken place in Yugoslavia."[48] It is conceivable that the CPP leaders might have found it possible to cooperate with certain PDK leaders if political exigencies demanded, but not with others, such as Pol Pot or Ta Mok. But in view of the implacable hostility that the PDK and CPP had shown to each other, and given the fervent revolutionary convictions of the PDK, it seemed improbable in 1993 that Hun Sen and the CPP would support a formula to bring the PDK peacefully into the national community. Yet individual leaders might negotiate personal deals.

PDK Perspective on Negotiations with the Interim Government

The PDK appeared to have been stunned by the outcome of the election.[49] Their radio broadcasts refrained from reaction for several days and there was no immediate comment from their embassies abroad. Their decision to withdraw from the peace process had not worked out to their advantage. They had failed to sabotage the election, and they had badly miscalculated the results. They were now, more than ever, excluded from the national political scene.

The PDK had lost whatever measure of legitimacy among the Cambodian population and among interested foreign powers that they may have gained upon signing the Paris Agreements. PDK public statements gave indications that the party was feeling isolated and vulnerable, and that they believed, with good reason, that the Western powers together with the other Cambodian parties were conspiring to destroy or further marginalize them. Pol Pot had recognized the danger of such a constellation of forces in his February 1992 speech to PDK cadres, and he had acknowledged the need for foreign support.[50] The outcome of the electoral process had rendered the PDK much weaker.

Besides their political loss, the PDK forces, according to UNTAC estimates, had declined to less than fifteen thousand from pre–Paris accords estimates of more than thirty thousand. Nevertheless, the PDK retained significant assets and were not expected to crumble. They controlled some 20 percent of the countryside (although with only some 5 percent of the population). The territory under their control, most of it adjacent to Thailand, was rich in gems, timber, and rice, and had easy access (with local

48. Phnom Penh Samleng Pracheachon Kampuchea Radio Network in Cambodian, April 7, 1993, in *FBIS-EAS*, April 8, 1993.

49. See Nate Thayer, "Whither the Khmer Rouge?" *Phnom Penh Post*, June 6–12, 1993.

50. Ibid.

Thai military cooperation) to commercial outlets in Thailand. They retained a strong-willed leadership, zealous to gain power, and a disciplined organization. Even though their numbers had declined, their military forces were thought capable of inflicting serious damage upon their adversaries, and were not believed to be susceptible to easy defeat by the forces that were likely to be mustered against them.

A few analysts disagreed with the assessment (noted above) that the PDK had been badly damaged by the UN-led peace process. For example, Craig Etcheson suggested in August 1993 that the Khmer Rouge "may be stronger than at any time since 1979." He noted that the Vietnamese were gone, and the "puppet regime" had been defeated, replaced by an unstable conglomeration. He asserted that the PDK retained a competent administration and military, and sufficient popular strength to sustain themselves in an autonomous zone covering one-fifth of the country. He added: "Pol Pot still has his army, and still has highly placed friends in Thailand and China. He is wealthy. He has hugely expanded his territory and population. He has deeply infiltrated the opposing parties, and again has both covert and overt operatives in Phnom Penh. And he has convinced most of the world that the Khmer Rouge threat is no more."[51] Ben Kiernan appears to have shared this assessment, writing that the PDK "gained the most" from the implementation of the Paris Agreements.[52] Yet, with the benefit of four more years of observation, it is clear that the PDK did indeed suffer a severe loss from the UNTAC-led peace process.

PDK Strategy and Tactics of Negotiation

It appears that the PDK moved to a strategy of watchful waiting, retaining exclusive control of their "autonomous" zone, applying intermittent military pressure on their adversaries and, at the same time, searching for political opportunities to gain access to a share of power without surrendering control of territory or military assets. They may have calculated that, in the long run, their opponents would weaken themselves through pervasive corruption and factionalism. The PDK would be ready to seize power, no matter how long it would take, when their enemies faltered. In the meantime, they

51. Craig Etcheson, "Pol Pot and the Art of War," *Phnom Penh Post*, August 13–26, 1993.

52. See Ben Kiernan's introduction and essay in Kiernan, ed., *Genocide and Democracy in Cambodia: The Khmer Rouge, the United Nations, and the International Community*, Southeast Asia Studies Monograph Series No. 41 (New Haven: Yale University, 1993). For critical reviews of this point of view, see Stephen Heder, *Phnom Penh Post*, June 16–29, 1995, and Laura Summers, "Cambodia: Kiernan, the Khmer Rouge, and Human Rights," on Internet, <SEASIA-L@MSU.edu.>

would continue to struggle for popular support based on an intensified chauvinistic campaign against the hated Vietnamese who, they asserted, still maintained a pervasive presence in their motherland. Opportunities for access to power in Phnom Penh, they appeared to calculate, were most likely to come through the mediation of King Sihanouk; and PDK spokesmen exhibited a respectful posture toward him, often responding positively to his propositions for national reconciliation. Even prior to the election they had hinted that they would respond favorably to Sihanouk's invitation to form a government of national reconciliation. Asked by an interviewer what the PDK would like, Khieu Samphan had responded: "We support the efforts of His Royal Highness. We want the withdrawal of foreign forces so we can have genuine national reconciliation. If there is national reconciliation I would like to tell you very clearly that after the Vietnamese withdrawal, we don't ask for important portfolios; even a folding chair would be acceptable. I want to make it clear that the DK does not want to come back to power."[53] Thus, the PDK had hoped to convince Sihanouk to use his leverage to cancel the elections which they believed, at the time, that the CPP would win, and to make a governing arrangement that would legitimize a role for them in Phnom Penh.

Following the elections, an indication of the PDK political strategy came with their endorsement of Prince Sihanouk's brief effort on June 3 to form a government under his own leadership, with Ranariddh and Hun Sen as joint deputy prime ministers, and with the PDK in an "advisory" role. In endorsing Prince Sihanouk's proposal, a PDK spokesman emphasized that the new arrangement under Sihanouk must strip the SOC from control of the key functions of power, particularly domination of the armed forces. The spokesman also denounced U.S. interference regarding this proposal, and added, "The object of the Paris Agreements was not elections. It is only a means to achieve national reconciliation, territorial integrity and the withdrawal of foreign forces. We cannot solve the problem of Cambodia without national reconciliation."[54]

For his part, Prince Sihanouk reciprocated the courteous approach of the PDK. By mid-June, after the formation of the Interim Joint Administration, he invited PDK representatives to meet with its new leaders. His letter to Khieu Samphan suggested that Samphan and the interim administration leaders meet "as a family" to discuss the issue of ethnic Vietnamese in Cambodia.[55] In his speech at the oath-taking ceremony before the Con-

53. *Phnom Penh Post*, April 9–22, 1993.
54. *Phnom Penh Post*, June 18–July 1, 1993.
55. UPI, June 17, 1993.

stituent Assembly, Sihanouk spoke of the desirability of a "gentle" policy toward the PDK. In a polite exchange of correspondence with Khieu Samphan later in June, Sihanouk wrote, "I am very happy and relieved to know that the [PDK] remains in our Cambodian national community and wishes to play a role in our unified Kampuchea."[56]

Later, however, Sihanouk made another typical reversal of style. In a speech to monks, nuns, and worshippers in front of Wat Butom, he noted that although the PDK's recent attitude had been flexible and he welcomed word that the PDK were now willing to be a "simple political party of simple people," "nevertheless, we should be careful with these simple people. We cannot trust such people 100 percent. We must be careful with such sweet words because we have already tasted the sweetness of the Khmer Rouge. We used to eat Pol Pot's fruits, which were quite sour and bitter and sometimes the fruits were even poisonous."[57]

Military Issues and the PDK

Military unity was as important as political cooperation—perhaps even more important—to the process of national reconciliation. By late in June 1993, after thirteen years of civil war, three of the four factions were discussing the formation of a unified army. As previously indicated, the CPP was estimated to control some 45,000 regular troops and 100,000 provincial militia while FUNCINPEC and the KPNLF controlled some 10,000 troops. The PDK were estimated at that time to have some 15,000 under arms.[58] The issue of military integration was, of course, intertwined with the question of political participation in the new government. Faction leaders agreed, at least publicly, to encourage the PDK to integrate their troops into the newly forming national army. General Pol Saroeun of the SOC said, "We leave the door open for any factions who have not joined us."[59]

The PDK responded respectfully to the entreaties of Prince Sihanouk for serious discussions about military integration, but there seemed little prospect that a compromise acceptable to the PDK and the government could be achieved. The PDK appeared unlikely to risk giving up control of their army, which protected them in the zones they dominated. Unless the PDK was willing to integrate its independent military force, the govern-

56. Ibid., June 25, 1993.
57. Reuter, June 27, 1993; *Phnom Penh Post*, July 2–15, 1993.
58. UPI, June 23, 1993. According to other estimates, 10,000 to 15,000 troops. Reuter, July 13, 1993.
59. UPI, June 24, 1993.

ment was unlikely to accept a compromise arrangement. A sort of shadow play ensued, in which the two sides carried on intermittent discussions about military integration, while they alternated with military offensives against each other. Thus, the practice so familiar from the earlier wars in Indochina—"fight, talk, fight"—continued.

During the negotiations, UNTAC weighed in as a force encouraging the PDK to return to the peace process. UNTAC's leverage was declining as the time approached for it to withdraw from Cambodia, following the constitution, the conversion of the Constituent Assembly into the National Assembly, and the formation of a permanent government. The UNTAC mission would be completed in September 1993 and it would withdraw. But Akashi and General Sanderson made another effort to encourage PDK participation in the new government and army. A UN radio announcer quoted Akashi as saying, "As for UNTAC, we regard Khieu Samphan as a part of Cambodian political life and as a party among the four factions and the Paris Peace Agreement, and a representative of the SNC."[60] Akashi met with two PDK representatives in Phnom Penh in talks aimed at paving the way for Khieu Samphan to return to the capital. Sanderson met with the same representatives to discuss the prospects for a cease-fire.[61]

Hardly ten days following these talks, the PDK launched an attack with one hundred soldiers and seized the cherished tenth-century Preah Vihear temple, in the first major PDK military challenge to the interim government.[62] This PDK move appeared to the government to be a bargaining chip in the military and political negotiations. Hardly a week after the seizure, Khieu Samphan, who returned to Phnom Penh for a meeting with Prince Sihanouk following a three-month absence, claimed that the PDK were willing to join the new national army.[63] Prince Sihanouk told reporters that Khieu Samphan had agreed that the PDK would return their "autonomous zones," including their base at Pailin and the Preah Vihear temple, if their demands were accepted by himself and the interim government. In Sihanouk's version, Khieu Samphan proposed the inclusion of the PDK army into the national army and called for PDK representatives to be named as permanent counselors to the government.

On July 15, the PDK radio broadcast Khieu Samphan's respectful report of his meeting with Prince Sihanouk, noting that he had "reaffirmed our PDK's support for the Prince's national reconciliation plan" and had added

---

60. Reuter, July 3, 1993.
61. Ibid., July 1, 1993.
62. Ibid., July 8 and 9, 1993.
63. Ibid., July 13, 1993.

a proposal and a promise to the prince: "1. To set up a quadripartite army to avoid armed confrontation and armed clashes. 2. The PDK asks for only an advisory role and will not demand a role in the government."[64] Sihanouk scheduled a roundtable during the second half of September for discussion of these issues between the PDK and the interim administration. Sihanouk added a warning to Khieu Samphan that the PDK should expect difficulties to be raised by the United States over these proposals. The U.S. ambassador to the UN, Madeleine Albright, had recently reiterated U.S. objections to a PDK role in the government or army.[65]

Joining the public dialogue, Prince Ranariddh added that "if the PDK want to join the national community, we welcome them, but they should not put up any conditions." Referring to a statement by Khieu Samphan that the PDK were prepared to return the territory under their control in exchange for joining the "quadripartite" army, Ranariddh noted, "If they want to join the army they must join it as a national army. . . . If they say 'quadripartite' army, it would mean that we still have factions. From now on we do not have any more factions." Commenting on Khieu Samphan's statement that the PDK were prepared to accept ministerial positions if offered, Ranariddh said, "Maybe later on we will have to provide them some ministerial posts, but for the time being it is simply the question of advisory roles. As advisors, they don't have the veto right."[66]

While keeping the door open for some sort of PDK cooperation, Ranariddh was clearly more skeptical than his father about the prospects of achieving it. His public posture in negotiations with the PDK retained a dose of cynicism. Noting that the PDK were now sending envoys to discuss issues of reconciliation with UNTAC's Akashi and General Sanderson, Ranariddh remarked, "It is very strange that now they [PDK] have become real allies of UNTAC after fighting it very seriously. I think they are trying to catch the train that not only they missed, but that they tried to sabotage. The train is going on, so why not try to catch the train of peace." Hun Sen, Ranariddh's partner in the interim government, retained a formal public stance that was polite about the prospects of PDK cooperation: "I do not oppose people who can work for the benefit of the nation. My personal view is that it is better to reconcile than to fight each other. This is exactly the aspiration of our people who want at all cost to avoid warfare."[67]

64. Voice of the Great National Union Front of Cambodia in Cambodian, July 15, 1993, in *FBIS-EAS*, July 16, 1993.

65. UPI, July 14, 1993; Reuter, July 14, 1993.

66. UPI, July 15, 1993.

67. Ker Munthit, "Will There Be a Role for the Khmer Rouge?" *Phnom Penh Post*, July 16–29, 1993.

During this postelection phase of negotiations with the PDK, in which Prince Sihanouk was the prime mover, U.S. Deputy Secretary of State Clifton Wharton again told the press that he had delivered a message to Prince Sihanouk that the U.S. would not support or provide aid to Cambodia if the PDK were included in a new government.[68] Once again Sihanouk was outraged by what he regarded as flagrant interference in his country's internal affairs by an imperialist power. Again, with characteristic bluntness and volatility, he publicly expressed his anger in pungent denunciations. (American diplomats, however, knew they need not take Sihanouk's outbursts too seriously. Drawing from experience they understood that he was capable of changing his mind and declaiming with equal fervor against his previous position in an argument.) In a statement issued from his residence in Beijing, Sihanouk denounced the US: "In spite of my repeated statements, the U.S.A. continues to threaten Cambodia with all sorts of hostile measures should the Khmer Rouge be accepted by me or the Cambodian government as government members or advisers or members of the Cambodian National Army."

Sihanouk added that he had always fought against foreign interference in Cambodian affairs. But in view of the country's devastated condition and its need for aid from rich foreign powers, "I am no longer up to fighting against the U.S.A. as I did from 1955 to 1975. . . . I am more and more angered by these incessant warnings from the Americans, which have made me even more ill than I was in the recent past. So as not to end my life in a mental asylum, I abandon plans to organise in September 1993 or later, a 'Round Table' with Mr. Khieu Samphan or other Khmer Rouge."[69] Interim government officials said that they would respect Prince Sihanouk's decision to break off talks with the PDK. FUNCINPEC leaders must have been relieved and CPP leaders pleased by this turn of events. Press reports suggested that foreign diplomats were expressing skepticism that Prince Sihanouk would abandon his efforts to work out a plan for reconciliation with the PDK.[70]

Indeed, hardly a week had passed since Sihanouk's blast at the United States and renunciation of his plans for negotiations with the PDK, when Sihanouk officially authorized the co-presidents of the interim government to have talks with the PDK, "if they consider that such talks are liable to help them resolve the problems of the partition of Cambodia and peace."[71]

68. Reuter, July 19, 1993.
69. Hong Kong AFP in English, July 20, 1993, in *FBIS-EAS*, July 20, 1993.
70. UPI, July 21, 1993.
71. Ibid., July 26, 1993.

During the lull in negotiations, military activities stepped up, with in-creased PDK guerrilla activities and selected government military initia-tives against PDK strongholds. The increase in hostilities induced Prince Sihanouk to issue an impassioned appeal for peace to the PDK from his headquarters in Pyongyang: "Cambodia's road to reconciliation has been marred by increasing incidents of violence by the Khmer Rouge in recent weeks. The army of the DK in the past few weeks has cut national high-ways, blown up bridges, attacked villages, trains, etc. . . . the property of our country and our people. . . . I would like to plead with Democratic Kampuchea (KR) and its troops to re-provide peace, security and happiness to our people."[72] Government forces launched new attacks in northwestern Cambodia in the latter part of July. The military clashes served to maintain tension between the two sides, but they did not substantially alter the posi-tion of either antagonist. The interim administration did not have strength enough to defeat the PDK, nor to expel them from control of their zone, and the PDK was not strong enough to overturn the government. Thus, ne-gotiations for political and military integration proceeded against a back-ground of military hostilities. As the government prepared to promulgate the constitution, a government spokesman asserted that it was not seeking a military victory over the PDK. The deputy information minister, a FUN-CINPEC member, noted that "the door is still open" for the PDK to join the peace process. He added that if the PDK showed sincerity by ending attacks and giving up territory, "maybe we can find some [government] role for them."[73]

The New Regime Assumes Power

During the three months following the election, the constitutional drafting committee completed its preparation of the constitution (discussed in the following chapter) and presented it to the Constituent Assembly for ratifi-cation. On September 21, the Constituent Assembly ratified the Constitu-tion of the Kingdom of Cambodia by a secret vote which amply fulfilled the two-thirds requirement for adoption. Prince Ranariddh expressed satisfac-tion with the vote, commenting that "it was better than a unanimous vote," the 5 against and 2 abstentions, with 113 in favor, indicating "that Cambo-dia is a very liberal democratic country." Son Sann praised the adoption of the constitution and issued a plea for national unity.[74]

72. Reuter, Aug. 11, 1993.
73. DPA, Sept. 8, 1993.
74. *Phnom Penh Post*, Sep. 24–Oct. 7, 1993.

The adoption of the constitution was followed by the coronation of the king. On September 24, 1993, Norodom Sihanouk once again mounted the throne that he had abdicated in favor of his father (Norodom Sumarit) in 1955, in order to take a more active role in politics as prime minister. When his father died in 1960, Sihanouk became chief of state, but he did not resume the title of king, preferring to be addressed as Prince Sihanouk. After being ousted from power in 1970 by a coup, Sihanouk had moved through a dazzling variety of political alliances in the succeeding twenty-three years. His re-installation as king was the culmination of a strange political journey.

The ceremony restoring Sihanouk to the throne reminded the solemn onlookers of the splendors of the ancient Khmer monarchy. Heralds blew conch shells as Prince Sihanouk and Princess Monique, his wife, arrived at the resplendently decorated throne hall of the royal palace. Sihanouk was clad in traditional royal attire, a long-sleeved, gold-buttoned white jacket and purple, knee-length silk pants over black stockings. Members of the National Assembly, seated before the throne in a row of golden chairs, dropped to their knees and clasped their hands to their foreheads as the Prince passed by. Sihanouk lit incense and candles, which he placed on two roasted pigs, laid on a table with six roasted ducks, mounds of rice, tropical fruits, and coconuts. Gongs and conch shells resounded in the hall (interspersed with the softer buzzing of cellular telephones muffled in the robes of some of the more important notables). As he took the oath as monarch, he swore "to abide by the constitution and respect all the interests of the Cambodian people from now on."[75]

As his first act, King Sihanouk named Prince Ranariddh as the first prime minister of the new government and Hun Sen the second prime minister. The newly appointed government was essentially the same as that of the interim administration. With the completion of this process—the promulgation of the new constitution, the inauguration of the king, the conversion of the Constituent Assembly into the National Assembly, and the assumption to power of the new government—the mission of the United Nations Transitional Authority in Cambodia (UNTAC) was completed. On September 26, his voice cracking with emotion, Yasushi Akashi, chief of the UNTAC mission, bade farewell to Cambodia in front of an honor guard at the airport, presided over by Prime Ministers Ranariddh and Hun Sen. Akashi expressed deep satisfaction that UNTAC had been able to fulfill its task of aiding the Cambodian people to begin their historic march toward peace.

75. Reuter, Sept. 24, 1993; *New York Times*, Sept. 25, 1993.

Composing the New Constitution, 1993

The drafting of a constitution was a critical element in the process of rebuilding the failed state. A constitution was necessary to create the structure of government, determine the nature of the political process, and establish the frame of reference for the protection of human rights. A well-composed constitution could not by itself guarantee the creation of an effective government or a democratic political process, nor could it ensure that human rights would be respected. However, it was a necessary, if not sufficient, component in the pursuit of these objectives.

The Paris Agreements of 1991, which were signed by leaders of the four Cambodian factions as well as outside powers, included specific instructions about the process of constitution drafting and prescribed certain elements of its content. The very first article of the agreement noted that the transitional period, during which UNTAC would carry out its functions, would terminate when the "constituent assembly elected through fair and free elections, organized and certified by the United Nations, has approved the constitution and transformed itself into a legislative assembly, and thereafter a new government has been created." Article 23 stipulated a set of basic principles, including respect for human rights and fundamental freedoms, that would have to be incorporated in the constitution.

Annex 5, "Principles for a New Constitution for Cambodia," noted that the constitution would be the supreme law, to be amended only by legislative enactment, popular referendum, or both. The initial constitution was to be adopted by two-thirds of the Constituent Assembly. Annex 5, article 2, gave special attention to human rights, with the following provision:

Cambodia's tragic recent history requires special measures to assure protection of human rights. Therefore, the constitution will contain a declaration of fundamental rights, including the rights to life, personal liberty, security, freedom of movement, freedom of religion, assembly and association including political parties and trade unions, due process and equality before the law, protection from arbitrary deprivation of property or deprivation of private property without just compensation, and freedom from racial, ethnic, religious or sexual discrimination. It will prohibit the retroactive application of criminal law. The declaration will be consistent with the provisions of the Universal Declaration of Human Rights and other relevant international instruments. Aggrieved individuals will be entitled to have the courts adjudicate and enforce these rights.

Further, the annex provided that the constitution would declare Cambodia an independent and "neutral" state. The most innovative provision for a nation with little experience with democratic government was the following, from article 4: "The constitution will state that Cambodia will follow a system of liberal democracy, on the basis of pluralism. It will provide for periodic and genuine elections. It will provide for the right to vote and to be elected by universal and equal suffrage. It will provide for voting by secret ballot, with a requirement that the electoral procedures provide a full and fair opportunity to organize and participate in the electoral process." Finally, the annex called for the establishment of an "independent judiciary."

These stipulations of the Paris Agreements, which had been agreed to by the Cambodian factions, ultimately found their way into the constitution. The critical question was whether they would be followed in practice. Most constitutions enunciate noble objectives and prescribe proper procedures. However, few countries extensively carry them out. The challenge of adhering to a "system of liberal democracy, on the basis of pluralism" was an enormous one for Cambodia. The country had just emerged from two decades of war and revolution, destructive agrarian totalitarianism, foreign invasion, devastating domestic strife, and transitional management by an international organization. Was "liberal democracy" an attainable goal, or even an appropriate aspiration? The Paris accords assumed that it was.

There were other obvious sources, besides the Paris Agreements, from which the constitution drafters would draw inspiration. Since the end of World War II in 1945, Cambodia had been ruled under six constitutions: the 1947 and 1956 constitutions of the Sihanouk period; the 1972 constitution of the Lon Nol regime (1970–75); the 1976 constitution of Democratic Kampuchea (the Khmer Rouge regime, 1975–78); and the two constitutions of the People's Republic of Kampuchea (later named the State of

Cambodia), as adopted in 1981 and amended in 1989. FUNCINPEC and CPP drafters were likely to look for inspiration to the Sihanouk constitutions, which had been strongly marked by the French Fourth Republic, and to the PRK/SOC constitutions, marked by the 1979 Vietnamese model.[1]

Yet there was one dominant personality on the political scene to whom all of the factions had been offering obeisance, Prince Sihanouk. He was likely to play a critical role in the preparation and final adoption of the new document. Just as the constitution of the French Fifth Republic reflected Charles de Gaulle's political preeminence, so the Cambodian constitution would surely show the imprint of the country's paramount national figure, Sihanouk.

The Drafting Process

On June 30, 1993, at the first meeting of the Constituent Assembly following its inaugural session, the assembly appointed a constitution drafting committee composed of twelve members and eight alternates and assigned five Cambodian "experts" to assist the committee. The formal chairman of the drafting committee was the President of the Constituent Assembly, Son Sann, leader of the BLDP Party; and the vice president of the assembly, Chea Sim, leader of the CPP, was the formal vice chairman. FUNCINPEC was allotted six members of the drafting committee, CPP five, and the BLDP one.[2] Most of the members were considered to be intellectuals and professionals. The working leader of the committee was Chem Snguon, the minister of justice.[3]

At the outset, the drafting committee met Mondays through Fridays from 8 A.M. till noon, and later extended their hours to include afternoons. The committee conducted its business in remarkable secrecy. No spokesman was appointed nor were committee members authorized to speak publicly about the work of drafting the constitution. Lt. General Tol Lah explained that the assembly had adopted regulations calling for the work of its committees to be "conducted confidentially," and that the work

1. John C. Brown notes in the *Phnom Penh Post*, July 16–26, 1993, that Cambodia has experimented with many forms of government: monarchical (King Sihanouk), republican (Lon Nol), radical socialist agrarian (Pol Pot), and communist (Hun Sen). If there is one feature common to all these governments, he notes, it is the centralization of power.

2. Stephen P. Marks, "The New Cambodian Constitution: From Civil War to a Fragile Democracy," *Columbia Human Rights Law Review* 26, no. 45 (1994): 61.

3. Michael Vickery, "The Cambodian People's Party: Where Has it Come from, Where Is It Going?" in *Southeast Asian Affairs 1994* (Singapore: Institute of Southeast Asian Studies, 1994), p. 113.

of a committee could not be revealed until it had presented its report to the assembly.

The Drafting Process and External Influence

It was apparent following the appointment of the drafting committee that the key players in the constitution-making process did not want foreign interference. This was to be a Cambodian enterprise. Sihanouk was understood to have clearly expressed his wishes that foreigners should not be involved in the drafting process.[4] The twelve-man drafting committee appeared to share the same conviction. The desire to keep foreigners at arm's length appeared not to be connected to substantive issues but rather to a nationalist sentiment that Cambodians should draft their own fundamental law.

There had been a variety of efforts by external actors to guide the Cambodian parties in the preparation of a constitution. As early as September 1992, UNTAC Special Representative Akashi had placed on the SNC agenda an item related to the drafting of the constitution. Prior to the meeting, he had distributed a brief factual analysis prepared by Professor Reginald Austin, head of the Electoral Component, who was a former dean of the University of Zimbabwe School of Law. The draft laid out certain issues that should be considered, such as name, flag, delimitation of territory, and form of government. The Austin draft was careful not to suggest that UNTAC intended to write the constitution. Akashi was suggesting that an SNC task force prepare the work for a future Constituent Assembly.[5] Stephen Marks, an observer at the SNC meeting, reported that following Austin's presentation Prince Sihanouk congratulated him and then enunciated his views on what the constitution should contain. Marks writes:

> He [Sihanouk] would punctuate each point by addressing the Special Representative [Akashi] with words to the effect of, "That's what we should do, isn't it, Mr. Akashi?" In this way he stated his position on the name, flag, national anthem, borders, type of government, institutions of government, independence of the judiciary, requirements for the presidency, and so on. While in fact anticipating the outcome of the work of the Constituent Assembly, formally Sihanouk was merely endorsing the idea of creating an SNC task force

4. Interview by Joseph J. Zasloff in Boston, April 30, 1995, with Louis Aucoin, professor of law, Boston University, engaged by the Asia Society to serve as adviser to the Constituent Assembly on constitutional matters in 1993.

5. Marks, "The New Cambodian Constitution," p. 60.

to study these issues, the importance of which was so great he felt that both he and Mr. Akashi should participate. In fact the Electoral Component did convene several working sessions on constitutional matters with party representatives and a few outside experts, but without the participation of either Sihanouk or Akashi.[6]

Following the election, UNTAC's Human Rights Component undertook an effort at promoting "constitutional literacy," disseminating information on popular participation in constitutional drafting to Cambodian NGOs as well as to the general public. The component prepared audiovisual materials, set up NGO discussion groups, and organized a "constitutional forum" in which three Cambodian activists (a monk, a representative of women's organizations, and the head of a human rights organization) joined a panel with three outside Asian experts who had been participants in popular organizations involved in constitutions in their own countries. An audience of more than one hundred activists engaged in a spirited discussion which revealed their interest in participating in the constitution-drafting process. At the conclusion of the forum, the participants formed a coalition of fourteen groups called Ponleu Khmer (Cambodian Illumination) and formulated a strategy to press for strong human rights provisions. According to Marks, "the strategy was implemented with a remarkable degree of courage, initiative and perseverance."[7]

UNTAC respected the desires of the Cambodian participants to write their own constitution and was careful not to try to impose its will. For example, the UNTAC Human Rights Component had prepared a Bill of Rights for the constitution. However, they did not insist upon its acceptance by the Constituent Assembly, but rather remained in an advisory role. Copies of the Bill of Rights had not been requested by any of the members of the assembly or political parties represented there.[8] The *Phnom Penh Post* reported in August 1993 that UNTAC was taking a "hands off" stance toward the writing of the constitution, a posture consistent with the desires of the Cambodian leadership. It quoted a high-level UNTAC source as saying that "the UN has so far not seen any reason to worry about the process by which the constitution is being written." Nevertheless UNTAC did provide logistic support to the Constituent Assembly, placing several aides within the assembly building under the leadership of Sam Borin, a native Cambodian who was an UNTAC employee.[9]

6. Ibid., pp. 60–61.
7. Ibid., p. 61.
8. *Phnom Penh Post*, July 1993.
9. Ibid., Aug. 13–26, 1993.

The U.S. government, operating through nongovernment organizations, offered assistance in promoting democratic government and constitution drafting. The National Democratic Institute and the International Republican Institute, sponsored by the Democratic and Republican Parties, sent experts who offered seminars and instruction on a variety of democratic themes, including the internal rules for legislatures. The Asia Foundation, supported by the U.S. government, sponsored experts in constitutional law.[10]

The Asia Foundation experts decided soon after their arrival following the election that, in view of the constitutional drafting committee's sensitivity about possible interference by UNTAC, they should clearly establish their identity independent from UNTAC as well as from the U.S. Embassy. They succeeded in developing a close relationship with the chairman of the drafting committee, Chem Snguon, who placed them at desks just outside his office in the ministry, and recommended to committee members that they consult the professors with questions about comparative constitutions. The professors found that members came to see them with questions and they provided information and research about the practices of other countries. At times members asked for assistance in the drafting of certain sections of the constitution. During the second week of August, the two professors were abruptly cut out of the advisory process, apparently due to an order from Prince Sihanouk that no foreigners (presumably other than those from whom he was drawing assistance) were to be involved in the constitution-writing process.[11]

It appears that a French professor, Claude Gille Goure from the Faculty of Law at the University of Toulouse, had an important role in drafting the version that was closest to the one that was adopted. Sihanouk, through his son Ranariddh, himself a former professor of law at the University of Aix-en-Provence in France, had engaged Goure following the election to prepare a draft constitution. Goure worked in Phnom Penh until sometime in July 1993, and left the draft with Ranariddh before returning to France. One might assume that the draft conformed to the positions of Prince Sihanouk and Ranariddh. According to a source who was closely following the drafting process in late July 1993, Ranariddh came before the drafting committee and said, in effect, "Here's the constitution. My father has agreed to it and so do I." It was substantially Goure's draft. According to this account, Ranariddh expected that a draft endorsed by Prince Sihanouk

10. Professor Louis Aucoin and Professor Dolores A. Donovan were such experts. Aucoin interview.

11. Ibid.

and himself would be immediately accepted. Instead, the chairman of the committee calmly thanked Ranariddh and noted that the committee would consider it, along with the draft that it had been working hard to develop.

As the above account suggests, there was an abundance of advice from foreign experts available to the key Cambodian actors in the constitution-writing process. They may have shaped the thinking of the participants with information, suggestions, and even drafts of segments of the constitution. But it seems clear that the final version was a Cambodian product, shaped primarily by the interplay of the key Cambodian political forces.

The Drafting Process and the Issue of Secrecy

The secrecy of the drafting process was the subject of vigorous criticism by Ponleu Khmer, the human rights coalition, which had been granted three seats as observers in the Constituent Assembly. The spokesman of Ponleu Khmer, the venerable Yos Huot, asserted that "democracy is participation" and "in the writing of the constitution there has been no participation by the people of Cambodia. How can this be democratic? Who will protect the rights of the Cambodian people?" [12] Yos Huot expressed concern that human rights, and especially the rights of women, would be slighted in the drafting of the constitution. Further, he had learned that Buddhism would be made the state religion and he expressed "fears that by doing so, the Buddhist hierarchy will again be the arm of the state." [13]

Ponleu Khmer sent a three-page letter to both the government and the UNTAC special representative, asserting: "We have the right to ask all the elected representatives about what they are going to include in the constitution. They should let us know openly what their intentions are. The drawing up of the constitution is not a secret thing. All citizens have the right to know about what will be written in the constitution. The people have the right to oppose what they think is inappropriate or should not be in the constitution." [14] Special Representative Akashi responded, urging the Ponleu Khmer members to continue to lobby members of the Constituent Assembly and their political parties on any matters of concern about the constitution. He added,

It is expected that, as a popularly elected Assembly debating issues of public concern, the Constituent Assembly will, as a general rule, conduct its pro-

12. *Phnom Penh Post*, Aug. 13–26, 1993.
13. Ibid.
14. *Phnom Penh Post*, Aug. 27–Sept. 9, 1993.

ceedings in public. This would enable members of the various groups, or any other member of the public, to attend and observe such proceedings. . . .

It should be emphasized, however, that it is the responsibility and prerogative of the Constituent Assembly, which represents the sovereign will of the people of Cambodia, to elaborate and adopt a new Constitution. UNTAC remains ready to respond in any appropriate, positive manner to any request which the Constituent Assembly may make regarding support for this crucial task.[15]

Despite the pressure from the human rights organizations for a more open process, the constitutional drafting commission persisted in its secrecy. This secrecy by a government agency seemed in keeping with a longstanding Cambodian cultural trait. Further, the drafters appeared to assume that few Cambodians, even members of Ponleu Khmer, understood the requirements of a constitution. American advisers could point out that the Founding Fathers of the United States, drafting the constitution at the constitutional convention in 1787, proceeded in full secrecy. In the Cambodian drafting process, time to produce an acceptable document was limited. According to the Paris Agreements, the constitution was to be adopted within three months of the election of the Constituent Assembly. The serious political divisions in the country might be exacerbated if the process were prolonged. The Cambodian constitution framers had reason to believe that demagogic appeals during this period of political turbulence might create mischief in the drafting process.

Monarchy or Republic?

There was no hint either at the drafting of the Paris Agreements or in the early preparation phase of constitution drafting by UNTAC that the monarchy might be restored in Cambodia.[16] Certainly a central role for Prince Sihanouk was envisaged, but he was assumed in most discussions to be a future chief of state, probably president. Different assumptions prevailed as to the powers to be accorded the chief of state. Even Sihanouk apparently saw himself not as a restored king but as a head of state above political parties, who could bring reconciliation to the nation. At the SNC session (discussed above) where he revealed some of his views regarding the constitution, he distinguished the role that Cambodia's chief of state should perform from that of the president of the French Fifth Republic, noting

15. Ibid.
16. Marks, "The New Cambodian Constitution," p. 65.

that President Mitterrand was affiliated with the Socialist Party, a partisanship that would not be suitable for Cambodia.[17] Sihanouk rejected the name "Kingdom of Cambodia" ("which would not please certain parties") as well as the "Khmer Republic" ("which would not please my son [Prince Ranariddh]"), and suggested that the country be called "Cambodia."[18]

In January 1993, as previously noted, Sihanouk had proposed that a popular vote for president, assuming himself as candidate, ought to be conducted by UNTAC before, during, or after elections for the Constituent Assembly. The proposal found little support among the Permanent Five, and UNTAC regarded it as a violation of the Paris Agreements. His proposal for the election of a president could be viewed as another bit of evidence that Sihanouk was not contemplating the restoration of the monarchy. However, Sihanouk and his key followers may have envisaged his return as monarch as soon as an opportunity presented itself. Sihanouk may have been dissimulating when he insisted to the SNC that he did not wish to be installed as king. Such a ruse would not be alien to Sihanouk's style of maneuver.

It is not clear when and how the minds of the critical actors changed regarding the restoration of the monarchy. It seems likely that Sihanouk had long cherished the dream of re-ascending the throne. He often referred to himself as the "father" of his nation and to its people as his "children." Resuming the role of king would vindicate his long struggle as leader of his nation. However, until the surprising electoral victory of FUNCINPEC, the so-called royalist party, a restoration of the monarchy seemed politically impossible. With the endorsement of Prince Sihanouk that FUNCINPEC's victory implied, restoring the king seemed a natural move. The other Cambodian parties, for reasons of their own, would be willing to accept Sihanouk's accession to the throne. And there would be little objection likely from the principal external powers or UNTAC. A constitutional monarchy was not at odds with the mandate in the Paris Agreements to establish a liberal democracy. The United Kingdom, Japan, and the Scandinavian countries had long-standing democratic constitutional monarchies. Spain had restored the monarchy following the demise of Franco and had reestablished a democratic polity. Sihanouk was recognized by the Permanent Five members as a venerated leader who, as king, might have the best chance to fulfill the UNTAC mandate of achieving unity and national reconciliation.

Two working drafts of the constitution emerged from the writing process, one prepared by the members of the assembly's drafting commit-

17. Ibid.
18. Ibid.

tee and another referred to in the press as the "FUNCINPEC draft."[19] The core of the latter, it appears, was the draft prepared by Professor Goure, the French expert who had been commissioned by Princes Sihanouk and Ranariddh to assist in its development. A Western adviser to the assembly's drafting committee has noted that the FUNCINPEC draft, at least through the end of July 1993, did not stipulate a monarchy. However, by the first week of August, agreement emerged between FUNCINPEC and the CPP members that the constitution should provide for a king.[20] A government spokesman said that the completed draft would be taken to Prince Sihanouk in Pyongyang, on August 31.[21]

Ranariddh and Hun Sen did indeed take the two drafts to Prince Sihanouk in Pyongyang, who is reported to have congratulated the drafting committee on its work and the next day returned both drafts with annotations, including an observation that he liked the monarchical draft. Upon their return to Phnom Penh, Ranariddh and Hun Sen announced that Sihanouk would be king. Despite having agreed to a restoration of the monarchy, Sihanouk reversed himself and put out word that the monarchy should not be restored and he should not be asked to serve as king.[22] Commenting on this curious behavior, a biographer of Sihanouk writes: "It was all very much of a piece with Sihanouk's behavior in the past. Once the members of the assembly begged him to change his mind, he graciously did so. He had shown that he was truly wanted."[23]

This draft, endorsed by Prince Sihanouk, went before the Constituent Assembly for five days of debate ending on September 21, the day the constitution was adopted by 113 votes in favor, 5 against, and 2 abstentions in the 120-person assembly. Speaking to journalists the next day, Prince Ranariddh characterized the powers of the reestablished monarchy: "The thing we have left to the king is simply what we call a nominal function of powers of any head of state. I have to say that the king has less power than any president in any republican regime."[24]

19. *Phnom Penh Post*, Sept. 10–23, 1993.

20. This timing is confirmed by press reports. A Reuter dispatch, Aug. 19, 1993, noted that Cambodia's leading newspaper, *Reasmy Kampuchea* (Bright Light of Cambodia) contained hints that the new constitution would provide for a monarch and called for a national referendum on the issue.

21. Reuter, Aug. 19, 1993.

22. *Phnom Penh Post*, Sept. 10–23, 1993.

23. Milton Osborne, *Sihanouk: Prince of Light, Prince of Darkness* (Honolulu: University of Hawaii Press, 1994), pp. 261–62.

24. *Phnom Penh Post*, Sept. 24–Oct. 7, 1993.

General Characteristics of the Constitution

The new constitution, with thirteen chapters containing 139 articles, could be seen both as a statement of aspirations as well as a fundamental law defining the governmental system and the rights of the Cambodian people. The constitution formally established a "multi-party liberal democratic regime guaranteeing human rights, abiding by law, and having high responsibility for the nation's future destiny of moving toward perpetual progress, development, prosperity, and glory." It created a parliamentary system, in the form of a constitutional monarchy. It called for the adoption of a "market economy." Its foreign policy was declared to be "permanent neutrality and non-alignment."

Combined with these "modern" features, the constitution enunciated elements drawn from Cambodian tradition. The country's motto was defined as "Nation, Religion, King." The preamble alluded to the country's "fine Angkor civilization," and the flag depicted Angkor Wat, the renowned temple built at the pinnacle of Khmer power. Buddhism was established as the state religion. The king was to be chosen from one of three branches of the royal family.

The bulk of the language of the new constitution came from several clearly identifiable sources. The provisions for the monarchy and the description of the parliamentary system drew heavily from the Cambodian constitution of 1947, the period of royal rule by King Sihanouk under French colonial tutelage. Sihanouk was said to have a particular attachment to this constitution, which he regarded both as his creation and as a symbol of Cambodia's progress toward independence.[25] The chapter on human rights was drawn, in some articles almost verbatim, from the 1989 Constitution of the State of Cambodia. There was also a strong imprint of the constitutions of the Fourth French Republic (1946–58), when Cambodia was under colonial rule, as well as of the Fifth French Republic (1958 to present). The impact of the French tradition was easily understandable. The small number of surviving Cambodian jurists, including Prince Ranariddh, were educated in French universities. Moreover, as noted above, there was assistance by a French legal expert in the Ranariddh draft. Despite the strong imprint of foreign sources, the Cambodian Constitution of 1993 was characterized by two American law professors who served as advisers to the drafting committee as "distinctly Cambodian."[26]

25. Memo by Professor Louis Aucoin to faculty of Boston University School of Law, no date, probably 1993.
26. Louis Aucoin and Dolores Donovan (University of San Francisco Law School), in a draft of "Cambodia," an essay prepared for Albert P. Blaustein and H. Flanz, eds., *Constitu-*

The Executive Branch

The King

The constitution accorded great prominence to the king, whose role was the first of the governing institutions to be described, in twenty three articles (Chapter II, art. 7–30). It was obvious that many of the articles were inspired by the Constitution of 1947, drafted by French colonial authorities, which accorded certain powers to King Sihanouk.[27] Despite the prominence given the king in the new constitution, his powers were limited. The first article of the chapter noted that the king "shall reign but shall not govern" (a phrase reminiscent of the oft-quoted observation made by Bagehot, an English counselor to Queen Victoria, who noted that the British monarch "reigns but does not rule"). So insistent upon the limitation on the powers of the king were the framers that they later asserted (art. 17) that this provision "absolutely shall not be amended."

The constitution described certain symbolic functions of the king which aptly suited Sihanouk's own self-image. He "shall be a symbol of unity and eternity of the nation." He shall be the "guarantor of the national independence, sovereignty, and territorial integrity [of the nation], the protector of rights and freedom for all citizens and the guarantor of international treaties." These symbolic powers might well be translated into real powers, particularly in foreign affairs. These particular conceptions of the king's powers appear to have been drawn from the description of the president of the French Fifth Republic, in article 5 of the French Constitution of 1958.

Seven articles (art. 10–16) were devoted to royal succession, an issue of great importance in view of Sihanouk's age (seventy-one in 1993) and serious health problems (rumored to be prostate cancer in 1992 and also rumored to be leukemia, although both were said in 1996 to be in remission.) The king was named head of state for life and was prohibited from appointing a successor (art. 7, 10). Upon the king's death, a Royal Council of the Throne—consisting of the president and two vice presidents of the National Assembly, the prime minister, and the chief dignitaries of two Buddhist orders—was instructed to choose an heir from one of three branches of the royal family (descendants of King Ang Duong, King Norodom, or King Sisowath).

If the king cannot perform his duties, or after the king dies and until a successor is appointed, the president of the National Assembly was desig-

---

tions of the Countries of the World (Dobbs Ferry, N.Y.: Oceana Publications, (update of November 1994 publication).

27. Aucoin, memo to faculty of Boston University School of Law.

nated to act as regent (art. 11, 12). (CPP leader Chea Sim was the president of the National Assembly in 1993.) Further, the president of the assembly was also designated by the constitution (art. 30) to serve as "acting head of state" in the absence of the king. In view of King Sihanouk's frequent absences in Pyongyang, Beijing, and elsewhere, this provision took on special political importance. In the summer of 1994, for example, the assembly debated a government proposal to outlaw the Khmer Rouge. Ranariddh and Hun Sen supported the proposal. A minority, which included Minister of Finance Sam Rainsy and Foreign Minister Prince Sirivuddh, opposed it as fruitless and unwise. Interestingly, King Sihanouk, who still cherished the hope of achieving national reconciliation, also opposed the measure. The proposal was adopted by the assembly by a comfortable majority. Article 28 required that the king sign the law prior to its promulgation, but in view of the king's absence in Pyongyang, the question arose as to whether the president of the National Assembly, Chea Sim, was empowered to sign the law. A fax was dispatched to the king in Pyongyang to inquire of his views. The king replied by fax, a frequent practice (inspiring the observation often made in Phnom Penh that the "king's fax is law"), with the pronouncement that the National Assembly could, if it wished, vote to outlaw the Khmer Rouge. However, he added, the constitution should be amended to prescribe that the president of the National Assembly, in the absence of the king, could sign laws only with the permission of the king. Ranariddh proposed the amendment and the assembly passed it with a sufficient majority.[28]

The constitution endowed the king with significant powers, although the elective authorities retained certain checks upon them. The king may proclaim a state of emergency when the nation is in danger, but only "after agreement with the Prime Minister and the President of the National Assembly" (art. 22). (As in the constitution of the French Fifth Republic, article 16, the Cambodian constitution stipulates that the National Assembly cannot be dissolved during a state of emergency.) The king is the supreme commander of the armed forces (art. 23). He can declare war, "after approval of the National Assembly" (art. 24). He may grant "partial or complete amnesty" (art. 27). The latter power takes on special importance in view of the assembly's vote in 1994 to outlaw the Khmer Rouge. (The king accorded amnesty to Khmer Rouge leader Ieng Sary in 1996.) As noted earlier, the constitution accorded the king substantial powers in foreign relations. He was to receive the credentials from ambassadors of foreign

28. Aucoin interview. See also Marks, "The New Cambodian Constitution," who cites Sue Downie, "Cambodia Delays King's Amendment," UPI, July 13, 1994. Available in Lexis, Nexis World Library, UPI File.

countries (art. 25) and to be the "guarantor of the national independence, sovereignty and territorial integrity" of the nation and the "guarantor of international treaties" (art. 8). His ratification of treaties must come "after a vote of approval by the National Assembly" (art. 26).

An important function of the king, as in any constitutional monarchy, was to be the appointment of the prime minister and members of the Council of Ministers. The king, upon the recommendation of the president and two vice presidents of the assembly, was empowered to designate from among the members of the winning party a "dignitary" who would form a royal government from "members of the Assembly or members of the political parties represented in the Assembly." This latter provision was inserted to ensure that the PDK, who refused to participate in the election for the assembly, could not acquire portfolios in the government.

A newly formed government was required by the constitution to request a vote of confidence (by a two-thirds majority of all the members of the assembly) (art. 100). The king was empowered to dissolve the assembly only if the government were to be twice deposed within a twelve-month period (a provision similar to one in the constitution of the Fourth French Republic, designed to protect against government instability), and only with the approval of the prime minister and assembly president (art. 78).[29]

Unlike the system of the 1947 constitution, the king was not called upon to preside over the Council of Ministers, a clear constraint on his executive power. Rather the constitution noted that the king "shall grant an audience twice a month to the Prime Minister and the Council of Ministers to hear their reports on the state of the nation" (art. 20).

In summary, the king was defined as a constitutional monarch with more limited powers than the language of the 1947 constitution accorded to the throne. But the language was broad and, as in all constitutions and particularly new ones, subject to development and interpretation. Moreover, King Sihanouk was an imposing personality in his country, held in deep reverence by many of his subjects, and had been known since his days as chief of state for his peremptory style. Some members of the political elite, who were not among his admirers, feared that he would be a volatile, un-

29. Aucoin notes that the power of dissolution was the subject of controversy among the drafters. Prince Sihanouk was known to favor the provisions laid out in the 1947 constitution, which granted unlimited powers to the king to dissolve the National Assembly, while also granting reciprocal powers to the National Assembly. Sihanouk was said to have a particular attachment to the 1947 constitution, which he regarded as his creation and also as a symbol of the beginning of independence from French rule. Aucoin memo to faculty of law members, Boston University. Regarding the 1947 constitution, see David Chandler, *The Tragedy of Cambodian History* (New Haven: Yale University Press, 1991).

predictable, and undependable monarch, given to frequent absences in Pyongyang and Beijing and to "rule by fax." Some were concerned that he might expand and abuse his power, taking advantage of the country's weak political institutions. In the first four years after the promulgation of the constitution, King Sihanouk was frequently absent for reasons of health, and perhaps a preference for distance, insulating himself from the daily pressures of kingly life in Phnom Penh (and possibly believing that his regal aura was enhanced by the mystery of separation). However, King Sihanouk generally respected the confines of the constitution and took seriously the admonition, which he frequently intoned, that the king "shall reign but not govern."

The Prime Minister and the Council of Ministers

The constitution invested the important executive powers in a Council of Ministers, to be led during normal times by a prime minister, and including deputy prime ministers, state ministers, and state secretaries (art. 99). Membership in this Council of Ministers was said to be "incompatible with professional activities in trade or industry and with the holding of any position in the public service" (art. 101). This exclusion, concerned with the Anglo-Saxon concept of "conflict of interest" and the French concept of *incompatibilité*, was the subject of controversy during the drafting process. Some drafters proposed that a member of the assembly who was named a minister in the government should, as in the French Fifth Republic, resign his seat in the assembly. Others argued that the paucity of educated people available for high political office in Cambodia made such a restriction unwise. The compromise provided that a member of the assembly could serve as a minister but he could not hold other posts (art. 78, 101).

Members of the government were said to be "collectively responsible" to the assembly and each member was "individually responsible to the Prime Minister and the Assembly" for his conduct (art. 102). The Council of Ministers was called upon to meet weekly, in sessions chaired by the prime minister.

An unusual final chapter was inserted in the constitution, entitled "Transitional Provisions." During the term of the first legislature, which was created upon the promulgation of the constitution (at which time the Constituent Assembly was transformed into the National Assembly), the king was called upon to appoint a first and a second prime minister, after securing consent from the president and two vice presidents of the assembly (art. 138). This "transitional provision" (Chapter XIV) continued for the first five years the curious coalition created, following the election of May

1993, by Sihanouk's appointment of Ranariddh and Hun Sen as "co-presidents" of the interim government. The constitution stipulated that the next election for the National Assembly would be held in 1998, five years after the first election, and a new government would be formed with a single prime minister.

The peculiar tandem executive arrangement, which had been initially engineered by the king, survived during the transitional period (May to September 1993) and was written into the constitution, thus becoming authorized legal practice. The arrangement drew endorsement from UNTAC officials. General Sanderson noted that Cambodia "needs to say to the international community that now 'we have stability, consensus, to start reconstruction, rehabilitation.' " He added that "in the fullness of time, there will not be two prime ministers . . . but right now they need consensus to ensure stability."[30] Hun Sen expressed satisfaction with his role as second prime minister, noting benevolently, "Though I am a co–prime minister I've already given the first position to Sdech Krom Luong [Prince Ranariddh] as you can see in protocol, or at least I respect his age because he is older than I am." He added that the work procedures of the two would be equal.[31]

Legislative Branch

Legislative power was vested by the constitution in an assembly of at least 120 members, elected for five years by a "free, universal, equal, direct and secret ballot" (art. 76, 78, 90). The assembly was instructed to hold ordinary sessions at least twice a year, for a period of three months. The king, prime minister, or one-third of the assembly members could call for an extraordinary session (art. 83). An issue of controversy during the drafting process was the size of the majority required for action in the assembly. The CPP, with 51 of the 120 seats, came out strongly for a two-thirds requirement while FUNCINPEC generally preferred simple majority rule. A compromise was struck, calling for two-thirds on some issues and a simple majority on others. For example, a two-thirds vote was required to validate a member's seat, to elect a president, vice presidents, and members of commissions (art. 82). Perhaps most important was the two-thirds majority of the entire assembly required for a motion of censure, which would result in dismissal of the whole cabinet or of individual members of the government,

30. *Phnom Penh Post*, Sept. 24–Oct. 7, 1993.
31. Ibid.

or a vote of confidence in the government (art. 90, 96, 98). An innovation adopted from European practice was the provision that one day each week assembly members might question government ministers (art. 96).

Despite the powers accorded to the assembly in the constitution, the first four years of experience under the new system showed that dominant power lay in the hands of the co–prime ministers and members of their cabinet, with a strong role of influence by the king. With the coup d'état of July 1997 (as Chapter 8 shows), Hun Sen violated the constitution, "dismissing" First Prime Minister Ranariddh and consolidating power for himself and his CPP.

The Judiciary

The constitution placed judicial power in a Supreme Court and a unified system of courts of general jurisdiction. The king was called upon to be the guarantor of the independence of the judiciary (art. 113). Following the 1947 constitution, and the French tradition, a Supreme Council of the Magistracy, headed by the king, was prescribed to recommend the appointment and removal of judges and prosecutors and to consider disciplinary matters in accordance with the organic law that was to be drafted (art. 114–16). The judiciary was to be independent and impartial, and would protect the rights and freedoms of the citizens (art. 109). It is noteworthy that the constitution calls for the protection of "citizens" and is silent on protection for noncitizens (e.g., migrant Vietnamese), an issue of serious concern to human rights monitors.

These constitutional assertions about the judiciary amounted at best to noble aspirations. Cambodia's limited judicial system was decimated during Khmer Rouge rule. A legal scholar notes that "legislators, prosecutors, judges and law professors were killed or forced to flee the country. Law books were destroyed and the buildings that had housed the courts and the law school converted to other uses. Estimates of the number of legal professionals remaining in Cambodia at the end of the massacres in 1978 range from six to ten. In short, Cambodia's formal legal system was completely destroyed by the Khmer Rouge."[32] The rebuilding of the judiciary proceeded slowly under the successor regime. In 1992, the total number of judges on the bench under the State of Cambodia was seventy to ninety. For the most part the judges had a high school education or a year or two of

32. Dolores A. Donovan, "The Cambodian Legal System: An Overview," in *Rebuilding Cambodia: Human Resources, Human Rights, and Law*, ed. Fred Z. Brown (Washington, D.C.: Foreign Policy Institute, Johns Hopkins University, 1993), p. 69.

university, and had passed through a five-month course offered by the Institute of Public Administration and Law between 1982 and 1989.[33]

An official of UNTAC's Human Rights Component wrote, prior to the drafting of the constitution, that to achieve judicial independence, "it would be necessary to abolish the judiciary as it exists now, completely."[34] He noted that "the whole concept of independence of the judiciary was alien" to the Cambodian judges with whom he discussed the issue.[35]

The Constitutional Council

Following the French tradition, the constitution created a constitutional council which was to exercise a form of judicial review (Chapter X). This council was designed to be the protector of constitutional supremacy, a concept that the Paris Agreements required to be guaranteed in the constitution. The council was to be composed of nine members, three appointed by the king, three by the assembly, and three by the Supreme Council of the Magistracy. The king, the prime minister, the president of the assembly, or one-tenth of the assembly members could submit to the council either draft bills or laws already promulgated for an opinion regarding their constitutionality (art. 121, 122). Further, citizens were given the right to appeal the constitutionality of laws through their representatives or the president of the assembly (art. 122).

Human Rights

The new constitution, as required by the Paris Agreements, contained a chapter on human rights that resembled the protections typically guaranteed in the constitutions of liberal democracies. The drafters pledged Cambodia to respect human rights in accordance with "the U.N. Charter, the Universal Declaration of Human Rights, the covenants and conventions related to human rights, women's and children's rights." Thus, virtuous promises were made, but questions remained about the extent to which they would be carried out.[36]

33. Ibid.

34. J. Basil Fernando, "The Inability to Prosecute: Courts and Human Rights in Cambodia and Sri Lanka," 1993, quoted in Marks, "The New Cambodian Constitution," p. 69.

35. Ibid., p. 10.

36. An in-depth assessment of the place of human rights in the Cambodian constitution can be found in Marks, "The New Cambodian Constitution." Our brief summary of human rights in the constitution draws from this article.

Stephen Marks examined the extent of the UN's success in fulfilling the mandate of the Paris Agreements to establish a regime capable of assuring "human rights, and the non-return to the policies and practices of the past." He noted that most of the required protections were inserted into Chapter III of the constitution, but he expressed disappointment that the drafters did not draw upon the language or the normative richness of the international standards.[37] It is not unusual, especially in new constitutions of countries emerging from chaos, for proclamation of the protection of human rights to be far more noble than the practice. This was clearly the case in Cambodia. Some examples from the first few years of the new state reveal the wide discrepancy between constitutional assertions and grim reality. Women were guaranteed equal rights with men in articles 34–36, 45, and 46. Article 45 promised that "all forms of discrimination against women shall be abolished." Yet, when a draft law to implement the protection of women's rights in labor, marriage, and divorce and to prescribe punishment for molestation, violence, and rape was introduced in the assembly by the secretary of state for women's affairs, Prime Minister Hun Sen was unenthusiastic. He disputed the notion that women needed protection from suppression or harassment by men.

The press, guaranteed freedom in the constitution (art. 41), was abused by the new government despite a promising start during the UNTAC transitional period. At least twenty newspapers were published in Khmer, English, French, and Chinese, some of which criticized the government and its leaders freely, and in December 1993, local journalists formed the Association of Khmer Journalists.[38]

At least three journalists who had published accounts of official corruption were killed during the first two years, and no one was arrested or charged with the murders.[39] On a number of occasions, the government confiscated printed materials that were critical and, in some cases, closed down the publication.

A noticeable gap in the constitution was the absence of protection provided to noncitizens. Most of the protections in Chapter III were designated for "Khmer citizens" (e.g., art. 32: "Every Khmer citizen shall have the right to life, personal freedom and security"). Article 44 prescribed that

---

37. Ibid., p. 75. Marks includes charts in his text that show the correspondence of the articles in the new constitution with those in the 1989 constitution, pp. 76, 83–84.

38. Ibid., p. 100, citing *Report of the Special Representative of the Secretary-General, Mr. Michael Kirby, on the situation of human rights in Cambodia submitted pursuant to Commission on Human Rights Resolution 1993/6*, Commission on Human Rights, 50th Session, Agenda Item 19, UN Documents E/CN.4/1994/73, E/CN4/1994/73/Add.1, 1994.

39. Reuter, May 19, 1995.

"only Khmer legal entities and citizens of Khmer nationality have the right to own land." This provision could raise problems with foreign investors. Insider observers at the drafting process attributed the silence about protections for noncitizens to a widespread animus among Cambodians toward Vietnamese residents. The issue of Vietnamese minority rights was too sensitive, too subject to inflammatory rhetoric, to raise and settle it in the brief period available for constitution drafting.[40]

Economy, Environment, Education, Culture, and Social Affairs

Chapter V, devoted to the economy and the environment, put Cambodia among the former communist states that have announced their intention to adopt a "market economy" (art. 56). Nevertheless, it noted that the state "shall promote economic development in all sectors and remote areas" (art. 61) and shall "protect the price of products for farmers and crafters, and find marketplace for them to sell their products" (art. 62). It also declared that the state "shall protect the environment" (art. 59). The weak fulfillment of this stipulation is a source of grave concern. The country's forests are being rapidly denuded; in fact, the pace of deforestation has dangerously speeded up in recent years.

Chapter VI, entitled "Education, Culture and Social Affairs," promises to "provide free primary and secondary education to all citizens" (art. 68), to preserve the national culture (art. 69), and to "guarantee" the health of the people (art. 72).

Conclusion

The constitution provided a framework for government consisting of a constitutional monarchy, parliamentary system, and unicameral legislature, with provision for separation of powers and judicial review by a constitutional council. The transitional arrangement that created joint prime ministers and a coalition among former enemies was a curious one. It brought together leaders of a former communist movement (CPP) which had been a tutee of a widely feared and much despised neighbor, Vietnam, and a royal party (FUNCINPEC), led by one of the King's sons. In the past, they had vilified each other. The partnership in leadership survived for four years, raising hopes that it might continue until the next election, pre-

40. Aucoin interview.

scribed to take place by 1998. These hopes were dashed by the coup d'état of July 1997.

The king performed in the style of a constitutional monarch. The co–prime ministers forged a working arrangement during the first few years, but it was dissolved by serious tensions and ended with the coup. (During the period the two prime ministers cooperated, critics charged that they were bound by a common, self-serving greed. The cement for their union was the opportunity it provided for generous graft and corruption.) Despite the provisions of power to the National Assembly, it proved to be a weak institution. The bulk of the political power was concentrated in the co–prime ministers, with the king wielding significant influence in the initial two years. This profile of power was fundamentally altered when Hun Sen accomplished his power grab in 1997.

The constitutional provisions for judicial independence, the protection of human rights, and guarantees of health, education, and welfare, as well as the promise to guard the environment, were at best grand aspirations, at worst cynical reminders in flowery language of what Cambodians are still denied.

The Cambodian Constitution of 1993 contained the underpinnings of a "liberal, democratic regime," which was the declared intention of its framers. It created a framework for democratic government and vowed respect for the concepts of constitutional supremacy, separation of powers, and human rights. It was a necessary component for the repair of a failed state. But the constitution was imported by French-trained constitutional law scholars, and its logic and aspirations were unfamiliar to most of the nation to which it was devoted. Its survival would rest in the hands of far too few political leaders who truly cared for constitutional government. Their voice and actions would need continuing attention by the world community, to make effective UNTAC's contribution.

CHAPTER SEVEN

Government and Politics of the New State

The political record of the first years of the new state was as surprising as the elections that preceded it. The curious combination of royalists and former communists who had fought each other for more than a decade held together until July 1997. The restored King Sihanouk abided by the constitutional injunction that he should "reign but not govern," and he served as a national arbiter, assisting reconciliation between the former adversaries. At the same time, the Khmer Rouge were withering on the vine. The new government succeeded in soliciting foreign assistance, and it showed a creditable record of economic growth in its early years.

On the other hand, power was concentrated in the executive branch, particularly in the hands of the two prime ministers, and the government was suffused with corruption. A leading Asian periodical labeled Cambodia a "narcostate" and described connections of high-level officials with narcotics traffickers. Several Cambodian newspaper editors and journalists who had published stories critical of the government were assassinated. Two members of the National Assembly who had spoken in opposition to the leadership were pushed out under dubious procedures. The opposition political party organized by one of them was denied authorization by the government. There was rapid degradation of the country's prime forests, as logging contracts were let to business interests in neighboring countries, for the individual profit of high Cambodian officials. The gap between rich and poor grew even wider. Thus, there was much that was deeply disturbing in the record of the new state.

The Government and Administration

When the government coalition was created in 1993, serious doubts were raised as to whether a prince of royal blood could long share power with a former communist revolutionary, whose party had placed second in the vote. There were bound to be both institutional and personal conflicts in the new governing arrangement, and these proved to be too divisive for the fragile new quasi-democracy to survive.

Until summer 1997, although minor adjustments had been made, the basic political distribution of government appointments between the two major parties had remained stable. Of the 23 ministerial posts in the Council of Ministers, FUNCINPEC and CPP each held 11, and the BLDP held 1. Of the 20 provincial governors' posts, FUNCINPEC and CPP each occupied 10. To fill the 3 deputy governor posts in each province (*khet*), FUNCINPEC and CPP were each allocated 29 appointments, and BLDP the 2 remaining. Significantly, the CPP retained almost all of the 172 posts of district (*srok*) governors and the more than 1,000 commune (*khum*) leaders, giving that party significant political control at the rice roots, an important asset for a future election (particularly if a single-member district electoral system were adopted).[1]

Political Leadership

While there was stability in the distribution of ministerial portfolios between the two major parties, and the partnership between the two prime ministers, though severely strained, endured until the summer of 1997, the government was beset not only by corruption but also by the tensions of intraparty factionalism and political adventurism of certain politicians.

The events of July 1994, which some described as an abortive coup attempt and others simply as political theater, exemplified the frailty of the regime. The two leading actors in the mysterious machinations were Prince Chakrapong, former CPP deputy prime minister (and son of King Sihanouk and half-brother of Prince Ranariddh), and General Sin Song, the "feared" former CPP minister of interior. Both actors had been involved in the secession attempt of seven eastern provinces in June 1993, following the announcement of the UNTAC-guided election results. They had been removed from their CPP posts when their maneuver failed. They attempted a coup in July 1994 which was described by some sources as an at-

1. Chheang Sopheng, "Rift Widens: No Solution in Sight to Power Sharing," *Cambodia Times*, March 31–April 6, 1996.

tempt to "bully their way back into power," using troops to extract concessions from the government. Others alluded to powerful figures in the government behind them who urged them to act and subsequently dropped them. Were they deliberately led into a trap, purposely laid to crush dissent? A senior diplomat described it as a non-coup, with no troops, no shots fired, and only one leader arrested. "The question remains," he asked, "who was behind it and what were they launching a coup to do? It is a theatre for something else."[2] Full explanation of these events is yet to be found, but the episode amply indicated the fragility of the new state.

The Two Prime Ministers: A Tenuous Coalition

When first appointed, the two prime ministers suffered a built-in potential for conflict. They had previously led political movements at war with each other. Ranariddh led the royalist party, whose plurality in the election offered him a democratic mandate to lead Cambodia. Hun Sen was the leader of the former communist party that was widely expected to win, not only by the CPP leadership but by foreign observers as well. The shock of placing second was great. CPP leaders had no ideological guidance or experience in accepting election results as the basis for exercising power. As former communists, they had no instinctive inclination to share power with monarchist and bourgeois politicians. Their first reflex was to declare fraud and reject the voting results. The CPP's immediate demand for a revote in four provinces failed to persuade UNTAC, and the secessionist attempt in seven provinces, engineered by disgruntled CPP freebooters, fizzled. Only after crafty political maneuvering by the newly restored King Sihanouk was the curious political marriage between Ranariddh and Hun Sen achieved.

Despite challenges and severe altercations, at times, in their relationship, Ranariddh and Hun Sen managed to maintain their dual prime ministership until July 1997 and to keep their two parties within the coalition government. Both may have been motivated to serve the Cambodian national interest, as they saw it, and their continuing partnership served the country's need for stability. Both clearly were eyeing the projected 1998 election, and each was seeking to build a base that would permit him to become the preeminent political leader. The temporary political unity served their common commercial interest; each appeared to have his own channels for self-enrichment and personal aggrandizement which the other respected for the first few years of the new regime. Thus, they had a common interest in sharing power, at least temporarily.

2. Nate Thayer, "Shadow Play," *Far Eastern Economic Review*, July 14, 1994, p. 14.

When strains in their relationship arose, they were assisted by the intervention of the king. The sources of these strains were both institutional and personal. Both leaders faced serious intraparty challenges, though Hun Sen could rely on a better-organized, more cohesive, more ideologically-directed party than Ranariddh. Ranariddh's FUNCINPEC was a loosely organized group, led by exiles who had lived abroad during the 1980s. The differing backgrounds and personalities of the two prime ministers made for friction. Prince Ranariddh grew up accustomed to deference in a royal household. He spent a good part of his mature life as an academic in France, moving through his studies of law into the Faculty of Law at the university in Aix-en-Provence. He was recalled by his father in the early 1980s and anointed as the leader of the Sihanoukist faction of the CGDK. Ranariddh divided his time between residences in Bangkok and on the Thai-Cambodian border, and representations abroad.

Hun Sen emerged through the ranks of a communist revolutionary movement. He reached the rank of regimental commander while serving with the Khmer Rouge, then defected to Vietnam in 1977 along with other dissidents who later became the leadership of the CPP. Not long after the People's Republic of Kampuchea was implanted in Phnom Penh by Vietnam in 1979, Hun Sen craftily maneuvered his way to dominance in the new government.

A composite picture of Hun Sen's political personality, drawn from interviews in Phnom Penh in May 1996, suggests that Hun Sen has operated on two levels. On one level, he is a risk-taker, willing at the outset of the new regime to experiment with multiparty democracy, an open market economy, and other reforms imposed on him by the new environment he confronted. He is an intelligent, clever political operative, a quick study, who moves easily among the peasantry, speaks their language well, and inspires enthusiasm among many admirers. A diplomatic observer who was familiar with his movements reported that people frequently reached out to touch him. He showed, on this level, qualities of the successful politician, moving easily among the people, flexible, and willing to go along with reform when not threatened. He grew more comfortable, if not fully at ease, with a critical press during the third and fourth year of the new state. He achieved greater ease, too, in interchange with the international community. In sum, he grew more skillful at operating with the quasi-democratic environment that was sprouting in Cambodia, and he appeared to learn from experience in dealing with foreign diplomats.

On another level, reflecting his past as a canny communist revolutionary who survived vicious internecine warfare and factional conflict—indeed, he emerged at the apex of his party—Hun Sen was suspicious of open competition, felt threatened by free speech, and was hostile to criticism. He worked hard, probably overworking, without pacing himself adequately, sometimes getting stressed out. (He was treated for "nervous exhaustion" in a hospital in France in September 1994.)[3] Some reported that he could grow exceedingly tense, sleeping only two to three hours, chain-smoking, and drinking cognac heavily. (One diplomatic observer testified that, despite the rumors about Hun Sen's drinking problem, he has never seen him drunk.) At times of excessive fatigue, he revealed the bully in him, lashing out at his critics in intemperate language. He seemed obsessed about personal security, deploying military units and sometimes tanks to guard his house) and appeared to believe there were plotters aiming to kill him. He was said to move from house to house when he felt besieged. One keen observer noted that Hun Sen, like many Cambodians, was extremely sensitive to condescending Western attitudes, and he could easily take umbrage at perceived insults, especially those from foreign diplomats. Hun Sen's personality traits were seldom analyzed in the Cambodian or foreign-language press. Even courageous critics were reticent about provoking a harsh reaction. Hun Sen's bi-level cluster of traits suggested that he had the potential to lead the country either to more authoritarianism or to greater democracy. His coup d'état in July 1997 may have revealed a fateful decision to take the authoritarian path.

The Role of King Norodom Sihanouk

King Sihanouk played a critical role in the politics of the new state. The king respected the constitution's definition of the monarch as one who "reigns but does not govern." Although the king did not interject himself into the day-to-day decision making, he exercised an important influence in promoting stability—such as it was—during the early years of the fragile new coalition government. His chief role was that of an arbiter, lending his great influence to the resolution of conflict and achievement of compromise among contentious political actors. Sihanouk intervened on behalf of his half-brother, Prince Sirivuddh, with a plea for exile rather than imprisonment, helping to cool tensions over this case. (See Chapter 8.) Also, he attempted to defuse the tensions—unsuccessfully, as it turned out—over Ranariddh's demand for a greater share of power for FUNCINPEC, and in the offer of amnesty for certain Khmer Rouge leaders.[4]

Sihanouk's ability to resolve disputes derived, in good measure, from the

3. Nate Thayer, "Enemies Everywhere: Heads May Roll in Political Power Struggle," *Far Eastern Economic Review*, Sept. 15, 1994, p. 15.

4. See "King Defuses Tension Among Factions," *Phnom Penh Post*, May 3–16, 1996.

awe he commanded from large segments of the Cambodian population. He was still regarded as a god-king by many of the country's traditional strata, especially among the peasantry and the urban poor, and his wishes carried substantial weight. Political leaders within the CPP, and even the Khmer Rouge, recognizing the hold Sihanouk had on a significant segment of the population, accorded him great deference.

However, many among the political elite did not trust Sihanouk and did not like him.[5] They blamed him for a history of political vacillation. Many could not forgive him for aligning himself with the Khmer Rouge from 1970 to 1975. They criticized him for his long absences from Cambodia, living lavishly in his residences in Beijing, Pyongyang, and Paris, while his beloved "children" suffered in poverty in Cambodia. They charged that he stayed abroad so long because he wished to avoid unpleasant circumstances at home. He was frequently labeled not a fighter but a political survivor, interested primarily in his own political power. Many were skeptical about his frequently announced, vague health problems, labeled cynically in Phnom Penh cafes as "political illnesses."[6] One heard frequently in Phnom Penh that only Sihanouk, and perhaps his doctors, knew his real state of health. Sihanouk was often characterized by his detractors as mercurial, volatile, unpredictable, and prone to changing his positions abruptly.[7]

Sihanouk's family was also the target of frequent reproach among Phnom Penh's political cognoscenti. Two of Sihanouk's sons, half-brothers Ranariddh and Chakrapong, were bitter enemies. Sihanouk was said (in the early 1990s) to have shown more favor to his wife and his two sons by her, Prince Norodom Sihamoni and Prince Norodom Norindrapong.[8]

Who will succeed King Sihanouk, if any royal person, when he passes

5. These observations are derived from interviews by the authors in Phnom Penh in June 1992, December 1993, and May 1996. Interviewees characteristically requested that their views be treated as confidential.

6. During the severe tensions between FUNCINPEC and the CPP, in May 1996, the seventy-three-year-old Sihanouk explained that "grave health problems" would keep him in Beijing, where he had to consult his doctors "for several months." Prince Ranariddh noted a few days later, upon his return to Phnom Penh from Paris where he had conferred with his father, that the king was in good health but "the atmosphere does not seem to be favorable for him in Cambodia." *Phnom Penh Post*, May 17–30, 1996.

7. Always sensitive to these criticisms, Sihanouk contends that his convictions have not swerved since his youth. "In my acts and decisions, I have never been guided by a caprice or whim . . . those who know me well or have observed me closely, know that I am far from being 'unpredictable.'" Reuter, "Sihanouk on Succession," <SEASIA-L@msu.edu>, March 13, 1996.

8. Sihamoni is a professional ballet dancer, living in Paris. Nate Thayer, "End of the Line," *Far Eastern Economic Review*, March 2, 1996, p. 21. Norindrapong is a Soviet-trained political scientist and had been working with the Khmer Rouge.

from the scene? The constitutional provisions requiring a royal successor from one of the three historic royal families do not inspire great confidence that the monarchy will survive. The Royal Council to the Throne was charged with naming an heir within seven days of the king's death. The council was to be composed of the two prime ministers, the National Assembly chairman, two supreme monks of Buddhist order, and the two National Assembly vice presidents. Among the candidates who qualify constitutionally would be Prince Ranariddh, who has said that he does not wish to be king.[9] Ranariddh was, of course, rejecting the notion of serving in the honorific role of a constitutional monarch at a time when he still held genuine political power. Others would qualify, including those in the royal family mentioned above, as would Prince Norodom Sirivuddh, Sihanouk's half-brother, now in Paris exile.[10] But none of those eligible appeared to attract the interest of the real wielders of power.

Early in 1996, King Sihanouk elevated the rank of his wife, Queen Monineath, to the status of Supreme Wife of His Majesty the King. This decree gave rise to speculation that he was preparing the ground for his wife to succeed him, which would require a constitutional amendment, since she has no royal blood. A few in Phnom Penh appeared to support such a move (including a recently formed research agency, the Khmer Institute of Democracy).[11] From time to time, Sihanouk despondently expressed the view that the monarchy as well as democracy was on the brink of collapse. In December 1995, a week after the arrest of Prince Sirivuddh, Sihanouk wrote British journalist William Shawcross: "I am very sad that I cannot save either democracy or the monarchy in my country."[12] Hun Sen's coup of 1997 made King Sihanouk's lamentation seem all the more prescient. Serious doubt about the future of the monarchy was cast by the coup—Hun Sen and his CPP are not admirers of royalty.

9. Ranariddh has said on numerous occasions that he has no desire to be King. See, for example, "Sihanouk on Succession," Voice of America, March 11, 1996, <SEASIA-L@msu.edu>, March 11, 1996 and Thayer, "End of the Line."

10. Succession to the throne was an issue for discussion in Phnom Penh when the King, at age seventy-three, in an interview published on March 11, 1996, reminded that in the case of his incapacitation, Chea Sim, president of the National Assembly, would be appointed regent. He noted that Ranariddh could succeed him, though he added that Prince Sirivuddh had more qualities befitting kingship. See Activity Report, Jan.–March 1996, Khmer Institute of Democracy, Phnom Penh, p. 5.

11. Ibid.

12. Associated Press, "Cambodia Kingdom Near Collapse," <SEASIA-L@msu.edu>, Dec. 1, 1995.

Weaker Branches: Legislature and Judiciary

The National Assembly

For those who hoped that a strong, independent-minded legislature would emerge from the founding of the new state, there was disappointment. During its first four years, the National Assembly was subservient to the executive branch. The top party leaders, particularly the two prime ministers, dominated the legislators. The assembly's expulsion of Sam Rainsy and Prince Sirivuddh, by overwhelming majorities (discussed below), demonstrated how firmly the leaders held sway over the National Assembly. Inasmuch as the two major parties had joined in a formal coalition, there was no organized opposition within the assembly.[13] A handful of members dared to challenge the leadership, but their political impact was small, particularly when the two prime ministers were in agreement on policy. An incipient opposition party, the Khmer Nation Party (KNP), was formed by Sam Rainsy, but it was not given official approval by the government and it held no seat in the assembly.[14]

Until the coup of 1997 further emasculated the National Assembly, it did serve as an arena for debate on some critical policy issues, and several issues promised contentious debate. One was the question of a new electoral law for the 1998 elections. The CPP was calling for replacement of the system of proportional representation that was used in the UNTAC organized election with a single-member district ("first-past-the-post") system.[15] A single-member district system tends to favor the larger parties.[16] FUNCINPEC's position on this proposal was not fully defined.

Another subject that aroused debate was the so-called dual nationality

13. A Western consultant to the Khmer political parties expressed cautious optimism about the threat of withdrawal from the coalition expressed by Prime Minister Ranariddh in March 1996. Though he did not approve of the brusque manner in which Ranariddh expressed his dissatisfaction, the consultant believed that the end of political partnership of the two leading parties would be healthy for the democratic process. Interview by J. J. Zasloff in Phnom Penh, May 1996.

14. It is interesting that the (U.S.) International Republican Institute (IRI) provided workshops during 1996 for the KNP, the only party it assisted. The IRI regarded the two incumbent parties, as members of the ruling coalition, as "non-democratic." The government did not interfere with these workshops.

15. "New Electoral Law Drafted," *Cambodia Times*, March 31–April 6, 1996.

16. For an intelligent essay proposing the maintenance of a system of proportional representation for the next election, see the article by Dr. Lao Mong Hay, executive director of the Khmer Institute for Democracy, "Elections Make or Break the Future of Cambodia," *Phnom Penh Post*, May 3–16, 1996.

issue. A Citizenship Bill was to be adopted prior to the communal elections in 1997 and the assembly elections scheduled for May 1988. The CPP leadership had proposed an article that would bar all ministers, secretaries of state, undersecretaries of state, and members of the National Assembly from holding citizenship in other countries. More than twenty-five members of the government, most of them FUNCINPEC members, held citizenship in countries to which they had fled during the Lon Nol and Khmer Rouge periods.[17] Most commonly held citizenships were American, French, Australian, and Canadian. Ranariddh holds French citizenship.

This issue was bound to be politically embarrassing to FUNCINPEC. Average Cambodian citizens might well feel that Cambodian citizenship alone should be good enough for their leaders. Why should leaders have a safe haven? Those with dual citizenship would be susceptible to the charge of divided loyalty, and the legitimacy of their leadership could be called into question. FUNCINPEC members responded that special historic circumstances had created the need for them to reach safety in a third country. Many still had families living abroad, and most appeared to be determined to hold onto their foreign citizenship. A number of FUNCINPEC and BLDP assembly members felt justified by their prudence in retaining foreign citizenship when the 1997 coup made their safety in Cambodia precarious. Some fled to their adoptive countries.

Judicial System

The judiciary (and even more, the police system) had a widespread reputation in Phnom Penh for being weak, incompetent, corrupt, and available for purchase or, more frequently, for domination by the politically powerful.[18] Judges were compliant in condemning newspaper editors and journalists who had been critical of the power structure. A Western lawyer, with

17. "MP's and Dual Citizenship," *Cambodia Times*, April 14–20, 1996. An article in the *Far Eastern Economic Review* (*FEER*) notes that some two hundred senior FUNCINPEC officials would no longer be able to hold office if the amendment passed. It adds that the CPP is "now understood to be considering inserting a softened version of the electoral law." Murray Hiebert, "Truce at the Top: Co-Premiers Tone Down Their War of Words," *FEER*, July 4, 1996, p. 24. Different figures were cited a year earlier by Nate Thayer, who wrote that at least ten ministers, including Ranariddh, are citizens of foreign countries. In addition, "the head of the powerful Cambodian Development Council, at least 30 members of parliament, numerous provincial governors, senior civil servants, ambassadors and military generals hold foreign passports." Thayer, "Saints and Sinners: Returned Khmer Exiles Fill the Halls of Government," *FEER*, March 23, 1995, p. 29.

18. This judgment is drawn from a variety of interviews by the authors in Phnom Penh in June–July 1992, December 1993, and May 1996.

experience in the three Indochina countries, was unrestrained in describing the pervasive venality in the Cambodian judiciary.[19]

The new government was especially slow about creating the judicial institutions that were prescribed in the new constitution. The Supreme Council of the Magistracy, which should have been established to recommend appointment and removal of judges and prosecutors and to consider disciplinary matters (art. 114–16), had not been formed by the end of 1997. Nor had the Constitutional Council, which was to be composed of nine members, three appointed by the king, three by the assembly, and three by the Supreme Council of the Magistracy. The intended purpose of the Constitutional Council, following the French tradition, was to exercise a form of judicial review.

A highly respected, long-term personal adviser to King Sihanouk, Samdech Chakrei Nhiek Tioulong, in a rare public interview, expressed disappointment at the failure of the government to establish these bodies. As one of the three royal representatives to the Constitutional Council (the three from the assembly and three from the Supreme Council of the Magistracy had not been appointed), Nhiek Tioulong contended in October 1995 that "legally, everything has been blocked." For example, he said: "The Assembly's internal rules should have been approved by the Constitutional Council. But because the Council does not exist, the internal rules have not been approved . . . so all the functioning of the National Assembly has been illegal . . . the deliberations, debates, even the laws are, if not illegal, unconstitutional."[20] The coalition government was not eager for judicial interference in its self-serving activities. The government dominated by Hun Sen and the CPP after the July 1997 coup was even less likely to promote judicial independence.

Important Policy Issues for the New State

From 1993 until 1997, the new state confronted a number of policy issues, discussed in the sections below, which revealed important challenges and its style in confronting them.

19. Interview by J. J. Zasloff, May 1996, in Vientiane, Laos.

20. Matthew Grainger, "King's Advisor Bemoans Lack of Constitutional Council," *Phnom Penh Post*, Oct. 6–8, 1995.

The CPP's Continuing Dominance

The CPP's domination of the rural bureaucracy raised a serious question as to whether the mandate for change that was inherent in the election results could be translated into political reality. This problem was exemplified by the situation in the province of Komphong Som, where a newly appointed FUNCINPEC governor, Bun Sron, complained that he could not even "get a letter signed" without CPP approval. He claimed that CPP cadres ignored his orders, still obeying their CPP leaders who, in practice, retained power. He charged that the long-standing former CPP governor Kim Bo, now his first deputy, retained authority over the cadres who had served under his patronage and refused to implement FUNCINPEC decisions. Bun Sron described their behavior as "passive sabotage" and contended that the SOC apparatus had not been dismantled after the election, noting: "The whole administration belongs to the CPP; it is their people and their system . . . the structure has not been changed. People have lived here many years under CPP leadership. They are still owed respect . . . but not as we know it in the West; this is respect, meaning fear." Bun Sron reported that he complained to the FUNCINPEC co-interior minister, You Hockry, who told him that nothing could be done— "this was the reality." [21]

Continued domination by the CPP in the countryside, as described above, was not the exception but the rule. Indeed the CPP maintained ascendancy in the army, police, judiciary, and government bureaucracy, both national and local.[22] This domination derived, in part, from the thirteen years in which the SOC had governed (albeit under Vietnamese tutelage) in Cambodia. CPP personnel were thus entrenched, and little had been done during the UNTAC period to dislodge them. Further, the relative strength of the CPP was compounded by the weakness of FUNCINPEC. Although it had been victorious in the election, the FUNCINPEC appeal was largely attributable to its identification with King Sihanouk, and the party lacked organizational strength. Its leaders were primarily members of the Western-educated elite who had been in exile in France, the United States, Canada, and Australia, and returned to Cambodia for the electoral campaign. Many left their families abroad, as they took up ministerial posts in Phnom Penh. They did little to maintain contact with their supporters in

21. Matthew Grainger and Moeun Chhean Nariddh, "Governor Hits Out Against CPP Control," *Phnom Penh Post*, Feb. 24–March 9, 1995.

22. See Nate Thayer, "Bitter Victory: Poll Winners Find It Hard to Grasp Levers of Power," *Far Eastern Economic Review*, Dec. 9, 1993, p. 24.

the countryside after the election, and they failed to build their organization. One astute Cambodian political insider contended, in May 1996, that the takeover of power by the CPP was more a product of FUNCINPEC corruption and the self-serving policies of its leadership than the strength of the CPP.[23]

An American political consultant who for two years headed the (U.S.) National Democratic Institute's Phnom Penh office wrote, in May 1996, of FUNCINPEC's weak political leadership and their failure to build the party organization in the provinces: "By remaining in the capital FUNCIN-PEC officials did not see signs of distress on the faces of local activists who pursued their tasks with single-minded dedication. . . . They didn't notice the anger of party workers who risked their lives for a victory that would never be theirs. . . . By abandoning provincial supporters with no explanation for why they won the election but have no power, FUNCINPEC broke the cardinal rule of electoral politics."[24] A survey of FUNCINPEC provincial leaders during country-wide training programs conducted by the (U.S.) International Republican Institute (IRI) in 1996 confirmed many of the criticisms noted above. Asked to list the strengths and weaknesses of FUNCINPEC, these grassroots leaders cited the items below (in no particular order):

Strengths
- popularity of H.R.M. King Norodom Sihanouk
- popularity of national leadership
- democratic party principles

Weaknesses
- campaign promises are unfulfilled
- people's needs are not met
- leaders are inexperienced in politics and governing
- party platform is neglected
- party financial resources are scarce
- internal party organization is weak
- communication between party offices is poor
- elected officials do not visit constituencies
- some national party leaders are corrupt
- some national party leaders are untruthful

23. Interview by J. J. Zasloff in Phnom Penh, May 1996.
24. Jamie Factor, "FUNCINPEC: Deaf to the Sounds of Dissatisfaction. CPP: Self Preservation Coveted Above All Else," *Phnom Penh Post*, May 3–16, 1996.

- internal conflicts divide the party
- party won the election but lost power to CPP
- party conducts few provincial political activities[25]

The IRI report pointed out that some provincial leaders complained that there was little communication between elected officials and their constituencies, leaving local cadres to bear the brunt of voter frustrations with FUNCINPEC. Others protested that campaign promises of jobs or water wells were unfulfilled, leading to a general mistrust of the party. Local leaders wanted greater support and interest from FUNCINPEC's national leadership. Some also expressed concern that FUNCINPEC was losing power in the name of "national reconciliation."[26]

It is true that the CPP also had its share of weaknesses, but its organizational cohesion and strength compared to that of FUNCINPEC are notable. The National Democratic Institute consultant summed up the CPP advantage over FUNCINPEC:

> Contrary to conventional wisdom, the CPP has developed a skilled core of cadres who work voluntarily in pursuit of a common goal. The party rewards their dedication much the way that any organization should by advancing people through the ranks to even greater positions of authority. This, more than coercion, helps maintain discipline. It also enables the CPP to safeguard its interests in the government and the parliament—and still have more than enough people left over to plan a winning strategy for the next election. Hun Sen, in his typically unrefined manner, is unequivocal on this point as well: "The CPP has resources, 100,000 armed forces and 10,000 police. In reality no political party has more people, more staff, more experience than CPP." These advantages, as he also put it, flow down from ". . . the reality of history." Indeed, the SOC's inexorable merger of party and state has found a new home in the Royal Government.[27]

If the CPP has such superior political strength, the consultant asked, why did they continue to rely upon the threat of violence? Habit is a powerful behavioral force and, despite its willingness to embrace the transition to a free market, the CPP "remains a communist party in structure, mindset and custom." They are uncomfortable with elections and with voluntary persuasion, and they regard the use of force as an acceptable political strat-

25. International Republican Institute, "FUNCINPEC," in *Final Report*, July 1995 to January 1996, p. 3.
26. Ibid., pp. 4–5.
27. Factor, "FUNCINPEC."

egy. Further and even more important, "the CPP is simply unwilling to risk defeat once again." Even though they possessed organizational superiority, they suffered a surprising and humiliating defeat in 1993 by those they regarded as the enemy.[28]

Corruption

Widespread disgust at what was perceived to be a high level of official corruption could be found at all layers of Cambodian society as well as throughout the international community. *The Far Eastern Economic Review*, in a cover story in November 1995, even raised the question as to whether Cambodia had become "Asia's New Narco-State." Its article noted: "Western governments, international law-enforcement officials and Cambodian sources say businessmen engaged in criminal activities have amassed immense power in Cambodia in the two-and-a-half years since the United Nations–run elections. Protected by senior government officials, they've turned Cambodia into a major centre for drug trafficking, money laundering and smuggling."[29] Further, these sources contended that numerous senior military and police officers were involved in transporting heroin through Cambodia and protecting the traffic that originated in Burma's segment of the Golden Triangle. The deputy head of the regional office of the UN International Drug Control project in Bangkok was quoted as saying, "It is clear that Cambodia is a new and rapidly increasing trafficking route." The absence of an effective legal system, lack of resources to combat drug smuggling, and official corruption, he said, "makes Cambodia very vulnerable."[30]

An end-of-tour report (mysteriously leaked to the press in 1994) by the retiring Australian ambassador, John Holloway, noted that corruption reached to the highest ranks of government. He wrote that "every business deal must have a cut for the relevant minister (or Prime Minister) and every transaction involves a percentage for the relevant official."[31] Government officials were paid a fee of US$10.8 million for the right to build a gambling casino near Sihanoukville, a payment Prince Ranariddh termed a "legal commission."[32]

28. Ibid.

29. Nate Thayer, "Medellin on the Mekong," *Far Eastern Economic Review*, Nov. 23, 1995, p. 24.

30. Ibid., p. 25.

31. "Cambodia: A Wired Warning," *The Age* (Melbourne), Oct. 5, 1994, p. 15. See also Nate Thayer, "Unvarnished Truth: Leaked Cable Portrays a Government in Danger," *Far Eastern Economic Review*, Oct. 20, 1994, p. 18.

32. "Ranariddh Cited on Commissions from Contracts," *Reaksmei Kampuchea* (Phnom Penh), Jan. 23, 24, 1995, p. 1, in *FBIS–East Asia*, Jan. 23, 24, 1995, p. 1, and Jan. 24, 1995, p. 58.

The military and the police were known to contain some of the most nefariously corrupt elements. A particularly odious group of military miscreants in Battambang Province was charged, in August 1994, with extortion and serious violations of human rights. A dispatch in the *Phnom Penh Post* reported:

Confidential investigations by government, United Nations and human rights organizations have revealed senior Cambodian military personnel—including the commanding officers of elite secret military intelligence units—control criminal rackets responsible for:
- systematically torturing and executing suspected political opponents;
- running a highly organized extortion and murder racket;
- abducting, robbing and executing traders;
- recruiting known criminals to engage in organized armed robbery for the profit of military officers;
- demanding "protection fees" from provincial fishermen and peasants.[33]

An interesting acknowledgment of the pervasiveness of official corruption came in an interview by Nayan Chanda, in March 1995, with a powerful CPP political leader, Co–Minister of Interior and Deputy Prime Minister Sar Kheng. Sar Kheng noted that "the Khmer Rouge is not the No. 1 issue, it is corruption." Government corruption, he said, had provoked widespread indignation among students and other members of the public. Sar Kheng's criticism of his government was an indication of the factionalism within his own CPP party. He may have been distancing himself from government corruption, Nate Thayer suggests, because he had "his eye on the prime minister's job."[34]

Even more severe criticism about government corruption poured forth from Sam Rainsy, the original minister of finance in the coalition government. Rainsy's dismissal from his critical post in September 1994 appeared to result, in important measure, from his advocacy of structural reforms that threatened revenue sources of some of his political colleagues.[35] In particular, he objected to a government decision that stripped the finance ministry of the right to control logging, the largest source of internal revenue, and gave it to the army.[36] After his dismissal, Rainsy vigorously

33. Nate Thayer,"Army's Dossier of Shame," *Phnom Penh Post*, Aug. 12–25, 1994.
34. Nate Thayer, "Enemies Everywhere," *Far Eastern Economic Review*, Sept. 15, 1994, p. 15.
35. See Nate Thayer, "Red Rag to a Bull: Minister's Anti-Corruption Drive Stirs Powerful Opposition," *Far Eastern Economic Review*, Feb. 24, 1994, p. 32.
36. Nate Thayer, "Matter of Conscience," *Far Eastern Economic Review*, Nov. 3, 1994, p. 16.

charged the government with pervasive corruption. He told a reporter in November 1995: "Cambodia is now a mafia state because there is a group of businessmen who consider themselves above the law, who have infiltrated all spheres, all aspects of government, the judiciary, the parliament. These people—these politicians—are at least protecting and at worst working for the mafia."[37]

Rainsy's charges were all the more devastating to the government when he made them in France and the United States, and especially at meetings of donor countries considering assistance to Cambodia. He urged donors to make their assistance conditional upon "greater transparency in public decision-making." He spoke fluently and backed his charges with documentation that he circulated to the donors. A thirteen-page, single-spaced document prepared by Sam Rainsy on the occasion of the International Conference on the Reconstruction of Cambodia held in Paris on March 14–15, 1995, summed up what he called "The Institutionalization of Corruption and the Negation of the State":

> Dubious contracts, dubious through their lack of transparency and their onesidedness, inevitably led to suspicions of corruption. The country's highest leaders speak openly of "gifts" or "commissions" or "tips" paid by private companies but they hasten to add the qualifier "legal" because the amounts in question are "mentioned in the contracts" and "included in the State budget." . . . The First Prime Minister has spoken of several "tips," of which the most important, paid or to be paid by the Malaysian company ARISTON, amounts to US$10.8 million.[38]

The government prepared an official press release in response, offering general observations and then responding to each specific allegation.[39] In reply to criticisms that appeared in the national and international press, First Prime Minister Ranariddh addressed charges of corruption: "Corruption, like prostitution, is as old as mankind itself. Cambodia is no exception and we have not denied the existence of corruption in our society. However, instead of just admitting the existence of corruption, the Royal Government is taking concerted steps to tackle the issue."[40] Optimism was surely not the dominant feeling among international observers.

37. Nate Thayer, "Medellin on the Mekong," p. 25.

38. "Rainsy's Note on ICORC" (part 1), March 28, 1995, Southeast Asia Discussion List <SEASIA-L@msu.edu>. This document was circulated to the participants at the conference, and more broadly on the Internet.

39. "The Royal Government of Cambodia Response to Sam Rainsy's Allegation," March 30, 1995, Southeast Asia Discussion List <SEASIA-L@msu.edu>.

40. "Prime Minister's Vital Issues," *Phnom Penh Post*, Aug. 25–Sept. 7, 1995.

Environmental Policy: Logging

The constitution declares that the state "shall protect the environment" (art. 59). The weak fulfillment of this stipulation is a source of grave concern. The country's forests are being stripped at a rapid pace that has only increased in recent years. In July 1994 the state secretary for the environment, Dr. Mok Mareth, characterized the deforestation resulting from illegal logging as a "catastrophe," and he admitted that his department was "powerless to act." He noted that the government had issued licenses for companies to cut 300,000 cubic meters of wood per year and that, according to his department's estimates, there was actually 1,700,000 cubic meters of illegal cutting per year. A Mekong River Committee report estimated that 60 percent of the country was covered by forest in 1992 but by mid-1994, according to a senior forestry official's analysis of satellite data, the figure was 49 percent.

In March 1995 a British environmental group, Global Witness, issued a report alleging that Cambodian government and military officials had granted concessions to Thai companies to log trees in Khmer Rouge–occupied territory. They also reported that the government had made other large logging concessions, such as its huge deal with the Malaysian Samling Corporation, signed in August 1994, granting Samling 800,000 hectares, equivalent to 12 percent of Cambodia's remaining forest. The contract included a total levy of only $100,000 for reforestation, barely enough, according to a Phnom Penh forestry expert, for 2,500 hectares at current seed prices. Global Witness warned of the dramatic impact that such unsustainable logging would have, causing soil erosion and exacerbating the damage of floods and droughts. The group claimed that of the 74 percent of Cambodia that was formerly covered with forest, only 30 to 35 percent was left and at current rates of destruction, it was likely that the remaining forest would be completely destroyed before the end of the century.[41]

Global Witness charged again, in December 1995, that the government was "proposing new concessions involving 19 companies largely from Taiwan, Malaysia, and Indonesia, that would almost wipe out Cambodia's dwindling forest areas."[42] A few months later Global Witness reported that the two prime ministers had signed agreements with twenty Thai companies to export more than one million cubic meters of timber, two-thirds more than the 330,000 cubic meters of trees cut before a ban on newly felled timber took effect. News reports about the agreements suggested that revenue from the log exports might make its way into the pockets of se-

41. *Phnom Penh Post*, March 24–April 6, 1995.
42. Voice of America, "Cambodia Logging," Dec. 1, 1995, <SEASIA- L@msu.edu>.

nior officials rather than into the state treasury. Once again Prince Ranariddh issued an angry denial of the charge that he and Co–Prime Minister Hun Sen had secretly violated the ban.[43]

A study of Cambodia's logging policies conducted in late 1995 by a joint World Bank, UN Development Programme, and Food and Agriculture Organization mission, confirmed the dire warning about Cambodia's deforestation.[44] The report noted:

> The deforestation of over one million hectares and degradation of over three million hectares has occurred in Cambodia over the last thirty years. Current policies risk deepening and accelerating this pattern by repeating mistakes made in other forest-rich developing countries. . . . This program, which appears to have allocated nearly all of the country's commercially viable timberlands to a small number of concessionaires, rests on a level of timber exploitation which is likely to be unsustainable and will, in any case, provide inadequate fiscal returns.[45]

This joint report by international development agencies, which usually avoid intrusion into matters judged politically sensitive by host governments, indicates how seriously they regarded the rapid despoliation of Cambodia's formerly rich forests.

Democratic Practice and Human Rights

Despite the emphasis on safeguards for human rights in the Paris accords, and the inclusion of these protections in the constitution, serious human rights abuses punctuated the first four years of the new government. A *New York Times* correspondent, who had covered Indochina in earlier years and returned at the end of 1995, wrote a disturbing summary of Cambodia's new political violence: "The offices of a struggling independent newspaper are ransacked by ax-wielding villagers, and the Prime Minister applauds. A new opposition party is declared illegal before it is formally launched. Grenades explode at the office of another independent-minded senior politician, and in the courtyard of a Buddhist temple that has been shelter-

43. AFP, "No Violation of Logging Ban, Says Ranariddh," April 7, 1996, <SEASIA-L@msu.edu>.

44. Matthew Grainger, "Government Rapped Over Logging Practices," *Phnom Penh Post*, April 5–18, 1996.

45. "Text of Report Damning the RGC's Logging Policies," *Phnom Penh Post*, April 19–May 2, 1996, p. 5.

ing his supporters." She added, ironically, "This is the newly democratic Cambodia."[46]

UN Center for Human Rights

By early 1995, the two prime ministers were clearly uncomfortable with the presence in Phnom Penh of the United Nations Center for Human Rights, which had been disseminating reports highly critical of human rights abuses by the government and the military, including allegations of torture and murder in secret prisons, forced conscription, and attempts to restrict freedom of expression.[47] In a letter to the UN secretary-general, dated February 28, 1995, Prime Ministers Ranariddh and Hun Sen announced that they did not intend to renew the mandate of the center. They wrote:

> The continued presence of a U.N. Center for Human Rights makes it appear [to the world] that the situation in Cambodia is still in crisis similar to the situation which continues to prevail in some countries where the UN also maintains such centers. This is not good for investor or donor confidence. Furthermore, we are finding that every charge against the Government, whether real, imagined or exaggerated, receives the imprimatur of the United Nations once it is received by the Center as a complaint. Whilst the Center is only doing its job, it is being used to make it seem as if there are a large number of UN-accepted charges against the Government, whereas the real number is negligible.[48]

A flood of protests, particularly from Western embassies and nongovernmental organizations (NGOs), followed this announcement. Twelve Cambodian human rights groups and international NGOs wrote to the government urging that the center be maintained. An official at LICHADO, a prominent Cambodian NGO, acknowledged that "we would be very vulnerable if the Center were to leave." The official reported disturbing visits during the previous few months of agents claiming to be from the Ministry of Interior, without official papers, seeking information about staff in Phnom Penh and the provinces. Other NGOs, including Vigilance,

46. Barbara Crossette, "Outsiders Gone, Cambodia Unravels," *New York Times*, Dec. 3, 1995.

47. Associated Press, "Cambodia Favors Human Rights," March 20, 1995, C-ap@clarinet.com (AP).

48. "Human Rights Watch Criticizes Request to Shut Down Cambodian UN Center," March 20, 1995, <SEASIA-L@msu.edu>.

Khmer Institute of Democracy, and Ponleu Khmer, reported similar investigations.[49] The U.S. and Australian embassies were especially committed to continuing the UN center in Phnom Penh. In face of the strong pressure to retain the center, and the criticism that would attend its expulsion, the two prime ministers finally agreed that it would remain.[50] After his coup-d'état in July 1997, Hun Sen, reacting to reports from the center that CPP troops had executed at least forty supporters of Prince Ranariddh, requested, unsuccessfully, the United Nations to replace its human rights team in Phnom Penh.[51]

Political and Press Freedom, 1994–1996

In its required yearly report on human rights in Cambodia for 1994, the first year of constitutional government, the U.S. Embassy noted a few optimistic elements. It described the "human rights climate" as "better than in past years, with a relatively open political atmosphere, a vigorous press, and an active human rights community." Nevertheless, many problems that affected human rights remained. Democratic institutions, particularly the judiciary, were weak. Serious abuses were perpetrated by the security forces, including intimidation, extortion, torture, and murder.

There were a few healthy signs regarding freedom of the press. Independent news organizations, launched during the UNTAC period, continued to operate. By the end of 1994, thirty-three newspapers and magazines functioned, and the Khmer Journalists Association, established at the end of 1993, drew up a code of ethics and served as an informal liaison between the press and the government. However, there was well-grounded fear and suspicion among journalists that criticism of officials would bring retaliatory violence encouraged by government or security forces.[52]

In the second year of the new state, there was clearly a deterioration in respect for human rights. Amnesty International reported that the government had become "increasingly intolerant of political opposition resulting in the rights to freedom of expression, association and assembly being undermined over the last two years."[53] Political intimidation and assassination

49. Ibid.
50. Reuter, "Cambodian PM Says U.N. Rights Office Can Stay," March 25, 1995, C-reuters@clarinet.com (Reuter/Mark Dodd).
51. Barbara Crossette, "Hun Sen Seeks to Oust U.N. Human Rights Team," *New York Times*, Aug. 21, 1997.
52. U.S. Department of State, "United States Human Rights Report 1994: Cambodia."
53. Amnesty International, "Kingdom of Cambodia: Diminishing Respect for Human Rights," May 1996, AI Index: ASA 23/02/96. The "United States Human Rights Report 1995," prepared by the U.S. Department of State, shared this assessment that human rights had deteriorated in 1995. See note 55 below.

increased. Security forces beat detainees. Prison conditions were deplorable and prolonged detention was common. The government lacked the capability and political will to act against malefactors, particularly those in the military. Sam Rainsy was summarily expelled from the National Assembly in June 1995; Prince Sirivuddh was arrested on dubious charges in November. A BLDP faction out of favor with the government was denied permission to hold a party congress in the Phnom Penh stadium. In September grenades were lobbed into the faction's headquarters and into a nearby Buddhist pagoda lodging faction members, injuring thirty party officials and followers. The BLDP faction defied the government ban and held a rally attended by two thousand supporters. U.S. Ambassador Charles Twining spoke at the rally, stating that he had come to support those who attended, praising their courage in the face of violence, and proclaiming that freedom of assembly should be a basic right. Twenty minutes after the departure of Ambassador Twining, military police raided and dispersed the rally.[54]

Freedom of the press presented an ambiguous picture in 1995–96. The number of newspapers increased to fifty, many of them independent, and they were sometimes critical of the government. Three journalists' associations were operating, lobbying for a liberal press law and against the detention of journalists. But the government continued to intimidate journalists and editors who were critical, sometimes through judicial actions with compliant judges, and also, it appeared, through naked violence. In February 1995, the editor of the *Voice of Khmer Youth* was sentenced to a year in prison for "disinformation." In May, the editor of *New Liberty News* was sentenced to a year in prison for publishing an article critical of the two prime ministers. In September, the office and home of an editor of the *Morning News*, critical of the government, was the target of a motorcyclist who hurled a grenade. No one was arrested following the episode. In October, some one hundred residents of a village where Hun Sen sponsored a development project ransacked the office of the *New Liberty News*, which had criticized the project. Hun Sen publicly praised the villagers, asserting they were justified in the attack.[55]

Political intimidation and assassination of critics continued into 1996. Workers for Sam Rainsy's newly organized Khmer Nation Party (KNP) were harassed as they attempted to recruit popular support. In January

54. Voice of America, "VOA Report US Ambassador Addressed BLDP Meeting," Oct. 1, 1995, <SEASIA-L@msu.edu>.

55. U.S. Department of State, "United States Human Rights Report 1995: Cambodia," and "Cambodia Report on Human Rights Practices for 1996," released January 30, 1997. See also Amnesty International, "Kingdom of Cambodia: Diminishing Respect for Human Rights."

1996 Cambodian police detained some 150 people for three hours inside the party's Phnom Penh headquarters as they ostensibly searched for weapons. Sam Rainsy reported numerous death threats leveled at himself and his family.[56] In May, Thun Bunly, editor of *Khmer Ideal*, a newspaper described as "fearless enough to challenge the government," was murdered by two men on a motorbike a few hours after he had attended KNP opening ceremonies at its first provincial office in Sihanoukville. In 1995 Thun Bunly had been twice convicted on "dubious charges" for publishing critical articles about the two prime ministers. But, according to a former member of the Human Rights Task Force in Cambodia, his murder could most likely be attributed not to his role as editor of *Khmer Ideal*, from which he had resigned in December 1995, but to his membership on the KNP steering committee.[57] No arrests were made in connection with the murder.

A brighter spot on the Cambodian human rights scene was the modest growth of a civil society arising from the expansion of human rights NGOs. By 1995 the number of Cambodian human rights NGOs had grown to forty, supplemented by international NGOs. The courageous chairman of the Committee on Human Rights of the National Assembly, Kem Sokha, himself a former NGO leader, served as liaison between the assembly and the human rights community. Interviews in Phnom Penh revealed that Cambodian NGOs were making valiant efforts to provide assistance to victims of unlawful arrest and detention, torture, sexual mistreatment and rape, assault, harassment, and a variety of other abuses by officials. Some intellectuals expressed the view that the hope for development of Cambodia's civil society lay with the leadership potential of the NGOs.[58]

Treatment of the Ethnic Vietnamese Minority

Treatment of the Vietnamese minority in Cambodia has presented a long-standing problem. While the Chinese minority has been generally accepted, Cambodians have long looked at Vietnam with suspicion and fear, and these sentiments have permeated their attitude toward Vietnamese residents in Cambodia.

During the sevententh and eighteenth centuries Vietnamese settlers expanded to the south, into present-day southern Vietnam (formerly known

56. Voice of America, "Police Siege," Jan. 29, 1996, <SEASIA-L@msu.edu>.

57. James D. Ross, "Fight Political Violence in Cambodia," *International Hearld Tribune*, June 13, 1996. Ross spent two years with the Human Rights Task Force on Cambodia.

58. Interview in Phnom Penh, May 1996. A Cambodian NGO that has been especially active in defending human rights is LICHADO (Cambodian League for the Promotion and Defense of Human Rights).

as Cochinchina), at the expense of the Khmer Empire, which once extended to the South China Sea. Thus, the Vietnamese gained the reputation among Khmer as "earth-swallowers." During the period of the French protectorate of Indochina from 1863 to 1953, France encouraged Vietnamese immigration into Cambodia. Vietnamese came to work in the French-owned rubber plantations, to engage in commerce and the trades, and, significantly, to serve in the second echelon of the bureaucracy (with French at the higher echelon). The Khmer tended to look upon the Vietnamese as agents of the colonial power, and further resentment derived from the fact that France established Cambodia as a protectorate and Cochinchina as a colony.

The Vietnamese population in Cambodia grew from 5,000 in 1874 to an estimated 230,000 to 250,000 in 1951.[59] Vietnamese residents were especially clustered in the cities, dominating trade and commerce along with the Chinese. After World War II Cambodian nationalism was suffused with antipathy toward the Vietnamese.[60]

During the Sihanouk years (1953–70), despite discriminatory legislation toward Vietnamese residents, the Vietnamese population grew to an estimated 450,000 in 1970.[61] In 1970 the overthrow of Prince Sihanouk was permeated with denunciations of his having offered sanctuary and support to Vietnamese troops during the Vietnam War. His deposition was accompanied by a vicious pogrom against the ethnic Vietnamese community, in which thousands were killed and others fled for their lives. By early 1971, some 250,000 ethnic Vietnamese from Cambodia had found sanctuary in Vietnam.[62]

The Khmer Rouge period (1975–79) imposed a bitter fate upon the surviving Vietnamese in Cambodia. Vietnam was seen by the Khmer Rouge as their foremost enemy, and policies toward Vietnamese residents were vicious. Some 170,000 Vietnamese managed to escape to Vietnam during the Khmer Rouge period.[63]

59. Ramses Amer, "The Ethnic Vietnamese in Cambodia: A Minority at Risk?" *Contemporary Southeast Asia* 16, no. 2 (Sept. 1994): 213.

60. Ibid. Amer draws from David P. Chandler, *A History of Cambodia*, 2d ed. (St. Leonards, NSW: Allen & Unwin, 1993), pp. 163, 171.

61. Amer, "The Ethnic Vietnamese," p. 214, citing Jacques Migozzi, *Cambodge faits et problèmes de population* (Paris: Edition du Centre National de la Recherche Scientifique, 1973), pp. 41–44.

62. Amer, "The Ethnic Vietnamese," citing Joseph Pouvatchy, "L'exode des vietnamiens du Cambodge en 1970," *Mondes Asiatiques*, no. 7 (Autumn 1970): 342–47.

63. Amer, "The Ethnic Vietnamese," p. 218, citing paper by J. R. Pouvatchy, *The Vietnamisation of Cambodia*, ISIS Seminar Paper (Kuala Lumpur: Institute of Strategic and International Studies, Malaysia, 1986), p. 9.

With the establishment of the People's Republic of Kampuchea under the domination of Vietnam in 1979, an ethnic Vietnamese community reemerged in Cambodia. Some of those Vietnamese who had fled earlier returned. Others emigrated from Vietnam, with expectations of benevolent treatment by a PRK which was beholden to Vietnam. The number of Vietnamese living in Cambodia was the subject of intense disputation. Members of the resistance charged that Vietnamese settlers were pouring in by the thousands, and that Cambodia was in danger of being "Vietnamized." Prince Sihanouk asserted in 1986 that 700,000 Vietnamese had settled in Cambodia and that it was Vietnam's objective to increase the number to 2 million over a four-to-five-year period. Son Sann stated in the UN General Assembly in 1986 that Vietnamese settlers had grown to between 800,000 and 1 million. The PRK dismissed these assertions as pure propaganda, and put the number of Vietnamese residents of Cambodia at about 56,000.[64] Most researchers put the figure between 300,000 and 450,000.[65]

During the UNTAC period (1992–93) rhetoric denouncing Vietnamese immigration into Cambodia increased. The PDK statements were the most virulent, charging that 700,000 Vietnamese had obtained Cambodian identity cards. UNTAC dismissed these assertions as spurious. Without question Vietnamese migrants, particularly construction workers and building-trade specialists, came to find work in Phnom Penh in jobs that 22,000 UNTAC personnel and construction and renovation needs helped to produce. Vietnamese prostitutes and other camp followers also found their way into Cambodia, though not in the inflated numbers asserted by Cambodian critics.[66] Khieu Samphan in 1992 claimed that the Vietnamese settler population had reached 2 million. The other factions, not to be outdone in anti-Vietnamese chauvinism, competed in inflammatory rhetoric denouncing the Vietnamese.[67]

Sporadic attacks against the Vietnamese minority broke out in 1992 and 1993. Some were instigated by the PDK, others by military elements of the other factions. A sense of terror grew by the end of April 1993, and more than 21,000 ethnic Vietnamese, many of them second- or third-generation

64. See Amer, "The Ethnic Vietnamese," pp. 219–22. KPNLF camp officers, during interviews at refugee camps in Thailand in the 1980s, claimed that the number of Vietnamese settlers reached beyond one million. KPNLF spokesmen often asserted that Cambodia was deliberately being "Vietnamized." Interviews by J. J. Zasloff in refugee camps in Thailand during the 1980s.

65. See Amer, "The Ethnic Vietnamese," p. 222, for a discussion of this debate about the numbers of Vietnamese settlers, and for his references to sources.

66. See Annuska Derks, "Vietnamese Prostitutes in Cambodia," *Cambodia Report* (Publication of the Preah Sihanouk Raj Academy) 2, no. 1 (Jan.–Feb. 1996): 4–6.

67. See Amer, "The Ethnic Vietnamese," pp. 222–28.

residents of Cambodia, fled their homes. The status of ethnic Vietnamese residents in Cambodia was not provided for in the Paris accords, and some within UNTAC's leadership were inclined to think of the situation as an internal security issue for the Cambodian authorities to resolve.[68] UNTAC made an effort to convince local authorities to provide security, but SOC officials "only reluctantly" committed police forces to protect Vietnamese refugees on their boats near the banks of the Tonle Sap and Tonle Bassac rivers in Phnom Penh. The other factions stated publicly that the Vietnamese "had no claim on Cambodian citizenship and should be deported to Vietnam."[69] Many of those ethnic Vietnamese who fled in early 1993, however, returned after the elections. Nonetheless, Cambodian authorities forbade several thousand boats to enter by the Mekong River. By the end of 1995, most ethnic Vietnamese were permitted to return and others reentered quietly over land, although some remained stranded in the border area. In the absence of a nationality law, the legal and constitutional rights of the ethnic Vietnamese remain unclear, since constitutional protection is extended only to "Khmer people." Though the Khmer Rouge continued their campaign of inflammatory propaganda against the ethnic Vietnamese after 1996, there were fewer reports of killings by the Khmer Rouge or others.

68. *The United Nations and Cambodia, 1991–1995*, with an introduction by Boutros Boutros-Ghali, Secretary-General of the United Nations (New York: UN Department of Public Information, 1995), p. 42.

69. Ibid.

PART 4

❀

THE BALANCE SHEET

CHAPTER EIGHT

Collapse of a
Quasi-Democratic State

Serious tensions plagued Cambodia's fledgling government during its first years. The curious coalition survived for four years following the UNTAC-administered election, but the strains in the body politic led to the eruption of Hun Sen's coup in July 1997. Even though Hun Sen offered ritualistic obeisance to the constitution after "dismissing" the first prime minister and intimidating his FUNCINPEC associates, his coup in fact crushed the fragile democratic framework of the new state and established Hun Sen and the CPP as the dominant political force in the country.

The international community that had been so deeply involved in bringing democracy to Cambodia reacted to the coup with varying expressions of disapproval, but no Cambodian group appeared to have the leverage to forestall Hun Sen's consolidation of power. By August 1997, it appeared that Hun Sen had created a political *fait accompli*, emasculating his internal opposition and neutralizing his foreign critics.

Three political issues emerged during the early years of the new state which exemplified the strains within and between the ruling parties. In fall of 1994, controversy arose over Sam Rainsy, a dissident political leader within the FUNCINPEC Party. This episode, paradoxically, demonstrated temporary cooperation of the first and second prime ministers in attempting to rid themselves of a serious political rival. The second indicative issue, in the fall of 1995, involved Prince Sirivuddh, half-brother of King Sihanouk, secretary-general of FUNCINPEC, and a foreign minister and a deputy prime minister in the new government. This dispute revealed a deep split between the two prime ministers and indicated the disproportionate power of Hun Sen. The third issue concerned Ranariddh's demand of the CPP for truly equal power sharing, made at a FUNCINPEC Party conference in March 1996. Hun Sen, in a white paper later issued to justify his 1997 coup, claimed that Ranariddh's speech at that party conference was the "turning point" responsible for the rupture of the coalition. Not long thereafter, as the disintegration of the Khmer Rouge advanced, competition between Ranarridh and Hun Sen to acquire Khmer Rouge military and political collaboration triggered the 1997 coup.

The Controversy over Sam Rainsy

Sam Rainsy was born in Phnom Penh in March 1949 to a distinguished political family. His grandfather had founded a political party, Khmer Serei, during French colonial rule and his father, Sam Sary, had served as cabinet minister in education, planning, and finance and had also served as deputy to Prime Minister Sihanouk. His mother was said to be the first woman in Cambodia to have completed high school. When Rainsy was ten, his father was assassinated and his mother sent to prison. At age sixteen Rainsy went into exile in Paris, where he completed high school and attended university, getting degrees in economics, business administration, and political science. After graduation he served as an investment manager and executive director at several banks in Paris. In 1976 he founded a newspaper named *Sereika* (Liberation), which denounced the Khmer Rouge. In 1981, when Prince Sihanouk formed FUNCINPEC, Sam Rainsy joined it, traveling to Cambodia from time to time on organizational assignments. He served as a member of the Supreme National Council in 1992–93. He was named finance minister in the new provisional government in June 1993.[1]

Rainsy was widely regarded, particularly in the international community, as an intelligent, energetic reformer, dedicated to structural reform of the economy. He launched a major campaign, supported by key donor countries and international organizations, including the Asian Develpment Bank, International Monetary Fund, and World Bank, to root out official corruption and centralize the tottering budget and revenue collection system. These efforts raised a storm of protest from entrenched business interests, and by the beginning of 1994, political adversaries made a concerted attempt to have him sacked. Particularly threatened were CPP ministers and officials who would lose control of money if revenues were centralized. Rainsy's growing popularity with the Phnom Penh populace did not endear him to Prince Ranariddh, who apparently felt challenged by Rainsy's bold-

---

1. "The 'Bad Boy' of Politics," *Cambodia Times*, March 17–23, 1996.

ness and outspokenness.[2] The co–prime ministers, on a visit to King Sihanouk in Beijing in January 1994, proposed that Rainsy be dismissed. Sihanouk refused to endorse the action and issued a public letter to Rainsy on January 21, expressing his "sincerest gratitude and warmest congratulations to your excellency and all your colleagues in the ministry for having performed your duty to serve the Cambodian nation with loyalty, effectiveness, and courage, for the higher interests of the Cambodian people."[3]

By October 1994 the two prime ministers agreed to reshuffle their cabinet, addressing a number of factional disputes, and used the occasion to sack Sam Rainsy. Following his dismissal, Rainsy issued a statement respecting the right of the two prime ministers to reshuffle the government and reaffirming his allegiance to the FUNCINPEC party, of which, he noted, he had been a member since the day of its inception.[4] This affirmation had special political significance in light of subsequent events.

Rainsy engaged in a vigorous campaign of criticism of the government, touring donor capitals, meeting with foreign political leaders as well as members of the Cambodian exile community, focusing particularly on the need to place rigorous conditions on the granting of foreign assistance to Cambodia. He emphasized, in particular, the high levels of official corruption and the need for transparency in Cambodian government decisions. A report in the Paris edition of *Le Monde*, on March 14, 1995, quoted Rainsy's estimate of the cost of high-level corruption in fiscal 1995 to be US$200 million, almost half the entire budget of $410 million. Ranariddh responded to Rainsy's challenge by mobilizing a rump meeting of the FUNCINPEC steering committee to expel Rainsy from the party on May 13 for breach of party discipline.

Following this expulsion, Ranariddh arranged an administrative judgment, to be made by the party leaders in the National Assembly, that Sam Rainsy must be expelled from the assembly on the grounds that he was elected as a member of the FUNCINPEC party list, which no longer included him. He must be replaced, they contended, by the next FUNCINPEC party member on that list. On June 22, 1995, the National Assembly was convened to hear an announcement from the interim chairman (permanent chairman Chea Sim was absent, and reported by an aide

2. A *Voice of America* broadcast on Oct. 20, 1994, noted that "during the past 15 months, international finance experts have warmly welcomed the minister's attempts to bring order to Cambodia's lawless economy. Many ordinary Cambodians have also loudly supported his efforts against inflation and especially against corruption."

3. Quoted in Nate Thayer, "Red Rag to a Bull: Minister's Anti-Corruption Drive Stirs Powerful Opposition," *Far Eastern Economic Review*, Feb. 24, 1994.

4. Oct. 23, 1994, <SEASIA-L@msu.edu>.

to be "embarrassed" by the whole affair), declaring "Mr. Nou Saing Khan as a new deputy from Siem Riep province, replacing Mr. Sam Rainsy." The chair ignored the hands that were raised to discuss the issue, and the assembly was immediately adjourned, a few moments after it was opened.[5]

The Paris peace accords required a "party affiliation" for candidates to stand for election. It is not clear from this language whether members of the assembly elected from a party list are to lose their seats if they subsequently leave the party. The UNTAC-composed electoral law, under which the assembly members were elected, states that a member who "dies or resigns or otherwise becomes unable to serve" should be replaced by the next person on the party's original list.[6] The National Assembly's internal regulations refer only to members being replaced if they die, resign, or abandon their work for three months. The official English translation of the constitution states that members can be replaced in cases of "death, resignation or dismissal." However, some specialists have said that the translation from the Khmer is not correct and that "dismissal" should read "departure" (although "departure" was not defined).[7]

The Western diplomatic community in Phnom Penh voiced pointed criticism of Rainsy's expulsion from the National Assembly. A U.S. statement announced "disappointment" at the expulsion and expressed concern that the case would "sully Cambodia's international image with regard to respect for the rule of law, due process and open political debate." It noted that it was now "more important than ever that freedom of expression in Cambodia be protected as well as "independence of the legislature and rights of legislators." Australia also protested the expulsion, and Foreign Minister Gareth Evans questioned whether the move was done in a "fully transparent manner." "It is not clear that this occurred in the case," he said. The chairman of the British House of Lords human rights group, Lord Eric Avebury,

5. Jason Barber, "Orchestrated End for Sam Rainsy, MP," *Phnom Penh Post*, June 30–July 13, 1995, p. 8. Kem Sokha, one of the few National Assembly members who courageously opposed the expulsion of Sam Rainsy from the National Assembly, told one of the authors that he called out at the June 22 meeting, along with several others in opposition, to get the attention of the chairman to speak in protest of the expulsion. They were ignored. Interview by J. J. Zasloff in Phnom Penh, May 7, 1997.

6. The chief author of the UNTAC-written electoral law, Reginald Austin, wrote an unfulfilled prediction to Sam Rainsy, prior to the expulsion: "I feel sure that in light of a proper consideration of the real long term advantages of open democracy, there will be no unlawful or unconstitutional action against you, or any other elected member of this historic Assembly." Quoted in Ker Munthit, "Rainsy on the Assembly Skids," *Phnom Penh Post*, May 19–June 1, 1995, p. 3.

7. Jason Barber and Sou Sophornnara, "International Pressure Mounts, Slowly, Over Rainsy," *Phnom Penh Post*, June 2–15, 1995, p. 3.

was particularly caustic in his criticism of this move.[8] The Geneva-based Inter-Parliamentary Union also expressed its concern, in a letter to the UN secretary-general, at the expulsion of Sam Rainsy from the assembly.[9]

Despite the criticism, which they knew would be forthcoming, the two prime ministers obviously had concluded that dealing with the challenge from Sam Rainsy in a politically expeditious manner was worth the cost. Prime Minister Ranariddh, in a statement issued on August 3, 1995, gave the following defense of Sam Rainsy's ouster:

> Sam Rainsy had been given ample warnings, friendly lectures and gentle persuasions to mend his wayward ways and toe the FUNCINPEC party line. We must not forget that the Royal Government is a coalition government. As such, FUNCINPEC Party members must resolve any issues within the party apparatus and not fight in public, giving unwarranted advantages to undesirable elements. In any political organization, party loyalty and allegiance to the leadership, especially the President, is a pre-requisite to party unity and stability. Disloyalty, resorting to blatant lies and demagogy to further enhance one's career is not within the interest of the party or the nation. As for expulsion from the National Assembly, it is FUNCINPEC's right under UNTAC law and the internal regulations of the National Assembly which is a sovereign and independent organization.[10]

Two years later Ranariddh himself would be expelled from the National Assembly.

Following his expulsion from FUNCINPEC Sam Rainsy launched into the formation of a new party, called Khmer Nation Party (KNP). The Ministry of Interior sent ambiguous signals concerning the new party, stating in November 1995 that Rainsy had failed to comply with certain legal provisions and indicating that setting up the party would be illegal.[11] Rainsy continued with his recruiting efforts. By the end of March 1996, he claimed to have enrolled 102,000 members. Despite the fact that the party was not sanctioned by the government, the (U.S.-based) International Republican Institute (IRI) gave the party's regional cadres training sessions in early

---

8. Jason Barber, "Party Secretary Wants Rainsy Back," *Phnom Penh Post*, June 30–July 13, 1996, p. 8.

9. AFP, Reuter, "Banned Cambodian Party 'Has More Than 100,000 Members,'" March 31, 1996, in *Straits Times* (Singapore), March 30, 1996.

10. "Ranariddh's 'Vital Issues' Report," *Phnom Penh Post*, Aug. 25–Sept. 7, 1995.

11. Reuter, "Rainsy Forms New KNP Political Party," *Hong Kong Standard*, Nov. 10, 1995.

1996. Indeed, it was the only Cambodian political party to which the IRI offered workshops in 1996, having opted to work only with "non-elected parties." The IRI, promoting the development of parties committed to the democratic process, had determined by early 1996 that FUNCINPEC and the CPP were no longer democratic. (The IRI's Democratic counterpart, the National Democratic Institute for International Affairs, had already suspended its operations in 1995.) By the end of May 1996, the government had not interfered with this training.[12]

The Dispute about Prince Sirivuddh

A second controversy, which revealed serious fissures within the coalition, was closely related to the tensions over Sam Rainsy. Prince Norodom Sirivuddh, a prominent personality in the FUNCINPEC party, resigned from his government portfolios on October 23, 1994, in a show of solidarity with Sam Rainsy. Although still FUNCINPEC's secretary-general, he opposed the expulsion of Sam Rainsy from the party, revealing how fractured the party had become.[13] His alliance with Sam Rainsy strained Sirivuddh's relations with his nephew, Ranariddh. In addition, he was a longtime political adversary of Hun Sen.

On November 17,1995, two tanks, four armored personnel carriers, and a unit of ground troops were summoned to Hun Sen's house near Independence Monument. That same evening, You Hockry, the FUNCINPEC co–interior minister, advised Sirivuddh that he was in danger and should leave the country. Sirivuddh refused. The following day, Sirivuddh was placed under house arrest "pending legal processes by the National Assembly." Sirivuddh was charged with threatening to kill the second prime minister. He denied the charges. On November 21, at a closed session of the National Assembly, a vote was taken by hand to lift the parliamentary immunity of Sirivuddh, and it was announced that the vote had been unanimously adopted by 105 votes.

Kem Sokha, a BLDP member of the assembly and chairman of its committee on human rights, told one of the authors that the vote had been rammed through the assembly without presentation of proof of any of the charges. Sokha asserted that he and Ahmed Yahya, a FUNCINPEC mem-

---

12. Interview in Phnom Penh by J. J. Zasloff, May 9, 1996.

13. Nate Thayer, "Matter of Conscience: Foreign Minister Sirivuddh Quits the Government," *Far Eastern Economic Review*, Nov. 3, 1994, p. 16.

ber, had voted against the move, but their votes were not recognized.[14] Another member of the assembly, Radsady Om, a FUNCINPEC member and chairman of the committee on foreign affairs, told the same author that he voted for the withdrawal of Sirivuddh's immunity in order to "retain political stability." The consequences of a negative vote were clear, he said. Hun Sen had brought out tanks and guns. Negotiation was impossible. The democratic structure would collapse if the members refused Hun Sen's demands to withdraw Sirivuddh's immunity. It was better to sacrifice one person, he maintained, for a more important purpose. This event, he said, was the "fruit of the conflict between Sirivuddh and Hun Sen."[15]

Ranariddh appeared to confirm the seriousness of Hun Sen's threat to the fragile democratic regime. He told a reporter that "all was done solely for one major goal: to save the Kingdom of Cambodia from the danger as a state." He added that had he not intervened, Sirivuddh might be dead and the situation could have ended in more bloodshed.[16] Following the lifting of his immunity Prince Sirivuddh was placed in prison (and later moved to confinement in the Ministry of Interior) and was confronted with three formal charges under (1) article 4 of the law outlawing the Khmer Rouge, applicable to anyone who seeks to destroy the royal government; (2) a State of Cambodia law on terrorism; and (3) UNTAC law concerning criminal conspiracy to create unlawful armed groups. He faced a possible life sentence, if convicted.[17]

Prince Sirivuddh continued to deny the charges and maintained his complete innocence. Hun Sen appeared to believe that his life was in danger and he gave the impression that he was incensed by the threat. Although Hun Sen seemed determined to bring Sirivuddh to trial, in early December King Sihanouk appealed to Hun Sen's Buddhist instincts and asked for "compassion for the three young children of Norodom Sirivuddh and a semi-pardon for my younger brother Norodom Sirivuddh in the form of expulsion from Cambodia and exile in France." The king added: "My younger brother Norodom Sirivuddh has said unjust, unjustifiable and unpardonable things against your excellency."[18] Hun Sen permitted Sirivuddh to leave for France, where he was expected to remain in exile. In February

14. Interview by J. J. Zasloff in Phnom Penh, May 7, 1996.
15. Ibid.
16. Ker Munthit, "Ranariddh Defends His Actions," *Phnom Penh Post*, Dec. 1–14, 1995, p. 3.
17. Jason Barber, "Sirivuddh Determined to Stay and Fight," *Phnom Penh Post*, Dec. 1–14, 1995, p. 1.
18. "Hun Sen Agrees to Exile King's Half-Brother," *Nando Times*, "World Briefs," Dec. 12, 1995, <SEASIA-L@msu.edu>, Dec. 13, 1995.

1996, Sirivuddh was tried *in absentia* in a four hour-trial, found guilty, and sentenced to ten years, imprisonment.[19]

The Sirivuddh case revealed key elements of Hun Sen's political personality. Hun Sen apparently was seriously worried—some would say obsessed or even paranoid—about being assassinated and he may have had reason for such fear. (Henry Kissinger once remarked that even paranoids have enemies.) Michael Hayes, publisher of the *Phnom Penh Post*, noted: "In a broad, informal survey of opinion from current and former CPP officials, human rights and NGO workers, MP's, diplomats, Cambodia watchers and the general public, the consensus is that Hun Sen does indeed have reason to fear for his life, that he has enemies both inside and outside his own party and that there are several if not numerous precedents for his fears of a plot against him."[20] When he feels besieged, he does not to hesitate to lash out, without regard to democratic niceties. He survived vicious internecine political struggles in the Khmer Rouge and the CPP, and he has battled fiercely for his turf and life. Michael Hayes, further observed:

> If there is one point on which most observers agree it's that Hun Sen is a consummate political tactician who spends most of his time keeping three steps ahead of both his allies and his opponents. One source said that Hun Sen had repeatedly outsmarted even his own critics within the CPP. Because of his charisma as a public speaker, because of his foresight in thwarting moves against him, and because of his skill as a political manipulator, the premier had managed to rise to the top and stay there.[21]

Hun Sen's Rhetoric

The Sirivuddh case provided insight into Hun Sen's sensitivities about foreign criticism and revealed how vituperative he could be in defending himself. Both French and American diplomats expressed public disapproval of

19. Matthew Grainger and Ker Munthit, "Trial Called 'Farcical' as Sirivuddh Gets Ten Years," *Phnom Penh Post*, Feb. 23–March 7, 1996, p. 3. The article noted: "The witnesses called were State Minister Ung Phan (a former CPP official who joined FUNCINPEC before the 1993 election), who testified in an affidavit that the Prince had told him by phone that he could kill Hun Sen; editor So Naro, who testified on the stand that Sirivuddh said similar comments that Naro eventually published in his newspaper; KJA president Pin Samkhon, who said he would not have written the story that Naro wrote and that he believed that Sirivuddh was joking; and, an advertising representative, Cheam Phary, who was with Naro during his meeting with Sirivuddh."

20. Michael Hayes, "The Politics of Fear: What's Next?" *Phnom Penh Post*, Dec. 1–14, 1995, pp. 1, 2.

21. Ibid.

Hun Sen's treatment of the Sirivuddh case, criticizing the withdrawal of his parliamentary immunity and the launching of court proceedings against him. In a speech in Kandal Province on December 4, 1995, Hun Sen was unrestrained in his denunciation of foreign, particularly French and American, critics. He defiantly asserted that he would not be intimidated by donors threatening to withdraw their aid and warned them not to interfere in Cambodia's internal affairs. With rhetoric that might appeal to the anti-colonial, anti-imperialist, small-nation-versus-big-power, and chauvinist sentiments of Cambodian listeners, Hun Sen's threats were scarcely veiled:

> I have already told the French and the Americans that in Phnom Penh there will be a grand demonstration against those supporting assassins. Availing myself of this opportunity, I wish to warn foreigners that they should look out for demonstrators who may storm their embassies.
>
> Look! This matter is an internal affair of Cambodia. Why are the Cambodians not allowed to sentence an individual since the Cambodians have already stripped him of immunity?

Hun Sen pointed in particular to a demonstration in Paris against the Cambodian embassy: "Yesterday there was demonstration against the Cambodian Embassy in France. I told the French ambassador: If your country has the right to stage demonstrations, so do I. Nevertheless, you should bear in mind that if I stage a demonstration, one million people will take part. They will be all over Phnom Penh. I do not mean to threaten you. If you want to give aid, you can." Asserting that he could not be intimidated by threats against two of his children studying in France, he declared: "I . . . have two children in France. If you do not allow them to study there, I will send them to another country or bring them back to learn in Cambodia. Cambodia also has schools now. You want me to help promote the French language; my children learning your language should be encouraging." Hun Sen was most vituperative in his denunciation of the American wartime policy toward Cambodia, blaming the United States for the coup d'état against Prince Sihanouk in 1970 and for the Khmer Rouge rise to power. Rhetorically he threatened to demand financial compensation for America's past crimes against Cambodia:

> We have not yet claimed compensation from the Americans; the latter killed 800,000 Cambodians between 1970 and 1975. This figure represents only loss of human lives; the number of disabled have yet to be counted. Who destroyed schools, hospitals, factories and enterprises? The Polpotists de-

stroyed a number of them, but don't forget—and I still well remember—that the Americans also destroyed factories. . . .

Now I want these words to be conveyed to the U.S. Senate: If you want to help, then help. If you do not want to help, it is fine, but you must compensate the Cambodians for overthrowing their king and creating war in Cambodia. . . .

How much? Only about $20 billion. Moreover, the Americans should also be tried in the international court like Pol Pot. If the Americans had not staged a coup d'état to topple his Majesty, the Khmer Rouge could never have come to power. . . . I want to give this warning to make you understand that you have problems: Never again act as a superpower and bank on sending your planes.

You were defeated once; do you want to be beaten again?

Alluding to his sons in the United States, including one at the U.S. Military Academy at West Point, Hun Sen added: "I am not afraid, although I have two children studying in the United States. They went there after passing their examinations and legally applying for admission. Nevertheless, if the Americans are displeased with my protest, I will take my children back in 24 hours."

Hun Sen forthrightly confronted the frequent criticism from his opponents that he was beholden to Vietnam. He contrasted Vietnam's respect for Cambodian independence with the subservience he claimed the United States was demanding. He closed his speech with praise for the unconditional aid offered by Japan: "We should not oppose Japan because it has never intervened. Japan is very good. Aid from Japan is completely unconditional. Apart from Japan, it is really an awful mess."[22]

Ranariddh's Demand of CPP for Equal Power Sharing

A third political issue within the ruling coalition was Ranariddh's demand of the CPP, in March 1996, that it share power genuinely with FUNCINPEC. Stung by criticism in the press as well as by dissatisfied elements within his own party that, despite the FUNCINPEC victory at the polls, the CPP continued to dominate the bureaucracy, the army, the police, and the judiciary,[23] Prime Minister Ranariddh acknowledged at a FUNCINPEC party conference that "two years have passed, but the Royal Government has not

22. Radio Phnom Penh, Dec. 4, 1995, in *FBIS–East Asia*, Dec. 4, 1995.
23. See, for example, Seth Mydans, "Cambodia's Real Boss Rules from the No. 2 Post," *New York Times*, March 25, 1996.

been able to fulfill even 50 percent of its promises." He asserted in his speech that he was "absolutely not happy" after his first two years of serving as first prime minister. He added: "Being first puppet prime minister, puppet vice–prime minister, puppet ministers, puppet governors and deputy governors and soon-to-be puppet chiefs of district . . . being a puppet is not so good."[24]

In comments later broadcast on FUNCINPEC radio and television, Ranariddh complained that FUNCINPEC cadres had been denied appointments at the district level and asserted that Hun Sen had told him that district power sharing was unjust and contrary to national reconciliation. Ranariddh stated that unless there was an agreement to share power with "balance, justice and equality," FUNCINPEC should consider other options such as withdrawal from the government and becoming an opposition party in the National Assembly. He warned that if the CPP did not take note of his comments, FUNCINPEC could choose not to wait until 1998 for the next election. It could vote to dissolve the National Assembly and have an election "before the end of 1996." He commented: "I deeply regret not being able to grab for FUNCINPEC and the entire Khmer people the brightest and greatest victory corresponding to their wish. . . . I think that we cannot continue the betrayal of the determination the people already made in 1993 and neither can we continue until 1998."[25] He demanded that the CPP live up to the power-sharing commitments and added, "If it is necessary, we are not afraid to withdraw [from the government.]"[26] Subsequent press reports noted that Ranariddh was demanding appointments for FUNCINPEC cadres to equal those of the CPP at province (*khet*), district (*srok*), and commune (*khum*) administrative levels.

Soon after the speech, Ranariddh departed for France, ostensibly to give lectures at his university at Aix-en-Provence, in order to maintain his tenure there. King Sihanouk was in Paris at the time, as were oppositionists Sam Rainsy and Norodom Sirivuddh. Several FUNCINPEC ministers were also reported to be visiting in France. Rumors quickly spread within Phnom Penh that a royalist plot was afoot to bring down the government.[27]

Hun Sen apparently suspected a plot to kill him brewing in Paris. He as-

24. Jason Barber and Kerk Munthit, "CPP Draws Line in the Sand," *Phnom Penh Post*, April 8–15, 1996, pp. 3, 10.

25. Ibid.

26. Ted Bardacke, "Power Play threatens to dethrone democracy. The coalition between Cambodia's royalist FUNCINPEC Party and Communists is at risk," *Financial Times*, March 17, 1996, p. 7.

27. One of the authors was present in Phnom Penh in May 1996 and witnessed the continuing tension and coup rumors. Members of the Cambodian political elite, as well as political watchers in the international community, spoke in spirited fashion about the possibility of

serted that if FUNCINPEC "destroys the constitution, we will dare to use force."[28] Hun Sen warned: "No matter how poisonous the reactionary forces will be, I can suppress them. And if they want to try, I'll show them . . . in order to ensure safety and security for the people."[29] Further, Hun Sen used the episode to complain, once again, about irregularities in the 1993 election, contending that the CPP had decided to "swallow a bitter pill" and accept the compromise reached under the "august leadership of His Majesty the King."[30]

Sensing the seriousness of Hun Sen's suspicions concerning a cabal in Paris against him, King Sihanouk once again intervened with a statement aimed at calming Hun Sen's nerves. He called for a meeting of the disputants and assured Hun Sen that he and his son, Prince Ranariddh, had no intention to conduct a coup, nor would FUNCINPEC quit the current government.[31] A tenuous truce was negotiated between the two prime ministers, which was evidenced by a public ceremony they attended together in June 1996 in the newly refurbished Than Pagoda. The truce endured only until July 5, 1997.[32]

In a white paper issued six days after his coup, Hun Sen labeled Prince Ranariddh's actions at the March 1996 FUNCINPEC party congress as a "tragic turning point" in the coalition government. He charged that Prince Ranariddh, sensing that he was losing political power, had embarked on a deliberate "strategy of provocation" aimed at "creating a crisis in which the Second Prime Minister would make a fatal mistake."[33]

Confronting the Khmer Rouge, 1993–1997

The situation that apparently triggered the Hun Sen coup of 1997 was the negotiations of FUNCINPEC with certain leaders of the disintegrating Khmer Rouge over military and political issues. Both FUNCINPEC and the CPP were suspicious that the other would gain advantage in attracting

a coup. A quiet evening on the street was sometimes cited as evidence that the public sensed heightened danger of politically inspired military action.

28. Rodney Tasker, "War of Words: Power-Sharing Issues Plague Fragile Coalition," *Far Eastern Economic Review*, May 23, 1996.

29. *Phnom Penh Post*, April 19–May 2, 1996, pp. 1, 3.

30. Phnom Penh National Radio of Cambodia, May 1, 1996, *FBIS-EAS*-96-086.

31. *Phnom Penh Post*, April 27, 1996, p. 3.

32. Murray Hiebert, "Truce at the Top: Co-Premiers Tone Down Their War of Words," *Far Eastern Economic Review*, July 4, 1996, p. 24.

33. "White Paper. Background on the July 1997 Crisis: Prince Ranariddh's Strategy of Provocation," <SEASIA-L@msu.edu>, July 11, 1997.

Khmer Rouge factions to their ranks as the KR organization was crumbling. The KR collapse which unfolded from 1996 to 1997 had not been anticipated by either side, or by the international community, when the newly formed government began functioning in 1993. Indeed, the Khmer Rouge threat to the fragile new state had still seemed substantial.

After the Election: Fight, Talk, Fight

During the early months of the new government, the Khmer Rouge seemed determined to maintain control over its "autonomous" territory, keep its forces intact, encourage instability in the countryside, exploit discontent among FUNCINPEC cadres, and seek opportunities for participation in the government.[34] There were clues that indicated eroding Khmer Rouge morale, with reports that 2,000 KR fighters had defected to the government since the election. But there were also indications that thousands of government troops had deserted during the same period, as many Cambodians of all factions appeared desirous to return to their villages.

In January 1994 military analysts estimated that the Khmer Rouge could field about 10,000 fighters and controlled some 20 percent of the territory.[35] Despite the reports of diminished morale and the desire of some Khmer Rouge soldiers to defect, the revolutionary organization was able to retain authority over the population in its zone and engage in insurgent raids against targets belonging to the newly formed government. It continued to profit from commerce in the timber and gems located near the Thai border, selling these resources to Thai military elements or businessmen. Although Thai officials denied that Thailand supported this commerce, or that arms were reaching the Khmer Rouge from Thai sources, it was clear that Thai military elements colluded with Thai entrepreneurs to purchase the valuable Khmer Rouge resources and to sell them weapons and materiel. Estimates of the value of the gem and timber trade ranged from $10 to $20 million monthly during the first year following the election.[36] Former U.S.

34. See Nate Thayer, "Bitter Victory: Poll Winners Find It Hard to Grasp Levers of Power," *Far Eastern Economic Review (FEER)*, Dec. 9, 1993, p. 94. See also Rodney Tasker and Nate Thayer, "Difficult Birth," and Thayer, "Survival Tactics: Khmer Rouge Plans Its Post-Poll Strategy," *FEER*, June 10, 1993, pp. 18–23.

35. Nate Thayer, "Defector's Dilemma: Broken Promises Hold Back Khmer Rouge Surrenders," *FEER*, Dec. 30, 1993–Jan. 6, 1994, p. 16.

36. An Associated Press report cited the higher estimate of $20 million per month for the Khmer Rouge gem and timber trade with Thailand. "Cambodia May Ban Khmer Rouge," Associated Press, July 4, 1994, Clarinews@clarinet.com (AP). Nate Thayer and Rodney Tasker cite $10 million a month that Thai businessmen spent to buy logs and gems. "The Plot Thick-

ambassador to Thailand Morton Abramowitz wrote in the *Washington Post* in May 1994, "Thailand has become Pol Pot's best ally."[37]

Even while applying military pressure on the new royal government, Khmer Rouge spokesmen continued to assert that they were prepared for integration into a national army and wished for participation in the national government. Of course, terms for such entry were to be negotiated. A senior Khmer Rouge official, justifying its military policy in the absence of an agreement, told a journalist: "Everybody wants peace. We want peace. But how can we go blindly? We must have a stick before entering the cage of the tiger. We have to discuss how to unify the army so we feel safe and they feel safe. We want an equilibrium of forces in Cambodia so that everyone can participate in national political life safely."[38]

The Government's Approach to the Khmer Rouge

The new royal government's approach to the Khmer Rouge duplicated the ambiguous policies that Sihanouk, Ranariddh, and Hun Sen had pursued in the interim provisional government following the election. King Sihanouk again supplied the initiative in reaching out for reconciliation, although in classic Sihanouk style he alternated polite entreaties to the Khmer Rouge with candid criticism. First Prime Minister Ranariddh remained skeptical about the peace initiatives, but he was willing to follow the lead of his father. Ranariddh was not dissuaded by the recalcitrance of his CPP coalition partner toward a political solution that included the Khmer Rouge in the government. He stated: "They prefer war. But the people want national reconciliation and I was elected to solve the Khmer Rouge problem peacefully, so I will try."[39] Second Prime Minister Hun Sen in 1994 was reluctant to endorse peace talks, assigning them a "one-percent chance" of ever being held, but he did not attempt to thwart the king's reconciliation initiatives.[40]

King Sihanouk proposed a renewed peace plan in November 1993. In early December Ranariddh softened his earlier demand that the Khmer Rouge first yield the territory they controlled to the government, now sim-

---

ens," *FEER*, July 21, 1994, p. 21. See also Rodney Tasker, "Thailand: Caught in the Act," *FEER*, Dec. 23, 1993, pp. 12–13; and Tasker, "Trading Charges: Phnom Penh Accuses Thais of Aiding Khmer Rouge," *FEER*, April 28, 1994, p. 20.

37. Quoted in "Thai Military Backing Khmer Rouge," July 28, 1994, odin@gate.net (PNEWS).

38. Nate Thayer, "Peace Pipe: Cambodian Government Reaches Out to Old Foes," *FEER*, Dec. 16, 1993, p. 18.

39. Thayer, "Defector's Dilemma."

40. Thayer, "Peace Pipe."

ply calling for an immediate cease-fire and inviting the Khmer Rouge to integrate their armed forces into the national army. While negotiations were under way for peace talks, King Sihanouk published an appeal to the Khmer Rouge in the form of a citizen's "essay" which included the following language:

> Since the beginning of the peace accord, the Khmer Rouge has destroyed bridges, cut roads and railway lines, planted mines and burned villages. The death and destruction caused by the Khmer Rouge have only helped to plunge our country further into the pit of underdevelopment while rich foreign powers have done very little to reconstruct our country.
>
> If the PDK has any concern for the welfare of Cambodia and its people, and if it has any patriotism at all, it should stop offering false justification for its separate existence. I call upon the Khmer Rouge to accept an immediate total cease-fire throughout the country; immediately transfer the Preah Vihear, Pailin and other zones to the Royal Government; dissolve their army and merge parts of it into the national army. In compensation the Khmer Rouge— minus Pol Pot, Ieng Sary, Nuon Chea and Ta Mok—should be given some role in the Royal Government.[41]

Even while the peace skirmishes were under way, the royal government launched a major military offensive, beginning during the dry season in January 1994, against Khmer Rouge strongholds in western Cambodia. The government rationale for its attack was obviously to gain leverage for its diplomatic efforts. A Khmer Rouge official noted: "No negotiation is successful at the negotiating table alone. What we get depends upon the fighting. Of course we want the maximum but that will depend upon whether we can defend ourselves."[42]

As large government forces attacked, the Khmer Rouge withdrew, in an orderly manner. Some 60,000 villagers fled as the government troops advanced. The Royal Army seized Anlong Veng and Pailin during the offensive, as the Khmer Rouge moved into defensive positions. The new "victors" lacked magnanimity in their occupation. The officers, in particular, were appalling in behavior. One report noted:

> Government troops and police interviewed at the front near Battambang speak with disgust about their officers. They say that while they had no medicine, food, or pay, their superiors were using military trucks to haul away war

41. Norodom Sihanouk, "Forging Cambodian Nationhood," *FEER*, Jan. 13, 1994, p. 26.
42. Nate Thayer, "Test of Strength," *FEER*, Jan. 27, 1994, p. 19.

booty—motorcycles, furniture and even window frames—from Khmer Rouge houses in Pailin. Some soldiers speak of the wounded being made to walk through jungles for days while military trucks took the loot back to the safety of Battambang.[43]

However, in February 1994 Khmer Rouge forces pushed the government troops out of Anlong Veng, and by April they had routed the new occupiers from Pailin.

This military victory by the Khmer Rouge revealed the fundamental weakness of the Royal Army. The army was officially said to number 140,000, but a Western ambassador estimated that close to one-half were "ghost soldiers." This doubtful quantity of troops was led by 2,000 generals and 10,000 colonels, many conniving to pocket the salaries of the phantom soldiers.[44]

The Khmer Rouge military achievement could be attributed less to their strength—although in discipline and cohesion they were clearly superior to their Royal Army adversaries—than to the weakness of the government forces. The motley Royal Army was not capable of dislodging the Khmer Rouge from their territory by head-on military assault. However, the Khmer Rouge were not capable of overthrowing the government, nor even of gaining control of significant amounts of territory.

The failure of the government's dry season offensive in 1994 triggered a new peace initiative by King Sihanouk. He called for a power-sharing arrangement with the Khmer Rouge and struck a gloomy note for his country's future, saying, "Cambodia could be a destroyed nation, a dead state," if this were not achieved.[45] Some elements within FUNCINPEC, including thirty members of the National Assembly, favored Sihanouk's accruing greater power for a "limited time" with "appropriate powers" to "save the country."[46] Sihanouk appeared to endorse this effort, stating in an interview on June 19, 1994, that the "current government has shown it is not capable of stopping the process of deterioration" and that he "might be obliged to intervene" to assume powers for a limited time.[47]

Hun Sen was quick to shoot down Sihanouk's trial balloon. In a blunt six-page letter to the king, Hun Sen denounced Sihanouk's maneuver toward benevolent dictatorship in language that resembled the critiques that

43. Nate Thayer and Nayan Chanda, "Things Fall Apart," *FEER*, May 19, 1994, p. 17.
44. Ibid., p. 17.
45. Nate Thayer, "One Way Out," *FEER*, June 2, 1994, p. 14.
46. Ibid., p. 15.
47. Nate Thayer, "Standing Up to Father," *FEER*, June 30, 1994, p. 14.

would be heard in July 1997 against himself. Hun Sen asserted that Sihanouk's "proposal was an outrageous concession tantamount to a legal coup to dissolve the constitution, to dismantle the National Assembly, and the royal government elected by the people, [which] I would certainly not go along with." [48] Nor did King Sihanouk find support for his proposal from his son, the other prime minister.

This severe reaction to Sihanouk's efforts to expand his power and to find a means to bring the Khmer Rouge into a government of national unity can be seen as a political turning point both in Sihanouk's role as a constitutional monarch and in his effort to achieve peaceful reconciliation with the Khmer Rouge. Following Hun Sen's stern letter, Sihanouk announced that due to his "serious illness" he would soon be entering a hospital in Beijing for two or three months, and he would then undergo medical treatment in China and North Korea until January 1995. Therefore, he added, "in 1995 and in the following years there will be no question of my seeking government power in Cambodia." [49] This interchange revealed that the CPP, which had been consolidating its power following its election loss, was acting to limit the power of the king. A senior CPP official told a journalist: "We recognize the king only as the [titular] king . . . this position has been adopted by the CPP politburo. This letter is a warning to the king. The king must understand the message: 'Don't go too far. Be happy with being king.'" [50] In the following years, as previously observed, Sihanouk confined himself to the classic role of a constitutional monarch, living most of his time abroad and possessing declining influence in internal political affairs.

Sihanouk's reconciliation role was blunted in 1994 by the government's decision to outlaw the Khmer Rouge. While the impetus for the bill to ban the revolutionary organization came from the CPP, it was supported by Prime Minister Ranariddh and most of the FUNCINPEC members. Supporters of the ban maintained that the law would weaken the Khmer Rouge by providing the government the legal basis to seize its assets and restrict travel by its members. They argued that such a law would encourage the Thai government to restrict the trade in timber and gems along the border. Some 15 opponents among the National Assembly's 120 members, led by Sam Rainsy, expressed anxiety that the bill outlawing the Khmer Rouge might be used to abuse human rights. Political opponents might be charged as Khmer Rouge collaborators. A few amendments were adopted which

48. Ibid, p. 15.
49. Ibid.
50. Ibid.

gave the king power to grant pardons to convicted KR cadres, lengthened an amnesty period for low-ranking KR soldiers to six months, and added protection against false accusations of being Khmer Rouge.[51] Opponents withdrew their opposition and the bill passed the National Assembly unanimously on July 7, 1994.

In response, the Khmer Rouge, a few days later, proclaimed that it was forming a provisional government based in the jungles of the country's northern Preah Vihear province. Khieu Samphan announced over Khmer Rouge radio that he would serve as premier and defense minister in the Provisional Government for Solidarity and Survival of Cambodia. The announcement added that the PDK had decided to form the provisional government because the Phnom Penh authorities' decision to outlaw them had proved that the government intended to continue the fighting.[52]

Erosion of Khmer Rouge Strength, July 1994 through 1996

The next three years brought significant erosion of Khmer Rouge strength. Until 1996, the Khmer Rouge retained control of their territory and could not be expelled by the hapless forces of the royal government. They could also still create havoc in the countryside. Nevertheless, they were beset by a variety of problems, including increasing defections from their ranks and an inability to replenish their numbers with new recruits.

Evidence emerged in early 1994 that purges had taken place in the leadership ranks as early as 1992. Ieng Sary, formerly considered to rank among the top three Khmer Rouge leaders, appeared to have been demoted to control of a small area. Ieng Sary had been linked to the Chinese, and when they terminated their support to the Khmer Rouge in 1991, his influence diminished. Son Sen, another top leader, who had served as minister of defense and had been a Khmer Rouge delegate to the Supreme National Council, was also demoted in early 1994.[53] The paramount leader, Pol Pot, was said accurately to be suffering from malaria and other diseases, and his

51. See "Text of Law Outlawing the DK Group," July 27, 1994, <SEASIA-L@msu.edu>. See also Associated Press, "Cambodia May Ban Khmer Rouge"; and John C. Brown, "Intense NA Debate Ends in Compromise," *Phnom Penh Post*, July 15–28, 1994.

52. Associated Press, "Cambodia Rebels to Start Government," July 11, 1994, clarinews @clarinet.com (AP).

53. Nate Thayer, "Out with the Old: Two Khmer Rouge Stalwarts Fade from View," *FEER*, Feb. 10, 1994, p. 26.

death was reported, erroneously, on several occasions.[54] Nuon Chea, a key theoretician, was reported in early 1995 to be very sick.[55]

By summer 1996 defections had taken a serious toll of the Khmer Rouge strength. Living conditions in the jungle were difficult and the soldiers were tired of fighting. The government had declared an amnesty program in 1993, which, according to government claims, had brought in 1,000 defectors in six months. Some 7,000 Khmer Rouge guerrillas and local militia were said to have defected in 1994. In January 1995 the government estimated Khmer Rouge strength at 5,000 to 10,000 and reported that almost 2,500 KR defectors had joined the RCAF, with equivalent rank and new uniforms.[56] In March 1995 Hun Sen asserted at a press conference: "The political situation has changed categorically. The Khmer Rouge no longer constitute a political and military organization. They have become an armed group—rebels." He claimed that Khmer Rouge combatants had been reduced from 8,000 to 2,000 and now occupied only 3 to 5 percent of Cambodian territory.[57] Prime Minister Ranariddh made similar assertions at a conference of aid donors in Paris, declaring that the government had reduced the Khmer Rouge to a ragged band of rebels.

Khmer Rouge strength was further eroded by the loss of important foreign support. The Thai government made it more difficult for its military and business elements to exploit the timber and gem resources in neighboring Khmer Rouge territory. Tighter restrictions were placed on the timber trade, and the gem fields were being depleted.[58] Chinese support for the Khmer Rouge rebels had ceased following the signing of the 1991 Paris Agreements, although the Chinese were thought by experts to maintain informal contact with the Khmer Rouge. But China's commitment to the royal government showed up in a grant of military assistance worth $1 million in early 1996.[59]

54. Sihanouk, in an interview in Paris in April 1996, said that Pol Pot was ill and might die soon. See Julian Nundy, "Sihanouk in France," *Voice of America*, April 22, 1996. A Singapore *Straits Times* cover story (June 7, 1996) reported that a deputy commander of the Khmer Rouge told an AFP reporter that Pol Pot had died after a prolonged battle with malaria.

55. Nate Thayer, "Money Man: Defector Could Hold Key to Khmer Rouge Defeat," *FEER*, Feb. 9, 1995, p. 16.

56. Michael Hayes, "Trading Places: Khmer Rouge Weakened by Defections," *FEER*, Jan. 19, 1995, p. 21.

57. Associated Press, "Khmer Rouge Near Gone," March 16, 1995, C-ap@clarinet.com (AP).

58. Nate Thayer, "Rebel without a Cause," *FEER*, April 27, 1995, p. 24.

59. Matthew Lee, "New-Found Generosity: China Offers Phnom Penh Military Aid," *FEER*, May 9, 1996, p. 28.

Any attraction that the Khmer Rouge brand of Marxism-Leninism may once have exerted had been dissipated by its horrible record of rule from 1975 to 1979. Further, because of the collapse of communism on the international stage, communist appeals became relics. A persisting ideological thrust of the Khmer Rouge was anti-Vietnamese "racialism,"[60] playing on the strong animus toward Vietnam that is built into the Cambodian psyche. The Khmer Rouge became the primary exponent of anti-Vietnamese slogans to mobilize political support, although FUNCINPEC, BLDP, and more recently Sam Rainsy's KNP—indeed all the parties except the CPP (who were inhibited by their recent linkage with Vietnam)—strayed into this chauvinist political territory.

While there was still political mileage to be gained from blaming the Vietnamese for Cambodia's ills and raising the specter of Vietnamese "earth-swallowers" again invading Cambodian soil, these slogans were bound to wane in credibility for a population that had alternate sources of information. It was difficult to sustain the charge that 4 million Vietnamese settlers had invaded Cambodia, or that thousands of Vietnamese soldiers had penetrated the countryside, when such charges were not supported either by observation or by authoritative sources. Thus, the Khmer Rouge had increasing difficulty maintaining the belief in their own cadres and population, and even greater difficulty convincing those outside their control, that the evil Vietnamese and their Khmer "puppets" were poised to seize the Cambodian patrimony.

Although the Khmer Rouge leadership tried in the early UNTAC period to make their organization appear to be an agent of benevolent change, dedicated to expelling foreign influence, achieving genuine freedom for Cambodians, and serving the poor, it could not shake its deeply engraved image as a brutal, wildly revolutionary movement.

During the 1996 dry season, as Khmer Rouge strength was eroding, the government undertook another large offensive, this time against Khmer Rouge strongholds surrounding Pailin. The offensive produced the same disastrous outcome as in 1994. RCAF troops advanced; Khmer Rouge forces retreated. RCAF soldiers, with the connivance of their officers, took booty and pillaged. A Cambodian observer reported to one of the authors, in May 1996, that the Cambodian villagers were more afraid of the government soldiers than of the Khmer Rouge. After some weeks, the Khmer Rouge attacked and again routed the RCAF. This RCAF failure came

60. See Ben Kiernan, *The Pol Pot Regime: Race, Power, and Genocide in Cambodia under the Khmer Rouge, 1975–1979* (New Haven: Yale University Press, 1996).

at a time of severe tensions, described earlier, between Hun Sen and Ranariddh. Hun Sen blamed the failure of the RCAF offensive on Ranariddh's threat to pull out of the government.[61] However, it appeared that the RCAF was more interested in looting and plundering than in fighting the Khmer Rouge.

Democratic Structures Give Way, 1996–1997

The unraveling of the Khmer Rouge as a viable revolutionary organization, which took place during 1996 and 1997, exacerbated the serious strains within the government of Prime Ministers Ranariddh and Hun Sen. They had agreed to hold national elections in May 1998 and each was focusing on building a dominant political base for winning. FUNCINPEC was inferior to the CPP in organizational cohesion and strength, but Ranariddh was creating political alliances that Hun Sen saw as threatening.

Despite Ranariddh's earlier collusion with Hun Sen to have Sam Rainsy expelled from the National Assembly, by spring 1997 Ranariddh was negotiating a compact with Rainsy's newly formed KNP (Khmer Nation Party), which was said to have 250,000 "card-carrying members" by summer 1997.[62] An indication of how seriously Hun Sen and the CPP viewed expansion of the KNP was seen in the grenade attack launched against a KNP political rally on March 30, 1997, which killed sixteen and wounded nearly two hundred, including an American political consultant. FBI agents who investigated the attack (since an American had been wounded) reportedly found that the culprits who lobbed the grenades were in the employ of the CPP.[63]

The Defection of Ieng Sary

Defections by Khmer Rouge leaders and troops became another area of uncertainty in the summer of 1996.[64] Ieng Sary, a former brother-in-law to

61. Hiebert, "Truce at the Top," pp. 24–25.

62. See testimony by Ron Abney, consultant to the KNP from the (U.S.) International Republican Institute in Summary of Hearing of House Committee on International Relations, July 16, 1997, camdisc @lists.best.com.

63. AP, June 29, 1997; <SEASIA-L@msu.edu>, June 30, 1997.

64. For news reports concerning the defections of Ieng Sary and the Khmer Rouge troops associated with him, see dispatches by Seth Mydans in the *New York Times*, Aug. 13, 19, 21, 1996; *New York Times* editorial, Aug. 16, 1996; AP, Aug. 17, in *NYT*, Aug. 18, 1996; Reuters, Aug. 8, 1996, camdisc@cambodia.org: VOA, Aug. 8, 1996, <SEASIA-L-@msu.edu>; Mary Baker, "Khmer Rouge Fighters 'Defect' en Masse," Aug. 9, 1996, and David Lague, "Signs of

Pol Pot, was negotiating his defection to the government along with two generals, Sok Peap and Mit Chien, who were said to command three thousand troops. A Khmer Rouge radio broadcast denounced Ieng Sary for treason, embezzlement, and betrayal of his trust as the individual responsible for managing Chinese aid in earlier years.[65] Hun Sen entered the game by offering the defecting soldiers integration into the Royal Cambodian Armed Forces at equivalent rank. He thanked Ieng Sary for his action "because he did a good job that is worth the lives of thousands of people," adding that past deeds must be kept aside.

In an initial statement Ranariddh compared Ieng Sary to Hitler and said that the public should decide whether to allow him to defect. Within a few weeks, however, he visited Ieng Sary's base area and agreed to the induction of Khmer Rouge troops into the RCAF. Ieng Sary was permitted to remain in control of his troops and to continue to dominate the area around Pailin, a gem center near the Thai border. Ieng Sary had been sentenced to death *in absentia* at a show trial in Phnom Penh after the overthrow of the Khmer Rouge in 1979. Both Hun Sen and Ranariddh asked the king in September 1996 to grant Ieng Sary an amnesty from charges under Cambodian law. Sihanouk signed it without public discussion.

The competition between Hun Sen and Ranariddh for the allegiance of Ieng Sary continued into the autumn of 1996. On October 22, Hun Sen made a visit to Pailin where he vowed to three thousand villagers that "no one can take your land," and he promised not to confiscate any weapons from the Khmer Rouge dissidents. He also promised that he would build new roads to Pailin and Phnom Malai, erect six new schools, and renovate Pailin's temple.[66] Ranariddh paid his own visit to Pailin in October, without informing Hun Sen, during the Festival of the Dead. He appeared on national television with Ieng Sary.[67] Yet it appeared Hun Sen acquired more Khmer Rouge defectors to the CPP ranks than Ranariddh achieved for

---

Welcome End to Infamous Band of Killers," Aug. 9, 1996, in <SEASIA-L@msu.edu>; Prasit Saengrueng, "Sok Pheap: Political Solution Possible," *Bangkok Post*, Aug. 11, 1996, <SEASIA-L@msu.edu>; "KR Forces Launch Attack on Renegades: Hun Sen," *Straits Times*, Aug. 11, 1996, <SEASIA-L@msu.edu>; "Breakaway Rebels Warn Thai Traders," *Bangkok Post*, Aug. 12, 1996, <SEASIA-L@msu.edu>; Mark Baker, "Khmer Rouge Gears for Fight," <SEASIA-L@msu.edu>.

65. "Cambodia: Khmer Rouge Brands Ieng Sary a Traitor," (Clandestine) Radio of the Provisional Government of National Union and National Salvation of Cambodia, in Cambodian, Aug. 7, 1996, *FBIS-EAS-96-154*.

66. Katya Robinson, "Hun Sen Talks Peace—and Terms—with Ieng Sary," *Asiaweek*, Nov. 3, 1996, <SEASIA-L-@msu.edu>.

67. Ibid.

FUNCINPEC. (Nine months later Hun Sen would "dismiss" Ranariddh for allegedly bringing Khmer Rouge soldiers into Phnom Penh.)

Government Negotiations with the Collapsing Khmer Rouge

The defection of Ieng Sary and his loyalists stimulated other Khmer Rouge elements, fatigued by their futile struggle, to attain a favorable accommodation with the government. A truculent holdout against negotiations was Pol Pot, who continued to exercise authority in the northwestern area around Anlong Vieng. Other Khmer Rouge leaders, including critical military commanders, were interested in striking a deal with the government. Sharp conflict arose among leaders and factions in the rump organization.[68]

In February 1997 fifteen government officials who flew by helicopter into Khmer Rouge territory for negotiations were ambushed by Pol Pot elements. Ten were executed and the others were imprisoned. Yet a government military delegation resumed negotiations on May 16, with Khmer Rouge officials led by Tep Kunnal, a French-educated engineer. Khmer Rouge interlocutors agreed in principle to integrate their army into the RCAF, accept the Cambodian constitution, and disband their provisional government. On June 1, Khieu Samphan, their "prime minister," met secretly with Ranariddh near the Thai border, and a follow-up meeting took place on June 5 at the historic temple at Preah Vihear, where the Khmer Rouge planned to stage an anouncement of national reconciliation. Once again Pol Pot loyalists apparently disrupted the peace process, murdering the defecting "defense minister," Son Sen, and twelve members of his family and aides.

The Polpotists attempted to purge the peacemakers. Intense confusion and fighting grew up within the fractionated Khmer Rouge leadership ranks, complicated by the tensions and competition for KR adherents of Ranariddh and Hun Sen.[69] Defections mounted from the hard-line holdouts, and by mid-July the Khmer Rouge opponents of the Polpotists had prevailed, making prisoners of Pol Pot and several close aides and scattering or eliminating his estimated three hundred committed followers. The

68. The account of government negotiations with the collapsing Khmer Rouge draws upon an excellent report by Nate Thayer, "Cambodian Peace Was Just a Day Away," *Washington Post*, Aug. 17, 1997.

69. See dispatches by Seth Mydans in the *New York Times*, July 14, 16, 19, and 22, 1997. For a chronology of the negotiations, see "Blow by Blow—Six Weeks of Drama," *Phnom Penh Post*, June 27–July 10, 1997.

triumphant KR rebels mounted a show trial of their formerly exalted prisoner (filmed by Nate Thayer, an American journalist) at which the peasant spectators were led in a denunciatory chorus of "crush, crush, crush!" A physically spent Pol Pot was convicted of the murder of Son Sen and sentenced to life imprisonment, which translated into house arrest.

Finally, negotiations between the Khmer Rouge group favoring reconciliation and Ranariddh's emissaries, led by General Nhek Bun Chhay, a FUNCINPEC loyalist, were reported to have reached agreement. On July 6 Khmer Rouge authorities were to announce a decision, in a formal "surrender" ceremony, to support the constitution, commit their army and territory to central government command, and recognize King Sihanouk as the country's sovereign. This announcement was preempted by Hun Sen's coup of July 5, 1997.

The Coup

Two weeks prior to the July 5 coup there were clashes in Phnom Penh between Ranariddh's bodyguards and Hun Sen's troops. Two days before the coup there was further fighting between FUNCINPEC and CPP troops.[70] A few days before the coup Ranariddh departed for France "to see relatives," according to his spokesmen, and the day before the coup, Hun Sen traveled to Vietnam, "purely on private vacation," according to Vietnam's foreign ministry.[71]

On July 5, Hun Sen's troops moved swiftly against FUNCINPEC party headquarters, military strongholds, and Ranariddh's residence. The coup appeared to have been well prepared in advance, with tanks, marines, and infantry units moving into Phnom Penh from bases elsewhere in the country. Hun Sen labeled his move a preemptive strike to enforce the law, accusing First Prime Minister Ranariddh of importing illegal weapons and bringing the Khmer Rouge into the city. Hun Sen announced the "dismissal" of Ranariddh and said the "government is ready to choose a new First Prime Minister."[72]

The triumphant CPP troops rampaged through Phnom Penh, carting off televisions, washing machines, and mattresses. Looters stripped the airport of vital apparatus and radio equipment. Soldiers drove off in new cars and

70. Robin McDowell, "Cambodian Factions Square Off" (AP), July 2, 1997, <SEASIA-L @msu.edu>.

71. "Hun Sen Visits Vietnam" (Reuter), July 5, 1997, <SEASIA-L@msu.edu>.

72. Statement by Hun Sen, camdisc@lists.best.com, July 7, 1997. See also Reuter, July 5 and 6, 1997, <SEASIA-L@msu.edu>.

motorbikes, some carting televisions and appliances. The offices of FUN-CINPEC and the KNP were ransacked. FUNCINPEC military and civilian leaders were pursued. Some forty political opponents, according to UN officials, were executed and hundreds were arrested. Many went underground or fled abroad, including, according to early reports, seventeen FUNCINPEC and six BLDP members of the National Assembly. Newspapers associated with FUNCINPEC closed and many editors fled. As the fighting raged in Phnom Penh, King Sihanouk called for the two premiers to meet with him in Beijing to resolve their differences. Hun Sen refused with the statement, "It is too late and it is not necessary."[73]

An uneasy calm was restored in Phnom Penh two days after the coup, but "extra-judicial killings" were being verified for several weeks after the coup by civil rights activists.[74] Fighting gradually subsided in August 1997 and the FUNCINPEC loyalist forces created a stronghold at O Smach, near the Thai border.

Why did Hun Sen perpetrate the coup? Ranariddh's near-completed negotiations with the rump Khmer Rouge were the trigger. Hun Sen was threatened by the prospect of defeat in the scheduled May 1998 elections, as an imposing political alliance against him was growing. Ranariddh and Sam Rainsy were negotiating an alliance, labeled the National United Front (NUF), which would couple FUNCINPEC and the KNP. Hun Sen could see that Ranariddh's pending peace pact with Khieu Samphan and the remaining Khmer Rouge factions would add another partner to the anti-CPP coalition. King Sihanouk's aura would contribute support to his son and the royalist FUNCINPEC, as in the UNTAC election.

Hun Sen was particularly offended by the impending peace pact with the Khmer Rouge, whose spokesmen referred to Hun Sen in their proposed peace pronouncements as "contemptible" and a "puppet of Vietnam." The Khmer Rouge were making it evident that they were concluding peace with FUNCINPEC, not the CPP.[75] Hun Sen had shown himself determined to acquire and hold power, and he was not deterred by democratic niceties.

Hun Sen may have calculated that Ranariddh's concessions to the odious Khmer Rouge, so reviled in the West and particularly the United States, offered him a propitious moment to seize power. If he moved rapidly, he would not encounter opposition that might reverse his dominance. The United States would probably not intervene independently from ASEAN,

73. Reuter, July 7, <SEASIA-L@msu.edu>, July 9, 1997.
74. AFP, July 8 and 31, <SEASIA-L@msu.edu>, July 9 and Aug. 2, 1997; AP, July 7, <SEASIA-L@msu.edu>, July 7, 1997; Reuter, July 7, <SEASIA-L@msu.edu>, July 9, 1997, AVOA, July 9, <SEASIA-L@msu.edu>, July 11, 1997; *New York Times,* July 16, 1997.
75. Nate Thayer, "Cambodian Peace Was Just a Day Away."

which would surely reaffirm its policy of nonintervention in the affairs of its members or prospective members. Japan would probably not intrude.

Hun Sen was careful to call his action legal, not a coup, and to assert that he was abiding by the constitution. A new "first prime minister" would be chosen, and he promised that "free and fair" elections would be held in May 1998. Such were his efforts to retain international legitimacy for his seizure of power.

Attempts to Legitimize the Coup

Only a week following his seizure of power, Hun Sen, asserting that the coalition government established under the constitution was still in place, convened a senior cabinet meeting. Two FUNCINPEC ministers attended. Hun Sen proclaimed at the meeting that Prince Ranariddh had not been expelled from the country but had left voluntarily. He could return if he wished, but he would face court proceedings.[76] On July 16, under prodding from Hun Sen, a rump group of FUNCINPEC leaders nominated Ung Huot, the FUNCINPEC foreign minister (who held dual citizenship in Australia), to replace Ranariddh as first prime minister. Ung Huot, who had been in Paris during the coup, accepted, saying, "Life must go on and Cambodia has suffered too much."[77]

While taking measures to legitimize his coup, Hun Sen also consolidated his control, purging diplomats, civil servants, and political appointees loyal to FUNCINPEC.[78] On August 6 the National Assembly was convened, with 99 of the 120 members attending. In a session closed to the media and foreign observers, 86 members voted in favor of replacing Ranariddh with Ung Huot as premier. Four voted against[79]—with 6 abstentions and 3 spoiled ballots.

The next step to legitimize the new prime minister was to secure the endorsement of King Sihanouk. Characteristically, the king's position fluctuated. Two days after the coup, Sihanouk had called upon both prime ministers to meet him in Beijing to work out an agreement, an invitation that Hun Sen refused. On August 7, Sihanouk said he would not recognize Ung Huot as prime minister, but he wrote to Acting Head of State Chea

---

76. VOA, July 10, 1997, <SEASIA-L@msu.edu>, July 11, 1997.
77. VOA, July 16, 1997, <SEASIA-L@msu.edu>, July 16, 1997.
78. *Straits Times*, Aug. 6, 1997, <SEASIA-L@msu.edu>, Aug. 16, 1997.
79. Mark Baker, "Coup for Hun Sen as Prince Voted Out," *Herald*, Aug. 7, 1997, <SEASIA-L@msu.edu>.

Sim telling him he could sign such a decree, if he wished.[80] On August 10, just hours before an audience in Beijing with Hun Sen's delegation, including Ung Huot and Chea Sim, the king stated that Hun Sen's coup was illegal and he offered to abdicate, conditioning this offer upon assurances from "strongman" (as Sihanouk labeled him) Hun Sen that he would not criticize the king "for adding greater difficulties to the country and people." Sihanouk said that he still regarded Ranariddh as the prime minister and described his removal as "illegal and unconstitutional."[81] Following a five-hour meeting with Hun Sen and his delegation, Sihanouk announced that Hun Sen had not accepted his offer to abdicate. Sihanouk withheld approval of Ung Huot's appointment, described him as a "puppet," and likened the situation in Cambodia to a "comedy."[82] Nevertheless, on September 5, King Sihanouk signed a letter to the UN secretary-general announcing that newly appointed First Prime Minister Ung Huot and Second Prime Minister Hun Sen would be representing Cambodia at the UN General Assembly session beginning September 16, 1997. This appointment precluded the possibility that Prince Ranariddh would lead Cambodia's UN delegation, another setback to his campaign for international support for his restoration as prime minister.[83] The General Assembly's credentials committee, however, under U.S. pressure, decided to recommend no delegation from Cambodia at the 1997 session.

International Reaction to the Coup

Hun Sen's coup was a stunning blow to the painstakingly negotiated Paris Agreements. It transformed UNTAC's enterprise from what many termed a "limited success" to a failed rescue of a failed state. Most of the signatories expressed concern about Hun Sen's "dismissal" of Prime Minister Ranariddh, and especially about the violence and executions, but none intervened with sufficient leverage to alter the outcome. Hun Sen had created a new political reality, neutralizing his opposition, both internal and external.

The most persistent criticism of the coup came from the United States. Immediately following the events of July 5, the U.S. condemned the killing and attributed responsibility for it to Hun Sen. A U.S. spokesman urged

80. VOA, Aug. 7, 1997, <SEASIA-L@msu.edu>, Aug. 8, 1997.

81. AP, Aug. 11, 1997, <SEASIA-L@msu.edu>, Aug. 11, 1997.

82. AP, Aug. 11, 1997, <SEASIA-L@msu.edu>, Aug. 11, 1997; *Straits Times*, Aug. 12, 1997, <SEASIA-L@msu.edu>, Aug. 12, 1997; Reuter, Aug. 14, 1997, <SEASIA-L @msu.edu>, Aug. 14, 1997.

83. AFP, Reuter, Sept. 5, 1997, <SEASIA-L@msu.edu>, Sept. 5, 1997.

Hun Sen and Ranariddh to "drop the swords and guns and get back to the negotiating table."[84] A consensus emerged from both the administration and Congress that aid, except for humanitarian assistance, should be suspended until democratic government was restored. U.S. aid was initially suspended for thirty days, followed by an unlimited cutoff of nonhumanitarian economic and defense assistance. These decisions withheld half of the budgeted $35 million in economic assistance and $7 million in defense expenditures, except for funds to remove mines.[85]

On July 18, Secretary of State Madeleine Albright named Stephen Solarz, former U.S. Congressman involved in Cambodian affairs, as a special envoy to seek a resolution to the political conflict. He scheduled visits to Beijing, Tokyo, Jakarta, Bangkok, and Phnom Penh, to search for a settlement formula in compliance with international law.[86] Following a meeting in Tokyo, Solarz reaffirmed that the United States would not recognize Ung Huot as a replacement for Prime Minister Ranariddh.[87]

U.S. strategy was to urge ASEAN to persuade Hun Sen to restore democratic government. Albright called for "broad international pressure" against Hun Sen's regime. She asserted that "the international community was right to invest in peace in Cambodia and we are right to insist now that the Government in Phnom Penh live up to its obligation to respect democratic principles."[88]

ASEAN appeared to have a singular opportunity to exercise influence during the Cambodian political turmoil since Cambodia was under consideration for membership in the regional organization. Yet ASEAN foreign ministers frequently intoned the "principle of noninterference" in the internal affairs of its members or prospective members.[89] Nonetheless, Cambodia's admission was postponed and a delegation of foreign ministers was assigned to meet with King Sihanouk and the two original prime ministers to mediate the crisis.[90] The delegation visited Phnom Penh but was rebuffed by Hun Sen, who asserted that he would abide no interference in

84. U.S. Dept. of State, Daily Press Briefing, July 9, 1997, <SEASIA-L@msu.edu>, July 11, 1997.

85. *New York Times*, July 16, 1997; VOA, July 14, 1997, <SEASIA-L@msu.edu>, July 16, 1997; AP, Aug. 8, 1997, <SEASIA-L@msu.edu>, Aug. 8, 1997.

86. *Washington Post*, July 18, 1997.

87. Reuter, July 21, 1997, <SEASIA-L@msu.edu>, July 21, 1997; *Wall Street Journal*, July 21, 1997.

88. Mark Baker, "ASEAN Bows to Cambodia," *Herald*, July 25, 1997, <SEASIA-L @msu.edu>, July 25, 1997.

89. See, for example, the editorial "It Is Up to Hun Sen," in *The Straits Times*, July 19, 1997, <SEASIA-L@msu.edu>, July 19, 1997.

90. Star Publications, July 20, 1997, <SEASIA-L@msu.edu>, July 20, 1997.

his country's internal affairs.[91] Subsequently, after ASEAN had accepted Ung Huot as Cambodia's observer at its meetings (as foreign minister, not prime minister), Hun Sen softened his tone, at Ung Huot's urging, and announced on July 23 he would accept ASEAN's mediation.[92] Ung Huot assured the ASEAN meeting that key state institutions would remain in place, including the monarchy, the constitution, the principles of liberal democracy, and the 1991 Paris accords. He contended that Hun Sen's action was not a coup d'état but a "legitimate action to prevent Cambodia from slipping into anarchy and a possible second genocide."[93]

The ASEAN delegation presented a proposal for a caretaker government until a general election to be held on March 23, 1998.[94] Meanwhile, Solarz met with Southeast Asian leaders, urging firmness against Hun Sen's consolidation of power. Prince Ranariddh visited each of the ASEAN countries in search of support, but he found very little. Hun Sen refused any proposal for a caretaker government, and ASEAN indicated it would accept Ranariddh's replacement as prime minister and settle for a commitment from Hun Sen to respect the constitution and to abide by the 1991 Paris Agreements. On July 23, ASEAN admitted Laos and Myanmar to membership but continued the delay of Cambodia's entry.[95] On August 20, provoked by Philippine President Fidel Ramos's meeting with Prince Ranariddh, Hun Sen warned Ramos not to interfere in Cambodian affairs and angrily asserted to ASEAN:

> We are still ready to join, but they have to tell us quickly in order to let us be ready to live alone or live with ASEAN . . . .
>
> If I win the election in 1998, I won't join ASEAN. Let ASEAN fail in its formula for Southeast Asia—seven plus three without one. If we don't join ASEAN, we won't die.[96]

Japan pursued its customary postwar policy of caution about appearing to intervene in the internal affairs of an Asian nation. Reluctant to be drawn into debate over whether the Hun Sen government was legitimate, Japan on August 21 asked Prince Ranariddh to reschedule a planned visit to Tokyo. A Japanese spokesman said it was more productive to focus on en-

91. *Herald*, July 22, 1997; *Bangkok Post*, July 22, 1997; both in <SEASIA-L@msu.edu>, July 22, 1997.

92. Reuter, July 24, 1997, <SEASIA-L@msu.edu>, July 24, 1997; VOA, July 23, 1997, <SEASIA-L@msu.edu>, July 23, 1997.

93. Reuter, July 24, 1997, <SEASIA-L@msu.edu>, July 24, 1997.

94. *Bangkok Post*, July 24, 1997, <SEASIA-L@msu.edu>, July 24, 1997.

95. Ibid.

96. *Straits Times*, Aug. 20, 1997, <SEASIA-L@msu.edu>, Aug. 20, 1997.

suring that national elections then set for May 1998 would proceed as scheduled. Japanese aid, although interrupted for a few weeks, resumed its flow to Cambodia, and Japan pronounced itself in favor of ASEAN efforts to find an acceptable solution.[97]

China adopted an indulgent attitude toward Hun Sen's coup. Hun Sen curried Chinese favor on July·23 by expelling Taiwan's Economic and Cultural Representative Office.[98] On July 25, the Chinese ambassador in Cambodia joined Hun Sen in hosting a discussion with the Chinese community in Phnom Penh aimed at restoring confidence. Hun Sen urged China to provide assistance for infrastructure projects.[99]

Vietnam maintained a low profile in statements about the coup. Hun Sen's presence in Vietnam, one day before he launched his coup, added to the suspicions held by many Cambodians that Vietnam was manipulating Hun Sen to serve their interests. At the ASEAN meeting in Kuala Lumpur, Vietnam, as a new member, insisted that ASEAN should not intervene in the internal affairs of any member or prospective member, a position clearly favoring Hun Sen's consolidation of power.

97. Kyodo, AFP, Aug. 21, 1997, <SEASIA-L@msu.edu>, July 21, 1997; "Japan and China Up Their Stakes in Cambodian Crisis," *The Daily Yomiura*, Aug. 7, 1997.

98. AFP, July 23, 1997, <SEASIA-L@msu.edu>, July 23, 1997.

99. "Japan and China Up Their Stakes," *The Daily Yomiuri*.

CHAPTER NINE

Critical Review of the International Endeavor

The international effort to bring peace and democracy to Cambodia was in some ways unique, but the experience was quite relevant for future peacemaking ventures. Lessons abound for future diplomats who may seek to negotiate a lasting cease-fire and create a transitional authority, under which to conduct a free and fair election for a new national government, in a "failed state." Both mistakes and originality are readily discernible in the implementation of the mandate set forth in the Paris Agreements of October 23, 1991, designed to settle the Cambodia conflict. In this chapter we revisit these features, and we also review the political behavior of the Cambodian nation with an eye to patterns uniquely Cambodian, which cannot be counted on in future peacemaking episodes.

Diplomacy

Diplomacy was unlikely to produce a settlement of the Cambodia conflict until Russia and China were prepared to pull out of the region for political and economic reasons of their own. Surely the ending of the Cold War facilitated the collaboration by the Permanent Five (P-5) members of the UN Security Council, which produced a formula for settlement after ten years of diagnosis and search for an acceptable basis for agreement. This formula was embodied in the P-5's November 26, 1990 "draft agreement for a comprehensive settlement," which they made more compelling by cutbacks in military and economic assistance to their clients. Prior to 1989 the Cambodian factions had little incentive to settle their differences by negotiation and no acceptable basis for ending the externally supported civil war. Yet the unavailing efforts to find a formula for agreement may highlight lessons for future negotiators, however much the decisive element of Cambodian peacemaking may have lain in the foreign ministries of the Permanent Five. Trevor Findlay has summed up eight "lessons for negotiators" of future accords, which reflect a management perspective. They add up to ways to cope with the unexpected, to engage the UN Secretariat early in detailed planning and practical goal-setting, and to maintain the commitment of the local parties in dispute.[1] His caveats deal with writing the mandate comprehensively; and most of the situations that he would avoid in the future will be touched upon in our evaluation of the implementation of the 1991 Paris accords.

For getting to a settlement, a variety of strategic options might have been selected rather than the route chosen by the Cambodian factions and their backers. Ben Kiernan, in 1992, doubted that a diplomatic agreement that included the Khmer Rouge was preferable to simply allowing the factions to slug it out militarily.[2] He felt confident that the State of Cambodia could prevail over the Khmer Rouge and make its peace with the parties of Sihanouk and Son Sann. The difficulty with this scenario was the assumption that the Khmer Rouge would lose the military contest, that China would acquiesce in the demise of its client, and that the Cambodian people would back a government installed by Vietnam (the SOC) which promised more bloodshed, more fratricidal warfare. The war weariness of the Cambodian people might well have made such military action against the Khmer Rouge more costly than beneficial to the nation.[3] Moreover, the sorry performance of the SOC's armed forces in fighting the Khmer Rouge both before and after the election raises serious doubts as to whether the SOC would have defeated their better-organized enemy.

It also has to be remembered that the Cambodia conflict had more dimensions than four factions contesting for national power and authority.[4] It

---

1. Trevor Findlay, *Cambodia: The Legacy and Lessons of UNTAC* (Oxford: Oxford University Press, 1995), p. 153.

2. Ben Kiernan, "The Failures of the Paris Agreement on Cambodia, 1991–93," in a report of a conference as the Aspen Institute, April 30–May 2, 1993: Dick Clark, ed., *The Challenge of Indochina: An Examination of the U.S. Role*, (Queenstown, Md.: The Aspen Institute, 1993). Kiernan believed in early 1992 that SOC had the upper hand militarily and should not have been restrained by the flawed Paris Agreements. Remarks at a conference, "Genocide and Democracy in Cambodia," Yale University Law School, Feb. 21, 1991.

3. See John C. Brown, "UN Success in Cambodia: Could a Standing UN Force Have Produced a Better Outcome?" (draft, 1996).

4. Patrick Raszelenberg and Peter Schier, *The Cambodian Conflict: Search for a Settlement, 1979–91* (Hamburg: Institute of Asian Affairs, 1995), p. 17, lists ten such dimensions of conflict, including Vietnam, Thailand, China, USA, USSR, and ASEAN.

significantly involved the power and role of other states in the region. Such a multiplicity of concerns generated many diplomatic initiatives, but it also complicated the issues to be resolved. Eventually, all the concerned parties reached an agreement, which Patrick Raszelenberg and Peter Schier have characterized as "one of the best and most debated plans in international conflict resolution so far."[5] The assistance of the five permanent nations on the UN Security Council and the UN Secretariat was sorely needed in achieving this result.

Some critics of the diplomatic effort have questioned why the UN did not take charge of the settlement process more decisively by administering Cambodia throughout the entire period of election preparation, constitutional convention, and new government formation. As already indicated, such a "trusteeship" arrangement for a UN member state is not authorized by the UN Charter. The idea of "getting around" the charter and somehow charging the UN with administration of a "failed state" in accordance with Chapter VII ("threats to the peace") would have generated fears of colonial domination. Moreover, the burden of finding professionally adept, Khmer-speaking, and culturally sensitive administrators, who would remain politically neutral, was greater than the UN could be reasonably expected to shoulder.

In any case, the SOC tenaciously held to the position that no interim government was needed—they already *were* the government—and the negotiators wrestled awkwardly with proposals that stepped gradually back from the original "trusteeship" proposal of U.S. Congressman Stephen Solarz and the Australian foreign minister, Gareth Evans. As we have seen, the final draft agreement on an interim UN authority delegated by a newly conceived Supreme National Council (SNC) included a mandate for the special representative of the UN secretary-general to exercise final authority if the SNC became deadlocked; and the UN Transitional Authority in Cambodia (UNTAC) was to exercise control or supervision over five key areas of administration, so as to ensure a politically neutral environment.

The failure to achieve a neutral political environment before the election cannot be attributed simply to drafting failures in the negotiated agreement, but surely those who composed the text of the comprehensive political settlement did not provide adequate language to preclude the SOC from retaining effective power in the provinces and the key "ministries." The agreements, in effect, remained open to negotiation by the incumbent government party (the CPP) and UNTAC; and the omissions and confusions in the organizational design were not readily corrected in the politically neutral direction intended by the legal technicians of the enhanced

5 Ibid., p. 18.

P-5. Nor did the SNC take on the leadership role that had been anticipated. SNC President Sihanouk spent weeks away from the brewing election, and the Khmer Rouge expressed growing dissatisfaction with the lack
of neutrality exhibited by the Phnom Penh authorities and with the slowly
arriving UNTAC. The dissatisfaction of the Khmer Rouge and the sterile
wrangles within the SNC were not simply the product of insufficient negotiation by the sponsors of the agreements, but they do illustrate the critical
importance in international peacekeeping of nailing down precise mean-
ings of key phrases such as "supervision or control" of administrative action,
or "free and fair" elections, or "directly influence the outcome of elections."
Of course, when agreements fail to serve their intended purpose the most
exact language will not guarantee their observance by disadvantaged parties. Yet the legitimacy claimed in a party's rejection of agreement obligations can be significantly reduced by precision in the text.

Notwithstanding textual uncertainties, the Khmer Rouge emerged from
the implementation of the Paris Agreements in 1992–93 without a seat in
the government—which it had enjoyed in the CGDK and the SNC—and
after being outlawed by the National Assembly in July 1994, with no claim
to political participation. This delegitimization rested on the foundation of
law that the Paris Agreements laid down, which the Khmer Rouge had first
agreed to and then considered unimplemented. The SOC survived the
election as the second-strongest party, but with its credentials as a democratic body seriously tarnished by the criticism directed at it by the UNTAC
Human Rights and Civil Administration Components. So, the Paris Agreements provided a means both to create a Royal Government of Cambodia
and to test the Khmer Rouge's readiness to play by democratic rules.

The diplomacy of the Cambodia peacemaking process demonstrated
some valuable innovations such as informal tête-á-têtes by the top personalities; monthly policy coordinating meetings of P-5 vice foreign ministers
and their "framework" and "draft agreements"; regional coordination and
ASEAN conference-organizing initiatives; UN and Australian information-
gathering missions in advance of final agreement; new institutions for assisting a "failed" state (SNC, UNTAC, special representative of the
secretary-general, a special representative for human rights); UN Security
Council embargo on economic transactions with an agreement-flouting
party (the Khmer Rouge); annual condemnatory resolutions in the General
Assembly calling for foreign troop withdrawal from Cambodia.

In the final analysis, the diplomatic process generated pressure for a
clearing out of Vietnamese troops and mentors (although believed by the
Khmer Rouge to be incomplete); and it fashioned a formula for legitimizing an independent Cambodia. The agreements as implemented soon pro-

duced disputes and interpretations that left the PDK unwilling to enter the military cantonment phase, as well as the election itself. The formula for a settlement had been implemented, but not fully in the Khmer Rouge's estimate, and UN Special Representative Akashi had been unable to satisfy Khmer Rouge's demands for remedies for the alleged presence of Vietnamese soldiers and the lack of UNTAC "control" over the SOC administration. The problem was not simply in the wording of the agreement rather in the imperfect efforts to implement it. At the very least, the negotiators did not think through realistically how difficult it would be to achieve "control or supervision" of government activity. At the very worst, the agreement was designed to fail—which few would suggest—in order to push the Khmer Rouge out of the national restoration effort and leave them politically marginalized. In fact, the imperfect neutralization of the SOC administration and the Khmer Rouge unwillingness to demobilize left them confined to their strongholds and their rivals positioned to legitimately share and expand national power. The Khmer Rouge rejection of UNTAC's imperfect implementation of the Paris Agreements left the movement on the outside with fewer options than before.

Two dubious hypotheses regarding the agreements are (1) that the PDK, like most communist parties, had no intention whatsoever to abide by the agreement, and it was foolhardy to bargain with them; and (2) that the P-5 foresaw the departure of the DK from the UNTAC phases and plotted matters in that direction. There is no substantial evidence supporting either hypothesis.

An unusual aspect of the negotiation phase of the Cambodia rescue effort was the variety of diplomacy initiators who tried to sponsor a comprehensive agreement creating a new Cambodia. Top foreign office personnel, from ministers themselves to expert subordinates, made proposals for a settlement or for hosting international peace conferences. One is struck by the dedicated efforts of Australia's Gareth Evans (kindled by U.S. Congressman Stephen Solarz), and Indonesia's Foreign Minister Ali Alatas, and France's Foreign Minister Roland Dumas, and the Japanese foreign service personnel who organized the Tokyo conference of June 1990, and Prime Minister Chatichai of Thailand who ploughed his own path through the garden of diplomacy, especially anxious to move Vietnam forces away from his border, and the unidentified Chinese foreign ministry personnel who worked hard to mediate the disagreements over the composition of the SNC. Within the UN Secretariat and the Security Council, critical research and consultation were devoted to concluding a lasting cease-fire and workable mandate for UN management of a free election. It does not appear in this case that too many cooks spoiled the broth. All the stirring and tasting was sometimes unsettling, but ultimately it paid off with a nourishing set of ingredients.

No individual earned a Nobel Peace Prize for spawning the Paris Agreements, in part because so many individuals were worthy of citation, without achieving the commanding role of a Henry Kissinger or Le Duc Tho in reaching the final agreement. The Cambodia settlement required attention to several levels of conflict (domestic, regional, and great power), and called for an unprecedented assignment of responsibility to international organizations (UN and nongovernmental). A single dominant actor during the diplomacy phase was wholly unlikely. Prince Sihanouk was too erratic and elusive to have filled such a bill, and others barely survived the sequence of hopes and rebuffs.

The Paris accords did not give clear and comprehensive attention to the period between the election and the formation of a new constitutional government. The elected Constituent Assembly was expected, after approving a constitution within three months, to transform itself into a legislative assembly and create a new government, but the language did not address the "transitional period" in much detail. Although the Australians had considered this question of transition, the Paris Agreements did not single it out in the exposition of the role of UNTAC and the SNC.

The lack of precision in the Paris stipulations regarding governance after the national election may have left a constitutional swinging door through which Sihanouk and the CPP were tempted to pass in search of political control. As previously related, Sihanouk announced on June 3, 1993, the formation of an interim administration with himself as prime minister and Prince Ranariddh and Hun Sen as co-chairmen of a coalition Council of Ministers. This move was accepted by France and Japan but rejected by Ranariddh and the United States, which saw it as violating the peace agreements. A week or so after this maneuver failed, Prince Chakrapong attempted a secession by seven eastern provinces, possibly with the connivance of the CPP, but it collapsed for lack of popular support. Could these squalid political maneuvers have been avoided if the Paris Agreements had clearly prescribed the system of governance during the period from the election to the installation of a constitutional government? The agreement made no distinction about administrative authority after the election, during the writing of a constitution. Presumably the SNC and the UN special representative were to continue exercising their authority unaffected by the election results.

In fact, the national poll shattered the assumption of political superiority of the CPP and registered the FUNCINPEC as the majority party. For the parties to sit on this unexpected power alignment for three months until the Constituent Assembly finished its work was beyond previous experience. Sihanouk received Chea Sim and Hun Sen of the CPP, and worked out his compromise to avoid the CPP threats of war.

There were two negative features of Sihanouk's action. First, it disregarded the language of the Paris Agreements. Second, Sihanouk's cavalier promotion of the two-prime-ministers device denied the fruits of electoral victory to FUNCINPEC and imposed a barely workable marriage of two hostile party leaders. The strains in the arrangement were clear enough to see, but the same structure was prescribed for five more years in the new constitution itself (art. 138)—which was longer than the feigned prime ministerial harmony could last. The availability of the father figure Prince Sihanouk to promote the two-headed coalition device, against the wishes of his son, the number one prime minister, was a circumstance peculiar to Cambodia. It may have lowered the resistance of the majority party to an arrangement that bought time for the early stage of building a civil society, but it had no lasting power once democratic party competition came into play again. The CPP's threat of civil war was less credible in the presence of UNTAC, in the postelection summer of 1993, than it was during the Hun Sen coup d'état, four years later.

Implementation of the Agreements

UNTAC Success Stories

The implementation of the Paris Agreements, quite apart from the quality of diplomatic negotiation and draftsmanship they rested upon, offers lessons for future peacekeeping and peace-building operations. The task is somewhat simplified by the manner in which the mandate for UNTAC was laid down in seven distinct components, plus an education and information division. A "report card" on fulfillment of the tasks set forth in the agreement is available in written critiques by several specialists in UN affairs. Another measure to judge success and failure could be a comparison with other peacekeeping operations such as those in Namibia, Angola, or the Congo. The opportunity costs imposed by the Cambodia operation at the expense of UN opportunities forgone might also be calculated.[6] Such mea-

6. Steven R. Ratner examines the problem of measuring success and identifies "impact upon Cambodia" as "the most analytically useful" criterion. See *The New UN Peacekeeping: Building Peace in Lands of Conflict after the Cold War* (New York: St. Martin's Press, 1995), chap. 8. Jamie F. Metzl, in reviewing four recent books about UNTAC, suggests several measures of assessment, including comparison with previous peacekeeping operations ("an enor-

surements are more subtle and subjective than *task fulfillment*. The latter measure may beg the question of whether the UN's mandate embodied in the agreements was itself a success, i.e., whether it achieved appropriate goals in a beneficial manner. Surely the objectives set forth by the agreements to maintain independence, peace, national reconciliation, and self-determination and liberal democracy in Cambodia were laudable, but at what cost to the UN itself and the Cambodian people? These are intricate questions, which political evolution in Cambodia in the next few years will help to clarify. Meanwhile, presuming that the agreements expressed a valid purpose properly agreed to, we examine here the mistakes and achievements of UNTAC in fulfilling its mandate.

Written critiques of the implementation of the Paris accords before the 1997 coup by Hun Sen show positive consensus regarding several functions spelled out by the agreements and annexes. Areas of disappointment were also evident and contributed to a judgment that UNTAC was a "partial success" or a flawed success, or that "the UN did rather well."[7] These overall evaluations have evolved from UNTAC's multiple assignments in the agreements, which were performed with varying degrees of proficiency. On the pursuit of "liberal democracy," however, the record turned suddenly sour in July 1997.

In simple terms of fulfilling its assignments UNTAC earned high marks in preparing and conducting the election, with 90 percent turnout, notwithstanding a relatively small but deplorable loss of lives in acts of political terrorism by the PDK and the CPP. The nation responded to the well-organized and steadfastly conducted election in a stunning fashion after decades of nondemocratic rule. The election became the centerpiece of UNTAC's mission after the failure to achieve disarmament and demobilization of the parties, and its widely accepted outcome made possible a new legitimate government of Cambodia, whose participants were formally bound by constitutional rules of democratic behavior. The adherence to such principles was far from perfect, and the nation's ability to undergo a second free and fair election, in 1998, remained a challenging test of the

mous success" by UN standards), task fulfillment, or socioeconomic impact on Cambodia itself. See Metzl, "The Many Faces of UNTAC: A Review Article," *Contemporary Southeast Asia*, June 1995.

7. See Brown, "UN Success in Cambodia" ("did rather well"); Janet E. Heininger, *Peacekeeping in Transition: The United Nations in Cambodia* (New York: 20th Century Fund, 1994), pp. 1 and 5 (a "qualified success"); Findlay, *Cambodia: The Legacy and Lessons of UNTAC* ("a flawed success"); Ratner, *The New UN Peacekeeping* ("a partial success"); William Shawcross, *Cambodia's New Deal*, p. 36 ("a social revolution").

UN endeavor in Cambodia, which was very much in doubt. UNTAC had made a real but fading imprint in this basic realm of political restoration.

A second area of commendable activity was the repatriation of more than 360,000 displaced persons and refugees from the Thai border regions without a single fatal incident. This gratifying achievement benefited from the prior engagement of the UN Border Relief Organization, as well as from the long-developed expertise of the UN High Commissioner for Refugees in refugee operations and the cooperation of all the Cambodian parties, including the Khmer Rouge. The most serious flaw in the operation was its failure to find mine-free land to satisfy the demand of the returnees. More timely investigation might have been applied to this problem before plans were made that could not be fulfilled.

A third consensus candidate for emulation is the Information and Education Division that evolved under the special representative without the benefit of component status in the secretary-general's initial implementation plan of February 26, 1992. The acquisition of radio broadcasting equipment for use in voter education was slow and ragged, yet the relatively small but zealous group of broadcasters and opinion surveyors played a key role in inspiring people to register and vote (by *secret* ballot). This element most assuredly merits inclusion in future election organizing, with procurement of equipment at the very beginning and careful recruiting of qualified personnel.[8]

A fourth item of significant implementation was the awareness campaign on behalf of human rights, which left behind a UN special representative, a Center for Human Rights, and numerous determined nongovernmental organizations alert to international standards of justice. Even though the post-election period echoed with governmental and Khmer Rouge violations of rights to free expression and humane treatment, the UNTAC period energized a dialogue between rights abusers and their victims, who previously remained silent and unknown, without a press to complain in. The tragedy is that their gains may have been wiped out by the events of July 1997, which produced purges and murders of political opposition leaders, muzzling of the opposition press, widespread looting by an undisciplined military, and general intimidation.

UNTAC's effort in the domain of human rights was an unprecedented undertaking. A nation and its governors were subjected to an intrusion of legal and political advocates from abroad, ready to assist ordinary citizens in petitioning and criticizing their officials in the name of universal rights. As

8. Zhou Mei, *Radio UNTAC of Cambodia* (Bangkok: White Lotus Co., 1994).

already described, the Human Rights Component of UNTAC augmented its original tiny staff so as to present itself in the provinces as well as monitoring the headquarters of other components in Phnom Penh. The scope of the human rights effort prior to the 1997 coup also grew by means of spawning Cambodian nongovernmental groups, which boasted more than 150,000 members at election time and continued pursuing their goals after UNTAC's departure. The multimember international donor community strongly and courageously warned about the loss of democratic structures during the July 1997 coup. Yet there were shortfalls in the overall effort that leave the verdict mixed on the Human Rights Component's performance. As William Shawcross summed it up, they made "considerable achievements"[9] in exercising an ambiguous mandate, which covered treacherous ground that Cambodians had great difficulty in traversing.

The resourcefulness of the component in getting its size tripled and adapting radio dialogues and video productions to their education and training mission was clearly commendable. The seminar conducted for 14,000 civil servants was also a step in the right direction, but a rather short one. Some investigative work regarding brutal prison administration also made a positive impact, if not an irreversible one. Conditions in prisons sometimes reverted quickly to the traditional pain and abuse. Investigations into denial of justice or abuse of rights often produced convincing grounds for punishment of corrupt officials, but no judicial system of any consequence was available to order remedies. The "corrective actions," such as dismissal of personnel, authorized to the special representative, however, were scarcely exercised, as Akashi preferred to work on reforming corrupt institutions with the consent of the factions rather than intruding on criminal behavior by individuals.[10]

Areas of only partial UNTAC success were de-mining and economic rehabilitation. The latter goal was not pursued widely in part because the Khmer Rouge opposed SNC approval of long-term international development aid projects that would be administered through the SOC and might elevate it to a "quasi-government" before the elections. Quick impact projects were a more workable undertaking, and civic action projects by UNTAC armed forces to repair the ravaged infrastructure were also activated. More rehabilitation might have been attempted even during the relatively short presence of UNTAC, and the same applied to de-mining. The task of deactivating an estimated 4 to 10 million mines was staggering, but

9. Shawcross, *Cambodia's New Deal*, p. 59.
10. Ibid., p. 75. CAM: NGO Forum Issues Statement, July 18, 1997.

the momentum started before the election was unfortunately not sustained after UNTAC's departure.

Such were the star performances in UNTAC's eighteen-month guardianship in Cambodia. Some were favored by the intrinsically rewarding nature of the tasks (e.g., repatriation and economic aid), but other factors also combined to create the "successful" exercise of the mandate. The areas of little or no success, however, were both numerous and complex.

Shortfalls

An element that will surely bring trouble again in UN peacekeeping was the tardy deployment of UNTAC following the signing of the agreement in October 1991. Five months passed without the arrival of substantial UNTAC military forces or civilian administrators. Their absence produced a severe let-down among Cambodians and a loss of credibility for the UN. The delay in filling offices and deploying troops left people confused and anxious, and the existing authorities were emboldened to resist administrative scrutiny by the slowly organizing UNTAC personnel.[11]

The origins of this sluggish deployment lay in the slow start in drafting the secretary-general's implementation plan of February 19, 1992, and the exigencies of enlisting military personnel from more than thirty nations—who were supposed to speak either English or French—and a civilian staff with various skills, from administration to engineering to human rights enforcement. A more selective recruitment of civilian staff is needed, in order to expedite deployment. Greater selectivity should be applied to avoid sending troops without training and discipline in relations with local populations. There should be no tolerance of, nor failure to anticipate, troop behavior that demeans or exploits the nation to be "saved." Discipline and codes of conduct for peacekeeping forces require closer attention than they received in UNTAC's highly diverse military formations. Useful proposals to upgrade training requirements for such peacekeeping service, which might include earmarking troops in advance for peacekeeping missions, have been made in *post hoc* assessments of UNTAC.[12]

The civil police, numbering 3,600 from thirty two countries, were univer-

11. Findlay, *Cambodia: The Legacy and Lessons of UNTAC*, p. 113, points to late deployment as "one of the biggest flaws of the UNTAC mission. It emboldened the Cambodian factions to violate the Paris Accords."

12. Brown, "UN Success in Cambodia: Could a Standing UN Force Have Produced Better Outcome?", concludes yes to his question.

sally criticized. They were called "disastrous" and the like,[13] and they seemed to lack a clear-cut definition of their mission. Their lack of sufficient language skills and the wide variety in their national political practice and values made them an often regrettable component, which reduced the Cambodian people's sense of favorable possibilities under a democratic form of government. Some inadequacies can be corrected by more selective recruitment, including the delicate dissuasion of some potential contributors, until they can better prepare their personnel.

Another organizational norm that cries out for flexibility is the procurement system for UN equipment, which at times precluded local or regional purchases, which could have assisted UNTAC's start-up.[14] The timetable for UNTAC's task fulfillment was a mere eighteen months, but the rains of June–September dictated the quickly-in, quickly-out schedule that the 22,400-member international operation adopted on February 28, 1992. Voting had to be scheduled prior to the summer rainy season to achieve a meaningful turnout. So, "no later than May 1993" became the deadline for the election, which became the centerpiece of the UN mission, after disarmament failed.

Just as the civil police relied on policemen with no experience in a democratic polity, so UNTAC's administrative echelons contained personnel with no previous experience in Cambodia and few qualified interpreters. The roster of skilled persons available for temporary assignment was short indeed. Multilingual specialists in Khmer language and history were extremely scarce, even though lawyers and veterans of UN election supervision missions in Namibia and Angola showed up for enlistment by UNTAC. On the other hand, the use of UN Volunteers as election organizers (via voter registration) proved to be a laudable and viable enterprise, which admirably symbolized an international readiness of brave individuals to take risks and endure hardships in behalf of peace-building.

A further element of difficulty in carrying out the Paris Agreements was the backing out of the PDK. In refusing to enter phase two of the cantonment and demobilization procedures in June 1992, the Khmer Rouge contended that the supervision and control of administrative authorities, to ensure political neutrality, had not been achieved, that tens of thousands of Vietnamese troops remained in Cambodia, and that the SNC had not been

13. Findlay, *Cambodia: The Legacy and Lessons of UNTAC*, pp. 144–47. Akashi, in a newspaper interview in 1993, called for tighter criteria for recruitment of civilian police in the future.

14. How procurement rules slowed the establishment of Radio UNTAC is told dramatically in Zhou Mei, *Radio UNTAC of Cambodia*, chaps. 2–4.

allowed to exercise its intended authority.[15] These alleged shortcomings of UNTAC's performance served as justification for Khmer Rouge noncompliance with the comprehensive political settlement. UNTAC itself can hardly be criticized for creating this impasse. The agreements may have lacked precision and depth of instruction to the signatories, but the disagreement over whether UNTAC was fulfilling its treaty obligations lay less in the text and its interpretation than in the Khmer Rouge's uncertain commitment to seeking a solution under the UNTAC framework. Khmer Rouge adherence to the demobilization and election provisions of the agreements was little dependent upon UNTAC's performance and more related to the Khmer Rouge's shifting estimates of its political loss or gain from sticking to the agreements. In repatriating displaced Cambodians from the Thai border, the Khmer Rouge cooperated minimally with the UNHCR out of a common interest. Voter registration in Khmer Rouge-dominated areas was also permitted briefly, but by June 1992 their willingness to disarm and demobilize and to submit to a fair election apparently was overtaken by their assessment of the risks to their power.

Khmer Rouge defectors reported that their party was at first prepared to abide by the Paris Agreements and disarm and canton their troops; they had many arms caches in their areas. In April 1992, however, they saw UNTAC as favoring the Hun Sen regime, and by May they felt insecure vis-à-vis the SOC. The bamboo pole that stopped Special Representative Akashi and General Sanderson from entering the Khmer Rouge area in May 1992 may have prompted them to see the UN as weak or susceptible to challenge. The question remains unanswerable—would the Khmer Rouge have adhered to the agreements had UNTAC not tolerated the famous denial of access to Akashi and Sanderson? Or, could UNTAC have made its investigations into alleged Vietnamese military presence in Cambodia even more convincing? Or, could truly penetrating "supervision and control" of key administrative areas (primarily SOC and Khmer Rouge) have induced the Khmer Rouge to join in a free and fair election?[16]

15. Y. Akashi, "The Challenges Faced by UNTAC," *Japan Review of International Affairs*, Summer 1993, outlines these three claims and finds them insubstantial. He further testifies to cease-fire violations by both the PDK and SOC which were hard to distinguish as defensive or offensive. Also see Nate Thayer, *Far Eastern Economic Review*, Feb. 10, 1994, regarding the intra-PDK struggle over whether to adhere to the agreements in 1992. Party documents apparently show an original DK intention to comply with the peace plan.

16. Findlay, *Cambodia: The Legacy and Lessons of UNTAC*, p. 137, cites a study of the "never realized supervision and control" of civil administration which lists seven contributing causes: lack of planning, no precedents, staff shortages, lack of resolve, absence of a legal system, language barriers, inaccurate assessment of the problem.

The answer to these queries seems to be "no." The Party of Democratic Kampuchea became implacable, and stricter implementation of the Agreement would have been to no avail so long as the SOC remained in place, or so long as the PDK believed that Vietnam would not permit them to share or exercise national power. The Khmer Rouge, it seems, would not have reached a level of security sufficient to encourage them to seek political gains through an election. In the end, the failure to bring along the PDK as a fully cooperating party to the agreement was not attributable to UN administrative failures, even though a stricter level of UNTAC "control" over the SOC might have raised the possibility of persuading the PDK to participate in a less than perfect neutral election. It can be argued that the determination to proceed with the election and the formation of a new government without Khmer Rouge participation made a valuable contribution to the later collapse of the revolutionary organization in 1996–97.

The departure of the PDK from the comprehensive settlement was a deep disappointment to UNTAC's leadership, but they decided to accomplish at least as close to a free and fair election as they could manage. The PDK were patiently heard out by the special representative, but their fixation about alleged camouflaged Vietnamese soldiers was unassailable, and it left UNTAC trying in vain to prove a negative. The Khmer Rouge conception of a politically neutral interim authority seems to have outrun the realm of the possible soon after UNTAC's inauguration in March 1992. UNTAC tried hard to institute a neutral administration and an active SNC, but the SOC was determined to maintain its authority, placing the UNTAC task beyond realization. The fault lay not so much in the implementation as in the aspiration. The creation of a supervisory administrative structure that was unwanted and understaffed highlighted a failure of conceptualization in the agreement itself as much as a faulty administration.

The chief technician for translating the agreements into creative action, Yasushi Akashi, was a Japanese career diplomat with thirty-six years of UN service, recently in disarmament affairs. Akashi, with no Southeast Asian experience, was a surprise choice by a newly elected secretary-general (Boutros Boutros-Ghali). The secretary-general passed over the deeply engaged Rafeeuddin Ahmed and Indonesia's Ali Alatas in favor of a UN veteran from Japan, a country that was anxious to play, and finance, a larger role in the perceived "new world order" of peacekeeping operations. Akashi received both criticism and praise, depending on the critic's attitude toward the use of force in peacekeeping operations. The hallmark of Akashi's political leadership was his Asian-derived consensus seeking. However, in dealing with two irreconcilable party adversaries he was unable to sustain agreement on a peaceful comprehensive political settlement and settled instead for conducting a more-or-less free election, during which the Khmer Rouge marginalized themselves, and hostilities were minimal.[17]

Akashi was seen by some critics as too indulgent of the SOC and DK defiance of the agreements, when he allowed UNTAC to be excluded from Khmer Rouge–controlled areas. Some saw him as too reluctant to use his powers under the agreement to make binding directives or to remove Cambodian officials. He exerted utmost patience before resorting to a special prosecutor and control teams, or using sanctions under the electoral law, during the five months before the election. Yet he was also criticized for showing personal anger over the thwarting tactics of the Khmer Rouge. He was unable to deliver the settlement outlined by the agreements, but he avoided pushing the parties to full renunciation of them, and he delivered an acceptable approximation of a democratic election. Akashi's cautious approach to carrying out an eroding mandate deserves more credit than criticism in view of the fragility of agreement among the Cambodian parties and the non-belligerency insisted upon by many countries in contributing troops to UNTAC.

Another area in which UNTAC performance fell short was the disarmament and demobilization program. The initial phase got under way slowly, and in June 1992 the Khmer Rouge officially rejected the second phase. The Khmer Rouge demands were beyond fulfillment, unless UNTAC had exerted such thorough penetration of the SOC administration as to virtually replace it in the five key areas. This would probably have ended cooperation by the CPP and left two hostile parties unwilling to disarm or demobilize, or exercise governmental responsibilities in a politically neutral way. In fact the refusal of the Khmer Rouge to enter phase two on June 13, 1992, led to the effective abandonment of cantonment altogether by November 1992. The failure of disarmament and demobilization can be attributed to a change in political strategy by the Khmer Rouge, not to the implementation efforts of UNTAC. The rival parties remained armed and militarily mobilized throughout the election campaign and the three months allotted to writing the constitution, but none of the parties made sustained attacks or significant territorial gains after cantonment was abandoned.

The UN suffered relatively light casualties, not directly related to the size, disposition, equipment, or training of UNTAC personnel. Redefining its role to provide security for the electoral process and safety for Cambo-

17. Ratner, *The New UN Peacekeeping*, chap. 8, p. 217, judiciously evaluates Special Representative Akashi's performance, which remains open to second guessing. His own assessment rates Akashi as doing "an admirable job." Findlay found Akashi was "in some respects perfectly suited for the role of Special Representative." *Cambodia: The Legacy and Lessons of UNTAC*, p. 110.

dian political parties, UNTAC made redeployments to protect voter registration teams stationed in remote villages and towns.[18] The level of casualties sustained by UNTAC from hostile action was 42 military and 42
civilians killed, plus 58 UN personnel seriously injured as of August 31,
1993 at of a total deployment of 24,000.[19] This was a small percentage of a
very large deployment in an undependable cease-fire situation. Yet casualties sustained in UN uniform are a new phenomenon for most national military forces and are very painful at home. UN operations have not often
confronted the chilling military reasoning of French General Jean-Michel
Loridon, whom Akashi eventually replaced as deputy commander. Loridon
made known his belief that with two hundred UN casualties he could put
the Khmer Rouge out of business. Akashi, the UN Security Council, and
the UNTAC troop contributors preferred to provide a free and fair election
(with minimal murder and intimidation), rather than attempt Loridon's
one-shot civil war victory over a badly wounded but probably still defiant
Khmer Rouge.[20]

Closely related to the breakdown of cantonment and disarmament was
the social damage imposed on the Cambodian people by the multinational
UNTAC personnel. The onset of rapidly spreading AIDS[21] via burgeoning
prostitution and the disrespect accorded to Cambodian people by some
poorly disciplined and underoccupied UN troops left ugly scars on an otherwise commendable venture. The size of the UNTAC force in relation to
its limited military engagements raises the question of how many foreign
troops are sustainable in a purely peacekeeping mode without becoming a
sort of occupying rather than sustaining force. The effects on Cambodia included insults and harassment of women and underutilization of local personnel. The economy was stimulated but distorted by the narrow band of
commerce created by the demands of UN personnel; and the UN-driven
inflation of real estate prices benefited a privileged elite of property owners.

The UNTAC forces, hampered by language barriers and cultural divides,

18. Fourth Progress Report of the Secretary-General on UNTAC, S/25719, May 3, 1993,
Doc. 79, *The United Nations and Cambodia, 1991–1995* (New York: UN Department of Public Information, 1995).

19. Findlay, *Cambodia: The Legacy and Lessons of UNTAC*, p. 156, n. 1.

20. Ibid., p. 131. Findlay succinctly concludes that "a military campaign to force KR compliance was out of the question." A counter-insurgency operation by UNTAC's diverse army
elements would have fared worse than the U.S. effort in Vietnam.

21. Estimates have suggested that 80 percent of the prostitutes in Cambodia were in-
fected with some form of sexual disease including HIV. Cf. Peter Utting, ed., *Between Hope
and Insecurity: The Social Consequences of the Cambodian Peace Process* (Geneva: UNR-
SID, 1994), p. 168.

received a mixed review among Cambodians.[22] They were associated for the most part with peace, but they could not readily reach their constituents. In future peacekeeping undertakings far more training of the troops in the history, culture, and language of the host country should be included. Less than three years after some regrettable UNTAC troop misbehavior in Cambodia came reports of abusive action by Canadian peacekeepers, from a seemingly exemplary army, in both Somalia and Bosnia.[23] The disgraceful incidents, it was suggested, stemmed from Canadian forces being "burned out" by repeated peacekeeping assignments.

A litany of secondary faults can be laid on the record of UNTAC, in what might be considered a normal shortfall for so large an undertaking. For example, land mine clearing for reopening fertile land for the repatriation operation was both late and inadequate, and three years after UNTAC's departure an estimated 4 to 10 million land mines remained, with only 20 square kilometers cleared between 1992 and 1996. The cost of clearing a single mine was estimated to be $300 to $1,000, which makes the task of clearing a beneficial portion of the total (which might reduce the heavy medical costs of accidental victims) a truly daunting enterprise.[24] In the absence of clear-cut goals, UNTAC and its successor organizations (international NGOs) have moved with unacceptable delay, to the point where the U.S. Department of Defense finally picked up responsibility in 1994 for funding, training, and equipping Cambodian military personnel for the job.

Nonetheless, the seven components of UNTAC worked hard and creatively to win the good-faith fulfillment of the Paris Agreements by mutually suspicious parties engaged in quite unaccustomed tasks. The election and political education achieved by UNTAC, and the repatriation of long-displaced people, clearly deserve commendation, even though the effort fell short of its intended design.

22. An analysis report by UNTAC Information/Education Division in September 1992 began: "The general population is angry at UNTAC" because of its perceived ineffectiveness and its treatment of civilians. P. Utting, chap. 5, Appendix I. A mixed opinion toward UNTAC is recorded in Timothy Carney and Tan Lian Choo, *Whither Cambodia? Beyond the Election* (Singapore: Institute of Southeast Asian Studies, 1993), p. 42.

23. *Boston Globe,* July 18, 1996, p. A2.

24. U.S. General Accounting Office, Briefing Report to the Chairman and Ranking Member, Committee on International Relations, House of Representatives, *Cambodia: Limited Progress on Free Elections, Human Rights, and Mine Clearing*, GAO/USAID-96-15BR, Feb. 1996, p. 21.

The Adoption of "Liberal Democracy"

According to the Paris Agreements, the new Cambodian government was to be a "liberal democracy." The agreements called for "periodic and genuine elections" to be conducted on the basis of universal and equal suffrage, with guarantees of a secret ballot and electoral procedures offering voters a "full and fair" opportunity to organize and participate in the electoral process. "Fundamental rights" were to be protected, including the rights to life, personal liberty, security, and freedom of movement, religion, assembly, and association. Freedom to organize and participate in political parties was to be guaranteed. Due process and equality before the law were to be ensured, as well as freedom from racial, ethnic, religious, or sexual discrimination. All of these protections were to be enforced by an independent judicial system.

It must be remembered that the Cambodian party leaders signed the final documents, embracing these democratic principles. Moreover, they were incorporated into the Cambodian constitution by a popularly elected Constituent Assembly. They could, therefore, be said to represent the aspirations of the Cambodian people.

The Coalition Government

Cambodia has enjoyed only scant experience in democratic government. Its new coalition government in 1993 was a tenuous partnership of former enemies who had emerged from strikingly different ideological and class backgrounds. That Prince Ranariddh and Hun Sen could serve as joint prime ministers in an association that endured almost four years, even though marked by strains, was itself noteworthy. This coalition was punctuated by bombast and confrontation, but it held out hope for a measure of political stability, a welcome alternative to the turbulence and instability that had preceded it. Had the CPP not been invited to share power, they would probably have been a disruptive political force and even a military threat contesting the stability that was emerging.

Was the formation of this coalition government, however, consistent with democratic practice? Ruling coalitions are a common phenomenon among democratic governments, particularly those with multiparty systems, and they are consistent with constitutional monarchies. The constitutional monarchy of Malaysia is governed by a coalition variously labeled "Alliance" and "National Front." The normal practice of a coalition government is for the leading party to appoint the prime minister, with a distribution of cabinet (ministerial) posts to the cooperating parties that stood in the election.

In Cambodia, however, the new constitution (art. 138) prescribed for the "first legislature" that the king should appoint a first and a second prime minister. This raised serious questions about adherence to democratic majority-rule procedures.[25] The distinction between the designated first prime minister, Ranariddh, and the second prime minister, Hun Sen, proved to be primarily in protocol rather than power.

Ministerial posts were supposedly divided equally between the two parties, FUNCINPEC and the CPP, even though the former had won a plurality of votes in the election. Moreover, despite this equal division of portfolios, the CPP emerged as dominant in decision making and administration, particularly in the countryside. The bureaucracy, the security services, the army, and the judiciary continued to be directed largely by former SOC cadres, loyal to the CPP leadership. Thus, the popular mandate expressed in the election, with its remarkable 90 percent voter turnout, was not translated into political power. The vote surely affirmed a desire for political change. Yet the former incumbents continued to exercise dominant power, and their style of rule remained much the same, until Hun Sen's aggressive "dismissal" of his co–prime minister in July 1997.

The Legislative and Judicial Branches

There were few checks or balances on the arbitrary authority of the executive branch. The National Assembly did not challenge the government; rather it was subservient to it. Important legislation was initiated by the government leadership, especially the two prime ministers, and most decisions in the assembly were dictated by the leaders in the executive branch. The two prime ministers showed little respect for political opposition. The cases of Sam Rainsy and Norodom Sirivuddh demonstrated the low tolerance that Hun Sen and Ranariddh had for political challenge. Dismissal of a dissident Rainsy from his post as finance minister by the prime minister could formally be portrayed as a legitimate parliamentary procedure; prime ministers have the right, as Rainsy publicly acknowledged, to choose members of their team and to dismiss those they judge to have violated party discipline. But expelling him from the legislature (after a rump party group expelled him from the FUNCINPEC party) went beyond the boundaries

25. The International Republican Institute (IRI), supported by the U.S. Republican Party, has contended, as pointed out in Chapter 7, that the ruling coalition in Cambodia is undemocratic since it fails to reflect the outcome of the election and makes no allowance for a loyal opposition. In 1996, the IRI provided training workshops only to the Khmer Nation Party, as the sole national party that was not participating in the coalition government. Interview in Phnom Penh by J. J. Zasloff, May 1996.

of usual democratic practice. The technical justification, that he had been elected on a political party list and had no individual right to the seat once he left the party, offered thin cover for this heavy-handed move by the two prime ministers against a challenging voice in the National Assembly.[26] Yet the new constitution and the election law were flawed by not defining whether members elected from a party list lose their seat upon leaving the party.

The case of Foreign Minister Norodom Sirivuddh presented an even more blatant disregard for due process of law. Sirivuddh may have spoken loosely, perhaps uttering malicious threats aimed at Hun Sen, which touched a sensitive nerve in the second prime minister, but Hun Sen's reaction was swift and punitive, quite disproportionate to the alleged crime. He ordered the house arrest of Sirivuddh and pressured National Assembly members in a closed session to lift his parliamentary immunity under threat of his death and possibly the demise of the assembly. A vote was demanded, and unanimously obtained, without debate. Although Hun Sen acceded to the intervention of King Sihanouk on behalf of his half-brother and allowed Sirivuddh to seek asylum in France, his trial *in absentia* three months later and his sentencing to ten years' imprisonment were a travesty of the judicial process.

Besides showing a disregard for democratic procedures, the treatment of Sam Rainsy and Norodom Sirivuddh showed the two prime ministers giving greater weight to political conformity than to retaining talent and experience. Both Rainsy and Sirivuddh were educated and experienced public officials. Individuals with such attributes are rare in Cambodia, whose educated class was decimated by the Khmer Rouge. Such talented and independent-minded individuals should be precious in the new Cambodia.

The current court system is far removed from the "independent judiciary" called for in the Paris Agreements and the constitution. Judges and their staffs have gained a well-deserved reputation for corruption, incompetence, availability for bribery, and, most importantly, for subservience to those in power. After four years, the new government had still not fulfilled the constitutional mandate to create the Supreme Council of the Magistracy, the body charged with recommending the appointment and removal of judges and prosecutors. Nor had the government created the Constitutional Council which, according to the constitution, is to exercise a form of judicial review, which might oversee unscrupulous activities.

26. In the Netherlands the practice gives elected members of Parliament the right to retain their seat even after leaving the party on whose list they entered.

Political Parties and Elections

Political parties, especially a loyal opposition, are important elements in developing a democratic polity. In the new Cambodian state, the political party record was ambiguous. FUNCINPEC scored highest in the election, probably thanks to its association with Sihanouk. Its leadership, composed largely of returnees from abroad, was weak and it failed to build a party organization throughout the country. Local cadres complained that the leader seldom appeared in the countryside and did little to help them build support in their constituencies. The party was pervaded by fragmentation and corruption. Its secretary-general during its first three years, Prince Sirivuddh, was expelled from the country, and one of its founders, Sam Rainsy, was expelled from both the party and the National Assembly. Thus, FUNCINPEC did not effectively institutionalize its party after an electoral victory based primarily on the charismatic appeal of Prince Sihanouk.

By contrast, the CPP showed much greater organizational cohesion and strength. It retained a greater sense of party discipline than its adversaries, and had greater reach within the bureaucracy and the army and throughout the countryside. The CPP (like FUNCINPEC) was pervaded by corruption and had its intraparty cliques and factions. But it had a greater ability to defend its interests than its competitors. The feeble BLDP, which emerged from the KPNLF, was rent by even greater cleavages than the two frontrunners and did not appear to have grown since its slim achievement in the UNTAC election.

After his expulsion from the National Assembly, Sam Rainsy founded the Khmer Nation Party (KNP) in 1995. Despite harassment of party organizers by government agents and the disruption of KNP meetings by security forces, Sam Rainsy claimed, in the spring of 1996, to have enrolled 102,000 members. Ron Abney, Republican Party consultant in Phnom Penh, reported that by July 1997 the KNP had 250,000 "card-carrying members."[27] The government's mistreatment of the KNP, a genuine opposition party, did not conform with the guarantees of freedom of assembly and association called for in the Paris Agreements and the constitution. Nonetheless, the government was ambiguous in its posture toward the KNP. Although it did not fully block KNP activities in the early months, it made trouble for the organizers. The intimidating impact of such incidents was widely felt.

---

27. Testimony before U.S. House of Representatives Committee on International Relations, Subcommittee on Asia and Pacific Affairs, July 16, 1997, reported in camdisc@cambodia.org, July 17, 1997.

A study for the U.S. General Accounting Office before the 1997 coup noted that, except for the CPP, Cambodian political parties lacked the leadership, organization, and financial resources to conduct effective national campaigns. The government had not taken adequate steps to develop the electoral framework (laws, regulations, and an independent commission) and resources (human and financial) needed to hold elections. Legislation was lacking for an electoral law, a nationality law and a political party law. Even if, as Prime Minister Ranariddh had proposed, an independent neutral commission under the king were formed to control the police and armed forces during the 1998 election, there was already room to doubt that such a commission could be effective. UNTAC, with over twenty thousand personnel, was unable to fully control the SOC police and armed forces before the 1993 elections, and it seemed unlikely that a fragile new observer corps could do better in 1998.[28]

The U.S. State Department had been mildly optimistic before Hun Sen's coup that the election would be held.[29] Hun Sen proclaimed after his July 1997 coup that the coalition government would be retained, albeit with a new FUNCINPEC prime minister (Ung Huot), and that the elections would be held as scheduled in 1998. However, the coup radically altered the political landscape, putting the second prime minister in the driver's seat and making the CPP the dominant political force in the country.

The Cambodian government had taken some measures in 1996 to advance the preparation for elections. A draft Communal Electoral Law included a provision for monitoring of elections by an organization of Cambodian NGOs, formed in July 1996. At each foreign aid donors meeting with Cambodian government representatives, questions about election preparations were posed, and it was clear that the legitimacy of the royal government would be closely tied, in their eyes, to the commitment to democratic rule.[30]

UNTAC had aimed not simply at stopping the fighting and conducting an election—both of which succeeded—but at laying the groundwork for a democratic state. Free elections were to be a vital test of the achievement of a democratic government. There could be a role for outside, perhaps UN-sponsored, election observers, which have been used successfully around the world, but it was important that Cambodians themselves take charge and demonstrate both a commitment to and a competence in the conduct of

---

28. U.S. General Accounting Office, *Cambodia: Limited Progress*, pp. 10–15.
29. Ibid., p. 32.
30. Chris Fontaine, "Election Watchdogs Gear Up," *Phnom Penh Post*, July 26–Aug. 8, 1996, p. 2.

truly free elections. The holding of a truly free and fair election in 1998, however, seemed far less likely after the Hun Sen coup of July 1997.

Corruption

Corruption was a nettlesome problem for the newly reconstructed Cambodia, and its pervasiveness raised special dangers. Decay into greater praetorianism, rather than development, could be the country's fate. Corruption erodes the legitimacy of a new government, which must achieve increasing levels of trust and respect to grow. The new coalition government from 1993 to 1997, and especially the Hun Sen government which succeeded it, often inspired comparisons with the Lon Nol government from 1970 to 1975, a regime riddled with corruption, which collapsed under the Khmer Rouge assault. Corruption adds to the cost of economic development. The endless "demand for bribes" in Cambodia, in the words of a foreign investor, is even a greater problem than finding capital and training workers. Corruption threatens the flow of economic assistance from foreign donors.

Corruption is, of course, a universal problem, particularly endemic in third world countries that lack effective political and social institutions. As a former communist-controlled government now in transition to a market economy, Cambodia shares the massive problems of corruption generally experienced by these formerly centrally planned economies. As a failed state, with its social and political institutions in shocking disrepair, Cambodia is particularly vulnerable to corruption. Foreign donors must search for strategies that help to curb it. These include the building of effective political institutions such as parties, interest groups, legislatures, courts, and bureaucracies. There must be measures to expand transparency in government, including vigorous news media that are free to criticize and unfettered NGOs that can probe and assist, and help civil society to expand. Perhaps most important are honest, dedicated, selfless, and committed leaders.

The Monarch: The Sihanouk Factor

A very special feature of the Cambodia rescue endeavor was the national father figure and political arbiter, Norodom Sihanouk. This royal survivor of more than half a century as variously king, prince, head of state, national arbiter, chief diplomat, and religious and national symbol clearly added dimensions to the UN peacemaking effort that cannot be replicated in future efforts to restore a failed state. No such political personage as Sihanouk is likely to exist, and no one is likely to match the personality traits that made

Sihanouk such a unique political player. His presence in his palace was un-predictable, and his moods, as well as his health, could not be counted upon. At times he seemed resigned to defeat by his opponents. At other times he moved dramatically to promote national reconciliation (by includ-ing the Khmer Rouge) or political compromise (by endorsing two equal prime ministers). He failed to achieve either an inclusive government—the Khmer Rouge boycotted the election—or a stable one—it lasted only until the July 1997 coup). He indulged his urge to find a compromise solution to his nation's political strife by promoting dual prime ministers for the period between the election and the installation of a constitutional regime. This system was then prescribed for the first five years of constitutional govern-ment. His initial plan, to have himself elected president, was rightly with-drawn as inconsistent with the Paris Agreements. Such legal niceties were not foremost in the calculations of the free-wheeling prince and father fig-ure. Yet his motives were not simple self-aggrandizement. By offering rather single-handedly to fill the lacunae in the Paris Agreements he was acting as the prince, but in so doing he may have weakened the respect ac-corded to UNTAC by lesser political operatives.

In 1997 his reaction to the Hun Sen coup was classic ambiguity, with cautious absence of condemnation but no official approval. He remained a potential arbiter in the struggle for legitimacy, in a fashion that no other player could match. Yet even a royal figure held in reverence and well prac-ticed in the politics of delay and ambiguity could only hope personally to momentarily deflect the course of Hun Sen's ambition. A constitutional chief of state suffused with royal reverence might slow the abuse of demo-cratic practices, but King Sihanouk himself showed no illusions about mili-tary power being the final arbiter.

In the matter of personal style, we have seen Sihanouk faulted as a volatile, self-serving, absentee monarch, who intervened by fax and suf-fered prolonged political illnesses. However, as an astute Cambodian intel-lectual critic put it in 1996, "When the two parties don't get along, we have depended upon a policy of national reconciliation. Our king has been seen as the incarnation of that policy, which has become a creed."[31] Without the king to resolve sensitive disputes, the observer thought there would be dan-ger of political polarization. A coup d'état would be possible, with the mili-tary playing a dominant role.

Failed or crumbling states cannot be expected to have a Sihanouk equiv-alent and are the less stable for it. For all his absenteeism and his swings of political mood, Sihanouk provided a respected royal personality who sym-

---

31. Interview in Phnom Penh by J. J. Zasloff, May 1996.

bolized and nurtured the national idea. Notwithstanding his disagreements with UNTAC and its policy makers, and with the Vietnamese, and his inconstant support of his political heir, Ranariddh, he worked for the reconciliation of his sorely rent nation and for political compromise. The risks of compromise may have proved to be too challenging, however, for such an inexperienced and reluctant leader as Ranariddh, despite the honest intentions of a mercurial king.

Like its neighbor Thailand, whose King Bhumibol Adulyadej celebrated his fiftieth year on the throne in 1996, Cambodia's polity is suited for constitutional royal rule. The Thai king's moral authority has provided Thailand a steady, continuous, and understandable source of authority during a period of rapid economic and social change. For Cambodia, the monarchy provides a link from the past to the tumultuous present, helping the nation psychologically to cope with disturbing forces of change. A danger of this symbolic royalist function, however, is that dependence on the dominant personality of King Sihanouk has inhibited the development of effective political institutions.

When King Sihanouk departs, Cambodia will face a very serious challenge. Despite his ambiguous legacy, he has played a dominant role in the country's contemporary history since 1941 and has provided a critical sense of continuity to the new state. Since the constitution requires that the royal successor must come from one of the three historic royal families, and none of those interested and eligible, up to the present, appear acceptable to the key political parties, it is possible to foresee a constitutional impasse. No individual on the political horizon possesses stature approaching the current king's, and the monarchy might even give way to a republic, as Sihanouk sometimes lamented during periods of depression. Even if the monarchy survives his departure—a condition that is not assured under Hun Sen's leadership—a new monarch will not be endowed with his grandeur and influence. The newly developing political institutions will be sorely challenged to replace the compromising functions he has performed.

Democratic Practice and Human Rights

The early record of the royal Cambodian government in protecting human-rights and democratic practice raised serious concern. The respected international human rights organization Amnesty International concluded that

> 1995 saw a steady deterioration in the human rights situation in Cambodia; political violence returned to the capital Phnom Penh, prisoners of conscience were detained in the country's prisons and newspaper editors were put on trial

for expressing their opinions, as the attitude of the Royal Government of Cambodia to political opponents became increasingly intolerant. Prominent government critics were threatened and intimidated. . . . Members of the armed forces and police committed human rights violations with impunity, and those responsible for past violations were not brought to justice. . . . The climate in which opposition politicians, journalists, newspaper editors and human rights workers must operate is increasingly harsh, and the political space afforded them by the Royal Government has narrowed significantly since the elections in 1993.[32]

There were a few encouraging signs from 1993 through 1995 to complement the sordid picture painted above. The UN Center for Human Rights continued to operate in Cambodia, after protests by the foreign diplomatic community and Khmer NGOs against its proposed expulsion. The government did sponsor some training in human rights standards for police and military personnel. As for freedom of the press, despite violence, intimidation, and even the murder of critical journalists, there were some fifty newspapers appearing in Phnom Penh in 1995, many of them independent. One editor, whose newspaper had been threatened by government authorities for publishing critical articles, noted that the press in Phnom Penh was more critical of the government than the press in Singapore, Kuala Lumpur, or Jakarta.[33]

It has been argued that the democratic standards for Cambodia, insisted on by the Western diplomatic community, were inappropriate for reconstructing a failed Asian state. A distinguished Southeast Asian diplomat serving in Cambodia advanced the premise that Western embassies were unrealistic in pressing Cambodia to reach a multiparty democracy. (The Cambodian constitution, he asserted, is "pie in the sky.")[34] This Western brand of democracy was not suitable for Cambodia, he argued. Westerners were too prone to criticize Cambodia (and other Southeast Asian nations) for abridging freedom of the press and abusing human rights. In an argument reminiscent of that of Lee Kuan Yew, the preeminent leader of Singapore, he stated that donors should understand the Asian approach to these issues, which is less concerned with individual rights and gives greater emphasis to economic development. Happiness is expanded when people have more to eat, more telephones for talking with their friends, better roads to

32. Amnesty International, "Kingdom of Cambodia: Diminishing Respect for Human Rights," May 1996, AI Index: ASA 23/02/96, p. 1.

33. Interview in Phnom Penh by J. J. Zasloff, May 1996.

34. These views were expressed to J. J. Zasloff in interviews in Phnom Penh, May 1996.

move about more freely, new schools for their children. These are more important, he pronounced, than radio time for Sam Rainsy.

On the other hand, democratic values are not the exclusive property of the West; indeed one might argue that it is demeaning to Asian, African, and Latin American nations to suggest that they are not "ready for democracy." It is, of course, reasonable to judge the government's application of democratic procedures and human rights in the Cambodian context. It was indeed unrealistic to expect a Denmark or Netherlands to emerge, full-blown, from the first years of a new state. But serious human rights abuses should not be condoned nor odious corruption tolerated on the grounds that Cambodia has faced tragic circumstances. Indeed, public opinion in Western democracies will not long tolerate the granting of assistance to abusive, corrupt governments.

Attitudes toward the Vietnamese

The Cambodian animus toward the Vietnamese is not found simply among party leaders. This deeply held antipathy transcends ideology and is embraced by Cambodian liberals and conservatives, royalists and communists alike. The authors have been struck by the passionate attitudes about the Vietnamese expressed by Cambodian intellectuals. Even those who share Western values regarding human rights and equal treatment of minorities seem to have a blind spot regarding the Vietnamese. They appear to have internalized a persistent anxiety that Vietnam threatens the very survival of Cambodia. They tend to see members of the ethnic Vietnamese minority in Cambodia as agents of a rapacious enemy, capable of wily dissimulation and subterfuge.

Antipathy toward theVietnamese has its source, in part, in the history of Cambodia's relations with Vietnam. Cambodians appear to internalize, with their mothers' milk, the story of the Vietnamese expansion during the seventeenth and eighteenth centuries into present-day southern Vietnam at the expense of the Khmer Empire, which stretched to the South China Sea. The Khmer regard the Vietnamese as "earth-swallowers," still intent on absorbing the remaining Cambodian territory. They are aware that Vietnamese immigration into their country expanded during French colonial rule, and they tended to regard the Vietnamese as agents of the colonial power. As a predominantly peasant society, Cambodians have looked upon the Vietnamese urban commercial class with suspicion and mistrust.

The tragedies that have befallen Cambodia in the past quarter century may have stirred even deeper dread about the society's future and the nation's survival. An insightful cultural analysis of the Cambodian preoccupation with the "Vietnamese problem" is offered by a former UN human rights officer:

> The social bonds uniting people, the willingness of individuals to make sacri-
> fices for the good of the country, and the spirit uniting the nation all seemed to
> be casualties of a national Post Traumatic Stress Disorder. Corruption by all
> factions was spinning the country off into environmental, economic, and polit-
> ical ruin. As conceptions of nationhood slipped away, Cambodians seemed to
> grab on to whatever they could find by which to define themselves as a nation.
> For many, hatred of the Vietnamese, the historical enemy perceived responsi-
> ble for the long decline in Cambodian power and prestige, filled this function.
> Hatred was not merely the residue of prejudice; it seemed a defining element
> of Cambodian identity.[35]

Cambodian politicians have lavishly tapped into the national animosity toward Vietnam for partisan benefit, thus keeping alive the popular preju-dice. Political groups have vied to outscore their competitors with inflam-matory anti-Vietnamese rhetoric. The Khmer Rouge have led the way in indoctrinating their cadres and propagating the notion that Vietnam contin-ues to dominate the new state.[36] FUNCINPEC and the KPNLF have fol-lowed close behind the Khmer Rouge in vituperative denunciation of Vietnam. More recently, Sam Rainsy's KNP joined the anti-Vietnam clamor.[37] Party spokesmen have used certain critical issues in relations be-tween Cambodia and Vietnam, particularly border disputes and illegal im-migration, to arouse chauvinist passions with their claims to be the defenders of the Cambodian patrimony against Vietnamese aggression or subversion. The CPP suffered from a liability in this contest, since it owes its origins to Vietnam's intervention on its behalf. The CPP's political oppo-nents targeted this liability, thereby challenging the very legitimacy of the CPP as a nationalist party. CPP leaders often responded defiantly—and

35. Jamie F. Metzl, "The Vietnamese of Cambodia," *Harvard Human Rights Journal,* 8 (Spring 1995), 275. For a study by the same author of Western responses to human rights vio-lations during the Khmer Rouge period, see *Western Responses to Human Rights Abuses in Cambodia, 1975–1980* (New York: St. Martin's Press, 1996).

36. When a Khmer Rouge officer, associated with Ieng Sary, who was negotiating the de-fection of his unit with RCAF officers was asked if he believed the Vietnamese still controlled the Cambodian government, he snorted, "Of course." Seth Mydans, "Split Puts Khmer Rouge Faction in Mood to Deal with Old Foes," *New York Times,* Aug. 19, 1996.

37. A Western political observer who has closely followed Sam Rainsy's efforts to build the KNP—and is generally an admirer of Rainsy's intelligence, skills, and goals—expressed dis-may at Rainsy's fiery anti-Vietnamese rhetoric during political speeches to recruit members for his KNP. Rainsy's inflammatory words appeared designed to arouse chauvinist passions in his Khmer audience. Interview by J. J. Zasloff in Phnom Penh, May 1996.

with good reason—that it was Vietnamese intervention that liberated the country from Pol Pot's tyrannous rule. This issue again aroused divisive passions when Hun Sen declared January 7 a national holiday, commemorating the date in 1979 when the Vietnamese "liberated" (others say "invaded") Cambodia.

It is difficult to determine the implications of this scapegoating of Vietnam. The anti-Vietnamese rancor appears to be the centerpiece of a larger xenophobia which inheres in many Khmer. Cambodians have a tendency— not unique to them—to look for outsiders on whom to blame their troubles or vent their anger. Besides slamming Vietnam, demagogues denounce other targets for political profit—the big powers, "imperialists," the UN, intrusive donors. The greater the malaise in the country, the greater is the use of these demagogic devices.

UNTAC, as we have seen, was constantly confronted with assertions, which they were powerless to disprove, that a Vietnamese military presence continued in Cambodia. The issue continued to corrode the legitimacy of the government and poison the climate of the political process.

Steady economic, social, and political development might normally offer hope and security to Cambodians, and the mischievous effects of this xenophobia may diminish. The donor community might use its influence to help provide realistic assessments of Vietnamese and other foreign intervention and to discourage inflammatory rhetoric and demagogic politics.

The Khmer Rouge

The Khmer Rouge insurgents once posed the most serious threat to the new state. The provisions in the Paris Agreements for Khmer Rouge participation in the UNTAC election had not been adhered to, nor were the prospects for reconciliation of the Khmer Rouge with mainstream Cambodian society at all promising. The Khmer Rouge seemed in 1993 to remain politically and militarily intact, in control of a segment of the population and territory, and enjoying a brisk commercial trade in gems and timber with Thailand that provided necessary funds to sustain their challenge. Some feared that a weak, fragmented, quarrelsome, corrupt coalition government with a bloated, undisciplined, inept army might, in time, fall to what appeared to be a cohesive, fervent revolutionary organization.

In the early months of the new state, King Sihanouk's peace initiative, accepted by First Prime Minister Ranariddh and reluctantly acceded to by Second Prime Minister Hun Sen, failed. The Khmer Rouge were distrustful of the new rulers and were unwilling to trade "autonomy" in their region for an uncertain share of power in Phnom Penh. Yet a few leaders on the government side, including King Sihanouk, continued to believe that reconciliation with the Khmer Rouge was possible. Some contended that significant elements in the Khmer Rouge were tired of fighting, discouraged by the lack of foreign support, and wanted to come out of the jungle and find opportunities to educate their children.[38]

The government's major military offensive against Khmer Rouge strongholds in western Cambodia in spring 1994 was a miserable failure, leaving a strong impression that the royal government's incompetent army was unlikely to be the principal instrument of defeat of the Khmer Rouge threat. A turning point in the struggle against the Khmer Rouge seemed to come following the legislation, adopted in July 1994, outlawing the revolutionary organization. The government's seizure of Khmer Rouge assets, the restriction of travel by Khmer Rouge officials, the diminution of support from Thailand, all promised by supporters of the law in the National Assembly debate, may have played a role in the weakening of the Khmer Rouge. Whatever the source of this diminished strength, defections started mounting in 1994.

The question of whether other Khmer Rouge leaders should be pursued for trial as war criminals was quite uncertain.[39] Pol Pot was given a brief show trial by former supporters at his base at Anlong Veng in July 25, 1997, but real international trials appeared unlikely, notwithstanding the extensive gathering of evidence by the U.S.-subsidized Cambodian Genocide Project under Ben Kiernan at Yale University.

The important Khmer Rouge defections starting in August 1996 added to the serious erosion of the revolutionary organization that was already far advanced. It was possible that the remaining Khmer Rouge (rump) organization would prove difficult for the sloppy Royal Cambodian Armed Forces to wipe out but in any case it no longer represented a credible threat to overthrow the government. Cambodia now confronted more serious threats. These included the combined impact of rising crime and common thuggery, pernicious corruption, a disorganized, bloated, top-heavy military still capable of political mischief, and a severely divided leadership.

The demise of the Khmer Rouge is an achievement that can be credited, in important measure, to the Paris Agreements and the UNTAC intervention. The process of negotiating the Paris Agreements induced the Khmer Rouge, under China's pressure, to sign the settlement and cease, if only temporarily, their guerrilla activity. When the Khmer Rouge withdrew from

38. These views were expressed to J. J. Zasloff in interviews in Phnom Penh, May 1996.
39. For news reports concerning the defections of Ieng Sary and the KR troops associated with him, see Chapter 8, note 64.

the electoral process and UNTAC continued the election without them, their legitimacy within Cambodia as well as in the international community further declined. The newly elected government was fully legitimized by the election and retained significant international sympathy and support. Those who had predicted that the Khmer Rouge would be legitimized and strengthened by their inclusion in the Paris Agreements proved to be wrong. In fact, the Khmer Rouge marginalized themselves by agreeing to the UNTAC intervention and then repudiating it, but without precluding the holding of a legitimizing election.

While the Khmer Rouge could not be defeated militarily by the RCAF, they nevertheless withered on the vine. Their supply of arms from China was severely cut back. Many of their soldiers grew tired of living in the jungle and wished to stop the fighting. Thus, the persistence of UNTAC in conducting the election and helping to reconstruct the failed state, despite Khmer Rouge obstruction, paid off handsomely.

For the UNTAC effort to be acclaimed even a "limited" success, the new state would have had to demonstrate that it has reasonably fulfilled the democratic aspirations embodied in the Paris Agreements. The international endeavor to save Cambodia quite clearly left an impact, in many respects unprecedented, and inspired hope during the first four years that it might reach many of its goals. The estimated cost of the UN presence, not including the voluntary economic rehabilitation assistance, was $1.876 million, but the final bill greatly exceeded this.[40] An election was conducted (which could be labeled "semi-free and fair"), a constitution was promulgated, a coalition government was established in theory and in working (if not incorruptible) order, refugees and displaced persans were repatriated, protection of human rights was put on the national agenda, and economic rehabilitation was initiated with foreign assistance. To be sure, military demobilization was not achieved among the DK and SOC forces, and UN personnel behavior was not always exemplary toward Cambodians, nor was it uniform in quality; and preelection violence, intimidation of the press, and arbitrary law enforcement swirled through the body politic. Economic management was corrupted from the very top down. The constitutional timetable for local and national elections gave some promise of being observed, and the idea of international observers was opened for debate.

The negotiating parties who fashioned the Paris accords of 1991, by their creative and generous efforts, set an example that neighbors, mentors, and

40. Addendum, Annex 1, UNTAC Provisional estimates of financial implications, Report of the Secretary-General on Cambodia . . . implementation plan for UNTAC, S/23613, Feb. 19, 1992, Doc. 30, *The United Nations in Cambodia, 1991–1995.*

the United Nations should be willing to consider again, where contending parties in a "failed state" are willing to work with a UN peacekeeping and peace-building operation. UNTAC put Cambodia on its feet and pointed it in the direction of "liberal democracy," at a cost of approaching $3 billion. Given the obstacles to lasting national salvation, UNTAC's achievements, notwithstanding the coup d'état perpetrated by Hun Sen in 1997, deserve to be recognized, refined, and under the right circumstances even tried again. Without genuine commitment by the political factions to abide by election results, as in Nicaragua, the peacekeepers and peacemakers will probably encounter disabling shortfalls such as those the international community experienced in its insufficient effort in Cambodia. The cost will not dimish, but the outcome can be improved.

UNTAC revealed how complicated and prolonged the negotiation of a comprehensive political settlement can be, as well as how fragile the resulting alignment of forces may be after the peacemakers depart. Cambodia confounded the aspirations and generosity of a host of nations and international organizations. Not only peace but also "liberal democracy" were put at stake, exposed to the hazards of single-minded leaders and movements which lacked a civil society of political associations and traditions to temper the ever present forces of ambition and greed. However disappointing the legacy of UNTAC may be in the five years since its departure, it is worth remembering that civil war is no longer fed by Cambodia's neighbors, and the Khmer Rouge has split apart, and human rights and constitutional procedure serve to shape much of the nation's political debate, if not its practice. The transformation of Cambodia to constitutional democracy could not be achieved in five years, but the failed state that it once was no longer exists to stunt the lives of its people. The democratic state that it may become will arrive the sooner because of UNTAC than otherwise could have been hoped for. The international effort was probably over-ambitious, but its basic decency of purpose and effort deserves recognition, and even reuse after acknowledgment of its shortfalls.

Epilogue

As the UNTAC-generated government of Cambodia broke apart in 1997, the constitution, particularly its requirement of a parliamentary election every five years, became a crucial instrument for the conduct of politics. Hun Sen, for all his ruthless ousting from office of Prince Ranariddh and his party followers, did not uproot this basic document, inspired in 1993 by UNTAC with the approval of Sihanouk. Staying on as Second Prime Minister and engineering a replacement First Prime Minister, Hun Sen accepted the constitutional obligation to put his purge-based regime to the test of a "free and fair, universal, equal, direct and secret ballot" in 1998.

Even though our manuscript was completed by the end of 1997, we delayed publication in order to encompass this critical election, the first since UNTAC was established. This delay permitted us to volunteer as official observers of the July 26 election with the team organized jointly by the National Democratic Institute and the International Republican Institute (NDI/IRI), research and training agencies that foster democratic institutions worldwide. We benefited greatly from this opportunity to see the election at the polling station level.

How did this second election in 1998 compare with the first in 1993? Obviously, there were no UN military and civil police to maintain security and law and order, nor was the government subject to international supervision or control. The Khmer Rouge were no longer a serious military threat. Three major parties contested the election, rather than two. Displaced persons along the border with Thailand did not constitute a major problem, as in 1993. Regrettably the government tightly limited the use of radio and television by opposition parties, and it faced no competition from a UN station, as it had in 1993.

More than 500 international election observers were recruited to serve in a Joint International Observer Group (JIOG), mostly from the European Union, with others from the Association of Southeast Asian Nations (ASEAN) and worldwide non-governmental organizations (NGOs). Equipment such as metal ballot boxes, plastic bags, cards, and voter booths was needed, along with training of local election personnel and observers. These volunteers were welcomed and respected, but this time the Cambodian government, not the United Nations, was in charge of the election. Was it sufficient to the task?

Feasibility of an Election

Why, one might ask, did Hun Sen agree to hold an election? A number of reasons appear plausible. Hun Sen was careful to abide, at least formally, by the letter of the newly promulgated constitution. After ousting First Prime Minister Ranariddh in July 1997 and hounding key FUNCINPEC political and military leaders into exile or hiding, in August Hun Sen maneuvered the appointment of a renegade FUNCINPEC member of the Assembly, Ung Huot, as First Prime Minister, thus retaining the façade of the constitutional bargain struck following the 1993 elections. Hun Sen contended that there had been no coup d'etat in July 1997. Ranariddh had broken the law in dealing in arms and military forces with the Khmer Rouge, and he would have to be judged by a court. The rule of law must be maintained, Hun Sen postured. Underlying his formalistic pursuit of democratic principles was his desire to avoid pariah status in the international community, which imposed sanctions upon Cambodia following Hun Sen's seizure of power.

The UN General Assembly refused to accept the reconstituted government as representing Cambodia at the United Nations.[1] ASEAN, despite admitting Laos and Myanmar (Burma)—hardly paragons of democracy—postponed its admission of the sole remaining Southeast Asian nonmember. Instead, ASEAN appointed a "troika" of the foreign ministers of

1. At the UN General Assembly Hun Sen's government failed to match the busy lobbying efforts of skillful American political operatives who overcame the early defeatism of Ranariddh's delegation and depicted the rival Hun Sen delegation as too blood-stained to replace the delegation led by the exiled prince. This public relations triumph and rejuvenation of the unhappy Ranariddh was described to the authors by one of its participants, an intriguing case of UN corridor politics.

Thailand, Indonesia, and the Philippines to mediate the conflict between Hun Sen and Prince Ranariddh, a maneuver that Hun Sen regarded as insulting. Various nations and international organizations halted or diminished their economic assistance, on which Cambodia was dependent for more than half its annual expenditures. The United States, for example, limited its assistance to humanitarian grants to NGOs.

An important endorsement of the proposed election by the international community came with Japan's taking the diplomatic initiative for the Friends of Cambodia, the successor group to the Perm 5, which included the United States, the European Community, Russia, China, Canada, Australia, and Japan. This group of nations interested in Cambodia's stability and development had coalesced following the July 1997 coup and made persistent efforts to guarantee a 1998 election. The Japanese formula for clearing a path was first floated in October 1997:

1. Prince Ranariddh would be tried in a Cambodian court *in absentia* for his alleged crimes.
2. Following the court's verdict, Hun Sen would request a pardon for Prince Ranariddh from King Sihanouk. (Sihanouk had announced that he would not grant a pardon without a formal request from Hun Sen.)
3. A cease-fire between FUNCINPEC and CPP forces would be consummated and FUNCINPEC military forces would be integrated into the Royal Cambodian Armed Forces (RCAF).
4. An election, in compliance with the constitution, would be scheduled, and Prince Ranariddh would be permitted to return to compete in it.

This arrangement was largely implemented (with the exception of the military clause). Ranariddh was convicted after two brief trials *in absentia*, sentenced to 30 years of imprisonment, and fined $54 million. The King, at the written request of the co-Prime Ministers on March 20, 1998, granted him a pardon, absolving him of the fine and prison term and making possible his return to Cambodia.

Thus, once again members of the international community helped provide a pathway to open Cambodia's deadlocked politics. Of course, Hun Sen did not transform himself into a model democrat with this compromise. He had reason to believe that he would triumph in the election. The CPP controlled the military, the police, the bureaucracy, and the judiciary. They dominated the media. They had smashed much of their opponents' political apparatus, decimated party lists, ruined office equipment, and expelled (or eliminated) party cadres in the days following the July 1997 seizure of power. Their thugs had spread intimidation among their rivals with some sixty "extra-judicial killings" (according to the UN Special Representative for Human Rights) during the coup, and another forty, including several opposition editors and journalists, in the subsequent period leading up to the election. Hun Sen could feel sufficiently assured of an electoral victory to risk what would appear to be a "free and fair" election, in order to win legitimacy in the international community.

Reception of the Election Proposal

Members of the opposition, particularly those who had fled into exile, were initially suspicious of the invitation to return to Cambodia. They feared a trap. Sam Rainsy was among the first to go back, returning to Phnom Penh in late November 1997, showing his daring and courage. He had a three-hour meeting with Hun Sen on December 8, and emerged smiling for the photographers, suggesting his willingness to make deals with the incumbent strongman. Other opposition assemblymen began their return from Thailand and elsewhere in early 1998, without encountering violence. Prince Ranariddh landed at Phnom Penh's airport in late March 1998, to be greeted by a cheering crowd of supporters, estimated at 10,000, even though his impending arrival was ignored in the government-controlled media.[2]

Opposition leaders publicly expressed doubt that credible elections could be conducted under Hun Sen's reign of fear. Sam Rainsy and Ranariddh threatened a boycott of the election, and called for a delay. But as Hun Sen persisted in scheduling an election, finally settling on July 26, 1998, the opposition leaders had to accept the challenge to compete. If they refused, they risked losing any chance for acquiring a share in power.

Among the Friends of Cambodia most active in the Cambodia arena, the U.S. Department of State remained skeptical that elections under Hun Sen's aegis could be "free, fair and credible." Some U.S. voices called for a postponement of the election, arguing that the opposition needed more preparation time. Opponents of delay, on the other hand, contended that little would change with Hun Sen in control, that the National Assembly's term of office would expire in September, and that a prompt election would be desirable.

The U.S. government decided, with a certain public reluctance, to offer

2. When queried by interviewers with the NDI/IRI team in July 1998 as to why the government-controlled TV did not televise this apparently newsworthy event, Hor Nam Hong, a high-level CPP party leader, lamely explained that Ranariddh was not the First Prime Minister but simply a National Assembly candidate, and government television personnel were prohibited from granting him special coverage.

limited support to the July 26 election effort. The sum of $2.3 million was pledged (after an earlier promise of $7 million), earmarked for international and Cambodian NGO election observers, voter education, and the UN electoral secretariat. Provisions were made to support some 50 to 75 U.S.-recruited election observers. The U.S. contribution to the election effort was substantially inferior to that of the European Union (EU), Japan, Canada, and Australia, which provided more than $20 million. Following an offer by Secretary General Kofi Annan to assist the election, the UN accepted the Cambodian government's invitation to coordinate (not manage, as in 1993) the international role. The Joint International Observation Group (JIOG) was formed, consisting largely of EU-recruited observers, with a Swedish diplomat serving as its spokesperson. Some 25 American "long-term" observers, recruited in Cambodia by the Asia Foundation, participated in the JIOG effort. A 35-member team recruited by NDI/IRI operated separately from the JIOG, and issued an independent report at the conclusion of the election.

The intervention of the UN, the Friends of Cambodia, and ASEAN in the Cambodian election reflected several interests. A large investment of energy and resources had been committed to achieve the Paris Agreements and the UNTAC-sponsored election, which followed them. There was disappointment among Cambodia's friends and neighbors that the 1993 settlement had disintegrated with the events of July 1997. Other countries in Southeast Asia, more important in size and influence than Cambodia, were now experiencing severe economic stress and demanding the attention of affluent nations. Cambodia was no longer entangled in the once compelling Cold War. Thus, Cambodia's claims for help were growing less urgent. But the UNTAC effort had accumulated sizeable "sunk costs," and the key international actors were not yet ready to abandon their endeavor to achieve a measure of stability in Cambodia.

The ASEAN nations were also prepared to endorse the proposed Cambodian election. The ASEAN troika's effort to mediate Hun Sen's conflict with Ranariddh had met Hun Sen's blunt rebuff. Offended by ASEAN's intrusion, Hun Sen pointedly told the ASEAN delegation to stay out of Cambodia's affairs.[3]

As the election period approached, it began to appear to the Cambodian participants, as well as international analysts, that the outcome was not a foregone conclusion. Despite the earlier abuses perpetrated by the CPP

---

3. Hun Sen, in an early meeting with the ASEAN delegation, told them testily that Cambodia had survived for centuries without membership in ASEAN. An ASEAN diplomat who had accompanied the troika in their meetings with Hun Sen told the authors that the ASEAN ambassadors noted that ASEAN had survived for thirty years without Cambodia.

regime, and the significant advantages of incumbency that it enjoyed, the opposition appeared to have a chance to share power if the campaign and election process were "free and fair." The constitutional requirement that a two-thirds vote in the National Assembly must authorize a government made it likely that the opposition would participate in forming the government, even if it did not emerge with a majority.

The Election

The pre-campaign period formally opened in April, with the exercise of voter registration (until June 15). Following in the footsteps of their UNTAC predecessors, who registered 97 percent of the eligible voters, the 1998 registration succeeded in registering the same remarkable 97 percent of the eligible voters.

However, as the campaign opened June 25, following the registration period, CPP attempts at voter manipulation were revealed. For example, the CPP conducted a widespread campaign in the countryside to recruit party members, taking thumbprints as a mark of membership. CPP cadres floated the proposition that membership in the party, signified by the thumbprint, required the member to vote for the CPP. Deviation from this requirement, it was asserted, would bring serious punishment. Still other assertions were that jobs controlled by the CPP would be endangered for families who did not vote correctly.

Despite these intimidating rumors, the campaign gained intensity as the candidates held rallies in their constituencies, and the leaders moved about the country. Enthusiastic crowds appeared at party meetings, including those of the opposition. At a Sam Rainsy Party rally in Phnom Penh attended by the authors and several thousand ardent supporters a week before the election, Sam Rainsy denounced the corruption and repression of the incumbent regime and promised wholesale change, to the delight of the crowd. We were spectators at a FUNCINPEC march, replete with sloganed banners and flags with party emblems, and watched a drive-by of colorful CPP trucks filled with laughing youth waving party pennants. Prior to an interview with the leaders of a small party, we observed a picturesque medley of costumed, traditional dances by the children of the party's supporters, which onlookers found engaging. The campaign mood, as most observers reported, was festive.

Parties were allocated only five minutes daily on government television. Critics charged that this limited availability of time for the parties favored the CPP, whose administrative allies controlled the balance of the programming. Nevertheless, in view of the profusion of banners and rallies, it would have been difficult for most of the population to be unaware of the election.

The vote on Sunday, July 26, appeared to proceed in an orderly, effective manner throughout most of the country. International observers (as reported by JIOG and NDI/IRI) were nearly unanimous in their judgment that local polling officials were conscientious, well-prepared by training and often by experience in the 1993 election, and in control of their tasks. They appeared to be respectful of the rules, insistent upon their own neutrality, and vowed devotion—often ritualistically—to a "free and fair" election. We found the officials invariably courteous toward international observers, willing to answer questions and provide explanations. They were welcoming and respectful, without seeming either haughty or obsequious. We were aware that most of the polling officials were CPP appointees, and they had reason to be suspicious of observers from the United States, which had a public record of criticism of the CPP. Nevertheless, they were polite and cooperative.

More important, polling officials were respectful and helpful to the voters. If there was a widespread fault, it was the failure at many stations to manage early morning crowds pressing at the entry point. The crowds lacked discipline—queueing up in orderly fashion is an alien concept in Cambodia—and only a minority of the polling chiefs developed a system of distributing numbers to regulate access. In other respects, however, administrators appeared competent in the conduct of their duties.

Except for those who were hassled by the early crowd, most voters were in a festive mood, proud to be casting a ballot in what was trumpeted as a "free and fair" election. Only a very few would disclose for whom they were voting. They jealously insisted that the vote was secret. Some voters went so far as to say that they were "voting for the King," a vote undoubtedly destined for FUNCINPEC, the royal party. Peasant women, asked by women observers if they would vote as their husbands instructed, responded with giggles and guffaws, accompanied by mirthful insistence that the vote was secret. The voters' comportment conveyed, along with its joy, a sense of seriousness and self-respect, giving the lie to pronouncements that simple peasants care little about the democratic process.

Notwithstanding the mounting claims by Sam Rainsy and Ranariddh of election irregularities—which held up the formation of a new government in August—the authors felt no doubt about the business-like, hospitable atmosphere that they witnessed in the polling stations (usually school rooms or pagodas) which they and their observer cohorts from dozens of countries visited. If fraud was afoot, they saw no evidence of it, and if violators of the rules were about, there was no visual sign of their furtiveness, or anxiety, or animosities toward voting officials. Villagers showed respect for expectant mothers, the aged, and the physically handicapped. Questions raised by local party observers were treated seriously and respectfully. Team after team of observers from the NDI/IRI operation reported on July 27 that a technically clean election had occurred in the stations they visited. Later countervoices recalled pre-election political intimidation, which seemed to resume in a post-election phase, and irregularities in ballot counting and storage were alleged.

As in the 1993 election, the turnout in 1998 was remarkably high. The 93 percent turnout surpassed the 89.56% percent turnout of 1993. International observers were impressed by the ready knowledge of polling officials about those who had not voted. Some cited names of people who were ill, or who had died since the registration period, or were incapacitated and could not appear. One might wonder if this official scrutiny was evidence of intimidation, specifically pressure to vote CPP. But the voters' happy demeanor left the impression with most observers that people were proud and pleased with the opportunity to vote, and that they were willingly casting their ballots.

Virtually all observers of the election saw it to be well organized and competently administered. Some noted occasional infractions of the rules and minor irregularities, but only a few, to our knowledge, cited incidents of major violations or significant evidence of fraud. It seemed that whatever violations might have occurred did not significantly affect the results. The JIOG reported that the election was "free and fair to an extent that enables it to reflect, in a credible way, the will of the Cambodian people." The NDI/IRI statement noted that the pre-election period had been characterized by fundamental flaws, including violence, intimidation, unfair media access, and ruling party control of the administrative machinery. But they noted that the voting on polling day went remarkably smoothly, the participation of more than 90 percent of the eligible voters was impressive, and that the election was "a successful exercise in self-determination." Indeed former Congressman Stephen J. Solarz, co-chairman of the NDI/IRI team, announced that the election had the potential for being considered a "miracle on the Mekong." Another NGO observer group composed of North Americans, Australians, and New Zealanders, led by former Australian Ambassador to Cambodia Tony Kevin, stated that the election was conducted "freely and fairly" and was an "authentic expression of the Cambodian people's choice."

It is impossible to determine what effect pre-election intimidation had on voting behavior. Some voters may have voted CPP out of fear. On the other hand, intimidation may have aroused a backlash among others, producing a vote against the CPP. During the campaign period, and clearly on voting day, opposition supporters revealed themselves. Thousands of voters turned out for the FUNCINPEC and Sam Rainsy Party rallies. On election day opposition party agents were present as observers at almost all polling stations, displaying their party affiliations on chest badges. Opposition party leaders campaigned as if they had a chance to win. Even seasoned analysts were unable to predict the outcome prior to the ballot counting.

International observers were also impressed by the efficiency and transparency of the counting that they witnessed on July 27. Despite later protests by the losing parties about irregularities in the counting process, these were not judged to be serious in early observer reports.

The Election Outcome

Preliminary results (released by the National Election Committee on August 5) showed that of 4.9 million ballots cast, 41.4 percent voted for CPP, 31.7 percent for FUNCINPEC, and 14.3 percent for the Sam Rainsy Party. The remaining 12.6 percent of the votes were scattered among 36 minor parties, none of which secured sufficient votes to win a seat in the National Assembly. The CPP was projected to win 64 seats, FUNCINPEC 43, and the Sam Rainsy Party 15.

Without the benefit of systematic polling data, we can provide only informed assumptions as to why the voters voted as they did.

The CPP Vote

The CPP had the advantage of incumbency. It dominated the bureaucracy, the military, the police, and the judiciary. It was the only party to possess an organized national network. The families of many voters were dependent on the CPP for jobs and security. A myriad of schools to which he had directed resources were named for Hun Sen. He promoted a variety of roadbuilding, well digging, and housing projects. Hun Sen did not appear to be personally popular. Indeed, some analysts believe that he adopted a low profile late in the campaign (even before his emergency appendectomy) upon advice from counselors worried about his heavy-handedness. Yet, many regarded him as an effective manager, especially when compared to the alternative choices. The CPP had more money and resources to spend on their campaign than their opponents. They were more lavish with their gifts, which included the payment of cash, the distribution of T-shirts and caps, food products and spices. The CPP enjoyed a propaganda advantage with its pre-election domination of TV and radio. And, as noted above, some people may have voted CPP out of fear. Some, too, may have voted for stability, believing that the CPP would seize power if they did not win the election.

The FUNCINPEC Vote

FUNCINPEC's primary appeal was its association with the monarchy, still a revered institution among the Cambodian peasantry. Prince Ranariddh was the beneficiary of this royalist support. His return to Cambodia gave assurance—in the minds of many voters—that the monarchy would continue. His reappearance was inspiring, representing a vindication of his right to rule.

In addition to benefiting from the aura of the royal presence, FUNCINPEC, as in 1993, must have also profited from negative sentiments against the CPP, seen by many as the controlling, corrupt, oppressive incumbent. However, in view of FUNCINPEC's own shoddy record of administration prior to Hun Sen's coup, this negative factor may have carried less weight than it did in the 1993 election. Sam Rainsy, the new political force on the election scene, must have drained off a segment of this sentiment. FUNCINPEC played upon Cambodians' deep suspicion of Vietnam during the campaign, in a manner the CPP could not, in view of its historical dependence on Vietnam. This strategy may have attracted votes as FUNCINPEC hammered on the dual themes of defending the Cambodian border with Vietnam and curbing Vietnamese immigration into Cambodia.

The Sam Rainsy Party Vote

Sam Rainsy profited from the anti-incumbency sentiment. Throughout his campaign, indeed throughout his career with the post-UNTAC government, he had sounded the alarm against government corruption, targeting both Hun Sen and Ranariddh. For this reason he lost his post as Finance Minister and National Assembly member. His defiance of the corrupt power-wielders attracted support, and he was widely admired for his personal courage. He organized a Khmer Nation Party (later the Sam Rainsy Party), and he was the first of the oppositionists to return, in November 1997, braving the wrath of possible CPP enforcers and organizing several public marches. He survived a grenade attack against one of his rallies, in March 1997, when 16 of his supporters were killed and many more were wounded. Sam Rainsy's intelligence, superior education, and independence were qualities that brought him support, particularly in Phnom Penh and other urban communities. He developed a populist manner, obviously enjoying the chanting urban crowds and haranguing his opponents in firebrand style.

Sam Rainsy's detractors labeled him "extremist" and charged that he was frequently carried away by his own rhetoric. He was particularly virulent on the Vietnamese issue. Some international observers thought him chauvinist, even racist, in denouncing Vietnamese immigrants and Vietnam's threat to Cambodia's border.

It is early to assess the impact of Rainsy's new party on the political scene. It is already clear that, in terms of the popular vote, he has divided the opposition. The Sam Rainsy Party vote of 14.3 percent, added to FUNCINPEC's 31.7 percent, totals 46 percent, as compared with the 41.4 percent for the CPP. Despite the use of proportional representation, the mathematics of the electoral system produced a majority of seats for the CPP.

The Smaller Parties

Unlike the outcome in 1993 when the smaller parties won 16.3 percent of the popular vote and 11 seats (BLDP 10, Molinaka 1), in 1998 the 36 minor parties garnered 12.6 percent of the popular vote but did not capture a single seat. Son Sann's Party and the BLDP were badly factionalized. Ung Huot's fragment of FUNCINPEC (which ran as the Populist Party) was compromised by its collaboration with the CPP following the 1997 coup. None of the smaller parties had a solid base in a particular region and none enjoyed the support of a particular ethnic group, as do small parties elsewhere.

Charges of Fraud

Immediately following the election, charges of fraud and irregularities burst forth from Sam Rainsy and Ranariddh. These protests led to recounts in a few communes, not enough to affect seriously the outcome of the election. Complainants were called upon to show evidence of malfeasance, and investigations were under way before the final results were to be announced in late August. The *New York Times*, on July 30, listed the following examples of the early complaints filed at the National Election Commission by Sam Rainsy:

- Overcrowded and disorderly. Staff cannot control normal procedure.
- Ballot box has no number on it.
- Doorkeeper is delaying by asking unnecessary questions, inspecting voters. Voters are complaining.
- Ballot papers are being torn off from bottom instead of the top.
- Ballot box loosely closed; lid is so loose you can stick your fingers in the sides.

A serious charge was the opposition's claim that the formula for distributing National Assembly seats via the system of proportional representation had been secretly adopted in an "unfair, arbitrary and unconstitutional manner." The formula used in the 1993 election, based on the highest average system, would have allocated 59 seats to the CPP (instead of 64), 45 to FUNCINPEC (instead of 43), and 18 to the Sam Rainsy Party (instead of 15). Thus, under the earlier formula, the opposition parties would have won a majority of the 63 seats in the 122-seat Assembly, and the CPP 59. Under the new formula, which benefits the leading party, the CPP acquired 52 percent of the seats with 42 percent of the popular vote. The government responded that the National Election Commission had adopted the new formula without opposition, on May 28, 1998, well before the election and that notice of it had been distributed to all parties. The CPP could not have been certain that it would benefit from the change. Critics of this charge suggested that the opposition had either not paid attention to the change when it was approved, or had thought they might profit from it. Whatever the substance of the complaints, the ambiguities and doubts created by them cast a pall on the legitimizing function of the election.

The protests can be given a variety of interpretations. It is reasonable to delay final judgment until evidence is presented to support the charges of serious corruption. However, it must be emphasized, as noted above, that the early reports of the international observers did not find serious faults in the voting or the counting. The protests may reflect, in part, a cultural attribute among the Cambodian elite. Losers do not easily acknowledge loss publicly. Cries of fraud may help reduce the loss of face—one can claim to have been cheated out of victory. Following the 1993 election in which FUNCINPEC won 45 percent of the vote compared to the CPP's 38 percent, the CPP shouted fraud and threatened secession of a number of provinces. In the end, the CPP bullied its way into a power-sharing arrangement in which Hun Sen was named co-Prime Minister and most of the ministries were divided between FUNCINPEC and the CPP.

Indeed, the current charge of fraud may be part of an opposition bargaining process, or "political theater" as a Western diplomat termed it. Since a two-thirds majority of the National Assembly membership is required by the constitution to approve a government and seven-tenths to convene the Assembly, the opposition may be negotiating for its share of power in a coalition government. The opposition does not have the leverage enjoyed in 1993 by the CPP, which controlled the state and security apparatus. But the opposition leaders can use the constitutional requirement as a bargaining tool.

Formation of the New Government

Since 82 votes of the 122–member National Assembly are constitutionally required to form a government, it was highly likely that a coalition government would be announced after bargaining. With 64 seats, the CPP could surely claim the most important ministerial portfolios, and Hun Sen was expected to become Prime Minister. Several options were available to Hun Sen in the makeup of the coalition. He might form a three-way coalition, offering portfolios to FUNCINPEC and Sam Rainsy Party leaders. Soon after preliminary election results were announced, Hun Sen told visiting Japanese parliamentarians that he had proposed a three-party coalition with himself as the sole prime minister. The CPP would control the five key ministries of defense, interior, finance, justice, and foreign affairs. Sam Rainsy hinted he would join a three-party coalition if that was the desire of the King. Rainsy also told journalists, however, "I shall never accept to be in a government led by the mafia." He added that he wanted to rid the country of "the drug-traffickers, the money launderers and Cambodia as a shelter for criminal activity."

A second option for Hun Sen was the formation of a coalition with only FUNCINPEC. In an interview with *Le Figaro* on August 5, Hun Sen said that a "coalition between the CPP and FUNCINPEC is simply an inevitable mathematical fact." He said he would offer FUNCINPEC 40 percent of the ministerial posts while the CPP would hold 60 percent. Cambodian insiders who know Ranariddh believe that it is unlikely that, as a Prince and a former First Prime Minister ousted by Hun Sen, Ranariddh would be willing to serve in a Cabinet under Hun Sen. They speculated that Ranariddh might be willing to commit FUNCINPEC to the coalition but that he would remain chairman of his party and assume the post of President of the National Assembly, biding his time until he would be chosen for the throne upon his father's departure.

A third option was a coalition between the CPP and the Sam Rainsy Party. The total seats available in this combination, however, would be only 79 (CPP 64 + SRP 15), 3 fewer than the 82 necessary to form a government. In a fourth option Hun Sen would entice a fragment of FUNCINPEC assemblymen to cooperate in a CPP government. Hun Sen has shown a canniness at splitting his opposition.

Each of these options required that former political enemies join with each other to cooperate in a new government. It stretches the imagination to envision rivals who have denounced one another in scathing rhetoric embarking upon a cooperative enterprise. But Cambodian political culture appears to encompass, almost as a given, curious combinations of bitter rivals.

One need only recall Sihanouk's liaison with the Khmer Rouge from 1970 to 1975, or FUNCINPEC's and the KPNLF's coalition with the Khmer Rouge from 1982 to 1991, to be reminded of the political contortions of which Cambodian politicians are capable. Western-style party politics is a relatively new game in Cambodia.

An important actor in the negotiation about these options is sure to be King Sihanouk. He told members of the diplomatic community that he was prepared to be active in the current political arena. The King avoided residence in Phnom Penh after the July 1997 events, preferring to reside in Siem Riep when he was not in Beijing or Pyongyang. However, Sihanouk retains an influential regal aura with a potential to help reconcile the disputing parties.

The Khmer Rouge

A major development of 1998 was the disappearance of the Khmer Rouge as a significant threat to the government. The Khmer Rouge ceased to exist as a national organization. Only scattered bands of fighters remained, numbering perhaps some 500, largely in the region of Anlong Veng, directed by a few old revolutionaries (Ta Mok, Nuon Chea, Khieu Samphan, among others), now essentially minor warlords. The KR had lost the patronage of China and the sanctuary of Thailand. The poor peasantry was appalled by the KR excesses and tired of war. KR cadres were ready to accept the government's inducements to defect, to make peace and rejoin the nation. Pol Pot was dead. Other former leaders were ill, and squabbling among themselves.

Some KR leaders concluded surprisingly attractive arrangements with the government. For example, Ieng Sary had been integrated, with some 1,500 of his followers, into the Royal Government, under an agreement with both Hun Sen and Ranariddh, while they still shared power. The two Prime Ministers requested that the King grant amnesty to Ieng Sary, and he retained control of civil and military administration in the region of Pailin. Journalists visiting his headquarters noted that he was profiting from his area's abundant timber stands and gem mines, whose products he traded to eager Thai businessmen, and his agents managed a casino where Thai and Cambodian customers came to gamble. Ieng Sary contended to all who inquired that he had no responsibility for the KR excesses during their reign of terror from 1975 to 1979.

There seemed to be little impetus within Cambodian society to bring Khmer Rouge malefactors to justice. While there is a nationwide abhorrence of the KR crimes, and hardly a family has not suffered some loss at their hands, no popular groundswell is evident to try those responsible. Indeed, little was said about the Khmer Rouge during the election campaign. The CPP approached the KR issue only tangentially, taking credit as the party of "peace." FUNCINPEC and the Sam Rainsy Party celebrated their capacity to provide for "reconciliation."

The political reality is that former Khmer Rouge functionaries are found throughout the Royal Cambodian Government and society. Some, like Hun Sen and other leaders of the CPP, abandoned the Khmer Rouge in 1978 and 1979. Others, including a cluster of intellectuals, defected as recently as July 1998. Many prominent leaders have cooperated with the Khmer Rouge over the past three decades. Sihanouk, Ranariddh, and Son Sann were their partners in the CGDK from 1982 to 1991. A lawyer defending selected KR leaders would surely attempt to make ties to many KR alumni, including Hun Sen and his CPP associates. Nevertheless, Hun Sen, from time to time, tells foreign journalists that he wishes for an international tribunal to try certain KR top leaders.

Some Future Dilemmas

Cambodia has little tradition of moving from an election to governance. The experience of government formation following the 1993 election offers an unfortunate precedent. The election results were not translated fairly in the distribution of power in the new government. This time, can they be clear of lingering bitterness?

Another question is whether, given putative legitimacy by the election, Hun Sen will be able to rise above his dark side—his suspicion, arrogance, and combativeness—to provide decent leadership for development and democracy. Can he steadfastly put his natural intelligence, his ability at canny political maneuver, and his nationalist dedication to work to create a healthier economy and society? Hun Sen has shown a talent for offering inducements to a variety of groups to attain their cooperation. In short, he has versatility at building coalitions to support his power. Some diplomatic observers believe that, if he feels sufficiently secure, he has the capacity and the interest to construct a "guided democracy," following the models of his regional neighbors Singapore and Malaysia. Such a prospect may seem too optimistic for a recently "failed state," but perhaps not beyond the realm of possibility.

Cambodian governments have little tradition of accepting the vital role of an organized opposition, which plays such a critical element in democratic government. Cambodian rulers have typically dealt crudely with critics.

With their exercise of majority power legitimated by the election, can Hun Sen and his CPP associates learn to tolerate the criticism of the opposition parties, which represent up to 46 percent of Cambodian voter opinion? Conversely, will the parties that are not vested with power learn to operate as a "loyal opposition," also a critical element in the functioning of a democratic system. Oppositionists in Cambodia are unaccustomed to offering measured, responsible criticism, or to accepting willingly the legitimacy of their governors. There are early seeds of a genuine opposition in the new party formed by Sam Rainsy. He has raised valuable issues in condemning corruption and environmental degradation. His party could provide a useful watchdog function. Will Sam Rainsy and his associates learn, and be permitted, to play a role as an effective and responsible opposition? These questions suggest the need for a modification of Cambodian political culture, which has not been congenial to political criticism.

Fully as much as selfless, incorrupt individual leadership, and alteration in its political culture, Cambodia needs institutional development. More effective political institutions—parties, legislatures, courts—must be developed. The growth of civil society, particularly NGOs committed to human rights, justice, and economic development, allowed to take off during the UNTAC period, must now be nurtured. More developed political institutions and an expanded civil society will be critical to reducing the plagues of avarice and corruption that have pervaded Cambodian public life.

The International Community and the New Government

With the formation of a new government, based on an internationally observed election, Cambodia can expect to enjoy international legitimacy. The UN is likely to accept the credentials of the new government, which will then resume its seat at the United Nations General Assembly. Likewise, ASEAN can be expected to invite Cambodia's membership, at least by its next plenary meeting scheduled for December 1998. The full restoration of economic assistance will depend on the policies of each bilateral donor, but constraints imposed by the events of July 1997 for most government as well as international organizations are likely to dissolve following the formation of a new government.

While the 1998 election in Cambodia has raised some confounding questions, it has also marked the political landscape in instructive ways. The national poll organized by Cambodians with international support has provided the CPP with a claim to "winning party" (Art. 100)—which must find two-thirds support in the Assembly to establish a new government.

The second- and third-ranked parties risk overwhelming the system with charges of irregularity and fraud. Their demonstrations raise the danger of provoking a violence that seems to lie just under the skin of many Cambodian political actors. The hopes inspired among the partisans of peace and liberal democracy for Cambodia have been sobered by the resumption of animosity between the contending parties.

What progress—or return on the UNTAC investment—can the international community discern after a second national election? Some markers are visible. Voter registration and turnout achieved a ninetieth percentile. The anti-election KR have disintegrated and lost their cohesion and effectiveness. Human rights, monitored by the UN, are now woven into the political dialogue. Non-governmental organizations, nurtured under UNTAC, now carry an impressive burden in developing social infrastructure and alleviating humanitarian needs. The most egregious economic injury to the nation, the ravaging of its forests, may have been slowed, if not halted.

So, Cambodia has benefited from the intervention of international organizations. However, disappointments loom large. Political violence and intimidation remain threatening. Racist campaign prejudice toward Vietnamese settlers tarnished the campaign dialogue. Pay-offs and theft of public assets continue to corrupt the economy. The Cambodian culture of venality and revenge remains resistant to change, inhibiting the development of values requisite for liberal democracy. Scant accountability is expected of public servants.

Some progress toward multi-party politics within constitutional constraints can be recorded. The main thrust of future advance will rest with the willingness of the Cambodian people and especially their leaders to draw on the gentler side of their cultural heritage, as well as on the goodwill of the international community. Few nations have suffered more and more clearly need international help.

Index